Laura Sabine class3

KW-491-431

WORDS
Warne's School Dictionary

WORDS

Warne's School Dictionary

Based on the former work by Isabel Mary McLean

Completely revised by
KIT PARRY and GEOFFREY PAYTON

FREDERICK WARNE

Published by Frederick Warne (Publishers) Ltd London 1979
© Frederick Warne (Publishers) Ltd 1979

Net edition ISBN 0 7232 2174 x
Non-net edition ISBN 0 7232 2407 2

Printed in Great Britain by
William Clowes & Sons Limited, Beccles and London
0244.679

PREFACE

This selective dictionary is designed for the use of children from 8 to 12 years of age. Words which the average 7-year-old should know and be able to spell are omitted. This also applies to words that are unlikely to be needed at the age of 12. The pronunciation is given for all words except those where there is no likelihood of error, e.g. *rib, carve*. Parts of speech are indicated in abbreviated forms (see page vi), but otherwise abbreviations have been avoided.

When a word has several meanings (e.g. *principle*) these are given under (a), (b) etc. Where a word can act as more than one part of speech (e.g. *print*), the definitions are shown separately and numbered 1., 2. etc. Derived forms, printed in italics, are often grouped under one head-word, especially if their spelling or pronunciation might cause difficulty. Where there are alternative accepted spellings or pronunciations only the most usual has been given, in order not to confuse the child.

A feature of this dictionary is the addition after many definitions of an example or examples (marked *Ex.*) of the usage of the word, so that its meaning, or the meaning of a derived form, may be more easily grasped. Both definitions and illustrative examples are given in simple language, although they sometimes include words that may have to be looked up elsewhere in the book.

With the older child in mind, more difficult words commonly encountered in newspapers, magazines and broadcasting are included (e.g. *relegate, sanction, redundant, picket*). There are also scientific words such as *nuclear, electronics, soluble, stamen, turbine* which can be explained in simple terms. In addition, words which have come into everyday use in recent years have been included (e.g. *spacecraft, duvet, stereophonic, motorway, digital*).

Abbreviations Used in the Dictionary

adj.	adjective
adv.	adverb
conj.	conjunction
Ex.	example
interj.	interjection
n.	noun
pl.	plural
prep.	preposition
pron.	pronoun
v.	verb

PRONUNCIATION

After most words a guide to pronunciation is given (in brackets), divided into syllables, with the stressed syllable in italics. For example: institution (in-sti-*tew*-sh'n). The aim has been to keep these as simple and self-explanatory as possible. Only four special symbols have been used:

y for the long *i* sound in line, tie, guy
dh for the *th* in there
U for the vowel in good, bull, put
zh for the sound in measure, division

The sounds are represented as follows:

Vowels	as in
a	hat
ay	hate
ah	father
aw	fall
e	bed
ee	creep
i	bit
y	bite
o	cot
oh	coat
u	cub
ew	cube
U	bull, put, look, good

Diphthongs	
ow	gout
oi	appoint

Vowels followed by r

ar	art
air	aquarium
awr	warm, choral
eer	mere
ur	urge, kerb and *er* when accentuated (pri-*fur*)
yr	*saf*-yr

Consonants

dh	their
ks	exit
ng-g	angle, anguish, mingle
ng-k	monkey, anchor
zh	measure

The use of other consonants is self-explanatory.

Every effort has been made to give the true pronunciation in use today, even though it may look bizarre in print. For example:

fortune (*for*-chen)—not *for*-tewn
message (*mes*-ij)—not *mes*-ayj
diary (*dy*-ar-i)—not *dy*-ar-ee
capable (*kay*-pa-b'l)—not *kay*-pa-bUl
motion (*moh*-sh'n)—not *moh*-shon
purchase (*pur*-chis)—not *pur*-chays

A

abandon (a-*ban*-d'n) *v.* To give up or leave entirely. *Ex.* She *abandoned* the idea of becoming a nurse.

abbey (*ab*-i) *n.* A monastery or a convent; the church belonging to either of these. An *abbot* is the head of a monastery, an *abbess* the head of a convent.

abbreviate (a-*breev*-i-ayt) *v.* To shorten. *Ex.* We *abbreviate* the word 'verb' by writing only '*v*'. '*V*' is an *abbreviation* (*n.*) for 'verb'.

abdicate (*ab*-di-kayt) *v.* To give up a position, especially a throne. *Ex.* King Edward VIII *abdicated* in 1936.

abdomen (*ab*-do-men) *n.* The part of the body containing the stomach and bowels. An *abdominal* (ab-*dom*-in'l; *adj.*) pain is a pain in that part.

ability (a-*bil*-it-i) *n.* The power to do things; cleverness. *Ex.* He is a boy of great *ability* and should do well.

abject (*ab*-jekt) *adj.* Miserable; pitiful; grovelling. *Ex.* He is an *abject* coward. He made an *abject* apology.

abnormal (ab-*nor*-m'l) *adj.* Not usual; strange. *Ex.* It is *abnormal* for a child not to want to play.

abolish (a-*bol*-ish) *v.* To do away with or put an end to. *Ex.* Some people want to *abolish* fox-hunting; others are against its *abolition* (ab-ol-*ish*'n; *n.*).

abominable (a-*bom*-in-a-b'l) *adj.* Hateful; detestable. *Ex.* It is *abominable* to treat animals cruelly.

aborigines (ab-or-*ij*-in-eez) *n.* The first people to live in a country. *Ex.* The *Aborigines* of Australia were the first people to live there.

abound (a-*bownd*) *v.* To be plentiful. *Ex.* Weeds *abound* in a neglected garden.

abreast (a-*brest*) *adv.* Side by side. *Ex.* You can walk only two *abreast* on this narrow path.

abridge (a-*brij*) *v.* To shorten. An *abridgement* (*n.*) of a book is a shortened version of it.

abroad (a-*brawd*) *adv.* In, or to, a foreign country; overseas.

abrupt (a-*brupt*) *adj.* Sudden; sharp; rudely brisk. *Ex.* John's *abrupt* way of speaking sometimes offends people.

abscond (ab-*skond*) *v.* To go away secretly to escape the law. *Ex.* The clerk *absconded* with his employer's money.

absent (*ab*-sent) 1. *adj.* Being away from; not present. *Ex.* Five of our class are *absent* today. 2. (ab-*sent*) *v.* To stay away deliberately (used with *oneself* etc.) *Ex.* He *absented himself* from the meeting because he felt ill. He was an *absentee* (ab-sent-*ee*; *n.*).

absent-minded (*ab*-sent *myn*-did) *adj.* Not paying attention; having a vague and wandering mind.

absolute (*ab*-sol-oot) *adj.* Complete. *Ex.* The play was an *absolute* failure and ran for only three nights.

absorb (ab-*sorb*) *v.* (a) To suck up. *Ex.* A sponge *absorbs* water. It is *absorbent* (*adj.*). (b) To occupy all one's attention or energy. *Ex.* He was completely *absorbed* in his book.

abstain (ab-*stayn*) *v.* To hold back or keep away from. *Ex.* In a drought we have to *abstain* from wasting water. This is an example of *abstinence* (*ab*-stin-ens; *n.*).

absurd (ab-*surd*) *adj.* Foolish; ridiculous.

abundance (a-*bun*-d'ns) *n.* Plenty. *Ex.* We have an *abundance* of food in the house, so we won't starve. There is *abundant* (*adj.*) food.

abuse (a-*bewz*) *v.* (a) To make bad use of. *Ex.* The king *abused* his powers and treated his people badly. (b) To swear at or insult. *Ex.* After the car accident the drivers *abused* each other. They were *abusive* (a-*bews*-iv; *adj.*). They exchanged *abuse* (a-*bews*; *n.*).

academy (a-*kad*-e-mi) *n.* A college at which a particular art or science, such as music or technology, is studied.

accelerate (ak-*sel*-er-ayt) *v.* To make quicker; to increase speed. *Ex.* The driver *accelerated* in order to overtake the bus.

accent (*ak*-sent) *n.* A particular way of pronouncing words. *Ex.* A Yorkshire *accent*. She speaks English with a French *accent*.

accept (ak-*sept*) *v.* To agree to take. *Ex.* He refused to *accept* any payment for his work. I gladly *accept* your invitation.

access (*ak*-ses) *n.* A way of reaching or entering. *Ex.* The only *access* to the roof is by a trap-door. A place is *accessible* (*adj.*) if it is easily reached.

accession (ak-*sesh*'n) *n.* Coming to the throne or any high office. *Ex.* Soon after his *accession* the king got married.

accident (*ak*-si-dent) *n.* An event that happens by chance; an unfortunate happening, as when people are injured in a *railway accident*. *Accidental* (*adj.*) means happening by chance.

accommodate (a-*kom*-o-dayt) *v.* To have or provide room for.

Accommodation (*n.*) usually means rooms in which to live. *Accommodating* (*adj.*) means ready to help.

accompany (a-*kum*-pan-i) *v.* (a) To go with. *Ex.* Will you *accompany* me on my walk? (b) To play music for a soloist (*see* solo). *Ex.* He *accompanied* the singer on the piano.

accomplice (a-*kom*-plis or a-*kum*-plis) *n.* One who helps another in a crime. *Ex.* Smith planned the crime; Jones was merely his *accomplice.*

accomplish (a-*kom*-plish or a-*kum*-plish) *v.* To succeed in doing; to complete. *Ex.* It took a year to *accomplish* this task. *Accomplishments* (*n.*) are skills that give pleasure to others, such as singing, drawing, dancing.

accord (a-*kord*) 1. *n.* Agreement. *Ex.* Their tastes were in complete *accord.* 2. *v.* To agree. *Ex.* His opinion *accords* with mine.

accordion (a-*kord*-i-on) *n.* A musical instrument with a small keyboard, whose reedy sounds are made by the air from a bellows.

account (a-*kownt*) 1. *n.* (a) A statement of money owing. *Ex.* The builder sent his *account* for work done. *Accounts* are a record of money received and paid, kept by an *accountant.* (b) A description. *Ex.* He gave an *account* of his wartime experiences. 2. *v.* To explain or give a reason for. *Ex.* His illness *accounts* for his absence.

accumulate (a-*kew*-mew-layt) *v.* To collect or gather together. *Ex.* We have *accumulated* too much furniture for this house. An *accumulation* (*n.*) is a collection, often one that is larger than is wanted.

accurate (*ak*-ewr-it) *adj.* Correct and careful. *Ex.* His spelling is *accurate. Accuracy* (*n.*) in spelling is important.

accuse (a-*kewz*) *v.* To blame. *Ex.* She was *accused* of telling lies but denied the *accusation* (*n.*).

accustomed (a-*kus*-tumd) *adj.* Having the habit of; become used to. *Ex.* I am *accustomed* to getting up early. I have *accustomed* myself to it.

ace (ays) *n.* (a) The 'one' on cards, dominoes and dice. (b) The name given to an outstanding fighter pilot, racing driver etc.

ache (ayk) 1. *n.* A dull pain. 2. *v.* To have a pain. *Ex.* My head has been *aching* since I bumped it.

achieve (a-*cheev*) *v.* To succeed in doing something. *Ex.* The army *achieved* victory after a hard struggle. It was a great *achievement* (*n.*).

acid (*as*-id) 1. *n.* A sour liquid—strong acids will burn the skin. 2. *adj.* Having a sour or sharp taste.

acknowledge (ak-*nol*-ij) *v.* (a) To admit. *Ex.* She *acknowledged* that she was guilty. (b) To express gratitude (*see* grateful) for. *Ex.* She *acknowledged* his kindness. If you *acknowledge* a letter you send a reply to show that you have received it.

acne (*ak*-ni) *n.* Pimples, usually on the face.

acquainted (a-*kwayn*-tid) *adj.* Known or familiar. *Ex.* These ladies are *acquainted* with each other, and have known each other for some time. An *acquaintance* (*n.*) is a person one knows, but not very well.

acquire (a-*kwyr*) *v.* To get. *Ex.* You can *acquire* a lot of information from books.

acquit (a-*kwit*) *v.* To set free from blame. *Ex.* The prisoner was not proved guilty at his trial and was *acquitted*.

acre (*ay*-ker) *n.* A measurement of land equal to 4840 square yards, or about 4047 square metres.

acrobat (*ak*-ro-bat) *n.* An entertainer who performs balancing tricks on the tightrope, trapeze etc.

action (*ak*-sh'n) *n.* Doing something; a deed. *Ex.* Giving money to the poor is a generous *action*. *Activity* is another word for action.

active (*ak*-tiv) *adj.* Lively; busy; able to move about. *Ex.* She is still very *active* although over eighty.

actor (*ak*-tor) *n.* A man who plays a part on the stage or in a film. An *actress* is a female actor.

actual (*ak*-tew'l) *adj.* Real. *Ex.* What is your *actual* intention— are you going or not?

acute (a-*kewt*) *adj.* Sharp. You can have *acute* hearing or an *acute* pain.

adapt (a-*dapt*) *v.* To alter for a different purpose. *Ex.* He *adapted* a wooden box to make a rabbit-hutch.

adder (*ad*-er) *n.* A poisonous snake, especially the viper.

addicted (a-*dik*-tid) *adj.* Unable to give up a habit, usually bad. *Ex.* Many cigarette smokers become *addicted* to smoking.

addition (ad-*ish*'n) *n.* Something added. *Ex.* The new baby was a welcome *addition* to the family.

addled (*ad*-l'd) *adj.* (Of an egg) Gone bad.

address (a-*dres*) 1. *n.* (a) A speech. (b) The place (town, street etc.)

where one lives. 2. *v*. (a) To make a speech. *Ex*. The politician *addressed* the crowd from the platform. (b) To *address* a letter means to write the address on the envelope.

adenoids (*ad*-en-oydz) *n*. Spongy lumps at the back of the nose which have become swollen and may interfere with breathing or speaking.

adept (*ad*-ept) *n*. One who is clever at doing something. *Ex*. My father is an *adept* (*n*.) at making bread; he is *adept* (*adj*.) at bread-making.

adequate (*ad*-i-kwit) *adj*. Enough. *Ex*. Our small garden is *adequate* for our needs.

adhere (ad-*heer*) *v*. To stick. You can *adhere* to a promise, or make a stamp *adhere* to an envelope.

adjacent (a-*jay*-s'nt) *adj*. Very near; next door. *Ex*. Our house is *adjacent* to a golf-course.

adjective (*aj*-ek-tiv) *n*. A word that describes a noun or adds to its meaning. *Ex*. In 'the black dog', 'black' is an *adjective*.

adjust (a-*just*) *v*. To put right. *Ex*. She *adjusted* her bicycle brakes, as they were loose.

administer (ad-*min*-i-ster) *v*. To manage the affairs of; to be in charge of. *Ex*. He is the man who *administers* the gasworks.

admiral (*ad*-mi-ral) *n*. The highest officer of a navy.

admire (ad-*myr*) *v*. To like the look of; to have a high opinion of. *Ex*. We *admired* the flower arrangements. They were *admirable* (*ad* mer-a-b'l; *adj*.) and filled us with *admiration* (*n*.).

admit (ad-*mit*) *v*. (a) To allow to come in. *Ex*. Dogs are not *admitted* in this food shop; there is no *admittance* (*n*.) for dogs. (b) To agree or confess. *Ex*. He *admits* that he is interested only in games. The act of admitting is *admission* (*n*.).

adolescence (ad-o-*les*-ens) *n*. The time of life when one is young but no longer a child; the teenage years.

adopt (a-*dopt*) *v*. (a) To take someone else's child by agreement and bring it up as one's own. (b) To take or choose. *Ex*. He *adopted* an attitude of hostility.

adore (a-*dor*) *v*. To love or worship. *Ex*. They *adore* their new baby. He is *adorable* (*adj*.).

adorn (a-*dorn*) *v*. To decorate or make more beautiful. *Ex*. The room was *adorned* with lovely new curtains.

adult (*ad*-ult or a-*dult*) *n*. A grown-up person.

advance (ad-*vahns*) *v*. To go forward; to progress to a further stage. *Ex*. The army *advanced* into enemy territory. He has done the easy exercises and is now on the *advanced* (*adj.*) course. *In advance* means beforehand.

advantage (ad-*vahn*-tij) *n.* A benefit that makes one person more fortunate than others. *Ex.* Being tall is an *advantage* when watching sport in a crowd. The opposite of *advantage* is *disadvantage*.

adventure (ad-*ven*-cher) *n.* An exciting experience. *Ex.* I like stories about the *adventures* of ordinary people.

adverb (*ad*-verb) *n.* A word that adds to the meaning of a verb. *Ex.* In 'Peter ran quickly', 'quickly' is the *adverb*.

adversary (*ad*-ver-sar-i) *n.* An enemy; the person one plays against in a game.

adverse (ad-*vurs*) *adj.* Unfavourable. *Ex. Adverse* weather delayed the ship's sailing.

advertise (*ad*-ver-tyz) *v.* To make known publicly. *Ex.* He *advertised* his car for sale. He put an *advertisement* (ad-*ver*-tiz-m'nt; *n.*) about it in the paper.

advise (ad-*vyz*) *v.* To give an opinion on what to do. *Ex.* Please *advise* me on this difficulty. Give me your *advice* (ad-*vys*; *n.*).

aerate (*air*-ayt) *v.* To put gas into a liquid and make it bubble like fizzy lemonade.

aerial (*air*-i-al) *n.* The rods, usually placed on the roof, by which a television or radio set receives programmes.

aerosol (*air*-o-sol) *n.* A pressure-filled can whose contents can be released in a misty spray.

affable (*af*-a-b'l) *adj.* Friendly and easy to talk to.

affair (a-*fair*) *n.* Something to be done or attended to; business; an event.

affect (a-*fekt*) *v.* To produce a change in something. *Ex.* Cold weather *affects* delicate plants; it has an *effect* (ef-*ekt*; *n.*) on them.

affectation (af-ek-*tay*-sh'n) *n.* A manner which is not natural but is put on to impress people. One who shows *affectation* is said to be *affected* (*adj.*).

affection (a-*fek*-sh'n) *n.* Love or fondness. One who is loving is *affectionate* (*adj.*).

affirm (a-*furm*) *v.* To state with certainty. *Ex.* He *affirmed* that he had never seen it. To answer in the *affirmative* (*n.*) is to say 'yes'.

affix (a-*fiks*) *v.* To fix on. *Ex.* You must *affix* a stamp to the envelope.

afflict (a-*flikt*) *v.* To cause suffering. *Ex.* He is *afflicted* with rheumatism.

afford (a-*ford*) *v.* To have enough money to buy. *Ex.* I can *afford* a new coat now.

afraid (a-*frayd*) *adj.* Frightened; fearing.

aft (ahft) *prep.* At or towards the stern (the back) of a ship.

aged (*ay*-jid) *adj.* Very old. *Ex.* We are collecting money to help *aged* people.

agenda (a-*jen*-da) *n.* A list of things to be dealt with at a business meeting.

agent (*ay*-gent) *n.* One who acts for another. *Ex.* My father uses an *agent* to sell his fruit.

aggravate (*ag*-rav-ayt) *v.* (a) To make worse. *Ex.* The pain of his wound was *aggravated* by the heat. (b) To annoy and irritate. *Ex.* She was *aggravated* by the gossip about her.

aggressor (a-*gres*-or) *n.* The one who begins a quarrel. *Ex.* Our cat is always the *aggressor* and attacks any dog she meets. She is *aggressive* (*adj.*).

aghast (a-*gahst*) *adj.* Horrified. *Ex.* Mother was *aghast* when I told her that I had left my job.

agile (*aj*-yl) *adj.* Able to move quickly and easily. *Ex.* The monkeys were very *agile*, leaping among the trees with great *agility* (a-*jil*-it-i; *n.*).

agitate (*aj*-i-tayt) *v.* To disturb or upset. *Ex.* He was very *agitated* when he heard of the accident.

agog (a-*gog*) *adj.* Excited and interested. *Ex.* The crowd were all *agog* to see the procession.

agony (*ag*-on-i) *n.* Very great pain of body or mind. *Ex.* Toothache can cause *agony*, or *agonizing* (ag-on-yz-ing; *adj.*) pain.

agree (a-*gree*) *v.* To consent or accept or be content. *Ex.* He *agreed* to pay a pound for it. A person or thing that is pleasant is *agreeable* (*adj.*). *Ex.* An *agreeable* surprise. An *agreement* (*n.*) is a promise between people to do a certain thing.

agriculture (*ag*-ri-kul-cher) *n.* Farming.

ail (ayl) *v.* To be ill. An *ailment* (*n.*) is a minor illness.

aim (aym) 1. *v.* To point at or try to reach. *Ex.* He *aimed* his rifle at the target. 2. *n.* An ambition or purpose. *Ex.* His *aim* in life is to be a doctor.

airport (*air*-port) *n.* The area where aircraft land and take off with passengers and cargo.

aisle (yl) *n.* The passageway between pews in church or seats in a theatre.

ajar (a-*jar*) *adv.* Partly open. *Ex.* Leave the door *ajar*.

akimbo (a-*kim*-bo) *adj.* With hands on hips and elbows out. *Ex.* He stood with arms *akimbo*.

alarm (a-*larm*) 1. *n.* A warning of danger. *Ex.* When he saw the fire he raised the *alarm*. 2. *v.* To frighten. *Ex.* She was *alarmed* by the noise.

album (*al*-bum) *n.* A book with blank pages for stamp collections, photographs etc.

alcohol (*al*-ko-hol) *n.* The pure spirit in whisky, wine, beer etc. which makes them intoxicating.

alert (a-*lurt*) *adj.* Quick to pay attention or to act. *Ex.* A ship's look-out must always be *alert*, or on the *alert* (*n.*).

alfresco (al-*fresk*-o) *adv.* In the open air. *Ex.* Let's have our lunch *alfresco*.

algebra (*al*-jeb-ra) *n.* A kind of maths in which letters of the alphabet are used to stand for quantities.

alias (*ay*-li-as) *n.* A false name. *Ex.* When arrested, the man gave an *alias* instead of his own name.

alibi (*al*-i-by) *n.* The excuse of an accused person that he was somewhere else when the crime was committed. *Ex.* When accused of burglary in Birmingham, his *alibi* was that he was in Jamaica at the time.

alien (*ay*-li-en) *n.* A foreigner, especially one who makes a long stay in a country not his own.

alight (a-*lyt*) 1. *adj.* Lit up or burning. *Ex.* When the camp fire was well *alight* we put the kettle on. 2. *v.* To get down from or to land on something. *Ex.* He *alighted* from the bus.

allege (a-*lej*) *v.* To state without proof. *Ex.* He *alleged* that she had cheated him; that was his allegation (al-i-*gaysh*'n; *n.*).

allegiance (a-*lee*-j'ns) *n.* Loyalty, especially to one's sovereign and country.

allegory (*al*-i-gor-i) *n.* A story with an underlying, unstated meaning. *Ex. Pilgrim's Progress* is an *allegory* in which people and places stand for virtues, vices, temptations etc.

allergy (*al*-er-ji) *n.* Unusual sensitiveness of the body to something normally harmless. *Ex.* Hay fever and asthma are due to an *allergy*. Some people are *allergic* (al-*urj*-ik; *adj.*) to shellfish, which give them skin rashes.

alleviate (a-*leev*-i-ayt) *v.* To make less or easier. *Ex.* This medicine will *alleviate* the pain.

alley (*al*-i)   *n.* A narrow passage between buildings.   *Ex.* The shop is in an *alley* near the Town Hall.

alliance (a-*ly*-ans)   *n. See* ally.

alligator (*al*-i-gay-tor)   *n.* An American reptile resembling, but larger than, a crocodile.

allocate (*al*-o-kayt)   *v.* To allot.   *Ex.* Each club was *allocated* two tickets.

allot (a-*lot*)   *v.* To distribute as a share. An *allotment* (*n.*) is a small piece of rented land used for growing vegetables etc.

allow (a-*low*)   *v.* To let something be done; to permit.   *Ex.* We asked if we were *allowed* to go inside. An *allowance* (*n.*) is a sum of money given regularly, such as pocket-money.

alloy (*al*-oi)   *n.* A mixture of metals.   *Ex.* Church bells are made of an *alloy* of copper and tin.

allude (a-*lood*)   *v.* To mention or speak about.   *Ex.* I will not *allude* to his mistake. I shall make no *allusion* (a-*loozh*'n; *n.*) to it.

ally (*al*-y)   *n.* A person or country united to another in friendship and by a promise to help one another.   *Ex.* Britain and America were *allies* in both World Wars. They formed an *alliance* (a-*ly*-ans; *n.*).

almanac (*awl*-man-ak)   *n.* A calendar that gives facts about the sun and moon, tides, holidays and other events of the year.

almond (*ah*-m'nd)   *n.* (a) A white, oval, edible nut. (b) The tree it grows on.

alms (ahmz)   *n.* Money or other gifts given to the poor.   *Ex.* An *almshouse* (*n.*) is a home for old people who are poor.

aloft (a-*loft*)   *adv.* High up.   *Ex.* The sailor went *aloft* to the mast-head.

aloof (a-*loof*)   1. *adv.* At a distance, taking no interest.   *Ex.* He stood *aloof* because the conversation bored him. 2. *adj.* Distant in manner, with a rather superior air.

altar (*awl*-ter)   *n.* (a) The decorated table which is the most sacred part of a church, at the east end of the chancel. (b) The slab on which animals were sacrificed to the gods of olden times.

alternate (*awl*-ter-nayt)   1. *v.* (Of two things) To follow each other by turns.   *Ex.* In April wet and sunny days often *alternate*. 2. (awl-*tern*-ayt) *adj.* Happening by turns, first one and then the other.   *Ex.* Jack and Jill did the shopping on *alternate* days; they did this *alternately* (*adv.*).

alternative (awl-*turn*-a-tiv)   *n.* A choice of two things.   *Ex.* You can walk or cycle; these are the only *alternatives*.

altitude (*al*-ti-tewd) *n.* Height. *Ex.* The plane flew over the Alps at a great *altitude*.

alto (*al*-to) *n.* and *adj.* The lowest range (called *contralto*) of a woman's singing voice, and the highest (called *counter-tenor*) of a man's.

aluminium (al-ew-*min*-i-um) *n.* A very lightweight white metal, used to make kitchen-ware, motor-car parts etc.

amalgamate (a-*mal*-ga-mayt) *v.* To mix or join together. *Ex.* The two firms *amalgamated* so that they could take on bigger orders.

amass (a-*mas*) *v.* To collect or heap up. *Ex.* One can *amass* a large fortune or a lot of rubbish.

amateur (*am*-a-tur) *n.* One who takes up a study or sport for the love of it, and not to earn money by it. *Ex.* He is an *amateur* (*adj.*) photographer in his spare time.

amazed (a-*mayzd*) *adj.* Very much surprised. *Ex.* He was *amazed* to find how large a jumbo jet is. It caused him *amazement* (*n.*).

ambassador (am-*bas*-a-dor) *n.* A minister of high rank who represents his country abroad.

ambidextrous (am-bi-*deks*-trus) *adj.* Able to use both hands with equal skill.

ambiguous (am-*big*-ew-us) *adj.* Having two possible meanings and not easily understood. *Ex.* His reply was *ambiguous*; we couldn't tell whether he meant yes or no.

ambition (am-*bish*'n) *n.* Desire for success and power. *Ex.* He works hard because he is *ambitious* (*adj.*).

amble (*am*-b'l) *v.* To go along at an easy pace.

ambulance (*am*-bew-lans) *n.* A van or car fitted to carry the injured and sick to hospital.

ambush (*am*-bUsh) *n.* (a) A group of people lying hidden and ready to make a surprise attack. (b) The place where they lie hid.

amen (*ah-men* or *ay-men*) *interj.* A Hebrew word meaning 'Let it be so', used at the end of prayers and hymns.

amend (a-*mend*) *v.* To improve or correct. *Ex.* He promised to *amend* his ways.

amenity (a-*meen*-i-ti) *n.* A pleasant feature of a place. *Ex.* A park may be one of the *amenities* of a city.

amethyst (*am*-eth-ist) 1. *n.* A purple jewel. 2. *adj.* Its colour.

amiable (*aym*-i-a-b'l) *adj.* Good-natured; friendly.

amicable (*am*-ik-a-b'l) *adj.* Friendly and peaceable. *Ex.* I broke one of her vases, but she was quite *amicable* about it.

ammonia (a-*mohn*-i-a) *n.* A strong-smelling gas, used in liquid form for cleaning etc.

ammunition (am-ew-*nish*'n) *n.* The bullets, shells etc. used in firing rifles or guns.

amount (a-*mownt*) 1. *n.* A quantity; the whole sum. *Ex.* There isn't a great *amount* of work to do now. 2. *v.* To add up to. *Ex.* The bill *amounted* to £7.

amphibious (am-*fib*-i-us) *adj.* Able to live on land and in water. *Ex.* The frog is an *amphibian* (*n.*).

ample (*am*-p'l) *adj.* Enough; spacious. *Ex.* There is *ample* room for our luggage in the boot.

amplifier (*am*-pli-fy-er) *n.* Apparatus used to increase the loudness of sound, and especially the strength of radio reception.

amputate (*am*-pew-tayt) *v.* To cut off a limb. *Ex.* The surgeon *amputated* the man's leg as it was too badly injured to save.

anaesthetic (an-es-*thet*-ik) *n.* A drug used to prevent the feeling of pain. *Ex.* I was given an *anaesthetic* before having my tooth out.

anagram (*an*-a-gram) *n.* A word or words made by changing the order of the letters in another word. *Ex.* 'Leap' is an *anagram* of 'pale'.

analysis (a-*nal*-i-sis) *n.* A breaking down into separate parts. *Ex.* The chemist *analysed* (*v.*) the water to see whether it was fit to drink.

anatomy (an-*at*-o-mi) *n.* The study of the structure of the body. Doctors study anatomy to find out how the body is made up and how it works.

ancestor (*an*-ses-tor) *n.* Any of our parents, grandparents, great-grandparents and so on into the past.

anchor (*ang*-ker) 1. *n.* A very heavy iron hook attached to a chain or rope, thrown over a ship's side to grip the sea bottom and keep the ship from drifting. 2. *v.* To fix with an anchor. *Ex.* The ship *anchored* in the bay.

ancient (*ayn*-sh'nt) *adj.* Very old; existing long ago.

anecdote (*an*-ek-doht) *n.* A very short story about a single happening. *Ex.* Uncle John is always telling us amusing *anecdotes* about the people he meets.

anemone (an-*em*-on-i) *n.* A spring flower. The *sea-anemone* is a soft-bodied sea creature with a flower-like form.

angle (*ang*-g'l) 1. *n.* A corner. The meeting of two lines forms an *angle* between them. 2. *v.* To fish with a rod, as an *angler* (*n.*) does.

anguish (*ang*-gwish) *n.* Very great pain or grief. *Ex.* The father suffered *anguish* when he thought his child was lost.

animated (*an*-i-may-tid) *adj.* Lively. *Ex.* Anne talks with such *animation* (*n.*) that all her stories come to life.

animosity (an-i-*mos*-i-ti) *n.* Hatred or ill-will. *Ex.* There was so much *animosity* between them that they began to fight.

anniversary (an-i-*vurs*-ar-i) *n.* The celebration each year of an event, on the date when it took place. *Ex.* Your birthday is the *anniversary* of your birth.

announce (a-*nowns*) *v.* To state publicly. *Ex.* At the party the hostess *announced* her daughter's engagement.

annoy (a-*noi*) *v.* To vex and irritate. *Ex.* James was *annoyed* that he had lost his torch. He felt *annoyance* (*n.*) about it.

annual (*an*-ew-al) 1. *adj.* Happening every year. *Ex.* Christmas is an *annual* festival. 2. *n.* (a) A book, such as a *Christmas annual*, that comes out every year. (b) A plant that lives for one year only.

anonymous (a-*non*-i-mus) *adj.* Having no name attached. *Ex.* She preferred to make her gift *anonymously* (*adv.*).

anorak (*an*-or-ak) *n.* A weatherproof jacket with a hood. Also called a *parka*.

answer (*ahn*-ser) *n.* A reply; a response to a question; the solution to an arithmetic question. *Ex.* We asked him the time, and he *answered* (*v.*) very crossly.

ant (ant) *n.* A small insect of a kind that lives together in great numbers and works hard in a very organized way.

antagonist (an-*tag*-on-ist) *n.* An enemy or rival. *Ex.* He was a powerful *antagonist* and hard to defeat. There was *antagonism* (*n.*) between the two footballers.

Antarctic (ant-*ark*-tik) *n. See* Arctic.

antelope (*an*-ti-lohp) *n.* A graceful grass-eating animal, rather like a deer, except that it does not shed its horns.

antenna (an-*ten*-a) *n.* (a) One of a pair of feelers which grows on the heads of some insects and shellfish. The plural is *antennae* (an-*ten*-ee). (b) A television or radio aerial.

anthem (*an*-them) *n.* (a) Words, sometimes from the Bible, set to music and sung in church or at a concert. (b) A national hymn, such as 'God Save the Queen'.

anthology (an-*thol*-o-ji) *n.* A collection of favourite pieces of poetry or prose.

antibody (*an*-ti-bod-i) *n.* A substance in our bodies which helps to fight an infection.

antipodes (an-*tip*-o-deez) *n.* The part of the world opposite to where one lives. Used especially of Australia and New Zealand, the *antipodes* of Britain.

antique (an-*teek*) *n.* Something, such as furniture or china, made long ago which people like to collect.

antiquity (an-*tik*-wi-ti) *n.* The far distant past.

antiseptic (an-ti-*sep*-tik) *n.* Any substance that prevents the spread of infection.

antlers (*ant*-lerz) *n.* The horns of a deer.

anvil (*an*-vil) *n.* The block of iron on which a blacksmith hammers metal into shape.

anxious (*ank*-shus) *adj.* (a) Worried. *Ex.* We are *anxious* about our grandmother's health. We feel *anxiety* (ang-*zy*-i-ti; *n.*). (b) Eager. *Ex.* He is *anxious* to succeed in his new job.

apartheid (a-*part*-hayt) *n.* The policy of keeping different races apart and under different rules and regulations.

apartment (a-*part*-ment) *n.* A single room, or a set of rooms, in a building.

apathy (*ap*-a-thi) *n.* Lack of interest or concern.

ape (ayp) 1. *n.* A large monkey without a tail. 2. *v.* To imitate. *Ex.* He tried to *ape* his father's way of walking.

aperture (*ap*-er-tewr) *n.* An opening. *Ex.* In a camera lens, a larger *aperture* is needed when the light is poor.

apologize (a-*pol*-o-jyz) *v.* To say sorry for what one has done. *Ex.* He *apologized* for arriving late. He made an *apology* (*n.*).

apostle (a-*pos*'l) *n.* A missionary, especially one of Christ's twelve disciples.

apostrophe (a-*pos*-tro-fee) *n.* A mark ', usually followed by 's' which shows ownership. *Ex.* Paul's pen. It may also show that letters have been left out of a word. *Ex.* Did*n't*.

appal (a-*pawl*) *v.* To shock or horrify. *Ex.* We were *appalled* at the news of the mining disaster.

apparatus (ap-ar-*ay*-tus) *n.* Equipment, especially in a science laboratory or gym.

apparent (a-*pa*-rent) *adj.* (a) Easily seen. *Ex.* The reason the tent collapsed became *apparent* when we found the guy-ropes cut. (b) Seeming, but not always real. *Ex.* The *apparent* cause may be different from the real one. '*Apparently* (*adv.*) he never got my letter' means that it seems that he never got it.

appeal (a-*peel*) 1. *n.* An earnest request. *Ex.* The prisoner made an *appeal* for mercy. 2. *v.* (a) To ask earnestly. *Ex.* She *appealed* to me for help. (b) To attract or please. *Ex.* Modern music does not *appeal* to me.

appear (a-*peer*) *v.* (a) To come into sight. *Ex.* A policeman *appeared* just in time. We greeted his *appearance* (*n.*) with relief. The opposite of *appear* is *disappear*. (b) To seem. *Ex.* He *appears* to be up to mischief; I don't like his *appearance* (*n.*).

appease (a-*peez*) *v.* To calm or satisfy. *Ex.* He was able to *appease* the indignant driver. His appetite was soon *appeased*.

appendix (a-*pen*-diks) *n.* (a) Something added, especially pages at the back of a book which give additional information. (b) A tiny part of the bowels, which may have to be removed when it becomes inflamed in *appendicitis* (a-pen-di-*sy*-tis; *n.*).

appetite (*ap*-et-yt) *n.* The desire for food. *Ex.* Marion lost her *appetite* when she had measles, and ate little.

applaud (a-*plawd*) *v.* To clap the hands to show approval and enjoyment. *Ex.* The audience was delighted and *applauded* loudly. There was great *applause* (*n.*).

apply (a-*ply*) *v.* (a) To put on. *Ex. Apply* a plaster to the cut. *Appliance* (a-*ply*-ans; *n.*) means apparatus. (b) To refer to. *Ex.* This rule does not *apply* to children. (c) To ask for. *Ex. Apply* for your tickets here. Make your *application* (*n.*).

appoint (a-*point*) *v.* To name or select. *Ex.* A new captain of the team has been *appointed.* Friday is the day *appointed* for the match. 'I have made an *appointment* (*n.*) to see the doctor' means that we have arranged to meet.

appreciate (a-*preesh*-i-ayt) *v.* To value highly; to be grateful for. *Ex.* We *appreciate* her kindness and have written to thank her. We feel *appreciation* (*n.*).

apprehensive (ap-ri-*hens*-iv) *adj.* Afraid; nervous about a future event.

apprentice (a-*prent*-is) *n.* Someone who agrees to work for an employer in return for being taught his trade.

approach (a-*prohch*) 1. *v.* To come near. *Ex.* We could see the ship's name as it *approached* harbour. 2. *n.* The *approach* to the house is by a narrow lane.

appropriate (a-*proh*-pri-at) *adj.* Suitable. A pound would be an *appropriate* sum to charge for the tickets.

approve (a-*proov*) *v.* To be pleased with and think good. *Ex.* I do not *approve* of your staying out so late. The opposite of *approval* (*n.*) is *disapproval*.

approximate (a-*proks*-i-mat) *adj.* Roughly correct. *Ex.* George gave an *approximate* answer before working out the sum.

apt (apt) *adj.* (a) Suitable. *Ex.* He gave an *apt* reply. (b) Inclined or likely. *Ex.* Our puppy is *apt* to chew to pieces anything he finds.

aptitude (*ap*-ti-tewd) *n.* Ability or skill in a particular activity. *Ex.* He has a natural *aptitude* for languages.

aqualung (*ak*-wa-lung) *n.* A diver's compressed-air supply carried on his back.

aquarium (a-*kwair*-i-um) *n.* (a) A tank to hold fish and other creatures and plants that live in water. (b) A building where such tanks are on view.

aquatic (a-*kwat*-ik) *adj.* Living in or connected with water. *Ex.* Seaweed is an *aquatic* plant. Water-skiing is an *aquatic* sport.

aqueduct (*ak*-kwi-dukt) *n.* A bridge which carries water across a valley.

arable (*ar*-a-b'l) *adj.* (Of land) Fit for growing crops in.

arch (arch) *n.* A structure of stone etc. built in a curve across an open space. A bridge is often in the shape of an *arch*. A cat may *arch* (*v.*) its back when it sees a dog.

arch- (arch) *prefix.* Chief or greatest, as in *archbishop.*

archery (*arch*-er-i) *n.* Shooting at a target with bow and arrow.

archipelago (ar-ki-*pel*-a-goh) *n.* A group of many islands.

Arctic (*ark*-tik) *n.* The area surrounding the North Pole. The *Antarctic* (ant-*ark*-tik) is the area round the South Pole. Arctic (*adj.*) means extremely cold.

arduous (*ard*-ew-us) *adj.* Hard; difficult. *Ex.* Sawing those logs was an *arduous* task.

arena (a-*reen*-a) *n.* An open space with seats round it for spectators at a bull-fight, circus etc.

argue (*arg*-ew) *v.* To give reasons for one's opinion or, especially, against someone else's opinion. *Ex.* Those two do love an *argument* (*n.*).

arid (*ar*-id) *adj.* Very dry. *Ex.* A desert is *arid* land.

armour (*ar*-mer) *n.* Protective clothing, usually of metal, once worn in war.

arms (armz) *n.* Weapons used in warfare. When men are given weapons they are *armed* (*v.*). An *army* (*n.*) is a body of *armed* (*adj.*) men trained for war.

aroma (a-*rohm*-a) *n.* A pleasant smell. *Ex.* I like the *aroma* of roasting coffee beans.

arouse (a-*rowz*) *v.* (a) To waken from sleep. *Ex.* He was *aroused* by the postman's knock. (b) To excite or stir up. *Ex.* His anger was *aroused* by what he saw.

arrange (a-*raynj*) *v.* (a) To put things in their proper places. *Ex.* Please *arrange* the chairs in rows. (b) To plan. *Ex.* A meeting has been *arranged* for Friday. That is the *arrangement* (*n.*).

arrant (*ar*-ant) *adj.* Complete or thorough, in a bad sense. *Ex.* He is an *arrant* thief. Don't talk such *arrant* nonsense.

array (a-*ray*) 1. *n.* Arrangement in order, sometimes for show. *Ex.* An *array* of troops. An *array* of wedding-presents. 2. *v.* To dress. *Ex.* The bride was *arrayed* in white.

arrears (a-*reerz*) *n.* Money that should have been paid, or work that should have been done, but has not. *Ex.* I must pay my *arrears* of rent, I am in *arrears*.

arrest (a-*rest*) *v.* To stop or seize. *Ex.* The police *arrested* the thief.

arrogant (*ar*-o-gant) *adj.* Conceited; haughty; bullying.

arsenal (*ar*-sen-al) *n.* A place where military weapons are made and stored.

arsenic (*ar*-sen-ik) *n.* A strong poison.

arson (*ar*-son) *n.* Deliberately setting fire to something.

art (art) *n.* (a) A skill in a particular subject. *Ex.* The *art* of pleasing people. The *art* of healing. (b) The use of the imagination in creating works such as an oil painting, sculpture or a piece of music.

artery (*art*-er-i) *n.* Any of the large tubes which carry blood from the heart to various parts of the body. *Ex. Arterial* (ar-*teer*-i-al; *adj.*) blood is bright red; the blood in veins is dark red.

artful (*art*-ful) *adj.* Cunning.

article (*art*-i-k'l) *n.* (a) An object; a thing. (b) In grammar the name for the word 'the' (the definite *article*) and the words 'a' or 'an' (the indefinite *article*). (c) A piece of writing in a newspaper or magazine.

artificial (art-i-*fish*'l) *adj.* Not natural; man-made. *Ex. Artificial* flowers can be made of plastic.

artillery (ar-*til*-er-i) *n.* (a) Big guns. (b) The branch of the army that uses them.

artist (*art*-ist) *n.* One who is skilled in a fine art such as painting or ballet. Such a person is *artistic* (*adj.*).

asbestos (az-*best*-os) *n.* A substance which can be woven into a cloth that will not burn, and is used in firemen's clothing etc.

ascend (a-*send*) *v.* To go up or climb. *Ex.* You *ascend* to the top floor by the lift. Many people have now made the *ascent* (*n.*) of Everest.

ascertain (as-er-*tayn*) *v.* To find out.

ash (ash) *n.* (a) A tall tree with grey bark and tough wood, useful as timber. (b) The dusty matter left when a fire has burnt out.

ashamed (a-*shaymd*) *adj.* Feeling shame or discomfort about one's failings. *Ex.* I am *ashamed* to think that I never tried to help them.

askew (a-*skew*) *adv.* Twisted to one side. *Ex.* That picture is hanging *askew*, I will put it straight.

asphalt (*as*-falt) *n.* A dark-coloured tarry substance, which is mixed with rock chippings to make a road or roof covering etc.

asphyxiate (as-*fiks*-i-ayt) *v.* To make breathing difficult or impossible.

aspire (a-*spyr*) *v.* To want to reach some higher position in life. *Ex.* He *aspires* to be Prime Minister.

assassinate (a-*sas*-in-ayt) *v.* To murder, especially for political reasons. The murderer is an *assassin* (*n.*).

assault (as-*awlt*) *v.* To attack violently. *Ex.* Two hooligans *assaulted* me on my way home. It was a brutal *assault* (*n.*).

assemble (a-*sem*-b'l) *v.* To come together in one place; to put together. *Ex.* A crowd quickly *assembled* at the scene of the accident. An *assembly* (*n.*) is a meeting of people for some special purpose.

assent (a-*sent*) *v.* To agree to. *Ex.* The doorkeeper *assented* when we asked if we could come in. He gave his *assent* (*n.*).

assert (a-*surt*) *v.* To state firmly. *Ex.* He *asserted* that his statement was true.

assess (a-*ses*) *v.* (a) To fix the amount of money to be paid as tax or for damage done. (b) To estimate. *Ex.* I am trying to *assess* our chances of winning the match.

asset (*as*-et) *n.* (a) Any property of value. *Ex.* When he died his *assets* came to £10,000. (b) Something or somebody useful. *Ex.* His knowledge of languages is a great *asset* to the firm.

associate (a-*soh*-shi-ayt) *v.* To keep company with. *Ex.* Rock fans usually *associate* with each other. An *association* (*n.*) is a group of people who have the same interest in something.

assorted (a-*sor*-tid) *adj.* Made up of various kinds.

assume (as-*ewm*) *v.* To take something upon oneself, or to take for granted. *Ex.* He *assumed* all the duties which his dead brother had undertaken when he was alive. He *assumed* that no one would object to this.

assure (a-*shoor*) *v.* To tell firmly. *Ex.* Janet *assured* her mother that she would come straight home. She gave that *assurance* (*n.*).

asthma (*asth*-ma) *n.* An illness which makes breathing difficult.

astonish (as-*ton*-ish) *v.* To surprise very much. *Ex.* Richard was *astonished* when he found that the birds had flown from the nest.

astound (as-*townd*) *v.* To amaze and astonish.

astride (a-*stryd*) *adv.* With one leg on either side of something, as most people sit on horseback.

astrology (as-*trol*-o-ji) *n.* The study of the stars and planets in the belief that they affect people's lives.

astronaut (*as*-tro-nawt) *n.* A space-traveller.

astronomy (as-*tron*-om-i) *n.* The science dealing with facts about the stars and the solar system. This is studied by *astronomers* (*n.*), using *astronomical* (as-tro-*nom*-ik-al; *adj.*) instruments.

astute (as-*tewt*) *adj.* Quick to understand; shrewd, often in a wily way.

asylum (a-*syl*-um) *n.* (a) A place of peace and safety. (b) A hospital for the mentally ill.

atheist (*ayth*-i-ist) *n.* One who believes there is no God.

athlete (*ath*-leet) *n.* A person who has physical skills in running, jumping etc., and competes in *athletic* (ath-*let*-ik; *adj.*) contests.

atmosphere (*at*-mo-sfeer) *n.* The air which surrounds the earth. *Ex.* Spacecraft go far beyond the *atmosphere*.

atom (*at*'m) *n.* (a) One of the tiny particles of which all matter consists. When an *atom* is split, a huge amount of energy is released. (b) Any tiny amount.

atrocious (a-*troh*-shus) *adj.* Wicked; horrible. *Ex.* Murder is an *atrocious* crime. It is an *atrocity* (a-*tros*-i-ti; *n.*).

attach (a-*tach*) *v.* To fasten to, or to join in some way. You can *attach* a trailer to a car, or be *attached* to an army unit for special work, or be *attached* to someone by bonds of affection.

attack (a-*tak*) *v.* To strike a blow or begin a fight. *Ex.* The enemy *attacked* the camp. Disease can also *attack*. *Ex.* Marion has just had an *attack* (*n.*) of measles.

attain (a-*tayn*) *v.* To arrive at; to gain by effort. *Ex.* He *attained* the rank of captain before leaving the navy.

attempt (a-*tempt*) *v.* To try. *Ex.* He *attempted* to save the kitten from drowning. He made the *attempt* (*n.*).

attend (a-*tend*) *v.* (a) To be present at. *Ex.* He *attends* church regularly. (b) To give thought to. *Ex.* Please *attend* to what I am saying. Give me your *attention* (*n.*). Be *attentive* (*adj.*). (c) To look after. *Ex.* The nurse was *attending* to the wounded.

attic (*at*-ik) *n.* A room right under the roof, with a skylight, often used as a storeroom.

attire (a-*tyr*) *v.* To dress. *Ex.* The dancers were *attired* in national costume. Their *attire* (*n.*) was attractive.

attitude (*at*-i-tewd) *n.* (a) A way in which a body is positioned. *Ex.* He stood in an *attitude* of keen attention. (b) A way of thinking or behaving. *Ex.* His *attitude* all through the week-end camp was unhelpful.

attract (a-*trakt*) *v.* (a) To arouse interest or admiration. *Ex.* Her beauty *attracted* the artist so much that he painted her portrait. The Christmas decorations were very *attractive* (*adj.*). They were an *attraction* (*n.*) to the crowds. (b) To draw to itself. *Ex.* A magnet *attracts* iron.

attribute (a-*trib*-ewt) 1. *v.* To consider as the cause or work of. *Ex.* He *attributed* her success to hard work. 2. *n.* (at-*rib*-yewt) A quality. *Ex.* Honesty is his most striking *attribute*.

auburn (*aw*-bern) *adj.* Reddish-brown (especially of hair).

auction (*awk*-sh'n) *n.* A public sale at which things go to the person who offers most money for them. The person who *auctions* (*v.*) the things is an *auctioneer* (*n.*).

audacity (aw-*das*-i-ti) *n.* (a) Boldness and daring. *Ex.* Nelson had the *audacity* to ignore his commanding officer's signal. He was *audacious* (aw-*day*-shus; *adj.*). (b) Impudence. *Ex.* He had the *audacity* to call me a liar.

audible (*aw*-dib'l) *adj.* Loud enough to be heard. *Ex.* Your radio should not be *audible* to your neighbours.

audience (*aw*-di-ens) *n.* A number of people who have come together to hear or see something.

audit (*aw*-dit) *n.* The examining of business accounts by specially trained people (*auditors*; *n.*), who *audit* (*v.*) them.

austere (aw-*steer*) *adj.* Stern; very simple and plain. *Ex.* An *austere* diet. An *austere* building.

authentic (aw-*then*-tik) *adj.* Real; genuine; correct. *Ex.* The Constable painting was found to be *authentic*, not a fake.

author (*aw*-ther) *n.* A writer of books.

authority (aw-*thor*-i-ti) *n.* The power or right to be obeyed. *Ex.* The headmaster has full *authority* in the school.

autobiography (aw-to-by-*og*-raf-i) *n.* The story of a person's life written by himself.

autograph (*aw*-to-graf) *n.* A person's own handwriting or signature. *Ex.* Several of the children asked for the cricketer's *autograph.*

automatic (aw-to-*mat*-ik) *adj.* (a) (Of a machine) Working without human control. *Ex.* The control of an aeroplane may be left to an *automatic* pilot. (b) Done without thinking. *Ex.* His immediate reply was an *automatic* 'no', but later he agreed.

automobile (*aw*-to-mo-beel) *n.* A motor-car.

auxiliary (awg-*zil*-i-ar-i) *adj.* Helping; additional. *Ex.* The *auxiliary* engine on our sailing-boat was a great help when the wind dropped.

avail (a-*vayl*) *v.* To make use of. *Ex.* He *availed* himself of the chance to come to London.

avalanche (*av*-a-lahnsh) *n.* A great mass of snow sliding down a mountain-side.

avarice (*av*-ar-is) *n.* A greedy love of riches. To have feelings of avarice is to be *avaricious* (av-ar-*ish*-us; *adj.*).

avenge (a-*venj*) *v.* To take revenge for a wrong done to oneself or someone else. *Ex.* Hamlet *avenged* the death of his father by killing the man who murdered him. He *avenged* his father.

avenue (*av*-en-ew) *n.* A wide, often tree-lined, street; a tree-lined approach to a house.

average (*av*-er-ij) 1. *adj.* Usual or ordinary. *Ex.* The *average* man does not want war. 2. *n.* In arithmetic the *average* of several quantities is their total divided by their number. *Ex.* The *average* of the three numbers 4, 6 and 8 (totalling 18) is 18 divided by $3 = 6$.

averse (a-*vurs*) *adj.* Feeling dislike. *Ex.* Most children are *averse* to going to bed early.

avert (a-*vurt*) *v.* To turn aside; to prevent. *Ex.* He *averted* his eyes from the blinding light. The accident was *averted* by the driver's skill.

aviary (*ay*-vi-ar-i) *n.* A place where birds are kept.

aviation (ay-vi-*aysh*'n) *n.* The science of making or flying aircraft.

avoid (a-*void*) *v.* To keep away from; to escape. *Ex.* To *avoid* a long journey, he took a short cut.

await (a-*wayt*) *v.* To wait for.

awake (a-*wayk*)   1. *adj*. Not asleep. 2. *v*. (Also *awaken*) To rouse from sleep.   *Ex.* I was *awakened* by the crash.

award (a-*word*)   1. *n*. A prize.   *Ex.* He won the mayor's *award* for the best-kept garden. 2. *v*. To give a prize.   *Ex.* The mayor *awarded* the prize.

aware (a-*wair*)   *adj*. Knowing and conscious of.   *Ex.* He was *aware* of the danger but still determined to go.

awe (aw)   *n*. Great respect; fear; wonder.   *Ex.* He was filled with *awe* when he first saw the Alps.

awful (*aw*-ful)   *adj*. (a) Causing awe; impressive. (b) Dreadful; terrible.   *Ex.* We had an *awful* thunderstorm last night. (c) Very great (in a bad sense).   *Ex.* I have an *awful* lot of work to do. I shall have to work *awfully* (*adv.*) hard.

awkward (*awk*-w'd)   *adj*. Clumsy; not graceful; difficult.   *Ex.* She is too *awkward* with her hands to make a good dressmaker. He is an *awkward* person to deal with. You have arrived at an *awkward* moment.

awning (*awn*-ing)   *n*. A covering of canvas or plastic to protect from the sun.

axe (aks)   *n*. A sharp-edged tool for cutting wood.

axis (*aks*-is)   *n*. The straight line (real or imaginary) round which any body, such as the Earth, turns.

axle (*aks*'l)   *n*. The rod on which a wheel turns.

B

babel (*bay*-b'l)   *n*. The confused noise of a lot of people talking at once.

baboon (ba-*boon*)   *n*. A large monkey with a dog-like face.

bachelor (*batch*-e-lor)   *n*. A man who has never married.

background   *n*. (a) The back part of a picture or of a crowd etc.; a place where one is not likely to be noticed. (b) The conditions in which one was brought up.   *Ex.* He came from a happy family *background*.

backwater   *n*. (a) A short branch of a river where the water is still (does not move). (b) A place or job where there is little going on, or chance of progress.

bacon (*bay*-k'n) *n.* The back and sides of a pig, cured and prepared for eating.

bacteria (bak-*teer*-i-a) *n.* Very simple microscopic creatures, some of which cause disease.

badger (*baj*-er) 1. *n.* An animal which lives in a hole in the ground and hunts at night. 2. *v.* To pester. *Ex.* He will do what you want if you don't *badger* him.

badminton (*bad*-min-t'n) *n.* An indoor game played over a net with rackets and shuttlecocks.

baffle *v.* To puzzle. *Ex.* The burglary *baffled* the police, as the most valuable things were left untouched.

baggage (*bag*-ij) *n.* The suitcases that one takes on a journey.

bagpipes *n.* A musical instrument; the *piper* (*n.*) blows air into a bag under his arm, and squeezes it through the reeds of various pipes.

bail 1. *n.* (a) Someone who guarantees that an accused person will attend his trial if he is freed in the meantime; the guarantee itself. (b) In cricket, one of the cross-pieces on a wicket. 2. *v. See* bale.

bait 1. *n.* Pieces of food used to catch animals in traps or fish on hooks. 2. *v.* To use food in this way. *Ex.* We *baited* the mousetrap with cheese.

balance 1. *n.* (a) A pair of scales for weighing. (b) What is left over. *Ex.* When you have paid for your ticket out of this pound you may keep the *balance*. 2. *v.* To keep steady. *Ex.* She can *balance* a water-pot on her head.

balcony (*bal*-kon-i) *n.* A sort of platform, with railings, outside a window, where people can sit.

bale 1. *n.* A bundle of things, such as hay. 2. *v.* (a) To make into bales. (b) (Also spelt *bail*) To scoop water out of a boat with a *bailer* (*n.*) or other container. (b) To *bale out* means to escape from an aeroplane by parachute.

ballad (*bal*-ad) *n.* A long poem which usually describes an adventure.

ballast (*bal*-ast) *n.* Something heavy, such as sand, placed in the hold of a ship to keep it steady in rough seas.

ballet (*bal*-ay) *n.* A performance in which a story is told, or a feeling is expressed, by dancing and miming to music.

balloon (bal-*oon*) *n.* A bag filled with gas that is lighter than air and enables it to rise and float in the air, often used to collect information about the weather. *Toy balloons* are inflated rubber bags.

ballot (*bal*-ot) *n*. A method of voting, in which a marked paper is put into a box.

bamboo (bam-*boo*) *n*. A tropical plant with big jointed hollow stems, much used in the East to build houses, make furniture etc.

ban *v*. To forbid. *Ex*. Smoking is *banned* in the concert-hall, but there is no *ban* (*n*.) on it in the restaurant.

banana (ban-*ahn*-a) *n*. A finger-shaped tropical fruit with a thick yellow skin and a soft inside.

band *n*. (a) A narrow strip of any material which can be used to hold things together, or as an ornament etc. (b) A number of people who are together for a particular purpose. *Ex*. A *band* of robbers. The *brass band* played military marches.

bandage (*band*-ij) 1. *n*. A band of cloth to bind up wounds etc. 2. *v*. To bind up in this way. *Ex*. She *bandaged* the cut on his leg.

bandeau (*band*-o) *n*. A band to bind the hair and keep it off the face.

bandit *n*. An armed robber.

bandy 1. *adj*. With legs bent apart at the knee. 2. *v*. To toss words from one to another. *Ex*. They began to *bandy* words, and gradually got angrier and angrier.

bangle *n*. A large ring worn for decoration around arm, wrist or ankle.

banish *v*. To send into exile; to drive away. *Ex*. Napoleon was *banished* to St Helena. She couldn't afford to go on the cruise, so she *banished* the idea from her mind.

banister (*ban*-ist-er) *n*. The railings, usually with a wooden top (the *banister rail*), on a staircase.

banjo (*ban*-jo) *n*. A plucked musical instrument with five strings, a long neck, and a round body covered with parchment.

bank 1. *n*. (a) The ground at the edge of a river. (b) An establishment which keeps, lends and exchanges money. 2. *v*. To put money in a bank. *Ex*. You had better *bank* that five pounds before you lose it.

bankrupt *adj*. (Of a person or business) Unable to pay the money owed.

banner *n*. A flag.

banns *n*. A notice, read in church, that a couple propose to marry.

banquet (*bang*-kwet) *n*. A rich dinner, usually given to celebrate some event and at which speeches are made.

baptize (bap-*tyz*) *v.* To admit to a Christian Church by the ceremony of *baptism* (*n.*), which usually includes sprinkling with (or dipping in) water, and the giving of a Christian name.

barbarous (*bar*-bar-us) *adj.* Not civilized; brutal. Also called *barbaric* (bar-*bar*-ik). *Barbarian* (*n.*) means a barbaric person; *barbarity* (*n.*) means brutality.

barbecue (*bar*-bi-kew) *n.* An open-air party at which meat is cooked on a grill over a charcoal fire.

barbed *adj.* Having sharp points on it. *Ex.* A *barbed-wire* fence.

bargain (*bar*-gin) 1. *n.* (a) An agreement, especially about the sale or exchange of goods. *Ex.* We made a *bargain* that he could use my garden if he gave me half the vegetables from it. (b) Something bought cheap, for example at a sale. 2. *v.* To argue or haggle about such a sale or other arrangement.

barge (barj) *n.* A flat-bottomed cargo-boat used on canals and rivers.

baritone (*bar*-i-tohn) *n.* A man's singing voice, higher than bass but lower than tenor.

bark *n.* (a) The outer covering of tree-trunks. (b) The cry of a dog.

barley *n.* A grain used for food and in brewing beer.

barn *n.* A farm building used to store corn and hay.

barnacle (*barn*-a-k'l) *n.* A small shellfish which clings fast to rocks and ship's bottoms.

barometer (bar-*om*-e-ter) *n.* An instrument which measures air-pressure and shows likely changes in weather.

baron *n.* A member of the lowest order of peers. His wife is called a *baroness*.

barrack 1. *n.* A building in which soldiers live. Also called *barracks*. 2. *v.* To make hostile noises at a team during a match.

barrage (*bar*-ahj) *n.* The firing of many guns at a small area for a long time, in preparation for an attack.

barrel *n.* (a) A wooden vessel used to store foods, beer etc. (b) The metal tube of a gun.

barren *adj.* Producing nothing. *Ex.* The land was *barren* and the people starved.

barricade *n.* A hastily put-up barrier across a street.

barrier *n.* Something put up to prevent anyone passing.

barrow *n.* A handcart. A street-trader's *barrow* has two wheels, and a *wheelbarrow*, used in gardening, has one. (b) An ancient burial-mound.

barter *v.* To trade by exchanging goods instead of using money. *Ex.* The fishermen *bartered* fish for tobacco.

base 1. *n.* (a) The lowest part of anything. *Ex.* A wreath was laid at the *base* of the war memorial. (b) An army headquarters where stores are kept. 2. *adj.* Of low character; mean. *Ex.* He turned out to be a *base* ungrateful fellow. *Basic* (*adj.*) means belonging to the first stages; essential. *Ex. Basic* cookery is simple cookery, learnt before going on to more difficult dishes.

baseball *n.* An American game developed from rounders.

basement *n.* The lowest part of a building, below ground level.

bashful *adj.* Shy; timid.

basis (*bay*-sis) *n.* The main quality from which other features develop or depend. *Ex.* The *basis* of courtesy is consideration for others.

bask *v.* To enjoy the warmth, especially of the sun. *Ex.* Cats like to *bask* by a fire.

basketball *n.* A team game in which goals are scored by throwing the ball into an iron ring (the *basket*) on a high pole. *Netball* is a similar game.

bass (bays) 1. *n.* (a) The lowest part in harmonized music. (b) Man's singing voice with the lowest range. 2. *adj.* Deep-sounding. *Ex.* A *bass* sound came from the great bell.

bassoon (ba-*soon*) *n.* The musical instrument that has the lowest tone of the woodwind family.

bastard *n.* The child of parents not married to each other.

baste *v.* (a) To cover roasting meat with melted fat etc. (b) To sew long loose 'holding' stitches in needlework; to tack.

bat *n.* (a) The heavy stick with which several ball games are played. (b) A small animal, rather like a mouse but with wings, which flies at night.

batch *n.* A collection of things of the same sort. *Ex.* A *batch* of loaves was taken out of the oven by the baker.

bath (bahth) 1. *n.* (a) A tub in which the whole body can be washed. (b) Washing one's body in this. 2. *v.* To give a bath, especially to a baby.

bathe (baydh) 1. *v.* To go swimming; to take a dip in the sea etc. 2. *n.* The act of swimming or taking a dip.

baton (*bat*-on) *n.* A short stick used by the conductor of an orchestra or choir to beat time.

battalion (ba-*tal*-yon) *n.* One of the units of an infantry regiment.

batter 1. *n.* A mixture of flour, milk and eggs used to make pancakes etc. 2. *v.* To beat. *Ex.* The police had to *batter* down the locked door.

battery *n.* (a) A unit of men and guns in the army. (b) An arrangement of cells for producing electricity. A *battery hen* is reared, with hundreds of others, in rows of small cages.

battlements *n.* A wall at the top of a castle, with regular openings from which its defenders could shoot.

bay 1. *n.* (a) A curving part of the shore. (b) A tree whose leaves are used in cookery for their flavour. (c) The deep cry of hounds. 2. *v.* To utter a deep howling sound. *Ex.* The hounds *bayed* when they scented the fox.

bayonet (*bay*-on-et) *n.* A short dagger that can be fixed to the end of an army rifle.

bazaar (ba-*zahr*) *n.* (a) An Eastern market-place. (b) A sale of goods, sometimes home-made, in aid of charity.

bazooka *n.* A rocket-firing anti-tank gun.

beacon *n.* (a) A warning light, such as a lighthouse. (b) A bonfire lit on a hill to celebrate an important event.

beagling (*bee*-gling) *n.* Hunting hares with hounds called *beagles*.

beam *n.* (a) A long piece of wood used in building a house or ship. (b) A ray of light or radiation. A *beaming* (*adj.*) smile is a bright smile that lights up the face.

bean *n.* (a) A kidney-shaped seed in a pod, used as a vegetable. *Runner beans* are cooked in the pod; the pods of *kidney* or *French beans* are not eaten. (b) Any similar shaped seed, such as the coffee *bean*.

bear 1. *n.* (a) A large clumsy furry animal, such as the grizzly of North America and the white Polar bear. (b) A bad-tempered person. 2. *v.* To carry.

beaver *n.* An animal of the rat family which works very hard building dams in rivers, and has a valuable fur.

beckon *v.* To invite a person to come near, by a movement of the head or hand.

bedlam *n.* A scene of loud confused noise; an uproar. *Ex.* After the teacher went out, there was *bedlam* in the classroom.

bedraggled *adj.* Wet and untidy.

bedridden *adj.* Obliged to remain in bed for a long time because of illness or weakness.

beech *n.* A tall tree with a smooth greyish bark, which provides timber used in furniture.

beer *n.* An alcoholic drink made from malted barley and flavoured with hops.

beetle *n.* An insect with a hard back.

beetroot *n.* A dark-red root vegetable.

begrudge *v.* To envy someone having something. *Ex.* Jim *begrudged* Charles his luck and said his win was unfair.

behalf *n.* Sake; benefit; cause. *Ex.* We are collecting on *behalf* of 'Guide Dogs for the Blind'.

behave *v.* To act in a certain way. You can *behave* well or badly. Your *behaviour* (be-*hayv*-yer; *n.*) can be good or bad.

behindhand *adv.* Not on time; with something still not done. *Ex.* She was *behindhand* with her rent and now had three months' rent to pay.

beige (bayzh) *adj.* A yellowish-brown colour.

belfry *n.* The part of a church tower where the bells are hung.

believe (be-*leev*) *v.* To accept as true. *Ex.* I *believe* his story as he is a truthful man. It is my *belief* (*n.*) that he spoke the truth.

belligerent (be-*lij*-er-ent) *adj.* (a) Being at war. *Ex.* The *belligerent* nations at last made peace. (b) Quarrelsome; aggressive. *Ex.* His manner was so *belligerent* that people were afraid of him.

bellow (*bel*-o) *v.* To roar like a bull.

bellows *n.* A kind of tool that blows air into a fire to make it burn, or into an organ so that it can be played.

belly *n.* The stomach.

bench *n.* A long seat such as those in parks; a table of the kind that a carpenter works on. The judges who sit in a lawcourt are called the *Bench*.

bend *v.* To force something into a curve or angle. *Ex.* When you *bend* a piece of wire it becomes *bent* (*adj.*). After a little way, the road took a *bend* to the right.

benediction (ben-e-*dik*-sh'n) *n.* A blessing.

benefactor *n.* One who gives help and shows kindness.

benefit *n.* Something which does a person good. *Ex.* Dick had been overworking and *benefited* (*v.*) from his holiday. He found it *beneficial* (ben-e-*fish*'l; *adj.*). *Sickness benefit* is money paid to those too ill to work.

benevolent (ben-*ev*-o-lent) *adj.* Kind and generous.

benign (be-*nyn*) *adj.* Kindly, good-natured.

bequeath (be-*kweedh*) *v.* To arrange to give something to someone after one's death. *Ex.* My aunt *bequeathed* most of her money to her family; she also made *bequests* (*n.*) to friends.

bereaved (be-*reevd*) *adj.* Having lost a relative or dear friend by death.

beret (*ber*-ay) *n.* A round, flat, woollen cap.

berserk (*bur*-serk) *adj.* Madly violent. *Ex.* When our dog went *berserk*, we suspected rabies.

berth *n.* The sleeping-place in a ship or railway sleeper, usually a bunk-bed.

beseech *v.* To ask or beg earnestly.

besiege (be-*seej*) *v.* To surround and try to capture. *Ex.* The city was *besieged* for months before it surrendered.

betray *v.* To be unfaithful to, or plot against. *Ex.* He *betrayed* his country by giving secret information to the enemy about the Navy. It was a serious *betrayal* (*n.*).

betrothed (be-*trohdhd*) *adj.* Engaged to be married.

bevel *n.* A sloping or slanting edge, as on a picture frame.

beverage (*bev*-er-ij) *n.* Any drink, but usually referring to tea, lemonade or other soft drinks.

beware *v.* To look out for and be careful about. *Ex. Beware* of that bull in the field.

bewilder (be-*wil*-der) *v.* To puzzle or confuse. *Ex.* She was *bewildered* by the crowds, as she had not visited a big city before.

bewitching *adj.* Charming.

bias (*by*-as) *n.* A leaning or slant to one side. One can be *biased* (*adj.*; one-sided) in behaviour. *Ex.* In the painting competition, the judge showed a *bias* in favour of water-colours. Material can be cut on the *bias* instead of straight up and down the weave of the cloth.

biceps (*by*-seps) *n.* The chief muscle of the upper arm.

bicker *v.* To quarrel, but not violently. *Ex.* Those two boys are always *bickering*, and don't get on well.

bigamy (*big*-am-i) *n.* The crime of having two wives or husbands at once.

bikini (bi-*keen*-i) *n.* A woman's swim-suit in two separate pieces.

bilious *adj.* Inclined to be sick.

billet 1. *n.* A house in which soldiers are lodged. 2. *v.* To lodge a soldier in a private house.

billiards (*bil*-yedz) *n.* A game played on a baize-topped table, in which balls are hit with cues into pockets at the side.

billion *n.* A million millions (1,000,000,000,000); in the USA it is a thousand millions.

bind (bynd) *v.* (a) To tie up or to fasten together, as with a rope.

(b) To put covers on a book. The covers are the *binding* (*n.*) of the book.

bingo *n.* A game with prizes, in which random numbers are called out and entered on cards by the players.

binoculars (bi-*nok*-ew-lerz) *n.* An instrument for looking at a distant object (with both eyes at once), which makes it seem nearer and larger. *Field-glasses* are used out of doors, and *opera-glasses* at the theatre.

biography (by-*og*-raf-i) *n.* A book telling the story of someone's life.

biology (by-*ol*-oj-i) *n.* The study of living things.

birch *n.* A graceful tree with smooth, often silvery, bark.

birth *n.* The producing of young; being born. The beginning of an idea or invention can be called its *birth.*

bisect (by-*sekt*) *v.* To cut into two equal parts.

bishop *n.* The chief clergyman of a large district.

bitter *adj.* (a) A sharp taste, the opposite to sweet. *Ex.* A lemon has a *bitter* flavour. (b) Harsh; distressing; unpleasant. *Ex. Bitter* weather; *bitter* sorrow; *bitter* reproaches.

blackbeetle *n.* A name for the common house cockroach.

blackguard (*blag*-ard) *n.* A very bad man; a scoundrel.

black-lead *n.* Graphite, a greasy mineral used in polishing grates, making pencils etc.

blackmail 1. *n.* Money obtained from a person by threatening to do him harm if he does not pay. 2. *v.* To try to get money in this way.

blacksmith *n.* A man who works in iron, making and fitting horseshoes, for example.

blame *v.* To find fault with or accuse. *Ex.* He was *blamed* for the disaster; he was to *blame.*

blancmange (bla-*monzh*) *n.* A flavoured jelly made with milk and cornflour.

bland *adj.* Smooth and mild in manner; (of food) smooth and not tasting of anything in particular.

blank *adj.* Having no writing or marks on it. *Ex.* Leave the first page *blank*, and begin writing on the second page.

blare *v.* To sound unpleasantly loud as, for example, a radio turned up too high.

blarney *n.* Insincere flattery.

blast 1. *n.* A great rush of wind or air. *Ex.* On the upper deck he was exposed to the full *blast* of the wind. 2. *v.* To blow up with explosives; to destroy. *Ex.* They were *blasting* out rock in the quarry. The oak-tree was *blasted* by lightning.

blaze *n.* The bright light from a fire. *Ex.* We could see the *blaze* of the burning house a long way off.

blazer *n.* A loose, buttoned jacket, often worn by schoolchildren and sportsmen.

bleach *v.* To make white by exposing to the sun, or by washing in a special liquid.

bleak *adj.* Cold; windy; gloomy. Weather is sometimes *bleak*, and a place or situation can be *bleak*.

bleary *adj.* (Of the eyes) Sore and red.

bleat *v.* To cry, used chiefly of sheep.

blemish *n.* A blot; something which spoils the appearance; a fault. *Ex.* She chose seven perfect pears with no *blemish* on them.

blend *v.* To mix well together. *Ex.* Different kinds of tea can be *blended*, and thus make a good *blend* (*n.*).

bless *v.* (a) To make holy by making the sign of the cross over. (b) To wish happiness to.

blight *n.* A disease in plants which makes them fade and die; something which causes hopes to come to nothing. *Ex.* Her hopes of going to America were *blighted* (*v.*) when she found how much it would cost.

blink *v.* To shut the eyes for a moment every now and then.

bliss *n.* Great happiness.

blister *n.* A piece of raised skin on the body filled with a watery fluid. A burn, insect-bite or a shoe rubbing a heel can cause one.

blizzard *n.* A heavy snowstorm and high wind combined.

bloated *adj.* Swollen, as from having eaten too much.

bloater *n.* A salted, smoke-cured herring.

block 1. *n.* (a) A solid mass, as of stone or ice. (b) Something which stops natural movement, such as a block in the traffic. 2. *v.* To stop or prevent movement. *Ex.* A fallen rock *blocked* the path.

blockade *v.* To besiege and prevent people or supplies entering or leaving a place.

blond *adj.* Fair-skinned and fair-haired. A *blonde* (*n.*) is a blond female.

bloodhound *n.* A dog with a strong sense of smell (a keen scent), trained to find missing people.

bloodshot *adj.* With eye red and inflamed, showing small streaks of blood in it.

bloodthirsty *adj.* Cruel and enjoying the sufferings of others.

bloom 1. *n.* A flower. *Ex.* The roses are in *bloom.* 2. *v.* To produce flowers. *Ex.* The roses are *blooming.*

blossom 1. *n.* The flower on a tree that comes before the fruit. *Ex.* Apple *blossom.* 2. *v.* To produce blossom.

blotch *n.* A patch on some surfaces where the colour has been altered. *Ex.* This paper is *blotched* with damp brown patches.

blouse *n.* A woman's loose-fitting outer garment, usually tucked in at the waist.

blubber 1. *n.* The fat of the whale. 2. *v.* To weep noisily.

blueprint *n.* A plan of something to be made (such as a building, machinery etc.), usually printed in white on blue paper, for use by builders or engineers.

bluff 1. *adj.* Kindly but rough in speech. *Ex.* The old seaman made them welcome in his *bluff*, outspoken way. 2. *v.* To deceive by giving a false impression, of being in a stronger position than one is, for example. *Ex.* He tried to *bluff* me into thinking he was rich.

blunder *n.* A stupid mistake.

blunt *adj.* (a) Having an edge that is not sharp. A knife or pencil may be *blunt.* (b) Speaking in a way that may be honest but not very polite. *Ex.* In his *blunt* way, he said he didn't want to see Jim ever again.

blurred *adj.* Not clear; smeared. *Ex.* The view through the windscreen was *blurred* by rain.

blurt *v.* To say something on impulse, without thinking of the effect it will have. *Ex.* Without warning, he suddenly *blurted* out the bad news.

blush *v.* To become red in the face through shame or feeling awkward.

blustery *v.* To talk, boast or threaten in a noisy way. A strong wind can be said to be *blustering* (*adj.*)

boar *n.* A male pig.

board *n.* (a) A thin flat strip of wood, such as a floorboard. (b) The food supplied to a lodger. A *boarder* is one who is supplied with *board* and lodging, as for instance at a *boarding-school* or *boarding-house.* '*On board*' means 'on a ship', 'plane' etc.

boast *v.* To talk about something that you have done, or possess, as if it were much better or bigger than it is. *Ex.* She is always *boasting* about her tennis. She is *boastful* (*adj.*).

boat *n.* A small, open vessel moved by oars, sails or a motor; another name for a ship.

bobsleigh (*bob*-slay) *n.* A racing sledge for two or more people, and steerable.

bodyguard *n.* A man or group of men who have to guard the life of someone.

bog *n.* A piece of sodden, spongy ground in which one might sink.

bogus *adj.* Sham; fake; not real.

bogy *n.* Something one fears, usually without reason.

boil 1. *v.* To cook in hot, bubbling water which is giving off steam. 2. *n.* An inflamed swelling on the skin.

boisterous *adj.* Rough; noisy. A wind or a game can become *boisterous*.

bolero (*bol*-er-o) *n.* A woman's very short, usually sleeveless, jacket.

bollard *n.* A short post on a quayside or ship, round which a rope can be tied; a low post on a road barring entry to cars etc.

bolster (*bohl*-ster) 1. *n.* A long narrow under-pillow on a bed. 2. *v.* To *bolster up* means to support.

bolt 1. *n.* A strong metal bar on a door for fastening it. 2. *v.* (a) To fasten a door with a bolt. (b) To break away and run. *Ex.* The horse *bolted* in fright. (c) To eat a meal in a great hurry.

bombard (bom-*bard*) *v.* To batter with gunfire. *Ex.* The city was in ruins after the long *bombardment* (*n.*).

bona fide (*bohn*-a *fy*-di) *adj.* In good faith.

bond *n.* Something which binds or holds people together. *Ex.* There are strong *bonds* of friendship between the two nations.

bondage *n.* Slavery; imprisonment.

bonus (*boh*-nus) *n.* An extra payment.

booby *n.* A stupid person. A *booby-prize* is sometimes given as a joke to the person who has come last in a race etc.

boom 1. *n.* A long pole which keeps the main sail of a boat stretched out. 2. *v.* To make a deep hollow sound, like the noise of distant gunfire.

boomerang *n.* A wooden weapon curved so that when thrown into the air it comes back to the thrower, used by Australian Aborigines in hunting.

boon *n.* A favour; a blessing; something one is glad to have; an advantage. *Ex.* A freezer is a *boon* to those who can't go shopping very often.

booth (boodh) *n.* A small covered area such as a market stall, a telephone *booth*, a stand at a fair or the place where one records one's vote at a polling station.

booty *n.* Things captured in war or stolen.

border *n.* The edge of anything. *Ex.* We have flower *borders* on two sides of the lawn.

bore *v.* (a) To make a hole with a tool. (b) To weary people by talking too much about uninteresting subjects. *Ex.* He *bores* me with his constant chatter; he is a *bore* (*n.*).

borough (*bur*-a) *n.* A town which has a mayor and corporation.

borrow *v.* To obtain the loan of something which you promise to give back. *Ex.* We *borrow* our books from the library.

bosom (*b*Uz'm) *n.* The breast. The *bosom of the family* means the affectionate centre of the family. A *bosom* (*adj.*) friend is a close friend.

boss *n.* (a) A knob, often ornamental. (b) The man in charge; the manager, foreman, etc.

bosun (*boh*-s'n) *n.* The seaman in charge of a ship's boats, anchors and rigging. *Bosun* is a contraction from *boatswain*, sometimes spelt *bos'n*.

botany *n.* The study of plants.

bother (*bodh*-er) 1. *n.* Something which is a little annoying or troublesome. 2. *v.* To make flustered or irritated. *Ex.* It *bothers* me if you come into the kitchen when I'm cooking.

bough (rhymes with *cow*) *n.* A large branch of a tree.

boulder *n.* A very large piece of rock. *Ex. Boulders* had rolled down the hillside and blocked the road.

bounce *v.* To spring back like a rubber ball when it is thrown to the ground; to make energetic leaping, jumping movements.

bound 1. *n.* A leap. 2. *v.* (a) To leap. *Ex.* The deer *bounded* across the road. (b) The past tense of the verb 'to bind'. To feel *bound* (*adj.*) to do something is to feel that you should. *Ex.* I feel *bound* to lend him the money. *Bound* is also used to mean 'certain'. *Ex.* It is *bound* to happen. 3. *adj.* On the way to. *Ex.* The ship is homeward *bound*.

boundary *n.* The line that divides one place from another; the edge. *Ex.* The city walls mark the *boundaries* of the city.

bounty *n.* What is generously given; generosity in giving.

bouquet (bu-*kay*) *n.* A bunch of flowers. *Ex.* At the end of the concert the singer was presented with a *bouquet* of roses.

bout *n.* A period of time or spell. *Ex.* A *bout* of hard work. A *bout* of malaria. A round in boxing etc. is also called a *bout.*

bow (bow) 1. *v.* To bend from the waist in respect as a formal greeting. 2. *n.* The forward part of a ship, often called *the bows.*

bow (boh) *n.* (a) A way of tying a tie or piece of ribbon etc. (b) The weapon from which arrows are shot. (c) A rod with stretched hair on it, used to play a violin etc.

bowels (*bow*-els) *n.* The series of tubes through which food passes while it is being broken down into various substances which are distributed to the blood-stream and other parts of the body.

bowls 1. *n.* A game played on a green, in which a wooden ball is rolled to hit a smaller ball. 2. *v.* To bowl in cricket is to deliver a ball to the batsman, or to get the batsman out by knocking the bails off with the ball.

boycott *v.* To punish someone by agreeing with others to have nothing to do with him.

brace *n.* (a) Something which holds things tightly together. (b) A wire used to pull back projecting teeth. (c) A pair, especially of game-birds. (d) Braces are shoulder straps to hold up men's trousers. (e) A tool to hold a bit, used in drilling holes.

bracelet *n.* An ornamental ring to go round the wrist.

bracing *adj.* Healthy and stimulating. *Ex.* The *bracing* sea air made us feel lively and strong again.

bracken *n.* A fern that grows mainly on moorland and heath.

bracket *n.* (a) A support for a shelf. (b) One of a pair of marks (like these) used to enclose words or figures.

brackish *adj.* Slightly salt, like the water near a river-mouth.

brag *v.* To boast. One who boasts is a *braggart* (*n.*).

braid *n* (a) A narrow strip of material (silk, gold thread etc.), used to trim clothing. (b) A plait of hair.

braille *n.* An alphabet of raised dots which the blind can read by feeling them with their hands.

brain *n.* The interior of the head, which controls learning, memory, thinking, speech, sensation, body movements etc. A clever person is said to have a good *brain.*

brake *n.* A fixture on a car, bicycle etc. by which motion can be slowed down or stopped. To *brake* (*v.*) is to use the *brake.*

bramble *n.* The blackberry bush.

bran *n.* The husk or outer skin of wheat or other grain, which is separated from the flour in making white bread but is used in brown bread and in cattle feeds.

brand 1. *n.* (a) A piece of burning wood. (b) The trade-name of a particular product, such as soap, to distinguish it from similar products made by other firms. 2. *v.* To mark cattle etc. with a hot iron, as a mark of ownership.

brandish *v.* To wave a weapon about in the air. *Ex.* The bully was *brandishing* a stick as he came towards them.

brass *n.* An alloy of copper and zinc.

brave *adj.* Without fear or not giving way to fear; having courage. *Bravery* (*n.*) is brave behaviour.

brawl *n.* A noisy fight or quarrel. To *brawl* (*v.*) means to fight in this way.

brawn *n.* Meat chopped up and spiced, and pressed into a mould, to be eaten cold.

brawny *adj.* Strong and muscular.

brazen *adj.* (a) Made of brass. (b) Bold and without shame. *Ex.* He lied *brazenly* (*adv.*), looking us in the face.

breach *n.* A hole made by something breaking. *Ex.* The flood was caused by a *breach* in the river-bank.

breaker *n.* A large wave hurled on to the shore.

breakwater *n.* A wall running out into the sea to break the force of the waves.

breath (breth) *n.* The air that we take into, and drive out of, our lungs. To do this is to *breathe* (breedh; *v.*).

breeches (britch-iz) *n.* Trousers reaching to, and buttoned, just below the knee, worn for riding.

breeze *n.* A light, gentle wind.

brevity *n. See* brief.

brew *v.* To make a drink, either by pouring boiling water over something (as in tea-making) or by boiling and fermenting (as in *brewing* beer).

bribe *n.* A payment, gift or other inducement made to a person to get him to do something he ought not to do. *Ex.* It is as wrong to offer as to accept a *bribe*. He *bribed* (*v.*) the doorman to let him come in.

bride *n.* A woman about to be married. The man she is marrying is her *bridegroom*.

bridge *n.* (a) A structure which carries a road over a river, railway etc. (b) A card game for two pairs of partners, in which one pair tries to win as many tricks as they said they would at the beginning of the game.

bridle (*bry*-d'l) *n.* The leather straps on a horse's head, together with the bit and reins.

brief *adj.* Short. *Ex.* Her *brief* letter surprised us, as she usually writes a long one. We were surprised at its *brevity* (shortness; *n.*).

brig *n.* A two-masted sailing ship with both masts square-rigged. In the brigantine (*brig*-an-teen; *n.*) only the foremast was square-rigged, the other being fore-and-aft rigged.

brigade *n.* (a) An army unit made up of three battalions. (b) A band of people formed for a special purpose. *Ex. Fire Brigade.*

brigand (*brig*-and) *n.* A bandit, especially one who robs people in wild places.

brilliant (*bril*-y'nt) *adj.* Very bright; sparkling; clever. A light or a jewel can be *brilliant*, and so can a person's mind. They all show *brilliance* (*n.*).

brim *n.* The edge of something, such as a hat or a volcano. *Ex.* Mary filled the cup to the *brim* (the very top).

brine *n.* Salt water. *Ex.* Pork is made into ham by soaking it in *brine* and then drying it.

brink *n.* The edge of something steep, such as a precipice; the sea-edge. *Ex.* He stood shivering on the *brink*, trying to pluck up courage to plunge into the sea.

brisk *adj.* Quick and lively. *Ex.* The nurse worked *briskly* (*adv.*), wasting no time.

bristle (*bris*'l) *n.* The stiff hair of a pig or other animal. Artificial bristles can be made of nylon. Toothbrushes have bristles.

brittle *adj.* Easily broken. *Ex.* The cup was made of fine china, almost as *brittle* as an eggshell.

broach *v.* To begin a new supply of something, or consider a new subject. *Ex.* When the others arrived, he *broached* a new bottle of lemonade. I thought it a good moment to *broach* the subject of my holdiay.

broadside *n.* The firing together of all the guns on one side of a warship.

brocade *n.* A heavy material with a raised pattern on it, sometimes in gold and silver threads.

brochure (*brohsh*-yewr) *n.* A pamphlet; a small booklet with paper covers.

brogue *n.* (a) A stout shoe for country walking. (b) A regional accent, especially an Irish one.

bronchitis (bron-*ky*-tis) *n.* A bad chest cold due to inflammation of the *bronchial* (*adj.*) tubes that lead to the lungs.

bronco *n.* A horse that has not yet been broken in (tamed).

bronze *n.* A metal made of copper and tin.

brood 1. *n.* A number of young birds hatched at the same time. 2. *v.* To spend much time thinking of one's troubles. *Ex.* Don't *brood* over your bad luck.

brook (brUk) *n.* A small stream.

broom *n.* (a) A brush used to sweep floors etc. (b) A shrub which bears sweet-smelling yellow flowers.

broth (broth) *n.* A thin soup of vegetables and meat.

brow *n.* (a) The forehead. (b) The edge of a hill.

browbeat *v.* To speak in a bullying way.

browse (browz) *v.* (a) To feed on growing plants, as some animals do (for example, giraffes, deer). (b) To read bits of first one book and then another, as cattle move from one patch of grass to another.

brunette (broo-*net*) *n.* A woman who has dark hair and complexion.

brunt *n.* The chief shock of an attack. *Ex.* All the others ran away and so he had to bear the *brunt* of her anger.

brusque (broosk) *adj.* Abrupt, sharp in manner. Usually applied to a way of speaking.

brutal *adj.* Savagely cruel.

bubble *n.* A balloon of liquid filled with a gas. *Soap bubbles* and *bubbles* of sea-foam are filled with air.

buccaneer (buk an *eer*) *n.* A pirate.

buck 1. *n.* The male of the deer, rabbit etc. 2. *v.* What a horse does when it tries to throw its rider by jumping in the air, arching its back and lowering its head.

buckle *n.* A metal fastening on a strap or belt, through which the belt is threaded.

bud *n.* A young flower or leaf before it is fully open.

budgerigar (*buj*-er-i-gar) *n.* An Australian parakeet, popular as a cage bird.

budget *n.* An estimate of future income and expenses, especially one made each year by the government. To *budget* (*v.*) is to plan how best to spend what money one has.

buffet (*buf*-it) *v.* To hit repeatedly with the fist. Also used of waves, high winds etc. *Ex.* He was *buffeted* by the wind as he walked along the cliff-top.

buffet (*bUf*-ay) *n.* A table or counter where food is laid out; the refreshment room at a railway station.

bugle (*bew*-g'l) *n.* A brass instrument like a small trumpet, used in the army to give commands, announce mealtimes etc.

bulb *n.* The roundish swollen underground stem of some vegetables and flowers (onion, daffodil), which stores food for the plant's growth. A bulb-shaped electric light is called a *light-bulb*.

bulge (bulj) *v.* To swell out. *Ex.* We saw the *bulge* (*n.*) which the conkers made in his pocket.

bulk *n.* Great size; the greater part of. *Ex.* The *bulk* of the work is now finished. A thing which takes up much space is *bulky* (*adj.*).

bulldozer *n.* A tractor for levelling and clearing land.

bullet (*bUl*-it) *n.* The piece of metal fired from a rifle, revolver etc.

bulletin (*bUl*-et-in) *n.* A public announcement. *Ex.* We can hear the news *bulletin* on the radio.

bull's-eye (*bUl*-zy) *n.* (a) The centre of a target, or a hit on the centre. *Ex.* Jim hit the *bull's-eye* with his airgun. (b) A boiled peppermint sweet.

bulrush (*bUl*-rush) *n.* A tall rush which grows in marshes and is used to make mats etc.

bulwark (*bUl*-werk) *n.* The parapet that surrounds a ship's deck as a protection against high waves; something put up as a strong defence.

bumper 1. *n.* A bar at the back and front of a car etc., to prevent damage on being bumped. 2. *adj.* Very plentiful. *Ex.* We shall have a *bumper* harvest this year.

bundle *n.* A number of things tied together. *Ex.* The Scouts collected *bundles* of old clothes for their jumble sale.

bungalow (*bung*-a-loh) *n.* A house with all its rooms on the ground floor.

bungle *v.* To do a job badly or clumsily. *Ex.* He was a poor workman and *bungled* the job.

bunk *n.* A shelf-supported bed in a ship or train. Similar small beds, one above the other, are often used in camps and children's bedrooms.

bunker *n.* The storage space for coal in a ship etc.

bunting *n.* Coloured cloth made into flags, used for signal-flags and for decorations on ship and shore.

buoy (boi) *n.* A floating object, anchored, and used to mark a channel, mooring etc.

buoyant (*boi*-ant) *adj.* Able to float like a cork.

burden *n.* Something very heavy, which has to be carried.

bureau (*bewr*-o) *n.* (a) A writing-desk with drawers and a flap for writing. (b) An office, for example, a *travel bureau.*

burglar *n.* One who breaks into a building to steal. Such a person commits a *burglary* (*n.*) by *burgling* (*v.*).

burly *adj.* Strongly built and stout. *Ex.* He is a big, *burly* fellow, and can carry heavy loads.

burnish *v.* To make bright by rubbing, especially metal.

burr *n.* The prickly seed-case of some plants which sticks to animals and clothing.

burrow 1. *n.* A hole in the ground made by an animal such as a rabbit. 2. *v.* To make a burrow.

burst *v.* To break into pieces suddenly and violently, like a pricked toy balloon.

bury (*ber*-i) *v.* To put something in a hole in the ground. This is called a *burial* (*n.*).

bush (bUsh) *n.* A thick woody plant with many small branches. *Bushy* (*adj.*) hair is thickly growing hair.

business (*biz*-nes) *n.* The trade or profession of a person. *Ex.* What is his *business?* He's a tobacconist.

bustle *v.* To move about quickly when doing something. *Ex.* She *bustled* about the kitchen, cooking the Christmas dinner.

busy (*biz*-i) *adj.* Having much to do; working hard.

butt 1. *n.* A large cask or barrel, such as a rainwater barrel. 2. *v.* To push with the head or horns, as a goat does.

buttress *n.* A support for the wall of a building.

buxom (*buk*-s'm) *adj.* A word usually applied only to a woman who looks plump, cheerful and healthy.

by-law *n.* A special law made by a town, for that town only.

C

The letter *c* is usually pronounced like *k* except before *e*, *i* and *y*. Before these letters it is pronounced like *s*. *Ex. Cat*, but *city*. When used before *h* it usually makes the sound *tsh*. *Ex. Church*.

cabin *n.* A very small house or hut; the room in which one sleeps in a ship.

cabinet (*kab*-in-et) *n.* (a) A piece of furniture with drawers, and with shelves to hold china etc. (b) *The Cabinet* consists of the Prime Minister and those Members of Parliament whom he selects to be chiefly responsible for the government of the country.

cable 1. *n.* A strong rope or chain like that attached to an anchor; a wire laid on the sea-bed, by which telegraph messages are sent. 2. *v.* To send a message by cable.

cache (kash) *n.* A secret store of food or treasure etc., such as pirates might hide away.

cactus *n.* A plant of dry climates, whose leaves are prickly spines, but whose stems store water and do the work of leaves.

cad *n.* A bad-mannered or dishonest person.

cadge *v.* To try to borrow; to beg.

café (*kaf*-ay) *n.* A place which serves tea, coffee and light meals.

cafeteria (kaf-et-*eer*-i-a) *n.* A self-service restaurant.

cajole (ka-*johl*) *v.* To coax by flattery.

calamity (ka-*lam*-i-ti) *n.* An event causing great suffering and distress. *Ex.* The colliery accident was a *calamity* for the whole village.

calculate (*kal*-kew-layt) *v.* To count up or think out by arithmetic. *Ex.* Can you *calculate* how many days there are till Christmas?

calendar (*kal*-en-dar) *n.* A table showing the days, weeks and months of the year.

calf (kahf) 1. *n.* (a) A young bull or cow. (b) The fleshy part of the lower leg. The plural is *calves* (kahvz). 2. *v.* To give birth to a calf.

calico (*kal*-i-ko) *n.* A coarse cotton cloth.

callous (*kal*-us) *adj.* Not caring how others suffer; hard-hearted.

calm (kahm) *adj.* Quiet, peaceful, not excited. *Ex.* A *calm* day; *calm* sea; *calm* person.

calorie (*kal*-or-i) *n.* A unit for measuring the heat and energy a body gets by eating and drinking.

calypso (kal-*ip*-so) *n.* A West Indian song, usually about something in the news, and often made up as the singer goes along.

camel *n.* A large browsing animal with a long neck and a hump on its back which stores food. This is the *Arabian camel* (found also in Africa). The *Asian camel* has two humps. Both kinds carry loads on long desert journeys.

camouflage (*kam*-oo-flahzh) *n.* Protective colouring which makes it difficult for an animal, thing or person to be seen at a distance. *Ex.* Troops wear *camouflaged* (*adj.*) battledress; aircraft are painted in *camouflage* colours; a leopard's spots act as *camouflage*.

camp *n.* A group of temporary homes, often tents, for troops, travellers or holiday-makers.

campaign (kam-*payn*) *n.* (a) The movements and battles of an army at war. (b) A planned operation, such as an *election campaign*.

canal (ka-*nal*) *n.* A man-made waterway cut through the land so that ships and barges may travel across country.

canary (kan-*air*-i) *n.* A small yellow bird which sings sweetly and is often kept as a pet.

cancel (*kan*-s'l) *v.* To cross out; to withdraw or take back (a command, request etc.). *Ex.* I have *cancelled* my appointment to see the dentist.

cancer *n.* A harmful growth in the body which may have to be removed by surgery.

candid *adj.* Honest, truthful. *Ex.* Please give me your *candid* opinion, as I want to know what you really think.

candidate *n.* A person who puts himself forward to be chosen for, or elected to, a job, office or qualification. *Ex.* An examination *candidate*. A *candidate* for Parliament.

canine 1. (*kan*-yn) *adj.* Connected with dogs. *Ex.* Distemper is a *canine* disease. 2. (*kayn*-yn) *n.* A pointed tooth, of which there are four in the human jaws.

cannibal *n.* Someone who eats human flesh.

cannon *n.* An old word for a large gun, once used to fire *cannon-balls*.

canny *adj.* Careful and shrewd.

canoe (ka-*noo*) *n.* A very light boat which is moved by paddles.

cantankerous *adj.* Quarrelsome.

canteen (kan-*teen*) *n.* A restaurant for members of an army unit, factory, office staff etc.

canter *n.* A horse's pace between a trot and a gallop.

cantilever (*kan*-ti-lee-ver) *n.* A projecting steel beam fixed at one end only. A *cantilever bridge* rests on *cantilevers* projecting from either side of each of two piers (pillars).

canvas *n.* A coarse cloth used in making tents, sails, schoolbags etc. A finer kind is used by artists for oil paintings, and can also be used for embroidery.

canvass (*kan*-vas) *v.* To go round asking people to do something you want done. *Ex.* Political candidates *canvass* for votes; firms send out salesmen to *canvass* for orders.

canyon (*kan*-y'n) *n.* A very deep cut in rocky country; a gorge.

capable (*kay*-pa-b'l) *adj.* Having ability, especially in practical matters. *Ex.* She is a very *capable* cook.

capacity (ka-*pas*-i-ti) *n.* How much a thing can contain. *Ex.* The *capacity* of that bottle is 1 litre. This is a *capacious* (*adj.*) concert hall which can hold a lot of people.

cape *n.* (a) A cloak, or a shoulder collar attached to a coat. (b) A piece of land jutting out into the sea. *Ex. Cape Horn.*

caper 1. *v.* To leap and skip about like a goat. 2. *n.* A pickled flower-head used to flavour a sauce.

capital *adj.* Chief; excellent. *Ex.* Paris is the *capital* city of France; it is the French *capital* (*n.*). I think that is a *capital* idea. A *capital* (large) letter begins names and some other words. *Ex.* We write 'Scotland' with a *capital* 'S'.

capitulate (ka-*pit*-ew-layt) *v.* To give in or surrender.

capsize (kap-*syz*) *v.* (Of a boat) To overturn.

capstan *n.* A large spindle or drum which can be turned round and round, used in ships to wind up the anchor etc.

capsule (*kap*-shool) *n.* (a) A little gelatine case which holds a dose of medicine. (b) A detachable part of a spacecraft.

captain (*kap*-tin) *n.* The chief officer of a ship, or of a company of soldiers; the chief member of a group. *Ex.* The *captain* of a football team.

captivate *v.* To charm; to win the affection of. *Ex.* Even those who don't like cats find kittens at play *captivating.*

captive *n.* A person who has been caught or captured and is a prisoner. He is kept in *captivity* (*n.*).

capture *v.* To takè prisoner.

caramel *n.* The substance sugar turns into when heated, used for flavouring. *Caramels* are sweets like soft toffee, made of sugar, butter etc.

carat *n.* A unit for measuring the fineness of gold. *Ex.* 24-*carat* gold is pure gold.

caravan (*ka*-rav-an) *n.* A covered wagon fitted up like a house, and used by gipsies etc.; a trailer used by holiday-makers.

carburettor (kar-bewr-*et*-or) *n.* A device in a motor-car which mixes air with petrol before it goes into the engine.

carcass (*kar*-kas) *n.* The dead body of an animal.

cardiac (*kar*-di-ak) *adj.* Having to do with the heart.

cardigan (*kar*-di-gan) *n.* A knitted woollen jacket which buttons down the front.

career *n.* A person's course through life, especially as regards the work he does. *Ex.* Teaching and nursing are *careers.*

caress (ka-*res*) 1. *n.* A movement of affection; an embrace. 2. *v.* To touch lovingly. *Ex.* The mother kissed and *caressed* her baby.

cargo *n.* The goods carried by a ship or aircraft.

caricature (*kar*-i-ka-tewr) *n.* A drawing of a person or thing which exaggerates and makes fun of a particular feature or way of behaving.

carnival *n.* A celebration with music, dancing and street processions.

carol *n.* A song or hymn, usually sung at Christmas.

carpenter (*kar*-pent-er) *n.* One who makes and mends things of wood.

carriage *n.* (a) A road-vehicle drawn by horses; a railway passenger car. (b) The carrying of something or the cost of this. *Ex. Air carriage* of goods is expensive. (c) The way someone holds himself in walking. *Ex.* People who have to carry loads on their heads always have a good *carriage.*

carrion (*kar*-i-on) *n.* The decaying flesh of a dead animal. *Ex.* A vulture feeds on *carrion.*

carrot *n.* A sweetish orange-coloured root vegetable, which is good to eat raw or cooked.

carton *n.* A cardboard box, usually large.

cartoon (kar-*toon*) *n.* A drawing, usually in a newspaper or magazine, making fun of something that has recently happened, especially in politics, or illustrating a joke.

cartridge *n.* The case containing the explosive material which is to be fired by a gun. *Ex.* After the rifle competition, we picked up some empty *cartridges.*

carve *v.* To cut into something; to shape something by cutting. *Ex.* Father *carved* the turkey. The artist *carved* the figure of a boy from the wood.

cascade (kas-*kayd*) *n.* A waterfall.

cashier (kash-*eer*) *n.* The person who receives and pays out money in a bank, shop etc.

cashmere (*kash*-meer) *n.* A very fine, soft, warm wool, originally made of goat's hair.

cask *n.* A kind of barrel.

casket *n.* A small box used to hold precious things such as jewels.

casserole (*kas*-er-ohl) *n.* A dish, often earthenware, in which food can be cooked and then brought to the table to be served. Food so cooked is also called a *casserole*.

cassette (kas-*et*) *n.* The container and its reel of magnetic tape played in a tape-recorder; the container of a camera film.

cassock *n.* A long robe worn by clergy and choristers in church, usually black.

cast 1. *v.* (a) To throw. *Ex.* The ship *cast* anchor (into the water). The fisherman *cast* his fly on to the river surface. To *cast* the blame on someone. To *cast* a look at something. (b) To give. *Ex.* In the election I *cast* my vote for Smith. (c) To shape in a mould. *Ex.* To *cast* a bronze figure. (d) To select for a part in a play etc. 2. *n.* (a) A throw. (b) Something moulded. *Ex.* They put his broken ankle in a plaster *cast*. (c) The actors in a play, film etc.

castanets (cast-a-*netz*) *n.* A pair of shell-shaped pieces of wood clicked together in the hand as an accompaniment, especially to Spanish dance music.

castaway *n.* A person cast ashore after a shipwreck.

castle *n.* A large fortified house.

castor *n.* (a) A bottle with small holes in the top, used for sprinkling sugar. (b) The small wheel fixed to the legs of armchairs, settees etc. so that they can be moved easily.

casual (*kaz*-ew-al) *adj.* (a) Careless, without attention. *Ex.* He gave the book only a *casual* glance. (b) Occasional. *Ex.* Fruit-growers employ *casual* labour to pick their crops. (c) Offhand; informal. *Ex.* He spoke to me in rather a *casual* manner. He was dressed *casually* (*adv.*).

casualty *n.* A person injured in an accident; someone wounded or killed in war.

catalogue (*kat*-a-log) *n.* A list of things arranged in order. *Ex.* A *catalogue* of the books in a library. A *seed-catalogue*.

catamaran (*kat*-a-mar-an) *n.* A boat with two hulls (bodies) fastened together.

catapult *n.* An ancient weapon worked by a lever and ropes to hurl stones. The *toy catapult* is a forked stick and elastic band, used to hurl stones.

cataract *n.* (a) A large waterfall. (b) A clouding of an eye through disease.

catarrh (ka-*tar*) *n.* A slight inflammation of the nose and throat; a cold.

catastrophe (ka-*tast*-ro-fi) *n.* A sudden great disaster.

cater (*kay*-ter) *v.* To provide food, entertainment etc. *Ex.* The library *caters* for most tastes.

caterpillar *n.* (a) The soft wingless grub which later turns into a butterfly or moth. (b) The endless steel belt round the wheels of a tank or bulldozer etc.

cathedral (ka-*thee*-dral) *n.* The chief church of a diocese.

catholic *adj.* (a) Including all Christians. Sometimes the word is used to mean *Roman Catholics* only. (b) Including everything. *Ex.* He had a *catholic* taste in music, liking classical, jazz and folk music.

catkin *n.* Any of the long tufts of tiny flowers that droop from the branches of the willow, hazel etc.

cattle *n.* Cows, bulls etc.

cause (kawz) *n.* (a) The thing which makes something happen. *Ex.* Black ice on the road *caused* (*v.*) the accident. (b) A matter of concern or interest to a group or to mankind. *Ex.* He died fighting in a noble *cause*. (c) Reason or grounds. *Ex.* You have no *cause* to complain.

causeway *n.* A raised road built to cross a wide stretch of marsh.

caustic (*kaw*-stik) *adj.* (a) Causing burns. *Ex. Caustic* soda. (b) Severe and cutting. *Ex.* He made *caustic* remarks about the book.

caution (*kaw*-sh'n) 1. *n.* Carefulness. *Ex.* You should approach that crossroads with *caution*. 2. *v.* To warn. *Ex.* We were *cautioned* not to go near the cliff-edge. We were told to be *cautious* (*adj.*).

cavalry *n.* Soldiers on horseback.

cave *n.* A large hollow place formed naturally in a hillside or under a cliff.

cavern. *n.* A cave.

celebrate *v.* To remember happily; to do honour to. *Ex.* We are *celebrating* Kate's birthday with a party.

celebrated *adj.* Famous.

celibacy (*sel*-i-ba-si) *n.* The state of being unmarried, especially referring to those monks, nuns and priests who have vowed not to marry.

cell *n.* (a) One of the tiny enclosed pieces of tissue in all living bodies, which are the units used in building up living matter. (b)

The compartment in a honeycomb. (c) A tiny room for one person, in a monastery, prison etc.

cellar *n.* A storeroom below the ground floor.

cello (*chel*-o) *n.* A bass member of the violin family. The full name is *violoncello*.

cellophane (*sel*-o-fayn) *n.* A transparent plastic wrapping material.

cement (se-*ment*) *n.* A powder containing ground limestone, which is mixed with sand and water in binding bricks, making floors etc.

cemetery (*sem*-e-tri) *n.* A place for burials other than a churchyard.

censor *n.* An official who examines films, books etc. and forbids the showing or publication of passages in them which he thinks might do harm.

census *n.* An official count of inhabitants.

centenary (sent-*een*-ar-i) *n.* A hundredth anniversary.

centipede (*sent*-i-peed) *n.* A small creature very like an insect. Some have over a hundred pairs of legs.

century *n.* A hundred years; a hundred runs at cricket.

cereal (*seer*-e-al) *n.* (a) Any kind of grain that is used for food, such as wheat or oats. (b) Food made from this (*breakfast cereals*).

ceremony (*ser*-e-mon-i) *n.* A formal way of celebrating an event or honouring someone. *Ex.* A *wedding ceremony.* A coronation is a very *ceremonial* (*adj.*) occasion.

certificate (sert-*if*-i-k't) *n.* A written statement which confirms the truth of a particular matter. *Ex.* A doctor's *certificate certifies* (*v.*) that statements about illness are correct.

chafe (chayf) *v.* To wear by rubbing; to fret or rage against. *Ex.* My shoe is *chafing* my heel.

chalet (*shal*-ay) *n.* (a) A wooden house with balconies, of the type common in Switzerland. (b) A small holiday house or hut.

chalk (chawk) *n.* A soft white limestone rock, formed in the distant past from shells. *Blackboard chalk* is made of a similar material.

challenge *n.* (a) A call to someone to ask who he is. Sentries on guard call 'Who goes there?'. (b) An invitation to a contest. *Ex.* He received a *challenge* to a duel. We *challenged* (*v.*) the school to play a return match.

chameleon (kam-*eel*-i-on) *n.* A lizard which can change its colour to match its surroundings.

chamois *n.* (a) (*sham*-wah) A kind of mountain deer. (b) (*sham*-i) A soft leather used in cleaning windows.

champion *n.* (a) One who takes the part of someone weaker than himself. *Ex.* He *championed* (*v.*) the cause of old-age pensioners. (b) The one who does best in a game or sport. *Ex.* A golf *champion.* The golf *championship* (*n.*).

chance *n.* 1. (a) What happens by luck or accident. (b) An opportunity. *Ex.* I have been waiting for a *chance* to take a holiday. (c) A possibility. *Ex.* We have a good *chance* of success. 2. *v.* To happen by accident; to risk. *Ex.* I *chanced* to meet him when shopping. I *chanced* my luck in the lottery.

change *v.* (a) To make or become different. *Ex.* I *changed* my plans when I heard the news. I made a *change* (*n.*) in my plans. (b) To take, give or use one thing instead of, or in exchange for, another. *Ex.* I am going to *change* my library book. When you pay for goods with a coin too big in value, you will get back some *change. Changeable* (*adj.*) means always changing, like the weather.

channel *n.* (a) The deeper part of a river. (b) A strip of water joining two seas. *Ex.* The *English Channel.* (c) In broadcasting, a frequency band reserved for a particular programme.

chant *v.* (a) To sing words on one note, as sometimes in church. (b) To shout altogether and repeatedly. *Ex.* The crowd at the demonstration *chanted* 'We Want Work'.

chaos (*kay*-os) *n.* Great disorder and confusion. *Ex.* After the hurricane everything was in *chaos.*

chapel *n.* A small place of worship, either standing alone or inside a larger building; the name for a Noncomformist church.

chaplain (*chap*-lin) *n.* The clergyman attached to a regiment, ship, college etc.

character (*kar*-ak-ter) *n.* The qualities (*characteristics*; *n.*) which go to make up a person's general nature, such as kindness, honesty. The people in stories and plays are called *characters.*

charade (shar-*ahd*) *n.* A game in which players act or speak the syllables of a word, one at a time, and the others have to guess the word. *Ex.* 'Car' and 'Go' acted to form the word 'Cargo'.

charcoal *n.* A fuel made by burning wood slowly. Sticks of *charcoal* can also be used to draw with.

chariot *n.* A cart used in ancient times in war and for races.

charity *n.* Generous giving of help or money to those who need it. To do this is to be *charitable* (*adj.*).

charm 1. *n.* Something carried or worn in the belief that it will bring luck. 2. *v.* To please by an attractive manner. *Ex.* She could not act well, but her *charm* (*n.*) delighted the audience.

chart *n.* (a) A map of a sea-coast showing depths of water, sandbanks and other hazards, for use by navigators. (b) A diagram which gives facts in an easily understandable form.

charter *n.* A document granting rights and privileges. *Ex.* Magna Carta is an important *charter* in British history.

chary (*chair*-i) *adj.* Cautious, wary of doing something. *Ex.* He was *chary* of offering help in case it seemed like interfering.

chase *v.* To run after and try to catch. *Ex.* The dog *chased* the cat out of the garden.

chasm (*kas*'m) *n.* A deep opening or split, such as may be seen in a glacier.

chauffeur (*shoh*-fer) *n.* The man employed to drive a private car.

cheat *v.* To deceive; to be dishonest.

check 1. *v.* (a) To stop or hold back. (b) To go over something to see if it is correct. *Ex.* Did you *check* this addition? 2. *n.* (a) A pattern of crossing lines forming squares. (b) In chess, if the King is exposed to attack he is *in check*. If he cannot escape he is *checkmated*, and the game ends.

cheer 1. *n.* A shout of joy or applause. 2. *v.* To make happier. *Ex.* It will *cheer* Mary if you go and see her now that she's ill.

cheese *n.* A food made from the pressed curds of milk.

cheetah *n.* A spotted member of the cat family with long legs, the swiftest of all animals.

chef (shef) *n.* A cook, especially in a restaurant.

chemistry (*kem*-is-tri) *n.* The science that explains what things are made of, their *chemical* (*adj.*) composition, and how the different *chemicals* (*n.*), such as oxygen and hydrogen, combine and behave. A person who dispenses (makes up) and sells medicines is called a *chemist* (*n.*).

cheque (chek) *n.* A written order to a bank to pay money to the person named on it.

cherish *v.* To love and take care of.

cherry *n.* A small shiny fruit with a stone in it, attached to a long stalk. Cherries vary from pale yellow to dark red, but *cherry-coloured* means bright red.

chess *n.* A game for two, played on a squared board with 32 *chessmen*.

chest *n.* (a) A large box with a lid, often used to hold clothes, tools etc. (b) The upper front part of the body.

chestnut (*ches*-nut) *n.* A tree with a sweet nut, whose reddish-brown colour is called *chestnut*. The *horse chestnut* tree bears conkers.

chew *v.* To bite into small pieces with the teeth.

chicken-pox *n.* An illness, common among children, which causes spots or blisters on the skin.

chilblain *n.* An inflammation, usually of hand or foot, caused by cold and poor blood circulation.

chill 1. *n.* (a) A severe feverish cold. (b) Coldness. *Chilly* (*adj.*) means cold. 2. *v.* To make cold.   *Ex.* I have *chilled* the lemonade in the fridge.

chime (chym) *n.* The musical sound of bells ringing or a clock striking.

chimpanzee (chim-pan-*zee*) *n.* An African ape.

china 1. *n.* Cups, plates etc.; the white clay of which they are made. 2. *adj.* Made of china.

chintz *n.* A glazed material printed with flowery patterns.

chipolata (chip-o-*lah*-ta) *n.* A thin sausage.

chisel (*chiz*'l) *n.* A tool with a sloped cutting edge, used in shaping wood, sculpture etc.

chivalry (*shiv*-al-ri) *n.* The qualities admired in knights of the Middle Ages, such as courtesy and gentleness. A person with such qualities is *chivalrous* (*adj.*).

chocolate (*chok*-lit) *n.* A sweet foodstuff made from cocoa-beans mixed with sugar to make a powder, paste or block chocolate.

choir (kwyr) *n.* A number of people trained to sing together. They sing *choral* (*kawr*'l; *adj.*) music.

choke *v.* To block up a narrow passage, such as the throat or a water-pipe.   *Ex.* If you take such large mouthfuls you will *choke*.

choose (chooz) *v.* (a) To pick out from among others.   *Ex. Choose* one of these books. Make your *choice* (*n.*). (b) To decide to.   *Ex.* He *chose* to walk, although he could have cycled.

chop 1. *v.* To cut, as with an axe. 2. *n.* A small piece of lamb or pork including a rib-bone.

choppy *adj.* With short, broken waves, making the water's surface look rather rough.

chopsticks *n.* Small ivory or wooden sticks used in the Far East to eat food with.

chord (kord) *n.* (a) The sounding together of different notes in music. (b) *See* cord.

chore *n.* An everyday odd job which may be boring but is necessary.

chorus (*kawr*-us) *n.* (a) A group of singers. (b) The part of a song that all can join in, at the end of each verse.

christen (*kris*'n) *v.* To name a child at its baptism. The name given is the *christian name,* and the ceremony is called a *christening* (*n.*).

chronic (*kron*-ik) *adj.* Lasting a long time, used especially of illness. *Ex.* He has *chronic* arthritis.

chronicle (*kron*-ik'l) *n.* A history of events in the order in which they took place.

chrysalis (*kris*-a-lis) *n.* The wrapped-up waiting stage an insect may go through while changing from a caterpillar to a butterfly, for example.

chute (shoot) *n.* A slope down which things can slide, such as a *waterchute* at a swimming-pool.

cider (*syd*-er) *n.* A fermented drink made from apples.

cinder *n.* Burned coal which has not quite burned to ashes.

circle (*sur*-k'l) *n.* A continuous curve drawn round a centre in such a way that any point on it is the same distance from that centre. A thing of this kind of shape, such as a ring or a round plate, is *circular* (*adj.*).

circuit (*sur*-kit) *n.* A journey round, such as the earth makes round the sun each year.

circular 1. *adj. See* circle. 2. *n.* A letter or advertisement sent round to a large number of people.

circulate *v.* To move round. *Ex.* The hostess *circulated* among her guests. (b) To pass something round. *Ex.* The collecting-box was *circulated* among the audience. The *circulation* (*n.*) of blood round our bodies is performed by the heart.

circumference (ser-*kum*-fer-ens) *n.* The boundary line of a circle; the length of this line.

circumstances (*sur*-kum-stan-ses) *n.* The state of affairs, the facts. *Ex.* We do not know all the *circumstances* of the case, so we cannot say he is to blame.

cistern *n.* A tank in which water is stored, usually at the top of a house.

citizen (*sit*-i-zen) *n.* A person who is not a foreigner.

civil *adj.* (a) Polite and obliging. (b) Not connected with, or a member of, the armed forces. *Ex.* A *civil* aircraft; a *civil* servant. A *civil* war is fought between fellow-citizens and not against a foreign country.

civilian   *n.* Anyone who is not in the Army, Navy or Air Force is a *civilian.*

civilization (siv-il-yz-*aysh*'n)   *n.* The condition of a community which has progressed from a primitive state to higher standards of orderly government, social organization, education and skill in the arts and sciences. *Civilized* (*adj.*) means having reached those standards; not primitive or barbarian.

claim   *v.* To ask for something because one has a right to it. *Ex.* As the match has been cancelled, you can *claim* your money back.

clammy   *adj.* Damp and sticky.

clamour (*klam*-or)   1. *n.* The loud noise of voices. *Ex.* I was kept awake by the *clamour* of a party next door. 2. *v.* To make such a noise.

clarinet (klar-i-*net*)   *n.* A musical instrument of the woodwind family with a mellow tone.

clasp   1. *n.* Something which fastens things together, such as a necklace *clasp.* 2. *v.* (a) To fasten with a clasp. (b) To hold tightly.

classic   *adj.* (a) To do with the world of Ancient Greece and Rome. (b) In a style of perfect proportion, harmony and simplicity. *Ex.* Mozart is a great *classical* (*adj.*) composer. (c) Of lasting greatness, as are some works of art. *Ex. Jane Eyre* is a *classic* (*n.*).

clause (klawz)   *n.* (a) In 'I'll come if I can', 'I'll come' is the *principal clause* and 'if I can' is a *subordinate clause.* (b) A paragraph in a legal document.

clay   *n.* Sticky earth which becomes hard when baked, used in making bricks, pottery etc.

clear   *adj.* Unclouded; letting light through; easy to understand. *Ex. Clear* skies; *clear* glass; *clear* instructions; *clear* radio reception.

clench   *v.* To close tightly. *Ex.* He *clenched* the coins in his hand.

clerk (klark)   *n.* A person who does office work. His work is *clerical* (*adj.*).

climate (*kly*-mat)   *n.* The sort of weather a place usually has.

climax (*kly*-maks)   *n.* The highest point. *Ex.* The *climax* to a story is its most exciting point.

clinic (*klin*-ik)   *n.* A private hospital; a group of doctors; a department dealing with one branch of medicine. *Ex.* An *eye clinic.*

cloak *n.* An outer garment like a coat but without sleeves; a covering to hide something. *Ex.* He escaped under the *cloak* of darkness.

clod *n.* A lump of earth.

clog 1. *n.* A shoe with a wooden sole. 2. *v.* To block up. *Ex.* The gutters were *clogged* with leaves.

clot *n.* A lump of something semi-liquid which has begun to harden. *Ex.* A *blood clot. Clotted* (*adj.*) cream.

clover *n.* A sweet-smelling wild plant, with white or pink flowers, often planted as a fodder crop.

clown *n.* A man in a circus or pantomime who amuses people with his antics (funny tricks).

club *n.* (a) A heavy stick for use as a weapon. (b) The stick used in golf. (c) A group who meet to do things that interest them all. *Ex.* A *tennis club.*

clue (kloo) *n.* Something which gives information or helps to clear up a mystery. *Ex.* Fingerprints can be *clues.*

clump *n.* A group of things clustered together. *Ex.* A *clump* of bushes.

clumsy *adj.* Awkward in movement; not graceful.

cluster *n.* A group of people or things close together; a bunch. *Ex.* A *cluster* of grapes.

coal *n.* A black fuel dug from underground beds formed from plant life buried under pressure millions of years ago.

coalition (ko-al-*ish*'n) *n.* A combining or alliance, especially of political parties in a government.

coarse *adj.* (a) The opposite of fine or smooth. *Ex.* This material is too *coarse* for a baby's dress. (b) Rough or rude in manner.

coast *n.* The land at the edge of the sea. A *coaster* (*n.*) is a cargo boat that trades only along the coast. A *coastguard* (*n.*) keeps watch for shipping in danger, smugglers etc.

coax *v.* To persuade someone by getting him into a good temper first.

cobble 1. *n.* A smooth round stone, once used for paving. 2. *v.* To patch up. A *cobbler* (*n.*) mends shoes.

cobra (*koh*-bra) *n.* A poisonous snake that swells its neck into a hood when alarmed.

cobweb *n.* The web spun by a spider to catch insects.

cockatoo (kok-a-*too*) *n.* The large crested parrot of Australia.

cockerel *n.* A young domestic cock.

cocoa (*koh*-ko) *n.* The ground beans of a tropical tree, used to make the drink of the same name, and also to make chocolate.

coconut *n.* The large hard-shelled fruit of a palm tree, rich in oil, with crisp white flesh and a sweet liquid inside it.

cocoon *n.* A chrysalis, especially of the silkworm.

code *n.* A set of letters, numbers or signs with a special meaning known only to one group of people, who know how to *decode* (*v.*) them (turn them into plain language). Also called a *cypher*.

coffee *n.* A plant whose seeds (beans) are roasted, ground, and used to make a hot drink.

coffin *n.* The wooden chest in which a dead body is placed before burial.

cogwheel *n.* A toothed wheel which fits in with the teeth of another wheel, as in motor-car gears.

coil *v.* To wind round into a ring. *Ex.* Sailors *coil* ropes; snakes often lie *coiled* round.

coincidence (ko-*in*-sid-ens) *n.* Something which happens by chance at the same time as another event, and is surprising. *Ex.* It is a *coincidence* that my parents' birthdays are on the same day.

colic *n.* A severe stomach-ache.

collaborate (ko-*lab*-or-ayt) *v.* To work together helpfully.

collapse (ko-*laps*) *v.* (a) To fall to pieces. (b) To give way or fall down from weakness, illness or shock.

colleague (*kol*-eeg) *n.* A fellow-worker.

college *n.* (a) A part of a university. (b) A school for advanced studies, often in a particular subject. *Ex.* A *college* of music.

collide (ko-*lyd*) *v.* To dash together or bump into. *Ex.* On the dodgem cars you are always *colliding* or causing *collisions* (*n.*).

collie *n.* A large, long-haired sheep-dog of Scottish origin.

colliery (*kol*-yer-i) *n.* A coal-mine. The men who work in it are called *colliers* (*n.*). Ships which carry coal are also called *colliers*.

colonel (*kur*-nel) *n.* An army officer in command of a regiment or with similar responsibilities.

colony *n.* A country ruled by another country.

colossal (kol-*os*-al) *adj.* Very large. *Ex.* An elephant is a *colossal* animal.

colt (kohlt) *n.* A young male horse.

column (*kol*-um) *n.* (a) A pillar. (b) One of the divisions of a newspaper page. (c) A row of figures arranged one below another.

combat *n.* A fight, usually with weapons. Those who take part are *combatants* (*n.*).

combine (kom-*byn*) *v.* To join together. *Ex.* As their teacher was sick, Class A had to *combine* with Class B. Things joined together form a *combination* (*n.*). A *combine harvester* reaps, threshes and winnows corn.

combustion *n.* A burning.

comedian *n.* An entertainer who makes jokes on stage.

comedy (*kom*-ed-i) *n.* A pleasant, amusing play.

comet *n.* A heavenly body with a tail of light which revolves round the sun. *Ex.* Halley's *comet* was last seen in 1910 and is not due back until 1985.

comfort (*kum*-fort) 1. *n.* A feeling of pleasant ease and well-being. A person with this feeling feels *comfortable* (*adj.*). 2. *v.* To console and support someone in distress. *Ex.* Kate *comforted* her sister when she was unhappy. She was a *comfort* (*n.*) to her.

command (kom-*ahnd*) 1. *n.* An order. 2. *v.* To give an order. *Ex.* The general *commanded* his troops to attack. To *commandeer* is to seize provisions etc. for an army's use.

commemorate (kom-*em*-or-ayt) *v.* To remind people of an important event in the past by a solemn ceremony. *Ex.* Remembrance Day services *commemorate* the dead of the two World Wars.

commence *v.* To begin.

comment *n.* A remark of explanation or criticism. *Ex.* I didn't *comment* (*v.*) on his extraordinary behaviour.

commerce *n.* The buying and selling of goods on a large scale, often between countries.

commit *v.* (a) To do something wrong. *Ex.* He *committed* murder. (b) To hand over. *Ex.* He was *committed* to prison. A *commitment* is a promise one has *committed* oneself to.

committee *n.* A group of people appointed to represent the organization they belong to, and who meet to deal with its business.

common 1. *adj.* Usual, ordinary, well-known. *Ex.* Birch trees are *common* on sandy soil. *Common sense* is ordinary, practical good sense. 2. *n.* A stretch of usually waste land which local people can make use of free.

commotion *n.* Noise, fuss or excitement. *Ex.* There was a great *commotion* when the lights failed.

communicate *v.* To pass on information; to succeed in getting others to understand one. *Ex.* The telephone is a means of *communication* (*n.*).

community *n.* A group of people who live in the same area and have the same rights, interests etc. *Communal* (*kom*-ewn-al; *adj.*) means shared by all.

commute (kom-*ewt*) *v.* To travel regularly between home and work, especially from suburb to city.

compact 1. (kom-*pakt*) *adj.* Closely packed or fitted together. *Ex.* The pocket calculator is a *compact* little gadget. 2. (*kom*-pakt) *n.* (a) Agreement; an arrangement. *Ex.* They made a *compact* to write to each other monthly. (b) A case for face-powder.

company (*kum*-pan-i) *n.* (a) A group of people; a *company* of soldiers, actors etc. (b) A business firm (short form is *Co.*). To be *good company* means to be a pleasant, amusing *companion* (*n.*) who offers *companionship* (*n.*).

compare (kom-*pair*) *v.* To look at things and see how they are like or unlike each other. *Ex.* If you *compare* these two stamps you will see that they are slightly different. *Comparative* (kom-*par*-a-tiv; *adj.*) means when *compared* with or in *comparison* (*n.*) with. *Ex.* This house is *comparatively* (*adv.*) quiet at night.

compartment *n.* A separate part. A drawer, a purse or a railway carriage may be divided into *compartments*.

compass (*kum*-pas) *n.* An instrument with a needle which always points north, and so helps travellers to find their way on land or sea. A *pair of compasses* is an instrument used for drawing circles.

compel (kom-*pel*) *v.* To force. *Ex.* He *compelled* the dog to give up the ball by holding its mouth open.

compensate (*kom*-pen-sayt) *v.* To make up for a loss or disadvantage. *Ex.* The insurance company *compensated* us for the damage to our house. They paid £1000 in *compensation* (*n.*).

compère (*kom*-pair) *n.* The master of ceremonies, or one who acts as host and announcer at an entertainment.

compete (kom-*peet*) *v.* To try to do better than someone else, for example in sport. There are many sports *competitions* (*n.*). *Ex.* They were *competitors* (kom-*pet*-i-torz; *n.*) in the sack-race.

competent (*kom*-pet-ent) *adj.* Capable.

complexion *n.* The colour and general appearance of the skin of the face.

complicated (*kom*-pli-kayt-id) *adj.* Difficult to deal with or understand because many different things are involved. *Ex.* This puzzle is too *complicated* for me.

compliment (*kom*-pli-ment) *n.* Words of admiration and praise to someone. To say such words to someone is to pay him a *compliment* or to *compliment* (*v.*) him. *Ex.* My father was *complimented* on his fine garden.

comply (kom-*ply*) *v.* To agree to what is demanded. *Ex.* You must *comply* with the rules of the game.

component (kom-*pohn*-ent) *n.* One of the parts which make up an object. *Ex.* The boiler is a *component* of a steam-engine.

compose *v.* To make by putting together; to write music. *Ex.* The bouquet was *composed* of sweet peas and roses. Mozart was a *composer* of operas. *Composed* (*adj.*) means quiet and calm in manner.

compound *adj.* Made up of parts.

comprehend *v.* (a) To understand. *Ex.* Why you did such a foolish thing is beyond my *comprehension* (*n.*). (b) To include. A *comprehensive* (*adj.*) school includes and combines different kinds of school which were formerly separate.

compress *v.* To press together into less space. *Ex.* A road-drill is worked by *compressed* air.

compromise (*kom*-prom-yz) *v.* To settle a dispute by each side giving way over some points.

compulsory *adj.* Forced; required. *Ex.* Maths is a *compulsory* subject in this exam. To do something under *compulsion* (*n.*) is to do it because one has to, or is made to, do it.

computer *n.* An electronic device which can perform in a second complicated calculations that would take the human brain hours to finish.

comrade (*kom*-rid) *n.* A close companion, especially in a particular activity.

concave *adj.* Curving in. *Ex.* The bowl of a spoon is *concave*; turn it upside down, and you are looking at its *convex* (bulging out) side.

conceit (kon-*seet*) *n.* A high opinion or admiration of oneself. To be *conceited* (*adj.*) is to think too well of oneself.

conceive (kon-*seev*) *v.* (a) To understand, to grasp the idea of. *Ex.* I can't *conceive* why he left. (b) To start the growth of a baby in the mother's body. The *conceiving* of something is its *conception* (*n.*).

concentrate (*kon*-sen-trayt) *v.* To think hard about one special thing, or give it all one's attention.

concern 1. *v.* (a) To relate or belong to. *Ex.* I am interested in anything that *concerns* flying. (b) To trouble or make anxious. *Ex.* I am *concerned* about him; he looks ill. 2 *n.* (a) An anxiety. (b) A business establishment. *Ex.* His firm is a prosperous *concern.*

concert *n.* A musical entertainment.

concise (kon-*sys*) *adj.* Short and easy to understand. *Ex.* He explained the fire-drill very *concisely* (*adv.*).

conclude *v.* (a) To end. *Ex.* The party *concluded* with a sing-song. (b) To come to believe or form an opinion because of some information one has. *Ex.* From his letter, I *conclude* that he won't come back; that is my *conclusion* (*n.*).

concoct *v.* To make up; to invent. *Ex.* He *concocted* some story about having seen a ghost.

concrete *n.* A mixture of cement, stones and sand which makes a hard building material.

concussion *n.* A state of shock due to a blow on the head.

condemn *v.* To find guilty; to declare unfit for use. *Ex.* The town council *condemned* the houses as unfit to live in.

condense *v.* To make compact or brief. *Ex.* He gave me a *condensed* (*adj.*) account of what happened.

condescend (kon-de-*send*) *v.* To behave in a superior way. *Ex.* She never *condescended* to explain why she hadn't come to my party.

condition *n.* (a) State. *Ex.* My bicycle is in good *condition.* (a) A part of an agreement that must be fulfilled. *Ex.* I will lend you the book on *condition* that you return it by Monday.

conduct 1. (kon-*dukt*) *v.* To lead or show the way. *Ex.* The manager *conducted* us over the factory. 2. (*kon*-dukt) *n.* Way of behaving.

cone *n.* (a) The fruit of conifers (fir, pine, yew etc.). (b) The *cone*-shaped wafer (cornet) which holds ice-cream. An object with a round base which tapers to a point is *cone-shaped* or *conical* (*adj.*).

confectionery *n.* Sweets and cakes.

confederate *n.* One who joins with someone else, often to do wrong. *Ex.* We think the thief had a *confederate* who left a window open for him.

confer (kon-*fur*) *v.* (a) To consult or discuss. *Ex.* They met to *confer* about the date of the match; they had a *conference* (*n.*). (b) To give or bestow a benefit or honour.

confetti (kon-*fet*-i) *n.* The tiny bits of coloured paper thrown at a wedding.

confide *v.* (a) To tell as a secret. *Ex.* She *confided* to me that she was leaving soon; she told me this in *confidence* (*n.*). (b) To trust. *Ex.* He *confided* the task to me; he was *confident* (*adj.*) that I could do it.

confine *v.* To force to stay in a limited space. *Ex.* The hens were *confined* in a small back yard.

confirm *v.* To assure somebody that a thing is so, or will be done. *Ex.* After I had phoned him I *confirmed* our arrangement in writing; I wrote in *confirmation* (*n.*).

confiscate (*kon*-fis-kayt) *v.* To take away with authority. *Ex.* Our matches and lighters were *confiscated* before we were allowed down the mine.

conflict *n.* A fight or struggle. *Ex.* The Battle of Bannockburn was a *conflict* between the English and Scots.

conform *v.* To behave as the others do, in the accepted way. *Ex.* We all have to *conform* to the rule about wearing gym-shoes in the gym.

confuse (kon-*fewz*) *v.* To mix up or fail to see the difference between. *Ex.* It is easy to *confuse* rooks and crows, as they are rather alike.

confusion *n.* Disorder, untidiness; shame and embarrassment. *Ex.* The room was left in *confusion* after the burglary. She was covered with *confusion* when she was found out.

congenial (kon-*jeen*-i-al) *adj.* To one's liking; of the same kind as oneself. *Ex.* One feels at home in *congenial* company.

congestion *n.* Overcrowding.

congratulate *v.* To express pleasure at someone's success or happiness. *Ex.* We *congratulated* him on his engagement; we offered our *congratulations* (*n.*).

congregate *v.* To come together. The people gathered together for a church service form a *congregation* (*n.*).

conifer (*kon*-i-fer) *n.* A cone-bearing tree, such as a pine, fir or yew.

connect *v.* To join together, either actually or in one's mind. *Ex.* They have at last *connected* a restaurant car to the train. I *connect* his laziness with the fact that he doesn't look well; but there may be no *connection* (*n.*).

conscience (*kon*-shens) *n.* The feeling inside ourselves which tells us whether we are doing right or wrong.

conscientious (kon-shi-*en*-shus) *adj.* Anxious to do what is right and trying hard to do it. *Ex.* No need to check his work—he is a *conscientious* worker.

conscious (*kon*-shus) *adj.* Awake to what is going on; aware. *Ex.* I was *conscious* that someone had crept into the room. If someone faints he becomes *unconscious.*

conscript *n.* A person called to enlist (join up) for national service. In wartime, people may be *conscripted* as soldiers, miners, farm-workers etc.

consecutive (kon-*sek*-ew-tiv) *adj.* Following on without break. *Ex.* I have to take tablets on three *consecutive* days: Monday, Tuesday and Wednesday.

consent *v.* To agree to. *Ex.* He *consented* to lend me his camera; he gave his *consent* (*n.*).

consequence (*kon*-si-kwens) *n.* Something which follows after, as a result. *Ex.* She stayed up very late and as a *consequence* (or, *in consequence*) overslept.

conserve *v.* To keep from decay or damage, or from being used up. Works of art and the natural beauty of the countryside are treasures that should be *conserved* (saved) for future generations.

consider (*v.*) (a) To think carefully about. *Ex. Consider* whether you can afford it before you buy it. (b) To think or have an opinion about. *Ex.* I *consider* this the most beautiful rose I've ever seen.

considerate *adj.* Thoughtful of other people's feelings or convenience. *Ex.* She is very *considerate* and won't bother you when you are busy.

consign (kon-*syn*) *v.* To hand over; to give to someone to deliver. *Ex.* I am going to *consign* these old letters to the bank.

consist *v.* To be made up of. *Ex.* Porridge *consists* of oatmeal and milk, cooked together. *Consistent* (*adj.*) means (a) always the same, not changing. *Ex.* You have been *consistently* (*adv.*) late all the week. (b) Agreeing with. *Ex.* His statements are not *consistent*—they don't make sense.

console (kon-*sohl*) *v.* To comfort or make happier.

consonant (*kon*-son-ant) *n.* (a) The sound made by a letter of the alphabet not a vowel, usually one you cannot go on making once you have pronounced it. (b) One of those letters.

conspicuous (kon-*spik*-ew-us) *adj.* Easily seen; noticeable. *Ex.* The lighthouse is a *conspicuous* landmark from far out to sea.

conspiracy (kon-*spi*-ras-i) *n.* A secret plot, usually against the law, made by *conspirators* (*n.*). *Ex.* The Gunpowder Plot of 1605 was a *conspiracy.*

constant *adj.* (a) Going on without stopping. *Ex.* There was *constant* rain, without a break all day. (b) Frequent. *Ex.* She is a *constant* visitor to our house; she comes to see us *constantly* (*adv.*). (c) Not changing, faithful. *Ex.* A *constant* friend.

constellation *n.* A group of stars that seem to us to make a shape or picture outline.

constipation *n.* Sluggish action of the bowels.

construct *v.* To build or make by putting the parts together.

consult *v.* To ask for advice or information. You can *consult* a doctor about illness or a railway timetable about train services.

consume (kon-*sewm*) *v.* To use up or eat up. *Ex.* This fire *consumes* logs very quickly.

contact *n.* Touch or nearness. To be *in contact* with someone is to be beside him or in communication with him. *Ex.* I was *in contact* with Charles when he had mumps, so I got them too. We *contacted* (*v.*) the doctor by telephone.

contagious (kon-*tayj*-us) *adj.* (Of diseases) Passed from one to another by contact or touch.

contain *v.* To hold, as a jug can *contain* water, or a book can *contain* several stories. What is contained is called the *contents* (*n.*) of the jug, book etc.

contaminate *v.* To infect or pollute with something which spoils. *Ex.* The floods *contaminated* the water-supply.

contemplate (*kon*-tem-playt) *v.* To think about seriously; to gaze upon something and think about it. *Ex.* He sat for a long time *contemplating* the beautiful scene. I *contemplated* retiring.

contemporary (kon-*tem*-por-ar-i) *adj.* (a) Of the same period. *Ex.* We were at school together, so we are *contemporaries* (*n.*). (b) Of this present period; modern. *Ex.* I don't think much of *contemporary* art.

contempt *n.* A feeling of scorn, or looking down on someone. We feel *contempt* for those who are cruel and think them *contemptible* (*adj.*).

content 1. (kon-*tent*) *adj.* Pleased, satisfied. *Ex.* I am *content* with my job; it suits me. 2. Contents *n. See* contain.

contest *n.* A struggle to decide which is better or stronger. *Ex.* There was a great *contest* between them for the prize.

continent *n.* One of the 7 great divisions of land on the globe, not broken up by seas. *Ex.* Asia is the largest *continent*. To the British *the Continent* means Europe.

contingency (kon-*tin*-jen-si) *n.* Something which may possibly happen. *Ex. Contingency (adj.)* plans are made so that if a thing happens there is a plan ready to deal with it.

continue *v.* To go on without stopping. *Ex.* The noise *continued* all through his speech; it was *continuous (adj.)*. Have you read the *continuation (n.)* of this story? *Continual (adj.)* means frequently repeated.

contort (kon-*tort*) *v.* To twist out of the usual shape.

contour (*kon*-toor) *n.* A line on a map which joins places of the same height above sea-level.

contraband *n.* Goods brought into a country illegally by smugglers.

contract 1. (*kon*-trakt) *n.* An agreement, especially in business matters and bound by law. 2. (kon-*trakt*) *v.* (a) To draw together; to become smaller. (b) To get. *Ex.* To *contract* a cold.

contradict *v.* To say the opposite. *Ex.* I said it was a good story, but he *contradicted* me and said it was not.

contralto *n. See* alto.

contraption *n.* An odd-looking machine or device, such as a very old bike.

contrary (*kon*-tra-ri) *adj.* Opposite; against. A *contrary* opinion is an opposite opinion. A *contrary* wind is one that blows the wrong way for you.

contrast *n.* A big difference between things when compared. *Ex.* There is a strong *contrast* in the sisters' appearance, the one so fair and the other dark.

contravene (kon-tra-*veen*) *v.* To break a law; to conflict with.

contribute (kon-*trib*-ewt) *v.* To add something, as money to a collection for charity. *Ex.* She made no *contribution (n.)* to the conversation.

control *v.* To restrain; to keep in order. *Ex.* Dogs should be kept under *control*.

controversy (*kon*-tro-ver-si) *n.* A long-continued argument or debate.

conundrum *n.* A riddle or puzzle; a difficult problem.

convection *n.* The distribution of heat by currents of air. *Convector (adj.)* heaters distribute heat in this way.

convenient *adj.* Suitable; helpful; not causing trouble. *Ex.* Would it be *convenient* if we called today? It is a great *convenience (n.)* to have a bus-stop near our house.

convent *n. See* abbey.

convention *n.* A generally accepted or traditional custom.

Conventional (*adj.*) means (a) normal, customary; (b) always following convention; not imaginative; not adventurous.

converse 1. (kon-*vurs*) *v.* To talk; to have a *conversation* (*n.*). 2. (*kon*-vers) *n.* The opposite.

convert *v.* To change something into a different form. *Conversion* (*n.*) means changing or being changed, for example from one religion to another.

convex *adj. See* concave.

convey (kon-*vay*) *v.* To carry; to communicate information. *Ex.* A bus *conveyed* us to the station. The letter *conveyed* bad news.

convict 1. *v.* (kon-*vikt*) To declare guilty. 2. *n.* (*kon*-vikt) A *convicted* criminal serving a sentence in prison. A *conviction* (*n.*). is a feeling of certainty; something one is convinced of.

convince (kon-*vins*) *v.* To make someone believe you. *Ex.* He *convinced* his mother that he could swim by swimming the length of the pool.

cooperate (ko-*op*-er-ayt) *v.* To work together helpfully. A *cooperative society* (or *co-op*) is one that sells goods and shares any profit among its members.

coral *n.* The hardened skeletons of tiny sea creatures, which may pile up high enough to form small islands. Pinky-orange *coral* is made into necklaces.

cord *n.* (a) Thin rope. (b) A cord-like part of the body such as the *spinal cord* (a mass of nerves inside the spine), or the *vocal cords* in the windpipe, which we use in speaking.

cordial 1. *adj.* Warm and friendly. *Ex.* A *cordial* welcome. 2. *n.* A sweet drink tasting of fruit.

cordon *n.* A line of people keeping others back. *Ex.* The police formed a *cordon* to keep sightseers from the fire.

corduroy (*kor*-der-oi) *n.* A ribbed cotton cloth with velvet finish.

core *n.* The centre or inner part, of an apple, for example.

cork *n.* Part of a cork-tree's bark which, being airtight and watertight, is used to keep things afloat, and to make into stoppers (*corks*) for bottles.

cormorant (*korm*-or-n't) *n.* A large diving sea-bird; also called a *shag*.

corn *n.* (a) Any grain, especially wheat. (b) A hard area of skin caused by rubbing, especially on the foot.

coroner (*kor*-on-er) *n.* An official who inquires into the cause of accidental or violent deaths.

corpse (korps) *n.* A dead body.

corral (kor-*ahl*) *n.* An enclosure for cattle and horses, especially on an American ranch.

correspond *v.* (a) To agree. *Ex.* The two accounts of the accident *corresponded.* (b) To write letters. *Ex.* My cousin and I *correspond* weekly.

corridor (*kor*-i-dor) *n.* A passage in a building from which rooms open off.

corrugated iron *n.* A sheet of zinc-coated iron or steel with a wavy surface, used for roofs.

corrupt (kor-*upt*) *v.* To ruin someone's character by persuading him to do wrong (to accept bribes, for instance).

cosmetics (koz-*met*-iks) *n.* Preparations used to beautify the skin etc., such as face-powder, lipstick.

costume *n.* (a) Another word for dress. (b) A particular way of dressing. *Ex.* Period (historical) *costume,* worn by actors. *Costume jewellery* is artificial jewellery worn on the clothes.

cotton *n.* (a) An annual plant with fluffy white cottonwool round the seeds. (b) The fine thread and the cloth made from this.

council *n.* A group of men and women who look after the affairs of a city, school etc. They are called *councillors.* A *council house* is one built and maintained by a *town council* etc., who let it to tenants at a low rent.

counsel 1. *n.* Advice. 2. *v.* To give advice.

counter *n.* The table in a shop or bank where money is paid. A *counter* is also a little disc used in many board games.

counterfeit (*kown*-ter-fit) *adj.* False, forged, imitation, especially of money.

county *n.* One of the parts into which a country is divided for purposes of government, and having its own *county council.* *Ex.* Essex and Cumbria are *counties.*

coup (koo) *n.* (a) A clever success. (b) A revolt against a government.

couple (*kup*'l) *n.* Two, or two that are connected; a pair. *Ex.* A *couple* of days. A married *couple.*

coupon (*koop*-on) *n.* A ticket entitling the holder to a payment, gift, service etc.

courage (*ku*-rij) *n.* Bravery; the quality of conquering fear in time of danger. *Ex.* The firemen tackled the blaze with *courage.* They were *courageous* (*adj.*).

court 1. *n.* (a) The place where law cases are heard. (b) The residence of a king or queen; their staff. (c) The prepared space for a game, such as a *tennis-court*. 2. *v.* To try to gain the affection or support of someone.

courteous (*kur*-ti-us) *adj.* Polite, well-mannered, showing consideration for others; showing *courtesy* (*n.*). The opposite of courteous is *discourteous*.

court martial *n.* The trial of a member of the armed services by his senior officers.

cousin (*kuz*'n) *n.* The child of one's uncle or aunt.

cove *n.* A small bay or inlet in the sea coast.

covet (*kuv*-et) *v.* To long for a thing that belongs to someone else.

coward *n.* Someone without courage.

cox *n.* The man who steers a boat in rowing races.

coy *adj.* (Of a girl) Shy or pretending to be shy.

crab *n.* A flat shellfish with 10 legs, including two dangerous pincers. A *crab-apple* is a small bitter apple.

cradle *n.* A baby's bed, usually on rockers.

craft *n.* (a) An occupation requiring skill with the hands. *Crafty* (*adj.*) means cunning or artful in a sly way. (b) A boat.

crag *n.* A steep rugged rock.

cram *v.* To crush into a small space; to fill very full.

cramp *n.* A tightened muscle, which causes sharp pain.

crane *n.* (a) A long-legged, long-necked wading-bird. (b) A machine for raising heavy weights.

crate *n.* A wooden packing-case with a nailed-on lid.

crater *n.* The open top of a volcano; the hole made by a bomb.

crave *v.* To long for; to earnestly beg for. *Ex.* The thirsty men *craved* for water.

crawl 1. *v.* To move on hands and knees, as babies do. 2. *n.* A swimming stroke in which the arms move alternately over the head and the legs do a scissor stroke.

crazy *adj.* Mad; silly.

cream 1. *n.* The fatty part of milk. 2. *adj.* Cream-coloured.

crease *n.* A line made by folding, as in paper, trousers etc.

create (kree-*ayt*) *v.* To make things exist or come to life for the first time. *Ex.* To *create* a work of art. A *creature* (*n.*) is a living being, whether animal or human.

credit *n.* (a) Something which increases a good reputation. *Ex.* He can take great *credit* for doing so well. It was very *creditable* (*adj.*). (b) Something to be proud of. *Ex.* He is a *credit* to his family, to his school.

creditor *n.* A person to whom one owes money.

creep *v.* To move quickly and stealthily. A *creeper* (*n.*) is a plant that clings to the wall it grows up.

cremate (kre-*mayt*) *v.* To burn a dead body to ashes instead of burying it.

crêpe (krayp) *n.* A gauzy, wrinkled dress material. *Crêpe soles* are rubber soles with a wrinkled surface.

crescent (*kres*-n't) 1. *adj.* Shaped like a new moon. 2. *n.* Anything made in that shape, such as a curved street.

cress *n.* A water-plant with leaves that taste mustardy, used in salads.

crest *n.* (a) The tuft (bunch) of feathers on top of the head of some birds, such as the lapwing, or on a knight's helmet. (b) The top of a hill or a wave.

cretonne (*kret*-on) *n.* A printed cotton cloth, heavier than chintz, used for curtains.

crew (kroo) *n.* A ship's company, or the staff of an aeroplane, train etc.

crick *n.* A muscle cramp, especially in the neck.

cricket *n.* (a) A team-game in which a batsman defends his wicket from balls bowled to him. (b) An insect like a grasshopper, which chirps.

crime *n.* An act punishable by law. Those who do such acts are *criminals* (*n.*).

crimson *adj.* Of a deep red colour.

cringe (krinj) *v.* To shrink away in fear or shame.

crinkled *adj.* Wrinkled up into little pleats, as crêpe paper is.

cripple *n.* One who is lame, who has difficulty in walking owing to an injury to a leg etc.

crisis (*kry*-sis) *n.* The point or time when an important decision or change takes place. *Ex.* When the miners went on strike, the Cabinet met to discuss the *crisis*; it was a *critical* (*adj.*) meeting.

crisp *adj.* Crackling and fresh; the opposite of limp.

criticize *v.* To give an opinion, or say what you think about something. *Ex.* He *criticized* their work, saying both good and bad things about it. It was fair *criticism* (*n.*). A *critic* is one who criticizes. One who is always finding fault is said to be too *critical* (*adj.*). To be *critically* ill is to be dangerously ill (*see* crisis).

crochet (*kroh*-shay) *n.* Needlework in which a hooked needle makes a series of loops to form a network, rather like knitting.

crockery *n.* China dishes, cups and saucers etc.

crocodile (*krok*-o-dyl) *n.* A large fierce reptile of tropical waters.

crooked (*krUk*-id)   *adj.* Bent or twisted; not straight.   *Ex.* Please put this picture straight, it is *crooked*.

crop   1. *n.* The grass, corn, vegetables etc. which farmers plant. 2. *v.* To cut, as to crop the hair, or crop the grass.

croquet (*kroh*-kay)   *n. See* mallet.

crouch   *v.* To stand with bent knees and tensed muscles, ready to spring, as an animal does. To *crouch down* means to bend the knees and sit back on the heels.

croup (kroop)   *n.* An inflammation of the windpipe causing a sharp high-pitched cough.

crowbar   *n.* An iron bar used for levering.

crucial (*kroos*-i-al)   *adj.* Decisive, critical.   *Ex.* The *crucial* moment in a game is when an event (such as a goal) makes the result seem certain.

crucifix (*kroo*-si-fiks)   *n.* An image of Christ on the Cross.

crude (krood)   *adj.* Unrefined.   *Ex. Crude* manners; *crude* oil.

cruel (*kroo*-el)   *adj.* Causing suffering to others; very unkind. *Cruelty* (*n.*) is cruel behaviour.

cruise (krooz)   *n.* A pleasure voyage.

crumble   *v.* To break or fall into pieces.

crush   *v.* To break or spoil by squeezing, as a dress or flower may be crushed.

crystal (*krist*-al)   *n.* (a) The solid state of many substances which have their atoms arranged in regular order. Syrup will become *crystals* of sugar when solid. (b) A clear quartz which can be made into gems (*rock crystal*). (c) High-quality hand-made glass.

cub   *n.* The young of some animals, such as a *lion cub*.

cube (kewb)   *n.* A six-sided solid object, such as a sugar lump or dice. *Cubic* (*adj.*) measurements are measurements of space taken up by something.

cuckoo (*kUk*-oo)   *n.* A migrating bird which lays its eggs in other birds' nests. Its well-known call gives it its name.

cucumber (*kew*-kum-ber)   *n.* The long green fruit of a trailing plant, with a distinctive flavour, used in salads.

cud   *n.* The partly digested grass which cattle bring back from their stomachs to chew again.

cuddle   *v.* To curl up in someone's embrace; to hold someone close affectionately.

cue (kew)   *n.* (a) A hint or guiding suggestion. (b) A signal to an actor to tell him when to start speaking. (c) The long stick used in billiards to strike the ball.

culprit (*kul*-prit) *n.* One who has done wrong. *Ex.* The flowers were flattened, the *culprit* being the cat.

cultivate (*kul*-ti-vayt) *v.* (a) To plough and prepare land for growing crops. (b) To make civilized and refined in taste. *Ex.* He is a well-educated, *cultivated* (*adj.*) man, interested in science and music.

culture (*kul*-cher) *n.* (a) The training of the mind in taste, 'to know the best that has been known and said in the world'. (b) The civilized state of a society.

cunning *adj.* Clever in a sly or deceitful way.

cur *n.* A mongrel dog, often bad-tempered.

curate (*kewr*-at) *n.* A vicar's assistant.

curb *v.* To control or check. *Ex.* She was very angry, but managed to *curb* her temper.

curd (kurd) *n.* The thick part of milk when it has turned sour (*curdled*), eaten as cottage cheese or made into hard cheese.

cure (kewr) *v.* (a) To make well again. (b) To preserve in salt, as is done with bacon.

curfew (*kur*-few) *n.* An official order that people must stay indoors after a certain hour (during a civil war or other crisis).

curious (*kewr*-i-us) *adj.* (a) Strange. *Ex.* The key was of a *curious* shape he had never seen before. (b) Eager to know something. *Ex.* He was *curious* to know how a microscope worked. He showed *curiosity* (*n.*) about it.

current 1. *adj.* Present, still going on now. *Ex.* My *current* hobby is model-making. 2. *n.* The flow of air, water etc. in a certain direction. *Currency* (*n.*) means the notes and coins used in a country.

curry 1. *n.* A meat and vegetable dish with peppery Indian spices, served with rice. 2. *v.* To rub down and comb a horse with a *curry-comb*.

curt (kurt) *adj.* So short as to be almost rude. *Ex.* He answered me very *curtly* (*adv.*).

custom *n.* A habit of doing something regularly. *Ex.* Hanging up mistletoe at Christmas is an old *custom*. A *customer* (*n.*) is one who comes to buy. *Ex.* Our milkman knows all his *customers* by sight.

cutlass *n.* A short curved sword, formerly used by sailors and pirates.

cutlery (*kut*-ler-i) *n.* The implements with which we eat at table: knives, spoons, forks.

cutlet   *n.* A thin slice of lamb or veal, cut from the neck and grilled or fried.

cycle   *n.* (a) The events which come round in a circle.   *Ex.* The *life cycle* of the butterfly, from egg to caterpillar to the adult, which lays eggs starting a new cycle. (b) A bicycle.   *Ex.* He *cycled* (*v.*) to school.

cylinder (*sil*-in-der)   *n.* A tube-shaped object, solid or hollow.   *Ex.* Hose-pipes or telescopes are *cylindrical* (*adj.*) in shape.

D

dabble   *v.* (a) To splash about with hands or feet in water. (b) To take up some hobby, but not energetically.

dainty   *adj.* Pretty, neat and delicate.   *Ex. Dainty* handkerchiefs.

dairy   *n.* (a) The place where milk is kept and butter and cheese are made. (b) A shop selling *dairy* produce.

dais (*day*-is)   *n.* A low platform in a hall, often for a lecturer to speak from.

dam   *n.* A wall which blocks the flow of running water, to form a reservoir etc.

damage   *v.* To hurt or spoil.   *Ex.* Frost *damaged* the fruit-blossom.

damp   *adj.* Slightly wet.   *Ex.* The ground is still *damp* from last night's rain.

dangle   *v.* To hang down, as do catkins on branches.

dank   *adj.* Damp and cold.

dare   *v.* To be bold enough to do something dangerous.   *Ex.* He showed great *daring* (*n.*) when he climbed the dangerous cliff to get help.

dart   1. *n.* (a) A pointed weapon which is hand-thrown. (b) A tapered fold stitched at the back of material in dressmaking to make for a good fit. (c) *Darts*, a game in which *darts* are thrown at a numbered *dartboard*. 2. *v.* To shoot quickly forward, as some birds do.

dash   1. *n.* A punctuation mark (—), either to show that something has been missed out or, if there are two of them, to take the place of brackets. 2. *v.* To rush off.   *Ex.* He *dashed* across the road and was nearly run over.

date   1. *n.* (a) The day, month and year, either today   (*Ex.* What's the *date* today?) or on which an event took place (*Ex.* The *date* of the Battle of Waterloo is 1815). (b) The fruit of the *date*-palm, rich in sugar. 2. *v.* To put a date on something. *Ex.* Did you *date* your letter?

daunt (dawnt) *v.* To frighten or discourage. *Ex.* The raging seas did not *daunt* the lifeboatmen; they were *undaunted* by the danger.

dawdle *v.* To do something slowly and without interest. *Ex.* Don't *dawdle* over your breakfast or you'll miss the bus.

dawn *n.* The beginning of daylight, when the sun rises. *Ex.* We got up at *dawn*.

dazed *adj.* Unable to think clearly, owing to a blow or shock etc. *Ex.* He seemed *dazed* after the accident and could not answer questions.

dazzle *v.* To make almost blind for a moment. *Ex.* The car's headlights *dazzled* us, so that we could scarcely see.

deaf *adj.* Unable to hear, or to hear properly.

deal 1. *n.* (a) A plank of soft wood, used to make boxes and cheap furniture. (b) A lot. *Ex.* I have a great *deal* of work to do. 2. *v.* (a) To give out. *Ex.* To *deal* the cards. (b) To do business with. *Ex.* They *deal* in exports. (c) To do what is needed. *Ex.* She promised to *deal* with the problem tomorrow.

debate (de-*bayt*) *n.* An argument on some subject of interest, usually in public. *Ex.* Before laws are passed in Parliament, they are *debated* (*v.*).

debt (det) *n.* Something one owes, or feels one owes, to another. *Ex.* I owe him a *debt* of gratitude for his kindness. He could not leave till he paid his *debts*.

début (*day*-boo) *n.* The first appearance before the public of an actor, pianist etc.

decay (de-*kay*) *v.* To become rotten and waste away, as may an apple or a tooth.

deceive (de-*seev*) *v.* To make someone believe what is not true. *Ex.* He *deceived* us by saying he was a club member, when he was not.

decent (*dee*-s'nt) *adj.* Suitable, good enough, respectable. *Ex.* He wore old but *decent* clothes. He was a *decent*, kindly old fellow.

declare *v.* To announce. *Ex.* Peace was *declared* after five years of war.

decline (de-*klyn*) *v.* To refuse. *Ex.* He *declined* our offer of a lift. (b) To go downward or become worse. *Ex.* His health *declined*.

decrease (de-*krees*) *v*. To become less. *Ex*. The membership of our club has *decreased*. There has been a *decrease* (*n*.) in numbers.

dedicate *v*. (a) To devote to some sacred or other purpose. *Ex*. The church is *dedicated* to St Andrew. He *dedicated* his spare time to writing a book. (b) To state that something is done in honour of someone. *Ex*. He *dedicated* his book to his wife.

deduce (de-*dews*) *v*. To draw a conclusion from what you have learnt or observed. *Ex*. From the look on your face, I *deduce* that you are angry with me.

deduct *v*. To take a part away. *Ex*. His employer *deducted* income tax from his wages.

defeat *v*. To win a victory over someone. *Ex*. Our football team has not had one *defeat* (*n*.) this season.

defect (*dee*-fekt) *n*. A fault; something not as it should be. *Ex*. The bicycle has one *defect*—the tyres are worn out; they are *defective* (*adj*.).

defend *v*. To protect or keep safe, sometimes by fighting. *Ex*. The army *defended* the city; it put up a good *defence* (*n*.).

defer (de-*fur*) *v*. (a) To put off till later. *Ex*. He phoned to say that he would have to *defer* his visit until next day. (b) To respectfully yield to someone else's opinion, judgement etc.

defiance *n*. *See* defy.

deficiency (de-*fish*-en-si) *n*. A lack or shortage. *Ex*. I have checked the money in the till; there is a *deficiency* of £1.

defy (de-*fy*) *v*. To disobey openly; to challenge someone to do something you think he cannot do. *Ex*. I *defy* you to tell him what you've just told me.

degree *n*. (a) The unit in which angles are measured; there are 90 *degrees* in a right angle. (b) An arc on the circumference of a circle (as on a compass or a globe of the world); there are 360 *degrees* in a complete circle. (c) A division on a measuring scale, such as a thermometer. *Ex*. The body's normal temperature is between 36 and 37 *degrees* (written as 36° etc.). (d) A stage in the progress of something. *Ex*. His photography is improving by *degrees* (little by little). (d) The title awarded to successful students by universities. *Ex*. The Bachelor of Arts *degree*.

dejected *adj*. Downcast, disheartened.

delay *v*. To put off till later; to make late. *Ex*. The ship was *delayed* by fog; fog caused the *delay* (*n*.).

delegate (*del*-e-gayt) 1. *n*. Someone who officially represents an organization or country, at a conference, for example. 2. *v*. To hand over some of one's work or powers to others. *Ex.* Mother was so busy cooking that she *delegated* the shopping to me.

deliberately (de-*lib*-er-at-li) *adv.* On purpose, not by accident. *Ex.* He *deliberately* went back into the blazing house to rescue the child.

delicate (*del*-i-kat) *adj.* (a) Fine and frail; easily broken, as is *delicate* china. (b) Not strong in health. *Ex.* She is rather *delicate*, and always catching chills. (c) Specially nice food is sometimes called a *delicacy* (*n.*).

delicious (de-*lish*-us) *adj.* Very nice to eat or smell.

delight (de-*lyt*) *n.* Joy and pleasure. *Ex.* He was *delighted* (*v.*) to see his family again after so many years.

delinquent (de-*link*-w'nt) *adj.* (a) Failing in one's duty. (b) Guilty of bad behaviour.

delirium (de-*lir*-i-um) *n.* A state of mind during illness when a patient talks in an excited, incoherent way, and seems to see and hear things which are not there.

deliver *v.* (a) To set free. *Ex.* Daniel, in the Bible, was *delivered* from the lions' den. (b) To hand over. *Ex.* The postman *delivers* the letters.

delta *n.* The muddy land at a river-mouth where it meets the sea.

deluge (*del*-ewj) *n.* A flood of water. *Ex.* The *deluge* flooded the whole valley.

demand *v.* To ask for something very firmly. *Ex.* The policeman *demanded* to see my driving licence.

democracy (de-*mok*-ra-si) *n.* Government by the people, who are represented by the Members of Parliament the majority have voted for.

demolish (de-*mol*-ish) *v.* To pull down or destroy, as may be necessary with an unsafe building.

demonstrate (*dem*-on-strayt) *v.* To show how. *Ex.* The crew *demonstrated* the way to put on a life-jacket. They gave a *demonstration* (*n.*). *Demonstration* can also mean a street march or other way of expressing strong approval or disapproval in public.

denim (*den*-im) *n.* A strong cotton material used to make overalls and jeans.

denote (de-*noht*) *v.* To show by a sign. *Ex.* The flag at the mast-head *denoted* that the ship would sail that day.

dense *adj.* Thick, or tightly packed together. *Ex.* A *dense* fog, or crowd or jungle. A *dense* person is one slow to understand.

dentist *n.* A person who treats teeth and looks after our *dental* (*adj.*) health.

deny *v.* (a) To say that a statement is not true. *Ex.* The accused girl *denied* that she had stolen the money, and we accepted her *denial* (de-*ny*-al; *n.*). (b) To refuse. *Ex.* The children begged so hard to be allowed to go, that it was impossible to *deny* them.

department *n.* A separate part. A large store (often called a *department store*) may sell clothes in one *department* and food in another.

depend *v.* (a) To rely on for support and help. *Ex.* Babies are *dependent* (*adj.*) on their mothers. (b) To have something influence what you will decide. *Ex.* Whether we can have the picnic *depends* on the weather.

depict (de-*pikt*) *v.* To show in pictures or describe in words. *Ex.* The painting *depicted* a sunset at sea.

deplore (de-*plor*) *v.* To be very sorry about or disapproving of. *Ex.* It is *deplorable* (*adj.*) to think that no one visited him when he was ill.

depose (de-*pohz*) *v.* To remove from a position of authority. *Ex.* There was a revolution, and the king was *deposed*.

deposit (de-*poz*-it) *v.* (a) To lay down. *Ex.* Soil is *deposited* by rivers on their way to the sea. (b) To put away for safety. *Ex.* They *deposited* their money in a savings-bank. Things which a buyer does not pay for in full are often kept for him if he pays a part of the price (a *deposit*; *n.*).

depressed (de-*prest*) *adj.* Unhappy and in low spirits. *Ex.* She is always *depressed* when her son is away at sea. A *depression* (*n.*) means (a) the state of being *depressed*; (b) the kind of weather that makes a barometer go down, indicating rain.

deprive (de-*pryv*) *v.* To take away or keep someone from having. *Ex.* The weather *deprived* us of the picnic we had planned.

deputy (*dep*-ew-ti) *n.* A person who acts for another. *Ex.* When the headmaster was away, a *deputy* took charge of the school.

derelict (*der*-e-likt) *adj.* Left ruined or abandoned; usually applied to a wrecked ship or a building.

descend *v.* To move downward. *Ex.* We *descended* by lift from the top floor.

describe *v.* To tell or write about something. *Ex.* The wedding was *described* in the newspapers. They gave *descriptions* (*n.*) of it.

desert (*dez*-ert) *n.* A large area of bare land, often sandy, where nothing grows. *Ex.* The *Sahara Desert.*

desert (de-*zurt*) *v.* To leave a person or place when one ought to stay. *Ex.* If a parent *deserted* a child, or a soldier *deserted* from the army, they would be guilty of *desertion* (*n.*).

deserve (de-*zurv*) *v.* To earn or be worthy of. *Ex.* He *deserved* to succeed because he worked so hard.

design (de-*zyn*) 1. *n.* A plan or sketch of how a thing is to be done. *Ex.* She made a beautiful *design* for a cushion, which she then embroidered. 2. *v.* To make such a plan or sketch. *Ex.* We asked him to *design* a small house.

desire (de-*zyr*) 1. *n.* A longing for something *Ex.* He had a great *desire* to travel. 2. *v.* To long for something. *Ex.* There is nothing I *desire* more than a little peace and quiet.

desolate (*des*-o-lat) *adj.* Lonely, dismal, gloomy, with no life about it. *Ex.* This is a *desolate* place to live in in winter. I feel *desolate* now my wife is in hospital.

despair 1. *n.* Loss of hope. *Ex.* She was in *despair* when she missed her train. 2. *v.* To have no hope. *Ex.* Don't *despair*—it may never happen.

despatch *v. See* dispatch.

desperate (*des*-per-at) *adj.* (a) Having or giving little hope of improvement. *Ex.* A *desperate* situation. (b) Reckless from despair. *Ex.* When arrested, he made a *desperate* attempt to escape.

despise (de-*spyz*) *v.* To look down on with contempt. *Ex.* They *despised* such cruel behaviour; they thought it *despicable* (*des*-pik-a-b'l; *adj.*).

dessert (de-*zurt*) *n.* A sweet course at the end of a meal, especially fresh fruit.

destination *n.* The place a person or thing is bound for; the end of the journey.

destitute (*des* ti tewt) *adj.* Having no money, and in great need.

detach (de-*tach*) *v.* To separate. Troops may be detached from the main body to form a *detachment* (*n.*) for special duty. Coupons can be *detached* from a booklet.

detail (*dee*-tayl) *n.* A small part of a whole; one item of many. *Ex.* Tell me in *detail* (item by item) exactly what he said. The artist made a rough sketch, intending to fill in the *details* later.

detain (de-*tayn*) *v.* To hold or keep back, and perhaps make late. *Ex.* I know you're busy, so I won't *detain* you for long.

detect (de-*tekt*) *v.* To notice or find out   *Ex.* The plumber soon *detected* what was wrong with the gas-pipe. A *detective* (*n.*) is a police officer trained to *detect* crime.

deter (de-*tur*) *v.* To stop or prevent. *Ex.* Barbed wire *deterred* the walkers from entering the wood.

detergent (de-*tur*-jent) *n.* A powder added to water which gets rid of dirt and especially grease, used in washing clothes, crockery etc.

deteriorate (de-*teer*-i-or-ayt) *v.* To get worse or make worse. *Ex.* His health has *deteriorated* since his accident.

determine (de-*tur*-min) *v.* To decide or make up one's mind on a subject. *Ex.* He *determined* that he would play better next time.

detest *v.* To hate or dislike very much.

detour (*day*-toor) *v.* A long way round, such as is made necessary when a road is closed.

devastate (*dev*-a-stayt) *v.* To lay waste, and make bare and useless, as a hurricane may *devastate* a town by destroying buildings.

develop (de-*vel*-op) *v.* (a) To grow. Living things *develop* if they have the right growing conditions. *Development* (*n.*) means growth. (b) To make a photograph visible on a film.

device (de-*vys*) *n.* An apparatus or machine for a special purpose. *Ex.* Nutcrackers are a *device* to crack nuts.

devil *n.* The spirit of evil, or any wicked spirit.

devise (de-*vyz*) *v.* To plan or invent *Ex.* The prisoner *devised* a way of escape.

devote *v.* To give up one's time, attention, care etc. to some person or thing. *Ex.* The nurse *devoted* herself to the care of the sick child.

devour (de-*vowr*) *v.* To eat greedily, leaving nothing over, as a wild beast may do.

dew *n.* The drops of water which form when warm air is cooled. *Dew* forms in the cool night air after a warm day.

dexterity (deks-*ter*-it-i) *n.* Neatness and skill with the hands.

diagonal (dy-*ag*-on-al) *adj.* Going from one corner to another, on a slant.

diagram (*dy*-a-gram) *n.* A drawing made to illustrate or explain. Many textbooks use *diagrams* to make the written explanations easier to understand.

dial (*dy*-al) *n.* The face of a clock or watch, or of a car's speedometer etc. *Ex.* A gas-meter *dial.* A *sundial* shows the time of day by using the shadow cast by the sun on a marked *dial.*

dialect (*dy*-a-lekt) *n.* A way of speaking and the words used, in a particular district. *Ex.* A Yorkshire *dialect.*

dialogue (*dy*-a-log) *n.* Conversation, usually referring to the words spoken in a play etc.

diamond (*dy*-a-mond) *n.* The hardest and most valuable of the precious stones. A *diamond wedding* is a 60th anniversary of a marriage.

diary (*dy*-ar-i) *n.* A written account of what has happened each day; a book for this.

dice *n.* (a) Small cubes marked with spots (1–6) on each side, which are thrown in many games. (b) A small cube of food etc. *Ex.* We *diced* (*v.*) cucumber and pineapple to make a salad.

dictate *v.* To tell someone what to do, say or write. *Ex.* When we learn a language, the teacher tests us by *dictating* sentences for us to write down; this is *dictation* (*n.*). A *dictator* (*n.*) rules a country as he likes, without considering the wishes of his people.

diesel (*deez*-el) *n.* A crude form of petrol used by many lorries and taxis. The sign '*derv*' means fuel for *d*iesel-engined *r*oad *v*ehicles.

diet (*dy*-et) *n.* Food, especially as ordered by a doctor, or as selected when slimming.

differ *v.* To be unlike in appearance; to disagree. To *differ* is to be *different* (*dif*-er-ent; *adj.*). *Ex.* Oranges and mandarins look rather alike but taste *different*; there is a *difference* (*n.*) between them.

digest (di-*jest*) *v.* To absorb food into the body so that it can nourish it.

digital (*dij*-i-tal) *adj.* Written in figures. Many watches and clocks now show the time as a row of figures (*digits*).

dignity (*dig*-ni-ti) *n.* Calm behaviour which commands respect. To behave thus is to be *dignified* (*adj.*).

dike *n.* (a) A ditch. (b) A barrier to stop flood waters flowing over the land.

dilapidated (di-*lap*-i-dayt-id) *adj.* In a state of decay, falling to pieces.

dilemma (di-*lem*-a) *n.* A difficult position, a fix. One is in a *dilemma* when undecided which of various things to do.

dilute (dy-*lewt*) *v.* To make a mixture thinner or weaker by adding more liquid, usually water; for example, to medicines, water-colour paints or bottled fruit-drinks.

dim *adj.* Not clear or bright. *Ex.* A candle gives only a *dim* light.

dimension (di-*men*-sh'n) *n.* Measurement. A sheet of paper has two *dimensions*: length and breadth; but a book has three: length, breadth and thickness.

diminish *v.* To become or make smaller. *Ex.* Icebergs *diminish* as they float into warmer seas; the gradual melting *diminishes* them.

dimple *n.* A little hollow, especially on the cheek, which some people make when they smile.

dinghy (*ding*-gi) *n.* (a) A ship's small boat, used to come ashore in. (b) A rubber boat, often used for sea rescue.

dingy (*din*-ji) *adj.* Dull, shabby, dirty-looking.

dinosaur (*dyn*-o-sor) *n.* A prehistoric reptile, often enormous.

diphtheria (dif-*theer*-i-a) *n.* A highly infectious inflammation of the throat.

diphthong (*dif*-thong) *n.* Two vowels which make a different sound by being put together, but make only one syllable. *Ex.* The 'ai' in 'paid'; the 'Ae' pronounced 'ee' in 'Aesop'.

diploma (di-*ploh*-ma) *n.* A certificate awarded to someone who has reached a certain standard in a subject.

direct (di-*rekt*) 1. *adj.* Straight. The most *direct* route is the shortest and straightest. A *direct* statement is a straightforward, clear one. 2. *v.* (a) To give information on the best way to get to a place. *Ex.* She gave them clear *directions* (*n.*) on how to get to the river; it was in a northerly *direction* (*n.*). (b) To control or manage. A person in charge of a firm's business is called a *director*.

dis- is a prefix which changes the meaning of a word, often making it the opposite of what it was. *Ex. Disagree, disappear.*

disable *v.* To injure or make unable to do something. *Ex.* She was *disabled* by rheumatism and could not use her hands.

disagreeable (dis-a-*gree*-a-b'l) *adj.* Not pleasant. *Ex.* It was a *disagreeable* day for us, as Anne was in a complaining, *disagreeable* mood.

disappoint *v.* To fail to fulfil the hopes of someone. *Ex.* She was *disappointed* at being left out of the team.

disaster (di-*zahst*-er) *n.* An unhappy or very unfortunate event, often happening suddenly, as a shipwreck or railway accident.

disc, disk *n.* (a) A round, thin, flat sheet of metal or wood.

(b) Something that looks like this. *Ex.* The sun's *disc.*
(c) A gramophone record.

discharge *v.* To dismiss; set free; fire a gun.

disciple (di-*syp*'l) *n.* A follower and believer of the teachings of someone; it refers especially to the Twelve *Disciples* of Jesus.

discipline (*dis*-i-plin) *n.* Training or way of living according to rules of law and order. The armed forces are trained to accept the *discipline* of the service to which they belong.

discord *n.* (a) Disagreement; unfriendliness. (b) Notes in music which, when sounded together, are not pleasant to the ear.

discount *n.* Part of the price of an article which the seller takes off, to make it cheaper and so encourage more sales.

discourage *v.* To dishearten and make less hopeful. *Ex.* Although she kept falling when learning to skate, she didn't let that *discourage* her.

discreet (dis-*kreet*) *adj.* Having the good judgement not to reveal things better kept secret. *Discretion* (dis-*kresh*'n; *n.*) means (a) being discreet; (b) freedom to act as one thinks best. *Ex.* Use your *discretion* in deciding what presents to give.

discuss (dis-*kus*) *v.* To talk or argue about. *Ex.* The girls *discussed* the chances of their team in the coming match. They had a *discussion* (*n.*) about it.

disgrace *n.* To be in *disgrace* is to be thought badly of. *Ex.* Some children were in *disgrace* because they had behaved badly.

disguise (dis-*gyz*) *v.* To change the appearance, especially by dressing up or putting on make-up, so as not to be recognized. People go to fancy dress parties *disguised* for fun.

disgust 1. *n.* Loathing and repulsion. 2. *v.* To fill with disgust. *Ex.* We were *disgusted* to hear they had left their cat to starve. The hotel food was *disgusting.*

dishearten *v.* To discourage, to make hopeless. *Ex.* He felt *disheartened* when he failed his test; it was *disheartening.*

disinfect *v.* To destroy the cause of infection.

dislike 1. *v.* To have no liking for. 2. *n.* A distaste for something or someone.

dismal (*diz*-m'l) *adj.* Gloomy or miserable. A person can be *dismal* or a place look *dismal.*

dismay *n.* Fear; a feeling of despair. *Ex.* They were *dismayed* to find how far they were from home.

dismiss *v.* To send away. *Ex.* He was *dismissed* from his job for slackness.

dispatch, despatch *v.* To send off. *Ex.* Mail is *dispatched* to its destination by the Post Office.

disperse *v.* To scatter in all directions. *Ex.* After the open-air meeting, the crowd *dispersed* to their homes.

displace *v.* To put out of place, to disarrange. *Ex.* I knew someone had been at my desk, as some of my things were *displaced*. A *displaced* (*adj.*) *person* is a refugee who no longer has a homeland.

display *v.* and *n.* To show, or a show. *Ex.* Have you seen a peacock *display* (*v.*) its beautiful tail? There was a fine *display* (*n.*) of fireworks last night.

dispose (dis-*pohz*) *v.* (a) To get rid of. *Ex.* He *disposed* of his old car before buying a new one. (b) To be inclined. *Ex.* I am not *disposed* to accept your word for it.

disposition (dis-po-*zish*'n) *n.* Nature or character. *Ex.* Her friendly *disposition* made her welcome everywhere.

dispute (dis-*pewt*) *n.* An argument or quarrel.

disregard *v.* To pay no attention to, to take no notice of. *Ex.* They walked over the grass, *disregarding* the notice telling them to keep off it.

disreputable (dis-*rep*-ew-tab'l) *adj.* Not having a good reputation or appearance. *Ex.* After getting so wet and muddy, the hikers felt they looked too *disreputable* to go into the restaurant.

dissolve (di-*zolv*) *v.* To melt in a liquid. *Ex.* Salt is easily *dissolved* in water.

dissuade (di-*swayd*) *v.* To persuade someone not to do something.

distance *n.* The space between two places or things. *Ex.* The *distance* between the villages was 2 kilometres; they are 2 kilometres *distant* (*adv.*) from each other. *Distant* can also mean far away. *Ex.* The *distant* (*adj.*) mountains could just be seen.

distaste (dis-*tayst*) *n.* Dislike. *Ex.* He found the idea of making fun of the handicapped *distasteful* (*adj.*).

distemper *n.* (a) A serious disease of young dogs. (b) A kind of paint used for covering the walls of a room.

distil (di-*stil*) *v.* To convert from liquid to steam and then back to liquid again. Alcoholic liquids are *distilled* in a *distillery* (*n.*).

distinct *adj.* Clear, easily heard or seen. *Ex.* The woodpecker makes a *distinct* tapping noise, easily recognized. The hills look very *distinct* after rain.

distinction (dis-*tingk*-sh'n) *n.* (a) The state of being *distinguished* or famous; an honour. *Ex.* It was a great *distinction* for him to be chosen to lead the expedition. (b) A difference. *Ex.* The farmer pointed out the *distinction* between barley and wheat.

distinguish (dis-*ting*-gwish) *v.* (a) To be able to tell the difference between one thing and another. *Ex.* The blind learn to *distinguish* things by touch. (b) To become well-known or famous. *Ex.* He *distinguished* himself as an artist; he became a *distinguished* (*adj.*) artist.

distort (dis-*tort*) *v.* To twist out of its true shape or meaning. *Ex.* His face was *distorted* by pain. His voice was *distorted* by a bad telephone line.

distract (dis-*trakt*) *v.* (a) To draw the attention away, so that one becomes confused. *Ex.* She was so *distracted* by the noise that she let the milk boil over. (b) To occupy pleasantly. *Ex.* Watching the cricket was a pleasant *distraction* (*n.*) while they waited.

distress *n.* Worry or suffering. *Ex.* The bad news caused us great *distress*; it *distressed* (*v.*) us.

distribute (dis-*trib*-ewt) *v.* To divide out. *Ex.* The sweets were *distributed* equally among the children; it was a fair *distribution* (dis-tri-*bew*-sh'n; *n.*).

district *n.* An area or region. *Ex.* This is a pleasant *district* to live in. The *Lake District*.

disturb *v.* To trouble, interrupt, agitate. *Ex.* Don't *disturb* us when we are trying to read.

ditch *n.* A long narrow space dug out of the earth, often for drainage purposes.

ditto *n.* The same as before or as above. Shortened in lists to *do* or a pair of commas (").

divan (di-*van*) *n.* A couch without back or sides, often used as a bed.

divert (dy-*vurt*) *v.* (a) To turn aside. *Ex.* The traffic was *diverted* because of the procession. '*Diversion* (*n.*) ahead'. (b) To occupy pleasantly; to amuse. *Ex.* Playing draughts was a pleasant *diversion* (*n.*).

divide *v.* (a) To split up into parts. *Ex.* We *divided* the cake between us. (b) To separate. *Ex.* The Cheviot Hills *divide* England from Scotland; they mark the *division* (*n.*) between them. A *division* can also be one of the parts that have been separated. *Ex.* This cupboard has two *divisions*—one for records, the other for cassettes.

divine (di-*vyn*) *adj.* Belonging to or coming from a god.

divorce 1. *n.* The legal ending to a marriage. 2. *v.* To legally end a marriage.

divulge (dy-*vulj*) *v.* To tell something that has been kept secret. *Ex.* She would not *divulge* where the presents were hidden.

dizzy *adj.* Giddy, feeling that everything is going round. *Ex.* It made me feel *dizzy* to look down from the church tower.

docile (*doh*-syl) *adj.* Obedient and easy to manage, as some domestic animals are.

dock 1. *n.* (a) The part of a harbour where ships load and unload. (b) A place where ships can be repaired or built. (c) The box in a law court where the prisoner stands. (d) A common weed. 2. *v.* (a) To take a ship into *dock.* (b) To cut short or make smaller. A horse's tail can be *docked* and so can a man's wages.

document (*dok*-ew-ment) *n.* A paper containing important, usually legal, information.

dodge *v.* To get out of the way of something. *Ex.* It was fun *dodging* the snowballs.

dogged (*dog*-id) *adj.* Determined to keep on trying.

dolphin (*dol*-fin) *n.* A sea mammal rather like a porpoise. It has a pointed snout and can do very clever tricks in an aquarium.

domestic *adj.* Connected with the house or home, as *domestic* work, *domestic* animals.

dominate *v.* To rule over; to be a controlling or chief influence.

domineer (dom-in-*eer*) *v.* To act in a masterful way, without considering the feelings and opinions of others.

doom *n.* Something unfortunate which is fated to happen. *Ex.* The *doomed* (*adj.*) ship was sinking fast and had no chance of reaching harbour.

dormant *adj.* Sleeping, not active. *Ex.* A dormouse is *dormant* when sleeping all winter.

dormitory (*dor*-mi-tor-i) *n.* A large sleeping-room, with beds for several people.

dose *n.* The quantity of medicine to be taken at one time.

dote *v.* To be over-fond, indulging someone as a child may be *doted* on by a fond grandparent.

double (*dub*'l) 1. *adj.* Twice as much. 2. *v.* My father is going to *double* my pocket-money. 3. *n.* A person exactly like another. *Ex.* The twins were exact *doubles* of each other.

doubt (dowt) 1. *v.* To be uncertain about, to be inclined not to believe. *Ex.* I *doubt* her story because she sometimes imagines things. 2. *n.* The state of *doubt.* To be in *doubt* is the opposite of being certain. *Ex.* It is *doubtful* (*adj.*) whether she could carry such a heavy parcel.

dough (doh) *n.* Flour, moistened, kneaded and ready for baking.

dove (duv) *n.* A bird of the pigeon family.

downcast *adj.* Sad and dejected.

doze *v.* To sleep lightly, not soundly.

drab *adj.* Dull and dreary. *Ex.* It was a *drab* street of old grey houses.

draft 1. *n.* The first rough form of a letter etc. before it is properly written or typed. 2. *v.* To write such a *draft.*

drag *v.* To pull along by force or with difficulty.

drain 1. *n.* A pipe to carry away water and waste matter. 2. *v.* (a) To supply with *drains,* as on farmland. (b) To drink till the glass or cup is empty.

drake *n.* The male of the duck.

drama (*drah*-ma) *n.* A play for acting; an exciting or *dramatic* (*adj.*) story or happening. One who writes plays is a *dramatist.*

drape *v.* To let material hang in folds over something. Material for dressmaking and upholstery is sold in the *drapery* (*n.*) department of shops.

drastic *adj.* Severe and strong in method. *Ex.* The headmaster said that he would deal *drastically* (*adv.*) with theft.

draught (drahft) 1. *n.* (a) A current of air. *Ex.* Do you feel a *draught* from this window? (b) A long drink. *Ex.* The thirsty horse enjoyed a cool *draught* from the river. (c) *Draughts* (*pl.*) is a board game for two players, with 24 pieces. 2. *adj.* Drawing along. A *draught* animal, such as a cart-horse, pulls a cart, plough etc.

dread 1. *n.* Fear or terror. 2. *v.* To be very frightened. *Ex.* I *dread* the thought of being in an earthquake. *Dreadful* (*adj.*) means terrible. *Ex.* I have a *dreadful* headache.

dreary *adj.* Dull, gloomy, lonely. *Ex.* The *dreary* road stretched over the moor for miles, with nothing to look at.

drench *v.* To make thoroughly wet. *Ex.* His clothes were so *drenched* that water could be wrung out of them.

dribble *v.* (a) To fall in drops, to trickle down. *Ex.* Babies *dribble* at the mouth when teething. (b) To move a ball gradually forward, as a footballer may do.

drift 1. *n.* Something heaped up by the wind. *Ex. Drifts* of snow blocked the road. 2. *v.* To be carried along by wind or tide. *Ex.* When the oars were lost, the boat *drifted* out to sea.

drill 1. *n.* (a) The training of soldiers in military movements and the handling of arms. *Ex.* We watched the soldiers *drilling* (*v.*). (b) A pointed instrument for boring holes. 2. *v.* To bore a hole with a drill. *Ex.* The dentist *drilled* my tooth before filling it.

drizzle *n.* Light rain.

droop *v.* To bend forward from weakness or want of nourishment. Plants *droop* for want of water; people may *droop* when tired.

drought (drowt) *n.* A long spell of very dry weather.

drown *v.* To die through remaining under water so long as to suffocate.

drowsy (*drow*-zi) *adj.* Sleepy. *Ex.* He was so *drowsy* that he could hardly keep his eyes open.

drudge *n.* One who is forced to go on doing hard work that he does not enjoy. This is *drudgery* (*n.*).

drug 1. *n.* A medicine or other substance that affects the body or mind, used to cure disease, lessen pain, help one sleep, and sometimes to poison or kill. 2. *v.* To give a *drug* to someone, especially to make them unconscious.

dual (*dew*-al) *adj.* Made up of two. *Ex.* A *dual* carriageway (where traffic has separate roads for opposite directions).

due *n.* Something one has a right to expect at a certain time, such as a payment, holiday, train etc. *Ex.* Our train is *due* to arrive at 5 p.m. *Due to* means because of, or caused by. *Ex.* Her stiff neck is *due to* her sitting in a draught yesterday.

duel (*dew*-el) *n.* A fight between two people arranged according to definite rules.

duet (dew-*et*) *n.* A piece of music for two to perform.

dumb (dum) *adj.* Not able to speak at all.

dumbfounded *adj.* So surprised as to be unable to speak at once.

dune *n.* A ridge or small hill of sand on the shore or in a desert.

dungeon (*dun*-jon) *n.* An underground prison in an old castle.

duplicate (*dew*-plik-at) *n.* Two of the same; double. *Ex.* This letter must be *duplicated* (*v.*) so that we can keep a copy. We need a *duplicate*.

durable *adj.* Hard-wearing.

duration (dewr-*ay*-sh'n) *n.* Length of time. *Ex.* The *duration* of the second World War was 6 years.

dusk *n.* The half-light before complete darkness at night.

duty *n.* What one ought to do; a task one knows one ought to perform.

duvet (*doo*-vay) *n.* A thick downy bed-quilt used instead of blankets.

dwell *v.* (a) To live in or make one's home in. A house is a *dwelling* (*n.*). (b) To keep thinking and worrying about something. *Ex.* Don't *dwell* on your troubles.

dwindle *v.* To grow less. *Ex.* As winter went on, our coal supply *dwindled.*

dye *v.* To change the colour of something by dipping it in a special liquid. *Ex.* I shall have these curtains *dyed* red.

dynamite (*dyn*-a-myt) *n.* A powerful and very destructive explosive.

E

eager (*ee*-ger) *adj.* Keen; anxious to do or have something. *Ex.* He was so *eager* to have a guitar that he saved up for one.

eagle (*ee*-g'l) *n.* A large bird of prey with a large hooked beak.

early 1. *adv.* (a) Near the beginning of some particular time. *Ex.* He left *early* in the morning. (b) In good time. *Ex.* We had lunch *early.* 2. *adj.* Before the usual time. *Ex.* I found some *early* primroses.

earn (urn) *v.* To get or deserve payment or reward. *Ex.* He *earns* good wages. He *earned* the good opinion of all.

earnest (*ur*-nest) *adj.* Serious or determined. *Ex.* He made an *earnest* effort to be on time.

earshot *n.* The distance at which one can hear or be heard. *Ex.* A Cockney is someone born within *earshot* of Bow Bells.

earthenware (*urth*-en-wair) *n.* and *adj.* Baked clay of which pots and tiles are made.

earthquake *n.* A shaking and splitting of the ground due to movements of rocks deep underground.

ease (eez) *n.* A state of comfort, without worry, difficulty or pain. *Ex.* He was quite at *ease* and felt relaxed. He lifted the heavy weight with *ease.* The medicine *eased* (*v.*) his pain.

easel (*eez*'l) *n.* A wooden frame that supports a blackboard, or a picture while it is being painted.

east *n.* The direction from which the sun rises. An *easterly* (*adj.*) wind comes from the east.

Easter (*ee*-ster) *n.* The Christian festival in March or April which commemorates the rising of Christ from the dead.

eaves (eevz) *n.* The bottom edge of a roof which overhangs the walls of a house. *Ex.* Swallows often build nests under the *eaves* of our house.

eavesdropper *n.* One who listens secretly to private conversation.

ebb *n.* When the sea moves away from the shore, gradually going farther out; this is the *ebb* (*adj.*) tide. The tide then turns and begins to come back (the *flood* tide). The tide *ebbs* and *flows* in turn.

eccentric (ek-*sen*-trik) *adj.* Odd in behaviour.

ecclesiastic (ek-lee-zi-*ast*-ik) *n.* A clergyman. *Ecclesiastical* (*adj.*) means having to do with the Church.

echo (*ek*-o) *n.* A sound, very like the original, made when sound waves are bounced back off a hard surface. You will hear your voice *echo* (*v.*) if you shout in a cave.

eclipse (i-*klips*) *n.* When our view of the sun is partly or wholly cut off for a time by the moon coming between it and our view of it, there is an *eclipse* of the sun. If earth passes between sun and moon, there is an *eclipse* of the moon.

ecology (ee-*kol*-o-ji) The study of how living things act on each other and on their surroundings.

economy (ee-*kon*-om-i) *n.* The careful management of money so as to avoid waste. A good housewife is *economical* (*adj.*); if she is spending too much she tries to *economize* (*v.*). *Economics* (ee-kon-*om*-iks; *n.*) is the study of the production and distribution of goods and their effect on the welfare of mankind.

edible (*ed*-i-b'l) *adj.* Fit to eat; eatable with safety. *Ex.* Not all mushrooms are *edible.*

edit *v.* To prepare books, newspapers etc. for publication. This is done by *editors* (*n.*).

educate (*ed*-ew-kayt) *v.* To teach or train. *Ex.* Most children are *educated* in school; this is where they get their *education* (*n.*).

eel *n.* A fish shaped like a snake.

eerie (*eer*-i) *adj.* Causing a strange feeling of uneasiness. *Ex.* The dark tunnel was *eerie*, and we were glad to get out of it.

effect (i-*fekt*) *n.* Result. *Ex.* We called the dog, but with no *effect*, for he didn't come. *Effective* (*adj.*) means having the *effect* wanted.

effervescent (ef-er-*ves*-ent) *adj.* Bubbling. *Ex.* Most of us like *effervescent* (fizzy) drinks.

efficient (ef-*ish*-ent) *adj.* Capable; able to do things well. *Ex.* The mechanic was *efficient* and soon repaired our car. He showed great *efficiency* (*n.*).

effort *n.* The use of energy; a trying hard; an attempt. *Ex.* The children made a great *effort* to raise money for the new theatre.

eiderdown (*y*-der-down) *n.* A quilt stuffed with the soft feathers of the *eider* duck.

either (*ydh*-er) *adj., pron.* and *conj.* One or the other. *Ex. Either* (*adj.*) boy is willing to go. You can ask *either* (*pron.*) of them. I will *either* (*conj.*) write or phone.

elaborate (e-*lab*-or-at) *adj.* Complicated; having many details or much ornament. *Ex. Elaborate* arrangements were made for the wedding. Many guests were *elaborately* dressed.

elastic (i-*last*-ik) *adj.* Having the power to spring back to its own shape after being stretched. A rubber band is *elastic*.

elated (i-*layt*-id) *adj.* Delighted and excited; in high spirits. *Ex.* He was *elated* by his success.

elbow (*el*-bo) *n.* The joint between the upper arm and the lower (forearm).

elder *adj.* Older. *Ex.* My *elder* brother. When people are getting old we say they are *elderly*.

elder *n.* A small tree with white flowers and purple berries.

elect (i-*lekt*) *v.* To choose, usually by vote. *Ex.* The cricket club met to *elect* a new captain. An *election* (*n.*) is the choosing of representatives, such as Members of Parliament or town councillors, by all who can, and want to, vote.

electricity (i-lek-*tris*-it-i) *n.* A kind of energy used for many things in our daily lives, producing heat, light, driving-power and means of communication (as by telephone) etc.

electronics (i-lek-*tron*-iks) *n.* The branch of physics to which we owe television, transistors, pocket calculators, computers etc.

elegant (*el*-e-gant) *adj.* Graceful; in good taste; fashionable. *Ex.* She looked very *elegant* in her new suit.

element (*el*-e-ment) *n.* One of the essential parts of something; the first and simplest part of a subject. *Ex.* We have to learn the *elements* of arithmetic before we can tackle algebra; and do *elementary* (*adj.*) piano exercises before we can play a piece of music.

elephant (*el*-e-fant) *n.* One of the largest animals, found in Africa and Asia. It has ivory tusks and a long trunk with which it puts food in its mouth.

elevate (*el*-e-vayt) *v.* To raise. A house in an *elevated* (*adj.*) position is one built on high ground.

elf *n.* A little fairy, full of mischief.

eligible (*el*-ij-ib'l) *adj.* Suitable, fit to be chosen. *Ex.* The young man was well-educated, and *eligible* for the job.

elopement (e-*lohp*-ment) *n.* The running away of two young people to get married without their parents' consent. Such couples *elope* (*v.*).

eloquence (*el*-o-kwens) *n.* The power of speaking well and in such a way as to stir the feelings of listeners. One who does this is *eloquent* (*adj.*).

elsewhere *adv.* In another place. *Ex.* He wasn't in the playground so I looked for him *elsewhere*.

embankment (em-*bangk*-ment) *n.* A long mound of earth built up at the side of a road, railway or river, to prevent flooding etc.

embark *v.* To go on board ship; to start on something. *Ex.* He *embarked* on a career of crime.

embarrass (em-*bar*-as) *v.* To make uncomfortable or shy. *Ex.* The returning hero was *embarrassed* by the great welcome at the station.

embers *n.* Pieces of coal in a fire which have not quite burned out.

embezzle *v.* To steal money left in one's charge. *Ex.* The treasurer *embezzled* the club's funds.

emblem *n.* A sign which represents or stands for some particular thing. *Ex.* The leek is the *emblem* of Wales.

embrace (em-*brays*) *v.* To clasp affectionately in one's arms.

embroider *v.* To decorate with stitches.

embryo (*em*-bri-o) *n.* A young creature before it is born.

emerald *n.* A green precious stone.

emerge (e-*murj*) *v.* To come out so as to be seen. *Ex.* It is exciting to see a chick *emerging* from its shell.

emergency (e-*mur*-jen-si) *n.* An unexpected happening which has to be dealt with right away; for instance, an outbreak of fire.

emigrate (*em*-i-grayt) *v.* To leave one's country and go and settle in another. One then becomes an *emigrant* (*n.*).

eminence (*em*-in-ens) *n.* (a) A hill or high piece of land. *Ex.* Edinburgh Castle is built on a rocky *eminence*. (b) Greatness or high position in life. *Ex.* He is an *eminent* (*adj.*) doctor, at the top of his profession.

emotion (e-*moh*-sh'n) *n.* A strong feeling, such as sorrow, joy, fear. *Ex.* The exciting film stirred the *emotions* of the audience.

emperor *n.* The ruler of an empire.

emphasize (*em*-fa-syz) *v.* To draw attention to, as being very important. *Ex.* The doctor laid *emphasis* (*n.*) on the need for exercise. He was very *emphatic* (em-*fat*-ik; *adj.*) about it.

empire (*em*-pyr) *n.* A group of states or countries ruled by an emperor, or all under one government.

employ (em-*ploi*) *v.* To give someone work to do, for wages or other payment. *Ex.* I am *employing* an electrician; he is my *employee* (*n.*); I am his *employer*; he is in my *employment*.

empty 1. *adj.* Having nothing in it. *Ex.* My purse is *empty*. 2. *v.* To make empty. *Ex.* I *emptied* the bucket of water.

emu (*ee*-mew) *n.* An Australian bird like an ostrich.

enable *v.* To make able. *Ex.* My bike *enables* me to get out into the country quickly.

enamel (en-*am*-el) *n.* A glassy coating put on some surfaces and heated, making a hard shiny surface, as on *enamel* (*adj.*) saucepans.

enchanting (en-*chahnt*-ing) *adj.* Delightful. *Ex.* There are *enchanting* views of the mountains from the windows. *Enchantment* (*n.*) is the use of magic arts, as in fairy stories.

enclose (en-*klohz*) *v.* (a) To shut in. *Ex.* High walls *enclosed* the garden. (b) To put in. *Ex.* I *enclosed* a photograph in my letter. That was an *enclosure* (*n.*).

encore (*ong*-kor) *n.* A call for a performer to repeat his performance, or to add another.

encounter *v.* To meet. *Ex.* He *encountered* a tiger at the jungle's edge. It was a frightening *encounter* (*n.*).

encourage (en-*kur*-ij) *v.* To make someone feel more hopeful; to try to persuade someone to do something. *Ex.* My father *encouraged* me to learn to swim.

encyclopaedia (en-syk-lo-*pee*-di-a) *n.* A book containing information on all sorts of subjects, usually arranged in alphabetical order.

endear (en-*deer*) *v.* To make dear or beloved. *Ex.* She had *endeared* herself to all by her kindness.

endeavour (en-*dev*-or) *v.* To try or try hard. *Ex.* I will *endeavour* to find out for you what he really said.

endless *adj.* Without end; lasting for ever. *Ex.* The road seemed *endless*, but at last we reached the village.

endure (en-*dewr*) *v.* (a) To put up with, to bear. *Ex.* I can't *endure* great heat. (b) To last or continue. *Ex.* I don't think my novel will win *enduring* (*adj.*) fame.

enemy (*en*-em-i) *n.* A person who wants to harm or defeat you; a hateful person. In war, the nation you are fighting against is called the *enemy*.

energy (*en*-er-ji) *n.* Force, power; ability and willingness to work hard or to be active. *Ex.* He is a man of great *energy*. He is *energetic* (*adj.*).

enforce (en-*fors*) *v.* To insist on rules being obeyed. *Ex.* A policeman's duty is to *enforce* the law.

engage (en-*gayj*) *v.* (a) To promise employment to. *Ex.* The firm *engaged* her as a typist. (b) To bind by promise. *Ex.* They got *engaged* to be married. *Engaged* can also mean occupied or busy.

engine (*en*-jin) *n.* A power-driven machine, such as a diesel engine, aero engine etc.

engineer (en-jin-*eer*) *n.* A person who designs, builds or repairs machinery, roads, bridges etc.

engraving *n.* A print of a picture etc. made by cutting into metal or wood, inking it, and then pressing it on to paper.

enigma (en-*ig*-ma) *n.* A puzzle; something hard to find an explanation for.

enjoy *v.* To like or find pleasure in. You can find *enjoyment* (*n.*) in food, a holiday, a rest etc.

enlarge *v.* To make larger. You can have an *enlargement* (*n.*) made of a photograph.

enlighten *v.* To make something clear by explaining and teaching. *Ex.* Oil painting was a mystery to him until some art classes helped to *enlighten* him.

enlist *v.* To join one of the armed services.

enormous (e-*nor*-mus) *adj.* Very large indeed.

enough 1. *adj.* As much as one needs; the right amount. *Ex.* Have you *enough* money for your bus fare? 2. *adv.* This bucket is full *enough*. 3. *pron.* I have eaten *enough*.

enquire *See* inquire.

enrage *v.* To make very angry.

enrol (en-*rohl*) *v.* To write a name on a list; to become a member of a group. *Ex.* Ten new pupils were *enrolled* in the class.

ensign (*en*-syn) *n.* A naval or military flag. *Ex.* The *White Ensign* is the flag of the Royal Navy.

ensure (en-*shoor*) *v.* To make sure or safe. *Ex.* The climbers were roped together to *ensure* their safety.

enter *v.* (a) To go in, or come in. The door or gate by which *entry* (*n.*) is made is called an *entrance* (*n.*). (b) To enrol, or put one's name down for a competition.

enterprise (*en*-ter-pryz) *n.* A task or adventure that is difficult or needs some daring. *Ex.* Landing on the moon was a great *enterprise. Enterprising* (*adj.*) people are adventurous and ready to take risks.

entertain (en-ter-*tayn*) *v.* (a) To amuse. *Ex.* He *entertained* the children by telling them stories. A performance meant to give pleasure and amusement is an *entertainment* (*n.*). Amusing people can be called *entertaining* (*adj.*). (b) To receive someone at one's house as a guest, for a meal, party etc.

enthral (en-*thrawl*) *v.* To delight and thrill. *Ex.* The girls were *enthralled* by the ballet.

enthusiasm (en-*thew*-zi-azm) *n.* Warm interest, liking or admiration. *Ex.* The boys greeted the idea of starting a boxing class with *enthusiasm.* They were *enthusiastic* (*adj.*).

entire (en-*tyr*) *adj.* Whole, complete. *Ex.* I have been working the *entire* day, without a break.

envelop (en-*vel*-op) *v.* To wrap up in, or cover completely. *Ex.* The town was *enveloped* in fog. An *envelope* (*en*-vel-ohp; *n.*) is a cover for a letter.

envy *v.* To grudge another's good fortune. To feel *envy* (*n.*) is to be *envious* (*adj.*) of what someone else possesses.

epidemic (ep-i-*dem*-ik) *n.* An illness that affects a great many people at the same time.

episode (*ep*-i-sohd) *n.* An event or incident, either in real life or in a story.

epitaph (*ep*-i-tahf) *n.* Words inscribed on a tombstone.

equal (*ee* kwal) *adj.* The same in size or numbers. *Ex.* We shared out the toffee *equally* (*adv.*).

equator (e-*kway*-tor) *n.* The imaginary line running round the earth, half-way between the North and South Poles.

equestrian (e-*kwes*-tri-an) *adj.* Mounted on a horse. An *equestrian* statue is one of a person on horseback.

equip (e-*kwip*) *v.* To fit out or supply what is necessary. *Ex.* The mountaineers were *equipped* with warm clothing. Their *equipment* (*n.*) was good.

equivalent (e-*kwiv*-a-lent) *adj.* Equal in value, amount or meaning. *Ex.* A pound note is the *equivalent* (*n.*) of 100 pence.

era (*eer*-a) *n.* A long period of time, with reference to a particular feature of that period. *Ex.* The *era* of sail (before the steamship); the Christian *era*.

erect 1. *v.* To set up, to build. *Ex.* A block of flats was *erected* near the river. 2. *adj.* Upright; not lying down.

erosion (e-*roh*-zh'n) *n.* Wearing away, especially the wearing away of the soil by water, wind etc.

err *v.* To make a mistake. If you *err*, you make an *error* (*n.*).

errand *n.* A short journey on which one is sent to deliver a message, buy something etc.

error *n. See* err.

erupt (e-*rupt*) *v.* To burst out, like a volcano.

escalator (*es*-kal-ayt-or) *n.* A moving staircase, such as one sees in large shops.

escape *v.* To get away, to get free, to avoid. *Ex.* They *escaped* from the burning building. We all had measles except Nancy, who *escaped* them.

escort (es-*kort*) *v.* To accompany, usually in order to guard a person, or prevent his escape. The police may *escort* a prisoner to the court. Troops may *escort* a king; they are his *escort* (*es*-kort; *n.*).

espionage (es-pi-on-*ahzh*) *n.* The work done by spies.

esplanade (es-plan-*ayd*) *n.* The walk or road along the sea-front of a town.

essay (*es*-ay) *n.* A piece of writing on a set subject.

essential (es-*en*-sh'l) *adj.* Necessary; what must be done. *Ex.* It is *essential* to be careful when crossing roads.

establish (es-*tab*-lish) *v.* To set up or set going. *Ex.* A scheme has been *established* to re-train the unemployed.

estate (es-*tayt*) *n.* (a) A large piece of private land surrounding a country house. (b) An area set aside for building new houses. *Ex.* A housing or council *estate*. (c) All of a person's property, especially that left at death.

esteem (es-*teem*) *n.* High opinion or respect. *Ex.* Beethoven is held in high *esteem*.

estimate (*es*-tim-ayt) *v.* To form a rough idea of the size of something, or the probable cost of building something etc. *Ex.* Before we have the roof repaired, I shall get *estimates* of cost from several builders.

estuary (*es*-tew-ar-i) *n.* A wide river-mouth.

eternal (ee-*turn*-al) *adj.* Lasting for ever, having neither beginning nor end. *Eternity* (*n.*) means an everlasting length of time.

evacuate (e-*vak*-ew-ayt) *v.* To go or send away from a place, leaving it empty. *Ex.* The police *evacuated* all the houses near the burning factory. They became *evacuees* (e-vak-ew-*eez*; *n.*).

evade (e-*vayd*) *v.* To avoid or get away from. *Ex.* The police set up a road-block, but the thieves *evaded* capture. *Evasive* (e-*vay*-siv; *adj.*) means not straightforward. *Ex.* He was so *evasive* that I couldn't make out whether he was coming or not.

evaporate (e-*vap*-or-ayt) *v.* To dry up. *Ex.* When the sun came out the pools of rainwater soon *evaporated.*

even *adj.* (a) Smooth, flat. (b) An *even* number is one which can be divided by 2 and have no remainder.

event (e-*vent*) *n.* A thing that has happened. A death is a sad *event,* a birthday a happy one.

eventually (e-*ven*-tew-al-i) *adv.* In the end, at last. *Ex.* We searched all day and *eventually* found our lost puppy.

evident (*ev*-i-dent) *adj.* Clear and easily seen. *Ex.* It was *evident* that he had been blackberrying by the stains on his hands; these were the *evidence* (*n.*) of what he had been doing.

evil (*ee*-vil) 1. *adj.* Bad, wicked. 2. *n.* Sin and wickedness.

evolve (e-*volv*) *v.* To develop. The *theory of evolution* (*n.*) states that all living creatures have developed from simpler forms of life in the distant past.

ewe (yew) *n.* A female sheep.

exact (eg-*zakt*) *adj.* Quite correct. *Ex.* The train arrived at the *exact* time it was due; it was *exactly* (*adv.*) on time.

exaggerate (eg-*zaj*-er-ayt) *v.* To make out that something is larger, better etc. than it really is. *Ex.* It is an *exaggeration* (*n.*) to say there were millions of people at the concert; you mean there were a lot of people.

examine (eg-*zam*-in) *v.* To look at closely; to find out by asking questions. *Ex.* You should *examine* your change before you leave a shop. An *examination* (*n.*) *paper* is one where questions are asked to test knowledge of a subject. A doctor *examines* patients to find out what is the matter with them.

example (eg-*zahm*-p'l) *n.* Something chosen either to be copied or to show what others of the same kind are like. *Ex.* This is an *example* of the kind of dolls I make. His calmness in the air-raid was an *example* for us all to copy.

exasperate (eg-*zahs*-per-ayt) *v.* To irritate and annoy. *Ex.* It was *exasperating* (*adj.*) to find that we had forgotten the keys.

excavate (*eks*-ka-vayt) *v.* To dig out. You can *excavate* to find the remains of ancient buildings under the ground, to rescue someone trapped in a landslide, or to dig a well. All these can be called *excavations* (*n.*).

exceed (ek-*seed*) *v.* To go beyond. *Ex.* He was fined for *exceeding* the speed limit. *Exceedingly* (*adv.*) means very or very much. *Ex.* The party was *exceedingly* enjoyable.

excel (ek-*sel*) *v.* To do something better than others. *Ex.* She *excels* at diving; her diving is *excellent* (*adj.*).

exceptional (ek-*sep*-shon-al) *adj.* Not like the others of its kind; unusual. *Ex.* The weather was *exceptionally* (*adv.*) dry for February.

excessive (ek-*ses*-iv) *adj.* Too much. *Ex.* I can't afford coffee, its price is *excessive*.

exchange (eks-*chaynj*) *v.* To change one thing for another. Some people *exchange* stamps. You can *exchange* seats with someone.

excited (ek-*syt*-tid) *adj.* Having strong feelings of happiness, agitation, hopeful expectation etc. *Ex.* He became *excited* as holiday-time drew near; it was *exciting* that he would soon be on holiday.

exclaim (eks-*klaym*) *v.* To call out suddenly, especially in surprise. *Ex.* Everyone *exclaimed* when the bird flew out of the conjuror's hat.

exclude (eks-*klood*) *v.* To shut out. *Ex.* Children were *excluded* from the cinema as the film was *exclusively* (*adv.*) for adults.

excruciating (eks-*kroo*-shi-ayt-ing) *adj.* Causing great pain.

excursion (eks-*ker*-sh'n) *n.* An outing or trip, usually for pleasure.

excuse 1. (eks-*kewz*) *v.* To overlook, to forgive. *Ex.* Please *excuse* me for being so late. 2. (eks-*kews*) *n.* A reason offered for doing something wrong. *Ex.* The teacher said he would accept no *excuses* for late work.

execute (*eks*-e-kewt) *v.* To carry out (orders); to put to death by law.

exempt (eg-*zempt*) *adj.* Freed from, excused. *Ex.* Those who had gone to the lecture were *exempt* from afternoon school.

exercise (*eks*-er-syz) *n.* Something done to improve knowledge, skill or health, such as a French *exercise*, a piano *exercise*, or gymnastics. One can *exercise* (*v.*) brain or body.

exert (eg-*zurt*) *v.* To use actively. *Ex.* He *exerted* all his strength to lift the weight.

exhaust (eg-*zawst*) *v.* To use up the whole of something; to wear out physically. *Ex.* The explorers had *exhausted* all their food before they were rescued; after their long, hard journey they were suffering from *exhaustion* (*n.*).

exhibit (eg-*zib*-it) *v.* To show, usually in public. *Ex.* The roses *exhibited* at the flower show were beautiful; it was a successful *exhibition* (*n.*).

exile (*eks*-yl) *n.* One who has been sent out of his own country and is not allowed to come back to it. *Ex.* Napoleon was *exiled* (*v.*) to St Helena.

exist (eks-*ist*) *v.* To be, to live. *Ex.* We wonder if life *exists* on other planets.

exit (*eks*-it) *n.* (a) The way out. *Ex.* When the match was over, we made our way to the *exit*. (b) The leaving of the stage by an actor.

expand (eks-*pand*) *v.* To grow larger and take up more space. *Ex.* Elastic *expands* when it is pulled, and a business *expands* when it is able to take more and more work. An *expanse* (*n.*) of land is a large area of land.

expect (eks-*pekt*) *v.* To believe that a thing will happen. *Ex.* We *expect* our mother will come home tomorrow.

expedition (eks-ped-*ish*'n) *n.* A party of people who set out on a journey for a special purpose, such as exploration, hunting etc.

expel (eks-*pel*) *v.* To drive out or send away. *Ex.* He was *expelled* from school for bad behaviour.

expend (eks-*pend*) *v.* To spend, especially money or energy. What you spend is your *expenditure* (*n.*).

expense (eks-*pens*) *n.* The cost. *Ex.* We cannot afford the *expense* of a holiday this year; it would be too *expensive* (*adj.*).

experience (eks-*peer*-i-ens) *n.* The knowledge and skill learnt through life by observing and doing. *Ex.* He is an *experienced* (*adj.*) lawyer and his advice would be valuable.

experiment (eks-*per*-i-ment) *n.* A test done to prove or discover facts. *Ex.* My brother has started doing chemistry *experiments*; he loves *experimenting* (*v.*).

expert (*eks*-pert) *adj.* Having great knowledge or skill in something. You might be an *expert* skater or an *expert* (*n.*) in gardening.

expire (eks-*pyr*) *v.* To die or come to an end. *Ex.* He *expired* at the age of 83. Our television licence has *expired* and we must renew it.

explain (eks-*playn*) *v.* To make clear; to give the meaning of or the reason for. *Ex.* The teacher *explained* the parts we couldn't understand. John *explained* why he was late; he gave an *explanation* (*n.*) for it.

explode (eks-*plohd*) *v.* To burst with a loud noise, as a bomb does. A bursting bomb makes an *explosion* (*n.*).

exploit (*eks*-ploit) *n.* A bold, adventurous or famous deed.

explore (eks-*plor*) *v.* To travel in unknown areas in order to find out about them. People who do this are *explorers* (*n.*). They make *explorations* (*n.*).

export (eks-*port*) *v.* To send goods to other countries for sale. *Ex.* Britain *exports* machinery. Machinery is one of her chief *exports* (*eks*-ports; *n.*).

expose (eks-*pohz*) *v.* To lay bare or leave uncovered. *Ex.* The tent was blown away, and the boys were *exposed* to the pouring rain.

express (eks-*pres*) *v.* To say in words. *Ex.* He found it difficult to *express* his thanks.

express (eks-*pres*) *adj.* Speedy. *Ex.* He took the *express* train so that he could get home quickly.

expression (eks-*presh*'n) *n.* (a) A phrase or set of words. *Ex.* The French speaker used unusual *expressions* we had not yet learnt. (b) The look on a person's face. *Ex.* She had such a pleasant *expression* that we asked her to help us.

exquisite (*eks*-kwiz-it or eks-*kwis*-it) *adj.* Most beautiful and excellent in every way. Food can have an *exquisite* taste and roses smell *exquisitely* (*adv.*).

extend (eks-*tend*) *v.* To stretch out; to make larger. *Ex.* The forest *extended* for 20 kilometres. We *extended* our garden to include some woodland. The *extent* (*n.*) of the garden was increased.

exterior (eks-*teer*-i-or) *n.* The outside. *Ex.* The *exterior* (*adj.*) walls of our house are painted white.

exterminate (eks-*tur*-min-ayt) *v.* To kill off entirely. *Ex.* The rats in our barn have now been *exterminated*.

external (eks-*turn*-al) *adj.* On the outside. *Ex.* His injuries were all *external*, being only bruises and cuts.

extinct (eks-*tingkt*) *adj.* Dead or no longer able to act. *Ex.* There used to be a bird called the dodo, but there is none now anywhere, so it is *extinct*. An *extinct* volcano is no longer active.

extinguish (eks-*ting*-gwish) *v.* To put out. You can *extinguish* a candle, or a fireman could *extinguish* a large fire.

extra (*eks*-tra) *adj.* Beyond what is usual or expected. *Ex.* It became colder at night, so we were glad of the *extra* blankets.

extract 1. (eks-*trakt*) *v.* To take out. *Ex.* A dentist *extracts* teeth. 2. (*eks*-trakt) *n.* A passage taken from a book for some purpose.

extraordinary (eks-*tror*-din-ar-i) *adj.* Beyond the ordinary, remarkable. *Ex.* A snowflake seen under the microscope is of *extraordinary* beauty.

extravagant (eks-*trav*-a-gant) *adj.* Wasteful, spending too much. *Ex.* Mother said that an electric mixer would be an *extravagance* (*n.*) as we could well do without one.

extreme (eks-*treem*) *adj.* Very great, or in very high degree. *Ex.* Though he was in *extreme* pain, he showed *extreme* courage.

exult (eg-*zult*) *v.* To rejoice in triumph. *Ex.* Everyone *exulted* in our team's victory.

F

fable *n.* A short story, usually about animals that act and speak like human beings, and which teaches a lesson. *Ex.* Aesop's *Fables*.

fabulous *adj.* (a) Not historically true but legendary. (b) Unbelievably amazing.

fact *n.* Something known to have happened or to have been done; information known to be true. *Ex.* Newspapers ought to make sure of the *facts* before they print news.

factor *n.* Something which helps to account for a result. *Ex.* An important *factor* in winning a war is keeping the troops well supplied. In maths a *factor* is one of the numbers which when multiplied together result in a given number. *Ex.* 5 and 6 are the *factors* which, multiplied together, make 30.

factory *n.* A building where things are manufactured (made).

faculty (*fak*-ult-i) *n.* Ability, especially one with which one is born, such as the *faculties* of hearing, sight etc., or for maths.

fad *n.* A silly like or dislike which won't last long. *Ex.* He is full of *fads* and fancies about food.

fade *v.* To lose colour or strength. *Ex.* Flowers *fade* and die if not given water. Coloured material may *fade* when exposed to the sun. Sound *fades* as we move away from it.

fail *v.* The opposite to succeed. *Ex.* I *failed* to clear 1½ metres in the high jump. Without *fail* (*n.*) means certainly.

faint *adj.* Weak. A sound or a light may be *faint*, or one may feel *faint*. To *faint* (*v.*) is to become unconscious.

fair *adj.* (a) Clear and pleasing to look at. *Ex.* A *fair* copy is one without mistakes, made from a rough copy. (b) With blond or golden hair. (c) With fine weather, free from rain. (d) Just and not biased. *Ex.* No one likes to play a game with *unfair* (not fair) players. (e) Pretty good but not very good. *Ex.* He is only *fairly* (*adv.*) good at games.

fair *n.* An open-air market, usually held once a year and including amusements such as roundabouts etc.

faith (fayth) *n.* Trust and belief in, such as trust in the beliefs of a religion. You can put your trust in someone who is *faithful* (*adj.*) to you.

fake *n.* Something which, in order to deceive, is made to look like the genuine article. *Ex.* This painting was supposed to be by Constable, but turned out to be a *fake*.

false (fawls) *adj.* Untrue, disloyal. You can make a *false* statement, or be a *false* friend. A *falsehood* (*n.*) is a lie.

falter (*fawl*-ter) *v.* To go unsteadily or hesitate, in walking, speech etc. *Ex.* Though he knew the danger, his courage never *faltered*.

fame *n.* Being well-known for good qualities. *Ex.* Mozart is a *famous* (*adj.*) composer.

familiar (fam-*il*-yer) *adj.* Well-known through personal knowledge. *Ex.* None of these songs is new to me; I am *familiar* with them all.

famine (*fam*-in) *n.* A dreadful shortage of food, usually due to poor crops. *Famished* (*adj.*) means in great hunger, starving.

fanatic (fan-*at*-ik) *n.* A person who is so enthusiastic about something that he acts without common sense. A *fanatic* for fresh air might want all windows kept open, summer and winter, which would be *fanatical* (*adj.*) behaviour.

fancy 1. *n.* (a) An idea passing through the mind. (b) A liking. *Ex.* I have taken a *fancy* to her. 2. *adj.* Ornamental, not plain. 3.

v. To imagine, to form a picture in the mind. *Ex.* He *fancied* he heard a ghost last night.

fang *n.* The long sharp tooth of a dog, wolf etc. *Ex.* A snake's *fangs* are sometimes poisonous.

fantastic (fan-*tas*-tik) *adj.* Strange and unbelievable. *Ex.* 'Sinbad the Sailor' is a *fantastic* story.

farce *n.* A play in which people act absurdly to make the audience laugh.

fare 1. *n.* (a) The price paid for a journey by public transport. *Ex.* The *fare* to London was £10. (b) Food. *Ex.* The tables were laden with good Christmas *fare*. 2. *v.* To get on (well or badly). *Ex.* He *fared* quite well in his exams.

farewell (fair-*wel*) *interj.* Good-bye! *Ex.* We gave her a *farewell* (*adj.*) present when she left.

farther *adv.* At a greater distance.

fascinate (*fas*-in-ayt) *v.* To charm and interest very much. *Ex.* He was *fascinated* by the escalators and kept going up and down on them.

fashion *n.* The shape, pattern or style in which a thing is made, especially clothes. *Fashions* are always changing; what is *fashionable* (*adj.*) today soon becomes *old-fashioned* (*adj.*). *Fashionably* (*adv.*) dressed means dressed in the latest style.

fast 1. *adj.* (a) Firm and secure. *Fast* asleep means sound asleep. (b) Quick, speedy. *Ex.* This is a *fast* train. 2. *v.* To do without food for a time, as a religious duty or simply to lose weight etc.

fasten (*fahs*-en) *v.* To shut or make secure, with a hook or catch etc. *Ex. Fasten* your seat-belts.

fatal (*fay*-t'l) *adj.* Causing death or disaster. A *fatal* accident is one in which someone is killed.

fate *n.* The power which is supposed to decide how everything is to happen, long before it does happen. *Ex.* I was *fated* (*v.*) never to meet him, though I tried hard.

fathom (*fadh*-om) 1. *n.* The unit used in measuring the depth of water. One *fathom* is 6 feet (1.8 metres). 2. *v.* To get to the bottom of and understand. *Ex.* I cannot *fathom* the mystery of his sudden departure.

fault (fawlt) *n.* A failing or mistake; an action for which blame must be taken. *Ex.* It was not his *fault* he was late; he was held up by fog. This torch is *faulty* (*adv.*), so I shall return it to the shop.

favour (*fay*-ver) *n.* (a) A kind act. *Ex.* Would you do me a *favour* and give me a lift into town? (b) Goodwill or approval. *Ex.* I won her *favour* by washing up for her. *In favour of* means liking the idea of. *Ex.* I am *in favour of* giving him some help.

favourable *adj.* (a) Promising good or advantage. *Ex. Favourable* weather. A *favourable* opportunity. (b) Showing friendly approval. *Ex.* A *favourable* reply.

favourite (*fayv*-or-it) *adj.* Most liked. *Ex.* My *favourite* colour is blue.

fawn 1. *n.* A young deer. 2. *adj.* Pale brownish colour.

fear *n.* A troubled feeling at the thought of meeting danger, pain or the unknown. *Ex.* She *feared* (*v.*) the dark; she was *fearful* (*adj.*) of it.

feast *n.* A specially rich meal, usually for some happy occasion.

feat *n.* A deed which requires special strength, skill or courage. *Ex.* It was a great *feat* to swim the flooded river.

feather (*fedh*-er) *n.* One of the horny stems, fringed on either side, which cover a bird's body; the soft fluffy *feathers* are for warmth and the larger stiffer ones form the wings and tail.

feature (*fee*-cher) *n.* (a) A part of the face, such as nose or chin. (b) An important, noticeable part of something. *Ex.* The special *feature* of the film was the lovely scenery.

fee *n.* Payment for services of a special kind. A doctor, a lawyer, a hired band can all charge *fees*.

feeble *adj.* Weak. *Ex.* The old woman was very *feeble*; she could hardly walk. That joke was a bit *feeble*.

feline (*fee*-lyn) *adj.* Of or like a cat.

fellow *n.* A man. *Ex.* A nice enough *fellow*. A silly *fellow*. Used with another noun *fellow* means 'of the same kind'. *Ex.* A *fellow-citizen*. I have a *fellow-feeling* (sympathy) for the deaf, as I am deaf myself.

felt *n.* Very thick fabric made not by weaving but by pressing wool very tightly, so that the tiny hairs cling together. Many hats are made of *felt*.

female (*fee*-mayl) *adj.* Belonging to the sex that produces young, whether babies, eggs or seeds. Women and girls belong to the *female* sex.

feminine (*fem*-in-in) *adj.* Of or like the female sex.

fencing *n.* A skilful sport in which men fight with foils (special light swords) to gain points, but not to injure.

fend *v.* (a) To stop something bumping into one, to ward off.

(b) To provide. *Ex.* While their parents were away, they had to *fend* for themselves.

fender *n.* (a) A piece of rope, rubber etc. fitted at a boat's side to prevent damage when coming alongside a quay etc. (b) An edging to a hearth, often of metal.

fern *n.* A feathery plant without flowers.

ferocious (fer-*oh*-shus) *adj.* Fierce, savage. *Ex.* A lion is *ferocious*; it shows great *ferocity* (fer-*os*-it-i; *n.*).

ferret (*fer*-et) *n.* A small white animal (a tamed polecat), used to chase rabbits and rats out of their holes.

ferry (*fer*-i) *n.* A boat which takes passengers, and sometimes cars, across a river or channel.

fertile (*fur*-tyl) *adj.* Able to produce good crops; fruitful. *Fertilizers* (*n.*) are spread on farmland to *fertilize* (*v.*) it, so that it will produce more.

fester *v.* To become infected with pus.

festival (*fes*-ti-val) *n.* A meeting held to express rejoicing or thanksgiving (*Ex.* A *harvest festival*); or a series of performances of music, plays etc., as at the Edinburgh *Festival* of the Arts.

festivity (fest-*iv*-it-i) *n.* A festival; the gaiety at a social gathering where people have the *festive* (happy) spirit.

fête (fayt) *n.* An outdoor festival, usually held to raise funds for a church etc.

feud (fewd) *n.* A bitter quarrel which goes on for a long time between two people or families.

feudalism (*few*-dal-iz'm) *n.* The system in the Middle Ages by which a man was allowed to farm land belonging to a landlord for whom he was obliged, in return, to work and fight.

fever (*fee*-ver) *n.* A state in which the body has a high temperature and a racing pulse.

fiasco (fi-*ask*-o) *n.* A complete failure. *Ex.* The open-air fête was a *fiasco* as it rained and few turned up.

fibre (*fy*-ber) *n.* (a) Anything thread-like in plant or animal tissue. (b) A substance from natural or artificial *fibres* which can be spun, such as cotton or nylon.

fickle *adj.* Changeable. A *fickle* person is one who may change his mind after making a promise, and so cannot be trusted.

fiction (*fik*-sh'n) *n.* A story which is imaginary and has been invented. Novels can be called *fiction*, and the people in novels are *fictitious* (fik-*tish*-us; *adj.*).

fiddle *n.* A violin.

fidget *v.* To move restlessly. *Ex.* It disturbs listeners at a concert if people *fidget*.

fiend (feend) *n.* An evil spirit, or a person who takes pleasure in being wicked and cruel.

fierce (feers) *adj.* Cruel, savage. Tigers are *fierce* animals.

fiery (*fy*-er-i) *adj.* Like fire; glowing. *Ex.* A *fiery* sky at sunset. *Fiery-tempered* means hot-tempered, easily made angry.

figure (*fig*-er) *n.* (a) The shape and form of a body. *Ex.* I saw the *figure* of a woman pass by in the gloom. (b) A number. *Ex.* '8' for 'eight'.

file 1. *n.* (a) A steel tool with a rough surface for rubbing off roughness in metal or wood. (b) A row of people one behind the other. *Ex.* They had to walk in single *file* because the path was so narrow.

filly *n.* A young female horse.

filter *n.* A strainer for liquids made so that the liquid pours through holes and leaves any solids behind. Coffee can be made by *filtering* (*v.*) hot water through coffee grounds.

filth *n.* Anything very dirty or nasty.

fin *n.* The part of a fish (like small wing) which helps it to swim, steer or balance.

final (*fy*-nal) *adj.* Last; at the end.

fine *adj.* (a) Excellent; extremely good. (b) Not coarse, heavy or thick. *Ex. Fine* thread is needed to go through the eye of a *fine* needle.

fine *v.* To make a person pay a sum of money (a *fine*; *n.*) as a punishment. *Ex.* People may be *fined* for parking offences.

fir (fur) *n.* An evergreen tree which bears cones and needle-shaped leaves, and whose wood is good for timber.

firearm *n.* A gun.

firm (furm) 1. *adj.* Strong and steady. *Ex.* A *firm* reply, a *firm* shelf, a *firm* friendship. 2. *n.* The persons who own and manage a business. *Ex.* Both these shops are managed by the same *firm*.

fist *n.* The closed hand.

fit 1. *n.* (a) A sudden violent attack of illness, coughing, temper etc. (b) A passing mood. *Ex.* I had a *fit* of laziness yesterday, so I haven't finished the job. 2. *adj.* (a) Suitable. *Ex.* This food is not *fit* to eat. (b) In good health. *Ex.* He is *fit* enough to work now. 3. *v.* (a) To suit; to be the right size and shape. *Ex.* The shoes *fit* perfectly. (b) To apply or supply. *Ex.* He *fitted* a new tyre to his bike.

fix *v.* To arrange, settle, make firm. *Ex.* To *fix* a date for the holidays. To *fix* a shelf on the wall. What is *fixed* is a *fixture* (*n.*).

flabby *adj.* Limp and floppy. *Ex.* His muscles are *flabby* from lack of exercise.

flake *n.* A thin flat piece of something, such as a *flake* of fish or a *snowflake*.

flame *n.* The gleam or tongue of fire seen when something is burning.

flank *n.* (a) The side of an animal. *Ex.* The horse's *flanks* were gleaming after being brushed. (b) Either end of a line of soldiers.

flannel *n.* Cloth made of soft wool, usually fine in quality.

flash 1. *n.* A sudden blaze of light seen only for a moment. *Ex.* A *flash* of lightning. 2. *v.* (a) To make a *flash*. *Ex.* He *flashed* his torch on and off as a signal. (b) To appear and disappear quickly, as does a lightning *flash*. *Ex.* The express train *flashed* past in a few seconds.

flask *n.* A small bottle, usually suitable to carry in the pocket. *Vacuum flasks* are bottles which keep liquids hot or cold for several hours.

flatter *v.* To praise insincerely, pretending more admiration than one feels. *Ex.* He *flattered* John by telling him he was a first-class cricketer, which John knew he was not. He realized this was *flattery* (*n.*).

flavour (*flay*-ver) 1. *n.* Taste. *Ex.* This ice-cream has an odd *flavour*. 2. *v.* To change the taste by adding something. *Ex.* I *flavoured* the custard with almond.

flaw *n.* A fault or defect. *Ex.* There is a *flaw* in your argument.

flax *n.* The plant whose stalks give us the material from which linen is made.

flea (flee) *n.* A very small jumping insect which bites animals and human beings.

flee *v.* To run away. *Ex.* When the bull broke loose, people began to *flee*; they *fled* for safety.

fleece *n.* The wool of sheep.

fleet 1. *n.* A number of ships or boats sailing together for one purpose. *Ex.* A fishing *fleet*; a naval *fleet*. The word is also used of a similar grouping of aircraft or cars. 2. *adj.* Very fast. *Ex.* Deer are *fleet-footed*.

flesh *n.* The soft parts of bodies under the skin and covering the bones; the soft inside of fruit.

flex 1. *n.* Flexible wire by which electrical appliances are connected to plugs etc. 2. *v*. To bend. *Ex*. The circus acrobats were *flexing* their muscles before their act.

flexible *adj*. Easily bent. *Ex*. Our arms are *flexible*, and so is wire. They have *flexibility* (*n*.).

flick *v*. To hit lightly with something soft, such as a cloth.

flicker *n*. A brief unsteady gleam of light, such as a candle gives before it burns out.

flight *n*. The passage through the air of flying creatures, aeroplanes and thrown objects. *Ex*. The fielder watched the cricket ball's *flight* as he ran to catch it. (b) A staircase or set of stairs. *Ex*. She climbed two *flights* of stairs to her room.

flimsy (*flim*-zi) *adj*. Weak; thin; not strongly made. *Ex*. This paper is *flimsy* and tears easily.

flinch *v*. To draw back in fear. *Ex*. He did not *flinch* when the dog rushed at him.

fling *v*. To throw or hurl, sometimes carelessly. *Ex*. He *flung* down his bat, in annoyance at being run out.

flint *n*. A very hard kind of stone. *Ex*. Steel struck on *flint* makes sparks.

flippant *adj*. Treating serious things lightly. *Ex*. We were told not to treat fire practice *flippantly* (*adv*.).

flit *v*. To fly lightly, as a butterfly does.

flock *n*. A number of animals or birds grouped together. *Ex*. A *flock* of sheep or sparrows.

flog *v*. To beat, especially with a whip.

flood (flud) *n*. Water that has overflowed from rivers or unusually high tides etc. *Ex*. The heavy rain caused *floods*; the area became *flooded* (*v*.).

florist (*flo*-rist) *n*. A shopkeeper who sells flowers. A *floral* (*adj*.) wreath is one made with flowers.

flounce 1. *n*. A frilled ornamental strip of material for dresses etc. 2. *v*. To move off impatiently, in an annoyed way. *Ex*. On hearing she had not been invited, she *flounced* out of the room.

flounder 1. *n*. A flat fish used for food. 2. *v*. To stumble about, as in mud and water; to stumble in speech. *Ex*. He had not thought out what to say, so he found himself *floundering* in his explanations.

flour *n*. Wheat or other grain ground into a fine powder.

flourish (*flur*-ish) *v*. (a) To grow well, or get on well. Plants can *flourish*, and so can a business. (b) To wave something about, to brandish. *Ex*. He *flourished* a stick at me.

flow (floh) *v.* (a) To run, as water does. (b) To move smoothly. *Ex.* The traffic *flowed* at a steady pace.

flu *n.* Influenza.

fluctuate (*fluk*-tew-ayt) *v.* To rise and fall, as one's temperature may do in illness.

flue *n.* A pipe which draws off the smoke from a stove or oven.

fluent (*floo*-ent) *adj.* With an easy flow of words. *Ex.* His French is *fluent.*

fluid (*floo*-id) *adj.* Able to flow as water or gas does. Water is a *fluid* (*n.*), except when it is frozen into a solid (ice). *Fluid* is the opposite of solid.

fluke (flook) *n.* A success due simply to good luck or chance.

flurry (*flu*-ri) *n.* Great hurry and agitation. *Ex.* My aunt gets *flurried* (*v.*) when preparing for a journey.

flush *v.* (a) To blush. (b) To wash out with lots of water.

fluster *n.* A word meaning much the same as flurry.

flute *n.* A wooden or metal musical instrument of the woodwind family, played by blowing across a hole in its side.

flutter *v.* To flap the wings, as a butterfly does; to flap in the air like a flag.

foal (fohl) *n.* A very young horse.

foam (fohm) *n.* Froth or bubbles on top of a liquid, such as the froth on top of a wave breaking on the rocks.

focus (*foh*-kus) 1. *n.* The point at which a thing must be placed to get a clear image of it with a camera, or with one's eyes. 2. *v.* To adjust a camera or binoculars etc. so that the object looked at is clear.

fodder *n.* Dried food given to cattle etc.

foe (foh) *n.* An enemy.

fog *n.* Thick mist.

foil 1. *v.* To prevent a person from doing something. *Ex.* He *foiled* all attempts to capture him, and escaped. 2. *n.* A very thin sheet of metal, often aluminium, used for wrapping food etc.

fold (fohld) 1. *n.* A part of a field enclosed by fences to keep sheep in. 2. *v.* To bend one part over another, as in *folding* paper or clothes.

foliage (*fohl*-i-ej) *n.* The leaves of trees or plants. *Ex.* In Canada, the autumn *foliage* is brilliantly coloured.

folk (fohk) *n.* People. *Ex.* Old *folk*, country *folk*, good *folk* etc.

folly *n.* Lack of common sense; foolishness. *Ex.* It was *folly* to give up his job before finding another.

fond *adj.* (a) Loving. (b) (With 'of') Enjoying greatly. *Ex.* He is very *fond* of swimming.

fondle *v.* To caress lovingly.

foolhardy *adj.* Taking foolish risks. *Ex.* It was *foolhardy* to take the boat out on such a rough day.

foothold (*fUt*-hohld) *n.* A place where one can put one's foot, especially while climbing.

footlights (*fUt*-lyts) *n.* The lights running along the front of a stage on the floor, to light the scene.

footprint (*fUt*-print) *n.* The mark left in soft soil by a foot.

forage (*fo*-rij) *n.* Food for cattle and horses. 2. *v.* To search for and carry off *forage.*

forbear (for-*bair*) *v.* To hold oneself back, to be patient. *Ex.* He showed great *forbearance* (*n.*) and did not once lose his temper with them.

forbid (for-*bid*) *v.* To order a person not to do something. *Ex.* He was *forbidden* to bathe in that dirty river. A *forbidding* look is a cross and uninviting look.

force 1. *n.* (a) Strength. *Ex.* He had to use *force* to get the door open. (b) A group of men trained for some active service, such as a *police force* or the *armed forces.* 2. *v.* To make a person do something. *Ex.* He *forced* the boy to give him the ball.

ford *n.* A shallow part of a river where a man or horse can cross without swimming. To *ford* (*v.*) a river is to cross it at a ford.

forearm *n.* The part of the arm between wrist and elbow.

forecast *v.* To tell beforehand. *Ex.* I *forecast* rain. A weather *forecast* for shipping.

forefather *n.* An ancestor or forebear.

forehead (*fo*-rid) *n.* The front part of the head above the eyes; the brow.

foreign (*fo*-rin) *adj.* Belonging to another nation. A *foreign* person is called a *foreigner* (*n.*), and he may speak a *foreign* language.

foreman *n.* The chief man of a group of workers, or of a jury.

foremost *adj.* The first or most important. *Ex.* The captain's *foremost* thought was for the safety of the passengers.

foresee (for-*see*) *v.* To realize beforehand and be prepared. *Ex.* My mother *foresaw* that we would run out of bread and bought some for us. She showed *foresight* (*n.*; thinking ahead).

foretaste *n.* A sample of what is coming. *Ex.* This lovely April sunshine is a *foretaste* of summer.

foretell *v.* To tell beforehand. *Ex.* The gipsy said she could *foretell* the future.

forewarn *v.* To warn beforehand.

forfeit (*for*-fit) *v.* To lose the right to something by one's own fault. In some games a *forfeit* (*n.*; penalty) has to be paid for failure etc.

forge *n.* A blacksmith's workshop; a furnace in which iron is heated.

forgery (*forj*-er-i) *n.* The crime of making documents, paper money, signatures etc. which look like the real or genuine thing.

forgive (for-*giv*) *v.* To pardon, and bear no ill-will to someone who has harmed you. *Ex.* When he said he was sorry he had broken the window, she *forgave* him.

forgo (for-*goh*) *v.* To give up and do without. *Ex.* She said she would *forgo* her holiday to look after him.

forlorn (for-*lorn*) *adj.* Lonely and unhappy. *Ex.* She felt *forlorn* when her brothers went to school.

form 1. *n.* (a) Shape. The flower-vase was in the *form* of a swan. (b) A school class. (c) A long seat or bench. (d) A printed paper with spaces to fill in. *Ex.* We had to fill in a *form* with details about our date of birth etc. 2. *v.* To make. *Ex.* We *formed* a chess club.

formal *adj.* Done according to the rules; correct; too correct to be natural. *Ex.* His letter of thanks was purely *formal*, so I don't know whether he really enjoyed his visit.

formation *n.* An arrangement; the way in which something is formed. *Ex.* The fighter aircraft flew in close *formation*.

former *adj.* Earlier, in the past. *Ex.* I remembered him from a *former* meeting.

formidable (*form*-id-a-b'l) *adj.* Rather frightening because of size, difficulty or a feeling of being overwhelmed. *Ex.* To get the two men to agree was a *formidable* task.

formula (*form*-ew-la) *n.* A combination of symbols and figures used in chemistry to state what a substance is made of. *Ex.* The *formula* for water is H_2O.

forsake (for-*sayk*) *v.* To leave, often in a neglectful way; to desert. *Ex.* The eggs were cold, so the bird must have *forsaken* the nest.

fortify (*fort*-i-fy) *v.* To make stronger, usually in order to resist an enemy attack. This is done by *fortifications* (fort-i-fi-*kay*-sh'nz; *n.*).

fortress *n.* A place fortified against attack. A *fort* is a small fortress.

fortune (*for*-chen) *n.* (a) A large amount of money. *Ex.* The rich man left a *fortune* to his son. (b) The kind of luck one has in life. One may have good *fortune* and thus be *fortunate* (*adj.*), or ill *fortune* and be *unfortunate*.

forward 1. *v.* To send on ahead. *Ex.* I am *forwarding* my luggage so that I shan't have to travel with it. 'Please *forward*' on a letter means send it on to a person's new address. 2. *adv.* Towards the front, or the future. *Ex.* He stepped *forward* when he was asked to come on to the platform. He was looking *forward* to the holidays.

fossil (*fos*-il) *n.* The remains or traces of prehistoric (very ancient) plant and animal life dug up from under the ground. *Ex.* A dinosaur is only found in *fossil* (*adj.*) form.

foster-parent *n.* Someone who brings up someone else's child.

foul 1. *adj.* Filthy, dirty. 2. *n.* A breaking of the rules of a game.

found *v.* To begin something such as a building, a business or a church. *Ex.* The *foundation* (*n.*) of this hospital has been a blessing to the town. It was *founded* 200 years ago. The *founder* (*n.*) was a rich merchant.

foundation *n.* (a) *See* found. (b) The part below ground on which a building is constructed.

foundry *n.* A factory or workshop where metals are melted and shaped.

fountain (*fown*-ten) *n.* A spout or jet of water coming from a pipe and falling into a basin. A *fountain-pen* is one with a supply of ink inside which flows to the nib when writing.

fowl *n.* A bird, especially of the kind reared for food.

fox *n.* A wild animal of the dog family, reddish-brown with a bushy tail. It eats rabbits and chickens and is hunted for sport.

fraction (*frak*-sh'n) *n.* A part of anything. A half or three-quarters are examples of *fractions*.

fracture (*frak*-cher) *v.* To break. Broken bones are called *fractures* (*n.*).

fragile (*fraj*-yl) *adj.* Easily broken or spoilt. *Ex.* This china is *fragile*, so be careful with it.

fragment *n.* A piece broken off. *Ex.* The cup was smashed into *fragments* on the floor.

fragrant (*fray*-gr'nt) *adj.* Having a pleasant smell. *Ex.* Sweet peas are particularly *fragrant*.

frail *adj*. Not at all strong. *Ex*. This chair is too *frail* to take your weight. Old people may become *frail*.

frame *v*. To surround with a border. *Ex*. This picture is *framed* in oak; it has an oak *frame* (*n*.).

frank *adj*. Candid, sincere and truthful. *Ex*. The doctor was *frank* with us and said it would be a long time before our sister was well again.

frantic *adj*. Wildly excited and agitated, usually with grief, fear or pain. *Ex*. She was *frantic* with anxiety for her lost child; her worry drove her into a *frenzy* (*n*.).

fraud (frawd) *n*. A trick; cheating. *Ex*. She got her money by *fraud*, pretending she was collecting for charity.

fray *v*. To wear away into loose threads by rubbing. *Ex*. His shirt cuffs were *frayed* by hard wear.

freak *n*. A creature which is not normal in appearance.

freckle *n*. A golden brown spot on the skin, commoner with fair people who have been much in the sun.

freeze *v*. To turn into ice, as water does when cold enough. It is then *frozen*.

freight (frayt) *n*. Cargo; the carrying of goods by ship, aircraft, train etc.; the charge for this.

frenzy *n*. *See* frantic.

frequent 1. (*free*-kwent) *adj*. Happening often. *Ex*. There are *frequent* buses to the city, so we shan't have to wait long. 2. (fri-*kwent*) *v*. To visit often. *Ex*. They soon got to know most of the children who *frequented* the park.

fresh *adj*. New; another one; not stale or preserved; bright and clean. *Ex*. A *fresh* tablecloth; *fresh* loaf; *fresh* orange-juice; a *fresh* breeze etc.

fret *v*. To worry. *Ex*. It was hard not to *fret* when we knew our mother was ill. *Fretful* (*adj*.) means complaining and irritable. *Ex*. Our baby is *fretful* because he is teething.

friction (*frik*-sh'n) *n*. Rubbing. *Ex*. The cathedral steps were worn by the *friction* of many pilgrims' feet.

frigid (*frij*-id) *adj*. Cold; chilly and unfeeling in manner. *Ex*. Her greeting was *frigid*, not at all warm and welcoming.

frill *n*. A decorative edging used to trim clothes, curtains etc., with one edge gathered up and attached to the garment etc.

fringe (frinj) *n*. A border of hanging threads such as one sees on a scarf. Hair is sometimes cut short across the forehead, and falls in a *fringe* down to the eyebrows.

frisky *adj.* Lively; inclined to leap about, like a young lamb.

fritter 1. *n.* A piece of meat or fruit fried in batter. 2. *v.* To waste time or money, bit by bit.

frivolous (*friv*-o-lus) *adj.* Not serious; inclined to be silly. *Ex.* She's a *frivolous* girl who never takes anything seriously.

frog *n.* A small animal with webbed feet and no tail, which lives partly in ponds and partly on land.

frogman *n.* A driver, who wears flippers, a rubber suit and breathing apparatus, so that he can stay under water to fish, photograph, do salvage work etc.

frontier (*frun*-ti-er) *n.* The border or dividing line between two countries.

frost *n.* Great coldness of the air which turns dew into ice, when the temperature is below *freezing* point; the *frozen* dew seen on a lawn, window, roof etc.

froth (froth) *n.* Foam, or the mass of tiny bubbles which forms on top of some liquids, such as beer.

frown *v.* To crease the forehead, drawing the eyebrows down, in anger or puzzlement.

frozen *adj. See* freeze.

frugal (*froo*-gal) *adj.* Careful not to spend more money than necessary, or to waste things. *Ex.* She is careful not to buy more food than is needed; she is a *frugal* housekeeper.

fruitful *adj.* Producing a good result, especially a good crop.

fruitless *adj.* The opposite of fruitful; having no good results, useless. *Ex.* Their search was *fruitless*; they could find no one who had seen their dog.

frustrate (frus-*trayt*) *v.* To prevent someone's chance of success; to bring to nothing. *Ex.* The barbed wire *frustrated* their attempts to get into the field. To feel *frustrated* is to be annoyed at being baffled or thwarted. *Ex.* It is *frustrating* (*adj.*) not to be able to help him.

fuel (*few*-el) *n.* Material for burning to produce heat or power, such as coal, peat, petrol.

fugitive (*few*-ji-tiv) *n.* One who runs away.

fulfil (fUl-*fil*) *v.* To satisfy or do what is required. *Ex.* The gardener *fulfilled* his duties, and *fulfilled* their hopes of having a perfect garden.

fumble *v.* To make awkward, unsuccessful attempts; to grope about. *Ex.* She *fumbled* in her bag for money.

fumes (fewmz) *n.* Smoke that is strong and bitter-smelling.

function (*fungk*-sh'n)   *n.* The natural action of anything. *Ex.* The *function* of a telescope is to make distant objects, such as stars, more easily and clearly seen.

fund   *n.* An amount of money set apart for a special purpose.

fungus (*fung*-gus)   *n.* One of the simpler forms of plant life, with no green colouring. Mushrooms, toadstools and mould are *fungi* (*fung*-gy; *pl.*).

funnel   *n.* (a) A kind of chimney on a ship to carry away smoke. (b) A cone-shaped vessel with a wide mouth opening into a tube, used to pour liquids into a bottle.

fur (fur)   *n.* The short soft hair of such animals as the squirrel or seal. A person who sells *furs* is a *furrier* (*fu*-ree-er; *n.*).

furious (*fewr*-i-us)   *adj.* Very angry. Those who are *furious* are full of *fury* (*n.*).

furl (furl)   *v.* To roll up a sail, umbrella etc.

furnace (*fur*-nis)   *n.* A closed fireplace for heating household water etc.; a very large oven-like construction where very great heat can be produced, used in the steel and glass industries etc.

furnish (*fur*-nish)   *v.* To supply, especially with *furniture* (*n.*) for a house. *House furniture* includes tables, chairs, beds etc.

furrow (*fu*-roh) *n.* The trench or groove dug by a plough.

furtive (*fur*-tiv)   *adj.* Secret, sly; deceitful-looking. *Ex.* We knew by his *furtive* manner that he was up to no good.

fuse (fewz)   1. *v.* To join pieces of metal etc. by melting them together. 2. *n.* The fine wire which easily melts and is put into electrical apparatus as a safety-device.

fuss (fus)   *n.* Unnecessary worry and bother about small things. *Ex.* Don't *fuss* (*v.*), don't make a *fuss* (*n.*); it's not important.

fusty (*fus*-ti)   *adj. See* musty.

futile (*few*-tyl)   *adj.* Useless; not likely to be successful. *Ex.* He made a *futile* effort to rescue the sparrow from the cat.

future (*few*-cher)   1. *n.* The time that is coming. 2. *adj.* That is to come. *Ex.* His *future* career depends on how he does in his exams.

G

gabble   *v.* To talk very fast and not distinctly.

gable *n.* The triangular part between the top of the side wall of a house and the roof.

gadget (*gaj*-et) *n.* A useful little thing made to serve a special purpose, such as a bottle-opener or a potato-peeler.

gag 1. *n.* Something pushed into a person's mouth to prevent him from speaking. 2. *v.* To silence someone in this or some other way.

gaiety *n. See* gay.

gain 1. *n.* What has been won or obtained; an increase or addition. 2. *v.* To obtain or win.

gala (*gah*-la) *n.* Festivity. A *gala* performance is a special performance to celebrate something.

galaxy (*gal*-aks-i) *n.* A huge cluster of stars. Our solar system forms part of the great Milky Way *galaxy*.

gallant *adj.* Brave. *Ex.* The crowd cheered the fireman's *gallant* rescue of the child.

galleon (*gal*-e-on) *n.* A large sailing-ship, especially a Spanish treasure ship of the 16th century.

gallery (*gal*-er-i) *n.* (a) A long narrow passage built above a room or hall so that one can look down from it into the room. Many churches and theatres have such *galleries*. (b) A hall or building where works of art are shown. *Ex.* The National *Gallery* in London.

gallon *n.* A measure for liquids, equal to 4.5 litres.

gallop (*gal*-op) 1. *n.* The fastest pace of a horse. 2. *v.* To go at a *galloping* speed.

gallows (*gal*-ohz) *n.* A wooden structure for hanging people sentenced to death.

galore (gal-*or*) *adv.* In great quantities. *Ex.* There were strawberries *galore* at the party.

gamble *v.* (a) To play a game of cards etc. for money. (b) To risk something for the sake of a possible gain. *Ex.* He resigned, and *gambled* on finding another job.

gambol (*gam*-bol) *v.* To leap about like a frisky lamb.

gamekeeper *n.* A man employed to look after *game* (birds and animals) on an estate.

gander *n.* The male of the goose.

gang *n.* A number of people acting together, either for a good purpose, such as a *gang* of workmen, or a bad purpose, such as a *gang* of thieves.

gangster *n.* One of a *gang* of criminals.

gangway *n.* A passage into, out of or through a place, especially on a ship or between rows of seats at a theatre. A *gangplank* is a plank set up as a temporary link between ship and shore.

gaol (jayl) *n.* A prison. Sometimes spelt *jail.*

gap *n.* An empty space between two things. *Ex.* A *gap* in a row of houses where one has been pulled down, or a *gap* between teeth where one is missing.

gape *v.* To stare with the mouth open, in surprise.

garage (*gar*-ahj) *n.* A shed where a car is kept; a repair shop for cars; a petrol station.

gargle *v.* To rinse the throat with liquid without swallowing it.

garish (*gair*-ish) *adj.* Showy; vulgarly bright. *Ex.* Everything in the fairground was painted in *garish* colours.

garment *n.* Any article of clothing.

garnet *n.* A dark-red gemstone.

garnish *v.* To decorate, especially food. *Ex.* The cold meats were *garnished* with parsley.

garret (*ga*-ret) *n.* A room at the top of a house under the roof, often poorly furnished.

garrison (*ga*-ri-son) *n.* Troops guarding a fortress or town.

garrulous (*ga*-rU-lus) *adj.* In the habit of talking too much; always chattering.

gash *n.* A long deep cut.

gasometer (gas-*om*-i-ter) *n.* A very large tank to store gas.

gasp (gahsp) *v.* To struggle for breath, usually when surprised or frightened. *Ex.* He *gasped* when he saw that the bull had got out of the field.

gathering *n.* A number of people who have come together for some purpose, such as a meeting or a party.

gauche (gohsh) *adj.* Clumsy from feeling ill at ease.

gaudy (*gaw*-di) *adj.* Showy, garish.

gauge (gayj) 1. *n.* (a) An instrument that measures something, such as temperature or pressure. *Ex.* A *tyre-pressure gauge.* (b) The measure of the width between railway lines, or of the thickness of wire. 2. *v.* To estimate. *Ex.* It is hard to *gauge* his sincerity.

gaunt (gawnt) *adj.* Thin and haggard. *Ex.* It was horrifying to see the *gaunt* faces of the starving garrison.

gauze (gawz) *n.* A very fine-woven material, like fine net.

gay *adj.* Feeling cheerful; having a cheerful, bright appearance.

Ex. The streets were *gay* with decorations. There was an air of *gaiety* (*gay*-et-i; *n.*) about the scene.

gaze (gayz)   *v.* To look at long and steadily.   *Ex.* They stayed on deck for a time, *gazing* at the sunset.

gear (geer)   *n.* (a) Equipment, usually for a particular activity.   *Ex.* Climbing *gear* (ropes, boots etc.). (b) A device in a car, bicycle etc. by which the relation between the speed of the wheels and the speed of the engine (or pedalling) can be varied.

gelatine (*jel*-a-teen)   *n.* A clear substance that can be used to make a jelly, to surround a dose of medicine or to make glue, photographic film etc.

gem (jem)   *n.* A jewel stone, such as a diamond.

gene (jeen)   *n.* One of the factors which together control how a living thing will develop. *Genes* are inherited from (passed on by) both parents.

general (*jen*-er-al)   1. *n.* A soldier above the rank of colonel. 2. *adj.* Usual; applying to many things and not one in particular.   *Ex.* As a *general* rule I get up at seven. A *general* store is a shop that sells many different kinds of things.

generate (*jen*-er-ayt)   *v.* To produce; to bring into existence.   *Ex.* Life was first *generated* on earth many millions of years ago. A *generator* (*n.*) is a machine that produces electricity. People of about the same age are of the same *generation* (*n.*), and their children belong to the next, or younger, *generation.*

generous (*jen*-er-us)   *adj.* Kind-hearted and willing to give things to other people.   *Ex.* They were rich, but also *generous* in helping those in need. They showed *generosity* (*n.*).

genial (*jee*-ni-al)   *adj.* Pleasant and cheerful.

genie (*jee*-ni)   *n.* A magical spirit, told of in the *Arabian Nights,* capable of good or evil.

genius (*jee*-ni-us)   *n.* (a) A special quality that a few people are born with, which makes them much better at using their brains, especially for artistic or scientific creation. (b) One who has the quality of *genius.*

gentile (*jen*-tyl)   *n.* and *adj.* A name in the Bible for anyone who is not a Jew, and especially for a Christian.

gentle (*jen*-t'l)   *adj.* Mild, quiet, not rough or severe.

genuine (*jen*-ew-in)   *adj.* Sincere; not false; not imitation.   *Ex.* Their grief for their uncle's death was *genuine,* for they loved him. These pearls are not *genuine,* but artificial.

geography (ji-*og*-ra-fi)   *n.* The description and study of all the features on the earth (mountains, rivers, climate, vegetation etc.) and of where people live and what they produce.

geology (ji-*ol*-o-ji) *n.* The description and study of the rocks of which the earth is made.

geometry (ji-*om*-et-ri) *n.* The branch of maths which studies shapes, such as circles and triangles, and also solids such as cylinders and cones.

germ (jurm) *n.* A very tiny living thing, too small to be seen, which causes disease.

germinate (*jur*-min-ayt) *v.* To begin to grow, as a plant does by putting out a shoot.

gesticulate (jes-*tik*-ew-layt) *v.* To use movements of the hand, arm or head to explain or emphasize what you are saying.

gesture (*jest*-ewr) *n.* (a) A movement of the body made in gesticulation. (b) Any act which indicates a feeling or intention. *Ex.* His friendly *gesture* in offering help made us feel happier.

geyser *n.* (a) (*gyz*-er) A natural spring of hot water, such as is found in New Zealand and Iceland. (b) (*geez*-er) Apparatus which heats water by gas, as it pours out.

ghastly (*gahst*-li) *adj.* Horrible, dreadful.

ghost (gohst) *n.* The spirit of a dead person which is sometimes believed to appear to the living.

giant (*jy*-ant) *n.* A person or thing of unusual size.

giddy (*gid*-i) *adj. See* dizzy.

gifted (*gif*-tid) *adj.* Having exceptional ability in some subject. *Ex.* Mozart was a most *gifted* musician.

gigantic (jy-*gan*-tik) *adj.* Extremely large, enormous.

giggle (*gig*'l) *v.* To laugh in a silly way, without good reason.

gild (gild) *v.* To cover with gold or gold paint. *Ex.* Picture frames which have been *gilded* are *gilt* (*adj.*) frames.

gill *n.* (a) (gil) The part of a fish through which it breathes. (b) (jil) A measure of liquid, about a small teacupful; one quarter of a pint.

gimlet (*gim*-let) *n.* A small tool with a spiral point, for boring holes in wood etc.

gimmick (*gim*-ik) *n.* A clever but possibly useless device intended to attract customers and increase sales; a meaningless slogan etc. intended to mislead. *Ex.* Prize offers printed on food packets may be *gimmicks*.

gin (jin) *n.* An alcoholic drink made from grain and flavoured with juniper berries.

ginger (*jin*-jer) *n.* The root of a plant with a hot taste, used in cookery and medicine and to flavour drinks. *Ex. Gingerbread*; *ginger beer*.

gingerly (*jin*-jer-li) *adv.* and *adj.* Very cautiously and carefully. *Ex.* He had to walk *gingerly* on the rotten floorboards in case they gave way.

gipsy (*jip*-si) *n.* One of a dark-skinned, originally Indian, race who live in caravans, moving from place to place.

giraffe (ji-*rahf*) *n.* An African animal with an extremely long neck and long legs, which grazes on trees.

girder (*gur*-der) *n.* A steel beam used in forming the main structure of a building, bridge etc.

girdle (*gurd*'l) *n.* A belt to go round the waist.

girth (gurth) *n.* (a) The measurement round a thing. *Ex.* This tree is of great *girth*. (b) The band round a horse's belly which keeps the saddle in place.

gist (jist) *n.* The main point of a statement. *Ex.* The *gist* of his message was that you are to join him as soon as you can.

glacier (*glas*-yer) *n.* A huge mass of ice which moves down a mountain-side so slowly that the movement cannot be seen.

glamour (*glam*-er) *n.* Charm which makes something seem more beautiful than it is. *Ex.* Moonlight cast a *glamour* over the scene.

glance (glahns) *n.* A quick look at something. *Ex.* I only just *glanced* (*v.*) at his letter and have not read it through.

gland *n.* One of several organs in the body which provide very important substances to help the body work properly. *Ex.* The liver is the largest *gland* in the body.

glare (glair) 1. *n.* Dazzling light. *Ex.* The *glare* of the sunlight on the sea made my eyes ache. 2. *v.* To stare angrily. *Ex.* The two boys were *glaring* at each other as if they meant to fight.

glaze (glayz) *v.* (a) To fix glass, as in a window. The man who does this is a *glazier* (*n.*). (b) To cover with a glassy material as pottery may be covered. *Ex.* A currant bun has a sugary *glaze* (*n.*).

gleam 1. *n.* A small beam of light; a glow. 2. *v.* To shine softly; to reflect light. *Ex.* The polished table *gleamed* in the candle-light.

glide *v.* To move easily and smoothly, as a skater on ice or a seagull riding the wind.

glider *n.* An aeroplane with no engine, which stays up by making use of rising currents of warm air.

glimmer *n.* A very faint light. *Ex.* They could see only a *glimmer* of light through the drawn curtains.

glimpse (glimps) *n.* A view of something for a moment only. *Ex.* The car was travelling so fast that I only got a *glimpse* of the driver.

glisten (*glis*-en) *v.* To shine, especially as wet things do.

glitter *v.* To sparkle with light. *Ex.* When the Christmas tree was lit, the ornaments on it *glittered.*

gloat (gloht) *v.* To gaze on or think about something, often with triumph or malice. *Ex.* The thief *gloated* over the stolen jewels.

globe *n.* A sphere; an electric light bulb; the earth, or a model of the earth with a map printed on it.

gloom *n.* Darkness; hopelessness. *Ex.* The foul weather cast a *gloom* over our spirits. We are in for a *gloomy* (*adj.*) winter now the coal strike has started.

glory *n.* Great praise, honour, fame; splendour, magnificence. *Ex.* The chestnut trees were in all their *glory*, covered with flowers. Trafalgar was a *glorious* (*adj.*) victory.

glossy *adj.* Having a shiny surface.

glow (gloh) *n.* (a) A low but steady light coming from heat. *Ex.* There was still a *glow* from the remains of the bonfire. (b) A look or feeling of warmth, as after outdoor exercise in cold weather. An excited face may *glow* (*v.*) with happiness.

glower (*glow*-er) *v.* To look at angrily. *Ex.* He *glowered* at me, too angry to speak.

glue (gloo) *n.* A sticky substance used to fix things together. *Ex.* I mended my model aeroplane with *glue*; I *glued* (*v.*) the pieces together.

glum *adj.* Gloomy-looking.

glut *n.* Too much of something—more than can be used. *Ex.* There was such a *glut* of fish at the market that some was given away.

glutton *n.* One who loves eating and eats too much.

gnarled (narld) *adj.* Knotted and twisted, as some old trees are.

gnat (nat) *n.* A small fly that bites.

gnaw (naw) *v.* To bite away with the teeth. *Ex.* Rats and mice *gnaw* through wood; dogs *gnaw* at bones to scrape all the meat off.

gnome (nohm) *n.* The bearded, hooded dwarf of fairy tales, who guards treasure in his cave.

goad *v.* To urge a person on to do something against his will; to torment.

goal *n.* The thing one is aiming to reach, either in one's work or in a game.

gobble *n.* (a) To swallow food greedily and in large lumps. (b) To make the noise a turkey-cock makes.

goblin *n.* The friendly but mischievous spirit of fairy tales.

gold *n.* A gleaming yellow metal of great value.

golf (golf) *n.* A game played on a grassy area (*golf-course*), in which a small ball is driven by a club (a long stick) into one hole after another in as few strokes as possible.

goose (goos) *n.* A large wild or domesticated water-bird with a long neck and a loud cackle.

gooseberry (*gUz*-be-ri) *n.* A juicy berry, usually green, with a hairy skin, eaten in tarts etc.

gore 1. *n.* Blood. 2. *v.* To pierce with horns. *Ex.* The bull came towards the boy, with lowered horns ready to *gore* him.

gorge 1. *n.* A deep and narrow passage or pass between high cliffs or mountains. 2. *v.* To eat greedily.

gorgeous (*gor*-jus) *adj.* Magnificent; having a very fine appearance. *Ex.* A *gorgeous* sunset; a *gorgeous* view.

gorilla (go-*ril*-a) *n.* The largest of the apes, which sometimes walks upright like a man.

gorse *n.* A prickly shrub bearing sweet-smelling yellow flowers throughout the year. Sometimes called *furze* or *whin*.

gosling (*goz*-ling) *n.* A young goose.

gospel *n.* The *Gospels* are the first four books of the New Testament, describing the life and teachings of Jesus Christ.

gossip *v.* and *n.* Chat about unimportant things or other people's private affairs. A gossip (*n.*) is also one who does this.

gout (gowt) *n.* A painful inflammation of the smaller joints, especially the big toe.

govern (*guv*-ern) *v.* To rule. A *governor* (*n.*) is an official appointed to rule over part of his country. A *governess* (*n.*) is a woman who looks after the education of children in their own home. A *government* (*n.*) consists of those who rule a country and make its laws.

gown *n.* (a) A woman's dress (a word not much used now, except for *ball gowns*). (b) A full loose garment worn over other clothes on certain occasions, by members of universities, clergy, judges and lawyers.

grab 1. *v.* To snatch. A *smash-and-grab* raid is one in which a shop window is smashed and goods *grabbed* by the thieves. 2. *n.* A double scoop, hinged like a pair of jaws, used to lift earth etc. when clearing land.

grace *n.* (a) Divine love or mercy. (b) A short prayer of thanks for food before or after a meal. (c) Beauty of appearance or movement. *Ex.* The *graceful* (*adj.*) dancer accepted our applause and flowers most *graciously* (*adv.*).

grade *v.* To arrange in groups or classes called *grades* (*n.*), according to ability, size etc.

gradual (*grad*-ew-al) *adj.* Going step by step. *Ex.* The improvement in her health was so *gradual* that we scarcely noticed it; she got better *gradually* (*adv.*).

graft *v.* (a) To put a shoot from a plant into the main stem of another, so that it can grow from that plant. (b) To transplant a piece of living tissue. Skin from other parts of the body is sometimes grafted on to a part which has been badly burned.

grain *n.* (a) The smallest quantity of anything solid. *Ex.* A *grain* of salt. (b) Various kinds of corn, such as wheat, barley, oats etc.

gram *n.* A metric unit of weight; an ounce is about 28 *grams*.

grammar *n.* The rules which govern the correct way of speaking and writing a language.

gramophone (*gram*-o-fohn) *n.* A machine which reproduces music and speech from discs (records); a record-player.

granite (*gran*-it) *n.* A very hard rock, much used in building.

grant 1. *n.* An allowance or gift of money etc., for a special purpose. 2. *v.* To give or agree to. *Ex.* I was pleased when he *granted* my request.

granulate (*gran*-ew-layt) *v.* To rub down into grains, as *granulated* (*adj.*) sugar is.

grape *n.* A sweet fruit which grows on a climbing plant (a vine), and from which wine is made.

graph (graf) *n.* A diagram which shows the rise and fall of some quantity, by a line marked against a scale. The population of a country over the years can be shown on a *graph*.

graphic *adj.* Very clear. *Ex.* We had a clear picture of what the house looked like, after hearing his *graphic* description of it.

grapple *v.* To seize and struggle to keep hold of. *Ex.* He *grappled* with the thief and brought him to the ground. To *grapple* with a problem is to struggle with it.

grasp *v.* (a) To take hold of firmly. *Ex.* If you *grasp* a nettle firmly it does not sting. (b) To understand. *Ex.* It is easy to *grasp* the meaning of a thing if it is clearly explained. To be *grasping* (*adj.*) is to be greedy and grabbing.

grasshopper *n.* A small greenish jumping insect which chirps and is found in long grass.

grate 1. *n.* The place in a room where a fire burns. 2. *v.* To rub down into small bits, as cheese etc. may be rubbed on a *grater* (*n.*).

grateful *adj.* Thankful for kindness. *Ex.* The campers were *grateful* to the farmer for letting them camp in his field; they expressed their *gratitude* (*n.*) to him.

gratify *v.* To please or satisfy. *Ex.* We felt *gratified* to have won after all our hard practising.

gratis (*gray*-tis) *adj.* Free of charge; costing nothing.

grave 1. *n.* The place in which the dead are buried. A *graveyard* (*n.*) is a burial ground. 2. *adj.* Serious, important. *Ex.* It was *grave* news to hear that he was a prisoner-of-war.

gravel (*grav'l*) *n.* A lot of very small stones, used to make garden paths etc.

gravity (*grav*-i-ti) *n.* (a) Seriousness; importance. (b) The pull (*gravitational force*) which attracts one mass of matter to another. Thus, the tides are pulled in and out by the influence of the moon and sun; and we do not fall off the earth's surface because we are pulled towards its centre.

gravy *n.* The juice which comes from meat while it is being roasted; a sauce made with this, or like it.

graze (grayz) *v.* (a) To feed on grass, as animals do. (b) To touch lightly when passing, as when *grazing* the skin of one's hand on a wall.

grease (grees) 1. *n.* Melted fat. 2. *v.* To put grease on, especially on parts of a machine to make it run more easily.

greedy *adj.* Wanting a great deal, especially food.

greenhouse *n.* A glass house, often heated, used to grow delicate plants and seedlings.

greet *v.* To welcome kindly; to send kind wishes to. *Ex.* We were warmly *greeted* on arrival.

grenade (gren-*ayd*) *n.* A small bomb.

grief (greef) *n.* Sorrow. *Ex.* It is natural to *grieve* (*v.*) over the death of a friend. *Grievous* (*adj.*) means painful and very sad.

grievance (*greev*-ans) *n.* A reason for complaining. *Ex.* The

farmer felt he had a *grievance* against people who left his field
gates open.

grill *v.* To cook under direct heat, as toast is cooked.

grim *adj.* Stern, unfriendly.

grimace (grim-*ays*) *v.* To twist the face in pain, disgust or fun; to
'make a face'.

grime *n.* Very black ingrained dirt.

grin 1. *v.* A wide smile that shows the teeth. 2. *v.* To smile in this
way.

grind (grynd) *v.* (a) To crush into small pieces. *Ex.* Coffee beans
are *ground* into grains or powder. (b) To sharpen by rubbing
against something hard. *Ex.* To *grind* an axe on a *grindstone* (*n.*).

grip *v.* To grasp.

gristle (*gris*'l) *n.* A tough substance in meat which cannot be
chewed.

grit *n.* (a) Dust, gravel or small bits of stone. (b) Strength of
character, plucky spirit.

groan (grohn) 1. *n.* A deep sound made by someone in pain. 2. *v.*
To make this sound.

grocer (*groh*-ser) *n.* A shopkeeper who sells tea, sugar, flour and
many other foodstuffs, which are called *groceries* (*n.*).

groom 1. *v.* (a) To look after a horse by brushing it etc. (b) To
make a person smart and tidy. *Ex.* The women were beautifully
dressed and the men *well-groomed.* 2. *n.* (a) The person who looks
after horses. (b) The husband-to-be at a wedding.

groove *n.* A line hollowed out. *Ex.* A wheel makes a *groove* in
soft ground; a carpenter can make a *groove* with a chisel.

grope *v.* To feel about when in the dark or unable to see. *Ex.* He
groped on the floor for his dropped torch.

grotesque (groh-*tesk*) *adj.* Fantastically shaped, unnatural, sometimes ugly. *Ex. Grotesque* figures parade through the streets at
carnival-time.

group (groop) *n.* A number of persons or things classed
together. *Ex.* A *group* of miners; a *group* of houses.

grouse *n.* A game-bird about the size of a small hen, living on the
moors and good to eat.

grove (grohv) *n.* A small wood.

grovel (*grov*'l) *v.* (a) (Of an animal) To crouch on the ground in
fear. (b) (Of a person) To humble oneself excessively.

growl *n.* The low rumbling sound made by dogs etc. when angry.
To *growl* (*v.*) is to make this sound.

growth (grohth) *n.* The act of *growing*; the amount that has been grown. *Ex.* There has been a rapid *growth* of population here in recent years. That creeper has made a lot of *growth* this summer.

grub *n.* A larva; an insect before it has grown wings and legs and become a butterfly, fly etc.

grubby *adj.* Rather dirty; not very clean.

grudge 1. *v.* To give unwillingly; to look enviously on. *Ex.* He *grudged* having to pay high wages for work badly done. She *grudged* him his good luck and was envious of him. 2. *n.* An old grievance. *Ex.* She bore him a *grudge* because he had once cheated her.

gruesome (*groo*-sum) *adj.* Horrible to look at or hear about.

gruff *adj.* Having a rough voice or manner.

grumble *v.* To mutter complaints. *Ex.* We *grumbled* at having to get up so early.

grunt *n.* The noise made by a pig.

guarantee (gar-an-*tee*) *v.* To promise to do certain things in certain circumstances. *Ex.* In the box of chocolates was a *guarantee* (*n.*) that they would be replaced if found faulty.

guard (gard) 1. *v.* To keep safe or defend from danger. 2. *n.* (a) A person or persons given this duty. *Ex.* At the airport the President inspected the *guard* of honour. (b) A safety device or protection. *Ex.* There was a *guard-chain* on the front door. A *guardian* (*n.*) is someone who looks after another, especially a child who has no parents.

guerrilla (ge-*ril*-a) *n.* A person who fights not as a regular soldier but alone or as a member of an armed band.

guess (ges) *v.* To give an opinion on, but not know for certain. *Ex.* You can *guess*, or make a *guess* (*n.*) at, the weight of a cake; you might *guess* rightly or wrongly.

guest (gest) *n.* A visitor invited for a meal or to stay at one's house; someone who stays at a hotel.

guide (gyd) *v.* To show the way; to give advice on the right thing to do. You could be *guided* through a museum or an unknown country; or *guided* in the best choice of books to read. A *guide* (*n.*) is one who guides. A *guide-book* (*n.*) describes a place and gives advice on what to go and see.

guile (gyl) *n.* Craftiness, cunning, deceit.

guilt (gilt) *n.* The fact or feeling of having committed a sin or broken a law etc. *Ex.* He was found *guilty* (*adj.*) and fined. She was full of *guilt* for neglecting her dog.

guinea-pig (*gin*-ee-pig) *n.* A small tail-less rodent, often kept as a pet. It is also used in scientific experiments, and a person who is experimented on for medical research is sometimes called a *guinea-pig*.

guitar (git-*ar*) *n.* A six-stringed musical instrument plucked by hand.

gulf *n.* A large or deep inlet of the sea. *Ex.* The *Gulf of Mexico*, from which the *Gulf Stream* comes.

gull *n.* A white sea-bird which glides on long wings and can swim.

gullet *n.* The passage in the body from mouth to stomach, down which food travels.

gullible (*gul*-i-b'l) *adj.* Easily taken in or duped.

gulp *v.* To swallow large amounts quickly or greedily.

gum *n.* (a) The flesh in which the teeth are set. (b) A sticky liquid found in plants, or made to fasten together pieces of paper etc. There is *gum* on the back of a postage-stamp.

gumption (*gump*-sh'n) *n.* Common-sense.

gurgle (*gur*-g'l) *n.* A bubbling sound. *Ex.* A stream may *gurgle* (*v.*) as it runs over stones; a happy baby may *gurgle* when too young to talk.

gush *v.* (a) To flow out suddenly. *Ex.* The water *gushed* out when the stopper was removed. (b) To speak with insincere friendliness or to praise insincerely. *Ex.* I knew I had played badly, so I didn't like his *gushing* (*adj.*) praise.

gust *n.* A sudden rush of wind. *Ex.* A *gust* of wind blew my hat off; it was a *gusty* (*adj.*) day.

gusto *n.* Enthusiasm and enjoyment. *Ex.* When the band started to play, they all joined in the dance with *gusto*.

gutter *n.* A groove or channel at the side of the road or at the eaves of a roof, to carry away rainwater.

gymnasium (jim-*nayz*-i-um) *n.* The place where physical exercises (*gymnastics*; *n.*) are performed.

H

haberdashery (hab-er-*dash*-er-i) *n.* Small articles to do with dress (needles, buttons, belts etc.), sold in the *haberdashery* departments of large stores.

habit *n.* Something done so often that it becomes usual; a usual practice. *Ex.* That dog has the tiresome *habit* of jumping up at every visitor. *Habitual (adj.)* means usual, continual. *Ex.* He is a *habitual* grumbler.

habitat *n.* The natural home of a creature. *Ex.* The *habitat* of the limpet is a rocky shore.

habitation *n.* A place in which one lives. A place that can be lived in is called *habitable (adj.)*.

hack *v.* To cut roughly and carelessly. *Ex.* The firemen had to *hack* down the door of the burning building with their axes.

haddock *n.* A sea-fish of the cod family, often eaten smoked.

hag *n.* An ugly old woman.

haggard *adj.* With a worn, tired face. *Ex.* Her long illness left her looking *haggard*.

haggle *v.* To argue more than is reasonable, about a price or the terms of a purchase.

hail 1. *n.* Frozen rain, which falls as little balls of ice. 2. *v.* To call or signal to; to greet. You can *hail* a taxi; or another ship when at sea.

hake *n.* An edible sea-fish rather like cod.

halibut (*hal*-i-but) *n.* A large edible flatfish, rather like turbot.

hallmark *n.* The mark stamped on gold and silver articles as a sign of quality. *Ex.* On the back of a silver spoon is a *hallmark* which includes symbols for the year and place of manufacture.

halo (*hay*-lo) *n.* A circle of light such as is sometimes seen round the moon. Artists often paint a *halo* of light round the heads of Christ and the saints.

halt 1. *n.* A stopping-place, especially a small railway station. 2. *v.* To make a temporary stop. *Ex.* 'Halt at the cross-road ahead'.

halter *n.* A rope, sometimes with a noose, for securing and leading horses and cattle.

ham *n.* The hind leg of a bacon pig, salted and dried in smoke.

hamlet *n.* A very small village, usually without a church.

hammock (*ham*-ok) *n.* A net or canvas bed hanging off the ground from hooks, used in the sleeping quarters of a ship. A *hammock* may also be slung between trees in a garden to make a pleasant resting place in summer.

hamper 1. *n.* A basket with a lid, often containing choice things to eat or picnic food. 2. *v.* To hinder or obstruct or make a difficulty. *Ex.* His large rucksack *hampered* him in getting through the narrow door.

hamster *n.* A small rodent like a guinea-pig, which keeps food in its cheek-pouches and is often kept as a pet.

handbook *n.* A small book which gives information on any one subject.

handcuffs *n.* A pair of steel rings fastened round the wrists of a prisoner and joined by a chain.

handicap 1. *n.* A disadvantage or disability *Ex.* He was *handicapped* in the car rally by not knowing the route well. 2. *v.* To place under a disadvantage, as is sometimes done in races to get a more equal contest.

handicraft *n.* Skilled work done by hand, such as carpentry, basketwork, lace-making.

handsome (*han*-s'm) *adj.* (a) (Of a man or boy) Good-looking. (b) Generous. *Ex.* A *handsome* present.

handy *adj.* (a) Useful, convenient. *Ex.* It is *handy* having a supermarket so near. (b) Clever with the hands.

hanker *v.* To long for. *Ex.* We *hanker* for cool drinks in hot weather.

haphazard (hap-*haz*-ard) *adj.* Left to chance. *Ex.* The camping arrangements were *haphazard*, as no one had planned the trip properly.

harass (*ha*-ras) *v.* To worry; to make weary. *Ex.* I'm a bit *harassed* at the moment, having too much to do.

harbour (*har*-ber) *n.* A place of shelter for ships, away from storms and rough seas.

hard-hearted *adj.* Cruel, not sympathetic.

hardly *adv.* Scarcely, not quite. *Ex.* There is *hardly* any bread left.

hardship *n.* Something that is hard to bear. *Ex.* The Antarctic explorers suffered many *hardships*.

hardware *n.* Ironmongery.

hardy *adj.* Strong, healthy. *Hardy* plants are those which can survive very cold weather.

hare (hair) *n.* A wild animal like a large rabbit, with long ears and long legs for leaping.

harm 1. *n.* Injury, damage. *Ex.* We skidded, but fortunately came to no *harm*. 2. *v.* To injure or damage.

harmony (*har*-mon-i) *n.* (a) Musical notes sounding pleasantly (*harmoniously*; *adv.*) together. The opposite of discord. (b) Agreement; friendliness. *Ex.* The meeting was *harmonious* (har-*moh*-ni-us; *adj.*) throughout, and ended in complete *harmony*.

harness (*har*-nes) *n.* The straps and chains put on a horse which draws a vehicle. The straps which attach a parachute to an airman, or a baby to a seat, are also called a *harness*.

harp *n.* A large musical instrument in a triangular frame, the strings of which are plucked by the harpist's fingers.

harpoon (har-*poon*) *n.* A sort of spear or dart used in whale-hunting.

harpsichord (*harp*-si-kord) *n.* A kind of early piano, on which the notes are sounded by quills plucking wires when the keys are pressed.

harrow (*har*-o) 1. *n.* A frame of metal spikes used by farmers to break up clods and level the soil after ploughing. 2. *v.* To distress or make very sad. *Ex.* The story of Robin Hood's death is *harrowing*.

harsh *adj.* Rough; hard-hearted and unkind. *Ex.* He has a *harsh* speaking voice but not a *harsh* nature.

harvest *n.* The gathering in of ripe crops on farms.

haste *n.* Quickness, hurry. To *hasten* (*v.*) means to hurry. *Ex.* She *hastened* to pick up her toys in case someone trod on them.

hatch 1. *n.* A sort of trap-door, especially in a ship's deck. *Ex.* The *hatches* were battened (fastened) down firmly as the storm approached; otherwise the water would have got below. 2. *v.* (a) To produce from eggs. *Ex.* Eight chicks have just been *hatched* from the hen's eggs. (b) To make a plan. *Ex.* These men had *hatched* a plot to murder the king.

hatchet *n.* An axe with a short handle.

hate *v.* To feel great dislike or *hatred* (*hay*-tred; *n.*). *Ex.* She *hated* the noise of big cities, so she moved to the country.

haughty (*haw*-ti) *adj.* Proud, disdainful. *Ex.* She was very *haughty* and treated us as if we were inferiors.

haul (hawl) 1. *n.* To pull. *Ex.* The fishermen *hauled* in the net. 2. *n.* The amount of something gathered in. *Ex.* A good *haul* of mackerel.

haunt (hawnt) *v.* To visit very often. *Ex.* He *haunts* the pier, wasting his money on fruit machines; it is his favourite *haunt* (*n.*). Ghosts are supposed to *haunt* certain places, which are said to be *haunted*.

haven (*hay*-ven) *n.* A harbour or any place of safety.

havoc (*hav*-ok) *n.* Great damage or destruction. *Ex.* The storm left a scene of *havoc* behind it, with many trees blown down.

hawk *n.* A bird of prey which attacks and kills other birds and animals for food.

hawker *n.* One who sells goods in the street or at the door.

hawthorn *n.* The may tree, with white or pink flowers and red berries (*haws*).

hay *n.* Dried grass used as food for cattle etc. in winter.

hazard (*haz*-ed) 1. *n.* A risk or a possible danger. 2. *v.* To take a risk. *Ex.* The lifeboatmen *hazarded* their lives when they put to sea in such stormy weather.

haze (hayz) *n.* Mist, which makes it difficult to see clearly. *Ex.* It is so *hazy* (*adj.*) today that I can't see the end of the pier. To be *hazy* in one's mind is to be muddled and vague.

hazel (*hay*-z'l) *n.* A tree, often found in hedges, which bears edible nuts in autumn.

headland *n.* A piece of land jutting out into the sea.

headline *n.* The heading of a newspaper article, in large letters.

headlong *adj.* Head first, usually of a fall. *Ex.* He fell *headlong* (*adv.*) into the river.

headquarters *n.* The chief or central office of an organization. *Ex.* The band's *headquarters* is the village hall, where it practises weekly.

headstrong *adj.* Wanting one's own way and not paying attention to advice.

headway *n.* Progress. *Ex.* Good *headway* has been made with the building of the new shops.

heal *v.* (a) To cure. *Ex.* Doctors *heal* the sick. (b) To become healthy. *Ex.* The wound has *healed* well.

health (helth) *n.* Being fit and well in body and mind.

hearsay (*heer*-say) *n.* Something one has heard; gossip; rumour. *Ex.* This court will not listen to *hearsay* (*adj.*) evidence.

hearse (hurs) *n.* A car or carriage for carrying a dead body to burial or cremation.

heart (hart) *n.* The organ which pumps the blood through the body.

heartbroken *adj.* Overcome by grief.

hearth (harth) *n.* The floor of a fireplace where the fire may be laid.

heartless *adj.* Having no pity; cruel.

hearty (*hart*-i) *adj.* In good spirits, cheerful; with good appetite; in good health. *Ex.* A *hearty* welcome.

heath (heeth) *n.* (a) Heather. (b) A large piece of uncultivated land, with wild shrubs growing on it.

heathen (*hee*-dhen) *n.* An old word for one who does not worship the Christian or Jewish God.

heather (*hedh*-er) *n.* A low shrub growing on moors and mountains. Its autumn flowers are pinkish-purple or sometimes white.

heave (heev) *v.* To lift and throw with difficulty.

heaven (*hev*'n) *n.* The sky; the region where God is or where good people go at death (often spelt with a capital H); great happiness. *Heavenly* (*adj.*) bodies means the stars, sun and planets.

heckle *v.* To interrupt a public speaker by shouting etc., as at a political meeting.

hectare (*hek*-tahr) *n.* A metric unit of area, 10,000 square metres (2½ acres).

hectic *adj.* Very agitated; excitedly busy. *Ex.* A *hectic* rush. People with a *hectic* colour have a feverish flush in their cheeks.

hedge *n.* A row of bushes or small trees set close together, to act as a barrier in fields and gardens.

hedgehog *n.* A small wild animal covered with prickly quills, which comes out at night to eat insects.

heed *v.* To pay attention to. *Ex.* He will not *heed* advice; he is quite *heedless* (*adj.*) of the consequences.

heifer (*hef*-er) *n.* A young cow.

heir (air) *n.* The person, usually the eldest son, who will inherit a title or estate on the owner's death. An *heiress* (*air*-es) is a female heir.

heirloom (*air*-loom) *n.* A valuable thing that has belonged to the same family for a long time and been handed down from generation to generation.

helicopter (*hel*-i-kop-ter) *n.* An aircraft with rotating blades (rotors) on top of it, which enable it to rise straight up into the air and, if required, to hover.

helm *n.* The wheel which controls the rudder that steers a ship.

helmet *n.* A specially strong head-covering to protect its wearer. Divers, firemen, motor-cyclists etc. have special *helmets*.

helpful *adj.* Kind and willing to help. *Ex.* She was very *helpful* to the bedridden old lady.

helpless *adj.* Not able to *help* oneself, needing the *help* of others.

hem *n.* The turned-under edge of material, usually sewn down.

hemisphere (*hem*-is-feer) *n.* Half of a globe either side of a line passing through its centre. The earth is so divided into northern and southern *hemispheres* by the Equator.

herald (*her*-ald) *n.* A state officer, formerly a royal messenger, who now superintends ceremonies, is an authority on coats of arms and family trees, and makes public announcements on behalf of the monarch.

herb *n.* A plant with a soft stem, used for medicine (as for example the foxglove), flavouring food (as mint), or scent (lavender).

herd *n.* A group of animals which live together, either in the wild (as elephants) or on farms (as cows).

hereditary (he-*red*-it-a-ri) *adj.* Passed on from one generation to the next. Some physical characteristics, such as hair or eye colour, are *hereditary*.

hermit *n.* A person who lives alone; one who avoids meeting people. Early Christian *hermits* lived alone in order to devote themselves entirely to religious thought (meditation).

hero (*heer*-o) *n.* (a) A person admired for great courage and brave deeds. A *heroine* is a female hero. Such persons are *heroic* (he-*roh*-ik; *adj.*) and have shown *heroism* (*he*-roh-izm; *n.*). (b) The chief character in a story. *Ex.* Robinson Crusoe is the *hero* of a famous story.

herring *n.* A small sea-fish, much used for food.

hesitate (*hez*-it-ayt) *v.* To pause in doubt. *Ex.* I *hesitate* to reply, as I'm not sure of the answer. He showed natural *hesitation* (*n.*) before diving from so great a height.

hibernate (*hy*-ber-nayt) *v.* To spend the winter in sleep, waking up in spring, as hedgehogs do.

hiccup (*hik*-up) *n.* The choking sound made when the entrance to the windpipe unexpectedly contracts in a series of spasms, sometimes brought on by eating or drinking too hurriedly.

hide 1. *n.* The skin of a large animal, such as a cow or a rhino. 2. *v.* To put or keep out of sight.

hideous (*hid*-i-us) *adj.* Very ugly and horrible to look at.

highway *n.* A main road. *Highwaymen* (*n.*) were robbers who used to stop travellers on the road and demand their money.

hilarious (hil-*air*-i-us) *adj.* Extremely funny or merry. *Ex.* He had never seen such a *hilarious* show, and laughed all through it.

hilt *n.* The handle of a sword, dagger etc.

hinder v. To get in the way of or delay. *Ex*. Our bus was *hindered* by a herd of cows; they were a *hindrance* (n.).

hinge (hinj) n. A metal fastening or joint on which a door or the lid of a box opens and shuts.

hint v. To suggest in a roundabout way. *Ex*. She *hinted* that there might be a surprise visitor, but she wouldn't say who.

hippopotamus (hip-o-*pot*-am-us) n. An enormous, thick-skinned African animal which spends most of its time in rivers or lakes.

hire v. To pay for the use of something for a time. You can *hire* a taxi, a boat on the river, a television set etc.

hiss v. To blow through the teeth making the sound 's', often as a sign of dislike, as cats, geese and snakes may do.

history n. An account of what happened in the past, either long ago or more recently. A *historian* (n.) studies the past. A *historical* (adj.) novel is fiction based on real events in history.

hitch 1. n. A small difficulty that holds things up. *Ex*. There was a *hitch* during the performance when the curtain would not come down. 2. v. To fasten. *Ex*. He *hitched* his horse to a tree.

hive n. A box-like home in which bees live and store their honey.

hoard (hord) v. To store secretly. *Ex*. The miser *hoarded* his money and spent none of it.

hoarding (*hord*-ing) n. A wooden wall on which advertisements are pasted.

hoarse (hors) adj. Having a rough voice, as when one has a cold or has talked too much in a loud voice.

hoax (hohks) n. A trick to deceive someone. *Ex*. On April 1st, April Fools' Day, many children *hoax* (v.) each other.

hobble v. To walk lame.

hobby n. What one likes to do in one's spare time. *Ex*. My *hobby* is making model aeroplanes.

hockey n. A game played on grass with long curved sticks and a ball, between goals. *Ice-hockey* is a similar game played on ice with a rubber disc (puck) instead of a ball.

hoe (hoh) n. A long-handled garden tool used in weeding and loosening the soil.

hoist v. To lift up high. *Ex*. The flag was *hoisted* to the top of the mast.

hold 1. n. The space below the deck of a ship where the cargo is stored. 2. v. To keep, to have in one's grasp.

hollow 1. adj. Not solid; having a space inside; empty. *Ex*. A *hollow* tree. 2. n. A little valley. *Ex*. We picnicked in a *hollow* sheltered from the wind. 3. *v.* To make a groove or hollow place. *Ex.* They *hollowed* out a log to make a canoe.

holy (*hoh*-li) *adj.* Sacred; connected with a god or with worship of a god.

homely *adj.* Like home; friendly, comfortable.

honest (*on*-est) *adj.* Just and fair in what one does, truthful; free from deceit; never stealing. The opposite of *honest* is *dishonest*. '*Honesty* (*n.*) is the best policy'.

honey (*hun*-i) *n.* A very sweet syrup made by bees from the nectar in flowers.

honeycomb (*hun*-i-kohm) *n.* A mass of waxy cells made by bees to store their honey.

honour (*on*-er) *v.* To show respect for someone. An *honourable* (*adj.*) man is worthy of *honour* (*n.*) as he has a high standard of honesty. *Dishonourable* is the opposite of *honourable.*

hood (hUd) *n.* A cloth covering for the head, often attached to an anorak, duffle-coat or cloak.

hoodwink (*hUd*-wink) *v.* To deceive by a trick.

hoof *n.* The hard horny part of the feet of horses, cattle etc.

hook (hUk) *n.* A piece of bent material, often metal, used to hold or catch something. *Ex.* A *coat-hook*, a *hook-and-eye*, a *fish-hook.*

hoot *n.* The cry of an owl, or the noise of a car-horn etc.

hop 1. *v.* To jump on one foot; (of birds) to jump on both feet together. 2. *n.* A climbing plant whose fruit is used to flavour beer.

horde *n.* A great crowd of people, wasps etc.

horizon (ho-*ry*-z'n) *n.* The line where earth (or sea) and sky seem to meet. *Horizontal* (*adj.*) means lying flat, level with the *horizon.*

horn *n.* (a) The pointed bony growth on the heads of cows, goats etc. (b) A musical wind instrument, once made of *horn*, now of brass. *Horny* (*adj.*) means like *horn*: a horse's hoof, for example.

hornet *n.* A kind of large wasp with a very painful sting.

horoscope (*ho*-ros-kohp) *n.* A chart of the positions of the planets at the time of a person's birth, from which astrologers claim to be able to predict (foretell) his likely future.

horrible (*ho*-ri-b'l) *adj.* (a) Causing physical fear. (b) Extremely unpleasant. *Ex.* What a *horrible* idea!

horrid *adj.* (a) Horrifying. (b) Disagreeable; rude; annoying. *Ex.* He is a *horrid* little boy.

horrify *v.* To fill with horror.

horror *n.* (a) A feeling of great fear or shock. *Ex.* It fills one with *horror* to see a serious accident. (b) Great dislike. *Ex.* I have a *horror* of spiders.

horsehair *n.* The hair from the tail or mane of a horse, used in stuffing the seats of furniture.

hose *n.* (a) A long, usually rubber, tube to convey water etc. Gardeners and firemen use *hoses.* (b) An old word for stockings.

hospitable (*hos*-pit-a-b'l) *adj.* Welcoming and kind to guests. *Ex.* He was very *hospitable* and offered to put us up for the night; we accepted his *hospitality* (*n.*) gladly.

hospital (*hos*-pit-al) *n.* A place where people suffering from illness or injury are cared for by doctors and nurses.

host (hohst) *n.* (a) A great number. *Ex.* He has a *host* of friends. (b) A man who receives and entertains guests. A *hostess* is a female *host.*

hostage (*hos*-tij) *n.* (a) A person handed over to the enemy as a guarantee (pledge) that promises will be kept. (b) A person seized by terrorists etc. to force someone to meet their demands for money etc.

hostel (*hos*-tel) *n.* A place where students or other groups of people can lodge.

hostile (*hos*-tyl) *adj.* Of an enemy; very unfriendly. *Ex.* The explorer found the villagers *hostile* and preparing to attack him; they showed *hostility* (*n.*). *Hostilities* (*n.*) are acts of war.

hound *n.* A dog trained for hunting.

household 1. *n.* All those living in one private house. *Ex.* We were a large *household* over Christmas, as the whole family were at home. 2. *adj.* Used by, or referring to, the household. *Ex. Household* repairs; *household* accounts.

hovel (*hov*'l) *n.* A hut; a small, poor, dirty house.

hover (*hov*-er) *v.* To stay up in the air, flapping the wings, in more or less the same spot, as a hawk or humming-bird can do.

hovercraft (*hov*-er-krahft) *n.* A wheel-less vehicle which travels on a cushion of air, usually over water.

however 1. *adv.* In whatever way. *Ex. However* you do it, it must be done. 2. *conj.* All the same. *Ex.* I don't want to go; *however,* I shall have to.

howl *v.* To cry loudly as do dogs or wolves, in a long whining way. The wind can *howl* during a storm, and people can *howl* with laughter.

hub *n.* The central part of a wheel. *Ex.* Car wheels have metal *hub-caps* in the middle of them.

huddle (*hu*-d'l) *v.* To crowd closely together. *Ex.* We *huddled* round the camp-fire to keep warm.

hug *v.* To put one's arms around someone, usually lovingly.

huge (hewj) *adj.* Extremely large.

hum 1. *n.* The sound made by bees etc. 2. *v.* To make such a sound; to sing quietly with the lips closed.

human (*hew*-man) *adj.* Belonging to mankind. The *human* race means all *human* beings; the whole of *humanity* (*n.*). *Humanity* also means a *humane* attitude or act.

humane (hew-*mayn*) *adj.* Kind, merciful.

humble *adj.* (a) Modest, not boastful. *Ex.* Although he was a good violinist, he was quite *humble* about it; his attitude was one of *humility* (*n.*). (b) Living in a very simple way.

humdrum *adj.* Dull and uninteresting.

humiliated (hew-*mil*-i-ayt-ed) *adj.* Made to feel ashamed or lowered in the esteem of oneself or others. *Ex.* It was *humiliating* (*adj.*) to have to ask for help after she had boasted that she would not need any.

humour (*hew*-mer) 1. *n.* (a) A playful but not unkindly attitude to the absurdities of life; playful imagination. A person with a *sense of humour* sees the funny side of things. *Humorous* (*adj.*) means (a) laughable, amusing; (b) having a sense of *humour*. (b) Mood. *Ex.* Is he in good *humour* today? 2. *v.* To give way to the whims of someone. *Ex.* We had better *humour* the old man and do what he wants.

hump *n.* A lump on the back, such as a camel has.

hunt *v.* (a) To search for. *Ex.* I *hunted* all over the house for my keys. (b) To chase animals for food or as a sport.

hurl (hurl) *v.* To throw with great force.

hurricane (*hu*-rik-an) *n.* A violent wind-storm; a cyclone.

hurry *v.* To act quickly or make someone else do so. *Ex.* Don't *hurry* me or I shall make mistakes. The doctor's visit was a *hurried* (*adj.*) one as he had other calls to make; he was in a *hurry* (*n.*).

husky *adj.* 1. (a) Big and strong. (b) Hoarse. 2. *n.* An Eskimo dog.

hybrid (*hy*-brid) *adj.* Produced from cross-breeding two different kinds of plant or animal. *Ex.* A mule is a *hybrid* (*n.*), being the offspring of a horse and a donkey.

hyena (hy-*ee*-na) *n.* A wild animal, rather like a wolf, which feeds on carrion and has a howl that sounds like a terrifying laugh.

hygiene (*hy*-jeen) *n.* The science of health and the prevention of disease; cleanliness. *Hygienic* (*adj.*) means clean and free from germs.

hymn (him) *n.* A song of praise, especially to God.

hyphen (*hy*-fen) *n.* A mark (-) between two words or syllables, to show they are connected. *Ex.* Paint-box.

hypocrite (*hip*-o-krit) *n.* A person who pretends to be better than he is, to be sincere or virtuous etc, when he is not so. *Ex.* Uriah Heep in Dickens's *David Copperfield* is full of *hypocrisy* (hip-*ok*-ris-i; *n.*).

hypnotize (*hip*-no-tyz) *v.* To put someone into a sleep-like state in which he may obey the *hypnotist*'s (*n.*) instructions or, sometimes, remember things long forgotten.

hysterical (his-*ter*-i-kal) *adj.* Inclined to laugh or cry uncontrollably, owing to over-excitement or emotional strain.

I

ice *n.* Water which is frozen solid. Very cold water or wind is said to be *icy* (*adj.*). A layer of moistened sugar on a cake is called *icing* (*n.*).

iceberg *n.* A huge mass of ice floating in the sea.

icicle (*ys*-i-k'l) *n.* A long, thin, hanging piece of ice, formed by water which freezes as it drips.

idea (y-*dee*-a) *n.* Something formed in the mind, a thought. *Ex.* Have you any *idea* how long this job will take?

ideal (y-*dee*-el) *adj.* The best that can be thought of; perfect. *Ex.* The weather in May is often *ideal* for a holiday.

identical (y-*den*-ti-kal) *adj.* Exactly the same. *Ex.* As these two boxes are *identical*, it doesn't matter which you choose.

identify (y-*den*-ti-fy) *v.* To recognize and give the name of. *Ex.* I can't *identify* these wildflowers; they are strange to me.

idiot (*id*-i-ot) *n.* A person whose mind is defective. When someone does a foolish thing we may say the person or thing is *idiotic* (id-i-*ot*-ik; *adj.*). *Ex.* It was *idiotic* to try to board a moving bus.

idle (*y*-d'l) *adj.* Not doing anything; not wanting to work; lazy.

idol (*y*-dol) *n.* A figure of a person or animal made to be worshipped as a god. To *idolize* is to admire someone excessively or blindly.

ignite (ig-*nyt*) *v.* To set fire to. *Ex.* You can *ignite* paper by focusing the sun's rays on it with a magnifying glass. You turn a car's *ignition* (*adj.*) key to start (fire) the engine.

ignorant (*ig*-nor-ant) *adj.* Having little knowledge of things in general; not aware of a particular thing. *Ex.* He is not altogether *ignorant*, but there are big gaps in his general knowledge. I was *ignorant* of the fact that today was your birthday.

ignore (ig-*nor*) *v.* To pay no attention to. *Ex.* It's silly to *ignore* danger notices on the beach.

ill *adj.* Not well; bad; unfriendly. *Ex.* He fell *ill* last week, but his *illness* (*n.*) is only slight. '*Ill*' (*adv.*) in front of many words means 'badly'. *Ex.* *Ill*-natured (unkind), *ill*-used (badly treated), *ill*-advised.

illegal (il-*ee*-gal) *adj.* Not lawful; against the law. *Ex.* Stealing is *illegal.*

illegible (il-*ej*-i-b'l) *adj.* Hard to read because badly written.

illiterate (il-*it*-er-at) *adj.* Not able to read or write.

illuminate (il-*ewm*-in-ayt) *v.* To light up. *Ex.* Floodlights *illuminated* the castle.

illusion (il-*oo*-zh'n) *n.* Something that is not what it seems to be. *Ex.* Conjuring tricks are often optical *illusions.*

illustrate (*il*-us-trayt) *v.* To make clear, to explain; to use pictures to do this or simply for decoration. *Ex.* This book gives examples of the use of a word to *illustrate* its meaning. The chemistry book is *illustrated* with diagrams. The artist won a prize for the *illustrations* in this book.

illustrious (il-*us*-tri-us) *adj.* Famous. *Ex.* England's most *illustrious* poet is Shakespeare.

im- *prefix.* This sometimes means *in*, as in *import, immigrate.* Placed before an adjective it means *not*, as in *impossible, impatient, immoral.* (*Im-* is used instead of *in-* before the letters b, m, p.).

image (*im*-ij) *n.* A likeness, such as a statue, or a reflection in a mirror. *Ex.* You can see your own *image* in still water.

imaginary (im-*aj* in a ri) *adj.* Not real; existing only in the mind or in the *imagination* (*n.*), like the characters in novels.

imagine (im-*aj*-in) *v.* To think, fancy or make a picture in one's mind. *Ex.* Can you *imagine* what it would be like to live on a desert island?

imbecile (*im*-be-seel) 1. *n.* A person with a weak mind. 2. *adj.* Foolish.

imitate *v.* To copy. *Ex.* Babies learn to speak by *imitating* what they hear. *Imitation* (*adj.*) jewels are those that look very like real jewels.

immediate (im-*eed*-i-at) *adj.* Without any delay. *Ex.* I want an *immediate* answer; I want it *immediately* (*adv.*).

immense (im-*ens*) *adj.* Very large.

immerse (im-*urs*) *v.* To plunge into liquid. *Ex.* We *immersed* the jars in hot water to remove the labels.

immigrate (*im*-i-grayt) *v.* To come into another country and stay there as a settler or *immigrant* (*n.*).

immoral (im-*or*-al) *adj.* Wrong, wicked. An *immoral* person is one who does wrong, knowing that it is wrong.

immortal (im-*or*-tal) *adj.* Never dying. The soul is said to be *immortal*. Shakespeare's plays are said to be *immortal* because they have won lasting fame.

immovable *adj.* That cannot be moved.

impact *n.* The striking of one thing against another; collision.

impartial (im-*par*-sh'l) *adj.* Fair and just; not favouring one side more than the other. *Ex.* An umpire must always show *impartiality* (*n.*).

impassable (im-*pahs*-a-b'l) *adj.* That cannot be passed. *Ex.* The swollen river was *impassable*, so the travellers had to turn back.

impatient (im-*pay*-shent) *adj.* Not patient; in a hurry; inclined to be irritated by slowness. *Ex.* He gets *impatient* if we are late to breakfast.

impede (im-*peed*) *v.* To hinder or hamper. *Ex.* His clothes *impeded* him when he plunged to the rescue of the drowning boy. A speech *impediment* (*n.*) is a stutter or other defect.

impel (im-*pel*) *v.* To drive or force. *Ex.* Wild animals are sometimes *impelled* by hunger to come near human beings.

impenetrable (im-*pen*-et-ra-b'l) *adj.* Too difficult to get through. *Ex.* The explorers' way was barred by an *impenetrable* forest.

imperceptible (im-per-*sept*-i-b'l) *adj.* Not visible. *Ex.* The growth of a plant is *imperceptible*, yet it goes on all the time.

imperial (im-*peer*-i-al) *adj.* Connected with, or referring to, an empire.

impersonate (im-*pur*-son-ayt) *v.* To pretend to be someone else by imitating him or his dress.

impertinent (im-*pur*-tin-ent) *adj.* Rude, cheeky.

impetuous (im-*pet*-ew-us) *adj.* Rash; inclined to act without thinking.

implement (*im*-ple-ment) *n.* A tool for doing a special piece of work, such as a hammer or a plough.

implore (im-*plor*) *v.* To beg very earnestly. *Ex.* He *implored* her to forgive him.

imply (im-*ply*) *v.* To suggest without actually stating clearly. *Ex.* He *implied* that he didn't believe me.

import (im-*port*) *v.* To bring goods in from abroad. Britain's imports (*im*-ports; *n.*) include New Zealand lamb and West Indian sugar.

important (im-*port*-ant) *adj.* (a) Mattering very much, or most; requiring attention; of great value. *Ex.* The *important* thing is, can you afford it? (b) Having great power, influence or authority. *Ex.* He knows many *important* people, people of *importance* (*n.*).

imposing (im-*pohz*-ing) *adj.* Impressive; very fine and grand, as a palace may be.

impostor (im-*pos*-tor) *n.* One who pretends to be someone else in order to get some advantage. *Ex.* The 'gasman' was an *impostor*, come to see if there was anything worth stealing.

impoverish (im-*pov*-er-ish) *v.* To make poor. *Ex.* War *impoverishes* all the nations engaged in it, whether they win or lose.

impress (im-*pres*) *v.* To have a powerful effect on the mind; to make people see the importance of. *Ex.* He made an *impressive* (adj.) speech, *impressing* on us the need to keep fit; his speech made a great *impression* (*n.*) on us.

impromptu (im-*promp*-tew) *adj.* Without preparation. *Ex.* An *impromptu* speech is an unprepared speech that a person may unexpectedly be called on to make.

improve (im-*proov*) *v.* To make better or become better. *Ex.* My health has *improved*; there has been a great *improvement* (*n.*) in it.

improvise (*im*-pro-vyz) *v.* (a) To make do with as a substitute, using such materials as are available. *Ex.* Robinson Crusoe *improvised* a shelter from the mast and sails. (b) To make up a piece of music as you go along.

imprudent (im-*proo*-dent) *adj.* Rash; not wise; not prudent.

impudent (*im*-pew-dent) *adj.* Rude, cheeky.

impulse (*im*-puls) *n.* A sudden idea or urge to do a thing. *Ex.* I bought these flowers on *impulse*. An *impulsive* (*adj.*) person is one who acts *impulsively* (*adv.*), without sufficient thought.

in- *prefix.* This may mean *in* (as *inlaid*, laid in); or *not* (as *incorrect*, not correct). In the following list of words the prefix means *not*.

For meanings, look up the words *without* the prefix; for example, look up 'accurate', and you will know that 'inaccurate' means the opposite of that:

inaccessible, inactive, inadequate, inappropriate, inattentive, inaudible, incapable, incautious, inconsiderate, inconstant, inconvenient, independent, indigestible, indirect, indistinct, inedible, ineligible, inexact, inexperienced, infrequent, inhospitable, injustice, inoffensive, insecure, insincere, insufficient, invisible.

inane (in-*ayn*) *adj.* Silly, foolish.

incense 1. (*in*-sens) *n.* Sweet-smelling spices etc. burnt in some churches during a service. 2. (in-*sens*) *v.* To make angry.

incentive (in-*sen*-tiv) *n.* A reward, promise etc. which encourages a person to do something. *Ex.* A large prize was offered as an *incentive* to us to enter for the competition.

incessant (in-*ses*-ant) *adj.* Never stopping. *Ex. Incessant* rain had flooded the fields.

incident (*in*-sid-ent) *n.* An event; something that happens.

incite (in-*syt*) *v.* To urge or stir up to action. *Ex.* Their leader *incited* them to rebel against the government.

incline 1. (in-*klyn*) *v.* (a) To lean, slope or bend. *Ex.* That tree *inclines* at a dangerous angle. (b) To tend towards; to be disposed to. *Ex.* I am *inclined* to make mistakes in mental arithmetic. I am *inclined* to agree with you. I have an *inclination* (*n.*) to go with you. 2. (*in*-klyn) *n.* A slope.

include (in-*klood*) *v.* To take in with, or add to, the rest; to reckon in. *Ex.* We must *include* her in the invitation; her *inclusion* (in-*kloo*-zh'n; *n.*) is necessary.

incognito (in-*kog*-ni-toh) *adj.* Using a false name. Well-known people sometimes travel *incognito* to avoid being pestered by journalists.

incoherent (in-ko-*heer*-ent) *adj.* (Of speech or writing) Muddled, not clear, difficult to follow.

income (*in*-kum) *n.* The amount of money a person earns or gets in any other way.

inconsistent (in-kon-*sis*-tent) *adj.* Contradicting oneself; not agreeing with what was said before. *Ex.* Your story now and the story you told me yesterday are *inconsistent*; they differ.

inconsolable (in-kon-*sohl*-a-b'l) *adj.* Not possible to comfort. *Ex.* She was *inconsolable* after her son's death.

increase (in-*krees*) *v.* To make or become greater.

incubator (*in*-kew-bay-ter) *n.* Apparatus for hatching eggs by artificial means.

incur (in-*kur*) *v.* To bring upon oneself. *Ex.* He *incurred* many debts.

indebted (in-*det*-ed) *adj.* Owing something, for example money, or gratitude for a kind act.

indescribable (in-des-*kryb*-a-b'l) *adj.* Not possible to describe. *Ex.* The sunsets were *indescribably* (*adv.*) beautiful.

index *n.* An alphabetical list of subjects dealt with in a book.

indicate (*in*-dik-ayt) *v.* To show or point out. *Ex.* His high temperature *indicates* that he is ill. An *indicator* (*n.*) at stations shows the times when trains arrive and depart.

indifferent (in-*dif*-er-ent) *adj.* Not interested; not caring what happens, one way or the other; not particularly good.

indigestion (in-di-*jest*-sh'n) *n.* Pain due to not being able to *digest* the food one has eaten.

indignant (in-*dig*-nant) *adj.* Scornfully angry about a thing one feels one has a right to be angry about.

indispensable (in-dis-*pen*-sa-b'l) *adj.* Not possible to do without; essential. *Ex.* Water is *indispensable* to all living creatures.

individual (in-di-*vid*-ew-al) 1. *n.* A single person, animal or thing. *Ex.* Most people stayed till the end, but one or two *individuals* left early. 2. *adj.* Belonging or referring to one only. *Ex.* We now have *individual* chairs instead of benches.

induce (in-*dews*) *v.* To persuade. *Ex.* I tried to *induce* him to come with us.

indulge (in-*dulj*) *v.* To give way to the desires of oneself or of others. *Ex.* He *indulges* his children's appetite for sweets; he is too *indulgent* (*adj.*). He *indulges* in bouts of extravagance.

industry (*in*-dus-tri) *n.* (a) The performance of work steadily and carefully. *Ex.* He is an *industrious* (*adj.*) worker. (b) Any branch of trade or manufacture. *Ex.* The cotton *industry*; shipbuilding *industry*.

inevitable (in-*ev*-it-a-b'l) *adj.* Certain to happen; impossible to avoid. *Ex.* If you go on eating sweets at that rate, it is *inevitable* that you will get fat.

inexcusable (in-ek-*skewz*-a-b'l) *adj.* Too bad to be excused or forgiven. *Ex.* Her lateness is *inexcusable*; she had plenty of time to get ready.

inexhaustible (in-egz-*aws*-ti-b'l) *adj.* Not possible to use up or come to the end of. *Ex.* There isn't an *inexhaustible* supply of coal in the ground; we shall *exhaust* it one day.

inexperienced (in-eks-*peer*-i-ensd) *adj.* Not having sufficient *experience*, knowledge or training. *Ex.* She is only a student nurse, too *inexperienced* to be of much use yet.

inexplicable (in-*eks*-plik-a-b'l) *adj.* Impossible to explain; puzzling.

infamous (*in*-fam-us) *adj.* Well-known for a bad quality; detestable. *Ex.* Nero and Hitler are examples of *infamous* men.

infancy (*in*-fan-si) *n.* The time of being a baby.

infantry (*in*-fan-tri) *n.* Foot-soldiers.

infect (in-*fekt*) *v.* To pass on a disease to someone. *Ex.* Measles is an *infectious* (*adj.*) disease; if you visit someone who has it, you may be *infected* with it.

infer (in-*fur*) *v.* To deduce; to form a conclusion from the evidence. *Ex.* From what you say I *infer* that you don't like me.

inferior (in-*feer*-i-or) *adj.* Lower in quality or rank. *Ex.* This cheap velvet is of *inferior* quality.

infest (in-*fest*) *v.* (Of pests etc.) To swarm over; to appear in large numbers. *Ex.* Our attic is *infested* with mice.

infinite (*in*-fin-it) *adj.* So great as to have no limits. *Ex.* He has *infinite* patience.

inflammable (in-*flam*-a-b'l) *adj.* Easily set on fire.

inflammation (in-flam-*ay*-sh'n) *n.* Redness, swelling and pain, caused by infection or injury.

inflate (in-*flayt*) *v.* To blow up or enlarge, as a balloon is *inflated* with air.

inflict (in-*flikt*) *v.* To cause to suffer something unpleasant. *Ex.* The court *inflicted* a heavy fine on him.

influence (*in*-floo-ens) 1. *n.* The effect which one person or event has on another. *Ex.* He has a good *influence* on her. 2. *v.* To have this effect. *Ex.* The weather *influenced* my decision.

influenza (in-floo-*en*-za) *n.* An infectious, epidemic disease caused by a virus, and marked by the sudden onset of a feverish cold, with aching limbs, followed by a long period of feeling tired and depressed.

influx (*in*-fluks) *n.* A flooding in of something, such as an *influx* of tourists into a town.

inform (in-*form*) *v.* To tell. *Ex.* Tourists can get *information* (*n.*) at an *information centre* about the area they are visiting.

informal (in-*form*-al) *adj.* Free and easy. *Ex.* An *informal* dance was quickly arranged. There was no *formality* (*n.*) of any kind.

infringe (in-*frinj*) *v.* To break a rule or law. *Ex.* Parking a car on double yellow lines is an *infringement* (*n.*) of the law.

infuriate (in-*fewr*-i-ayt) *v.* To make furious.

ingenious (in-*jee*-ni-us) *adj.* Clever at inventing; cleverly invented, made or thought out. *Ex.* He was an *ingenious* man, full of *ingenious* new ideas. The tiny watch was *ingeniously* (*adv.*) put together by a watchmaker who showed great *ingenuity* (in-jen-ew-i-ti; *n.*).

ingratitude (in-*grat*-i-tewd) *n.* Lack of gratitude for kindness received.

ingredient (in-*gree*-di-ent) *n.* One part of a mixture. *Ex.* The chief *ingredient* of toffee is sugar.

inhabitant (in-*hab*-it-ant) *n.* A permanent resident. *Ex.* The *inhabitants* of Siberia have to put up with great hardships; they *inhabit* (*v.*) a region of intense cold.

inhale (in-*hayl*) *v.* To breathe in. *Ex.* We *inhale* air when we breathe.

inherit (in-*he*-rit) *v.* To receive as an heir. An heir *inherits* and what he inherits is his *inheritance* (*n.*).

initial (in-*ish*-al) 1. *adj.* First. *Ex.* The *initial* match of the season is the opening match. 2. *n.* The first letter of a word, especially of a name. *Ex.* Jeremy Fisher's *initials* (J. F.) were put on his suitcase.

inject (in-*jekt*) *v.* To force something in; for example, by the *injection* (*n.*) of medicine into the body with a syringe.

injure (*in*-jer) *v.* To hurt. *Ex.* The *injured* (*adj.*) people were taken to hospital, but their *injuries* (*n.*) were not serious. *Injurious* (*adj.*) means harmful.

inkling *n.* An idea of something, or a hint of it. *Ex.* If we had had any *inkling* that you were coming, we would have stayed at home.

inland *adj.* In a part of the country away from the coast. *Ex.* Birmingham is an *inland* city.

innocent (*in*-o-sent) *adj.* Free from sin; not guilty; harmless. *Ex.* The prisoner said he was *innocent* of the crime.

innovation (in-o-*vay*-sh'n) *n.* Something new. *Ex.* Tea-bags were an *innovation*, when first introduced.

innumerable (in-*ew*-mer-a-b'l) *adj.* Too many to be counted. *Ex.* There are *innumerable* reasons why you can't go, so stop arguing!

inoculate (in-*ok*-ew-layt) *v.* To introduce disease germs, viruses etc. into the body so as to produce a very mild attack of a disease that will protect one from catching the disease in the future.

inquest (*in*-kwest) *n.* An official inquiry into a person's death.

inquire (in-*kwyr*) *v.* To ask a question; to seek information; to make an *inquiry* (*n.*). A person who is always asking questions, especially about other people's business, is called *inquisitive* (in-*kwiz*-i-tiv; *adj.*).

insane (in-*sayn*) *adj.* Not *sane*; mad.

insect *n.* A small creature with six legs, no backbone and a body divided into three sections. Most have wings and change form during their lives, for example from caterpillar to butterfly.

inseparable (in-*sep*-ar-a-b'l) *adj.* Impossible to separate; not wanting to be separated. *Ex. Inseparable* friends.

insert (in-*surt*) *v.* To put in. *Ex.* You *insert* a key in a lock.

insight (*in*-syt) *n.* Deep understanding.

insignificant (in-sig-*nif*-i-kant) *adj.* Trifling, not important.

insinuate (in-*sin*-ew-ayt) *v.* (a) To hint, especially at something unpleasant. *Ex.* She *insinuated* that I would never be any good at tennis. (b) To gain entrance craftily; to creep into. *Ex.* He *insinuated* himself into her favour.

insist (in-*sist*) *v.* To state firmly; to demand. *Ex.* The accused man *insisted* that he had not committed the crime. My mother *insists* that we tell her if we are going to be back late.

insolent (*in*-so-lent) *adj.* Rude, impertinent.

inspect (in-*spekt*) *v.* To look at carefully; to examine. *Ex.* Aircraft are *inspected* before they take off; mechanics make an *inspection* (*n.*) of them.

inspire (in-*spyr*) *v.* To influence in an encouraging and heartening way, by example or by words etc. *Ex.* Winston Churchill's wartime speeches *inspired* the people of Britain; they were an *inspiration* (*n.*).

install (in-*stawl*) *v.* To place a thing where it will be used; to place in office; to establish. *Ex.* The new cooker is now *installed* in the kitchen. He was *installed* as president.

instalment (in-*stawl*-ment) *n.* One of the parts of something which is not yet complete. *Ex.* We are paying for the record-player by *instalments*. This serial story is to appear in eight *instalments*.

instance (*in*-stans) *n.* A particular example. *Ex.* The blackbird is one *instance* of a bird with a fine song.

instant (*in*-stant) *n.* A moment. *Ex.* The paper was alight in an *instant*; the match produced an *instant* (*adj.*) flame.

instantaneous (in-stan-*tay*-ni-us) *adj.* Done in an instant; occurring at once.

instep (*in*-step) *n.* The arched upper part of the foot.

instinct (*in*-stinkt) *n.* A natural inclination or inward feeling which makes people and animals do a thing without having been taught. *Ex.* Birds fly by *instinct*. We all have an *instinctive* (*adj.*) fear of uncontrolled fire.

institution (in-sti-*tew*-sh'n) *n.* A society or organization set up for a certain public need or use, such as a hospital, prison etc.; the building which it occupies. *Institute* (*n.*) has the same meaning. *Ex.* The Royal National Lifeboat *Institution*.

instruct (in-*struckt*) *v.* To teach; to give orders to. *Ex.* I instructed the delivery-man to come before one o'clock. Paul is being given *instruction* (*n.*) in life-saving.

instrument (*in*-stroo-ment) *n.* Something made for doing a particular kind of work. *Ex.* Surgeons, dentists or pianists have *instruments* for their special needs.

insulate (*in*-sew-layt) *v.* To isolate or cut off; to cover electrical wiring with material through which electricity will not pass.

insult (*in*-sult) *n.* A remark that is rude and meant to give offence. To make such a remark is to insult (in-*sult*; *v.*) someone.

insure (in-*shoor*) *v.* To pay a small sum of money regularly in order to make sure of getting a large sum if a certain misfortune happens. *Ex.* The house is *insured* against fire for £25,000, the sum we should get if it was completely destroyed. This is called *fire insurance* (*n.*).

intact (in-*takt*) *adj.* Whole, with no parts missing or damaged. *Ex.* He dropped the radio on the floor, but it was still *intact* and in working order.

intellect (*in*-tel-ekt) *n.* The power of reasoning and thinking out ideas. *Ex.* Newton, the scientist, was a man of great *intellect*; he was *intellectual* (*adj.*).

intelligence (in-*tel*-i-jens) *n.* (a) Intellect, understanding. (b) A natural ability to grasp ideas quickly and to adapt to new circumstances. *Ex.* He is very *intelligent* (*adj.*); although he had never used a typewriter before, he soon saw how it worked.

intend (in-*tend*) *v.* To mean to do a thing; to have as one's aim or purpose. *Ex.* He *intends* to be a doctor when he grows up; that is his *intention* (*n.*). I didn't break it *intentionally* (*adv.*), it was an accident.

intense (in-*tens*) *adj.* Extreme, very great. *Ex.* It was a day of *intense* heat.

intercept (in-ter-*sept*) *v.* To seize or stop a person or thing while on the way from one place to another. *Ex.* The fighter squadron *intercepted* the bombers before they reached their target.

interest (*in*-ter-est) *n.* (a) Keen attention and curiosity. *Ex.* She is very *interested* (*adj.*) in bird-watching; it is her main *interest*. (b) Payment to someone of an agreed sum for the loan of his money. *Ex.* The Post Office pay me *interest* on the money I put in the savings bank.

interfere (in-ter-*feer*) *v.* To meddle in other people's affairs; to get in the way. *Ex.* I can tackle this problem myself; I don't want any *interference* (*n.*) from you.

interior (in-*teer*-i-or) *n.* The inside. *Ex.* The *interior* of the house is well decorated; the *interior* (*adj.*) decorations are beautiful.

interjection (in-ter-*jek*-sh'n) *n.* An exclamation expressing the feelings, such as 'Oh!' or 'Ouch!'.

interlude (*in*-ter-lewd) *n.* An interval, for example during a performance; the music etc. which may fill such a time.

intermediate (in-ter-*meed*-i-at) *adj.* Coming between. An *Intermediate* Piano test, for instance, comes between Beginners' and Advanced.

intern (in-*turn*) *v.* (In wartime) To imprison someone who belongs, or is friendly, to an enemy country.

internal (in-*tur*-nal) *adj.* Inside; referring to the inside of something. *Ex.* He had cuts and bruises as well as some *internal* injuries.

international (in-ter-*nash*-on-al) *adj.* Taking place between two or more nations. *Ex.* The Olympic Games are *international* events.

interpret (in-*tur*-pret) *v.* (a) To explain or bring out the meaning of. *Ex.* I don't know how to *interpret* your reply; are you refusing to obey? An actor *interprets* his part, a conductor gives his *interpretation* (*n.*) of the music played. (b) To translate. An *interpreter* (*n.*) translates a conversation from one language to another to help those who do not speak each other's language.

interrupt (in-ter-*upt*) *v.* To break into something that is going on; to get in the way of. *Ex.* The programme was *interrupted* to broadcast a gale warning; this was an *interruption* (*n.*).

intersect (in-ter-*sekt*) *v.* To cross. Where roads cross there is an *intersection* (*n.*).

interval (*in*-ter-val) *n.* The space, usually of time, between two things. *Ex.* We saw a flash of lightning and, after an *interval*, heard distant thunder.

interview (*in*-ter-vew) *n.* A formal meeting at which the *interviewer* (*n.*) questions the person being *interviewed* in order to learn certain facts about him, such as his suitability for a job.

intimate 1. (*in*-tim-at) *adj.* Private, personal, friendly. *Ex.* Letters between friends are more *intimate* than business letters. 2. (*in*-tim-ayt) *v.* To hint or make known.

intolerable (in-*tol*-er-a-b'l) *adj.* Unbearable.

intolerant (in-*tol*-er-ant) *adj.* Refusing to put up with; being severe and unfriendly towards ideas and attitudes which differ from one's own. *Ex.* He is *intolerant* of foreigners and of any religion but his own.

intoxicated (in-*tok*-si-kayt-ed) *adj.* Drunk.

intricate (*in*-trik-at) *adj.* Involved, entangled; full of detail. *Ex.* This is an *intricate* knot and I can't undo it.

intrigue (in-*treeg*) 1. *n.* A secret plot. 2. *v.* (a) To make such a plot. (b) To arouse curiosity.

introduce (in-tro-*dews*) *v.* (a) To formally make one person known to others. *Ex.* The chairman *introduced* the speaker to the audience. (b) To bring forward to people's notice; to start something new. *Ex.* When was the old age pension first *introduced*? Its *introduction* (*n.*) was a good idea.

intrude (in-*trood*) *v.* To go where one is not wanted. *Ex.* We won't *intrude* on our neighbour now, as she is busy; it would be an *intrusion* (*n.*).

intuition (in-tew-*ish*'n) *n.* An immediate understanding of something, without having to reason it out; insight. *Ex.* She had an *intuition* that all was not well; she sensed it without being told.

invade (in-*vayd*) *v.* To enter a country by force.

invalid 1. (*in*-va-leed) *n.* A sick person. 2. (in-*val*-id) *adj.* Having lost its value. *Ex.* An out-of-date ticket is *invalid* and cannot be used.

invaluable (in-*val*-ew-a-b'l) *adj.* Very valuable. The word really means 'so valuable that it is impossible to put a value on it'.

invariable (in-*vair*-i-a-b'l) *adj.* Not changing; always the same.

Ex. Summer months in the south of France are *invariably* (*adv.*) hot.

invent (in-*vent*) *v.* To design or produce something quite new. *Ex.* Television was an important *invention* (*n.*); several people claim to have *invented* it first.

invest (in-*vest*) To put money where it is expected to make a profit or earn interest—for example, in a building society or a business.

investigate (in-*vest*-i-gayt) *v.* To inquire into or examine with care. *Ex.* Scientists all over the world are *investigating* new ways of increasing food production; their *investigations* (*n.*) are making progress.

invigorating (in-*vig*-or-ayt-ing) *adj.* Giving health and strength.

invite (in-*vyt*) *v.* (a) To ask someone to a meal or to stay. *Ex.* He has sent us an *invitation* (*n.*) for his birthday party. (b) To attract; to tempt. *Ex.* That cake looks *inviting* (*adj.*).

invoice (*in*-voys) *n.* A list of goods supplied, with their cost.

involve (in-*volv*) *v.* (a) To draw into or entangle in. *Ex.* He got *involved* in debt. (b) To require as a necessary consequence. *Ex.* This job will *involve* much hard work. *Involved* (*adj.*) also means complicated or muddled.

iridescent (ir-id-*es*-ent) adj. Shining with all the colours of the rainbow. *Ex.* A starling's feathers are *iridescent*.

iris (*yr*-is) *n.* (a) A tall waterside plant, also grown in gardens; often with blue and yellow flowers. (b) The coloured part of the eye which surrounds the pupil in the middle.

irksome (*erk*-sum) *adj.* Tiresome and troublesome.

iron (*y*-ern) *n.* (a) A hard metal much used in making tools etc. Steel is an alloy of *iron* and carbon. (b) An implement used to smooth creases from cloth.

ironmongery (*y*-ern-mong-ger-i) *n.* Domestic metal goods such as saucepans and tools, not necessarily made of iron.

irrelevant (ir-*el*-e-vant) *adj.* Not related to or concerned with the subject being talked or thought about. *Ex.* The chairman asked us to keep to the point and not to waste time on *irrelevancies* (*n.*).

irrigate (*ir*-i-gayt) *v.* To water farmland by artificial streams.

irritate (*ir*-i-tayt) *v.* (a) To annoy or make rather angry. *Ex.* It was *irritating* (*adj.*) to find that the 'short cut' was in fact the long way round. *Irritable* (*adj.*) means easily annoyed, impatient. (b) To inflame or make uncomfortable. *Ex.* Gravel in the shoe can *irritate* the foot.

island (*y*-land) *n.* A piece of land surrounded by water. Sometimes called an *isle* (*yl*; *n.*). An *islet* (*y*-let; *n.*) is a very small *island.*

isolate (*y*-sol-ayt) *v.* To place alone or apart. *Ex.* People with dangerous infectious diseases are put in an *isolation* (*adj.*) ward.

issue (*is*-ew) 1. *n.* (a) The act of coming out; the result. *Ex.* A new *issue* of postage stamps. The *issue* of the match was in doubt till near the end. To die *without issue* is to die leaving no children. (b) A matter for discussion. 2. *v.* To come out or send out. *Ex.* The government has *issued* a statement about the strike.

isthmus (*is*-mus) *n.* A narrow piece of land joining two large masses of land. *Ex.* The *Isthmus of Panama.*

italic (it-*al*-ik) *adj.* Printed in sloping type (*like this*), often used when emphasis is needed.

item (*y*-tem) *n.* A single article on a list. *Ex.* Each *item* in the storeroom had to be checked against a list.

ivory (*y*-vor-i) *n.* The hard white bony material of which the tusks of elephants and other animals are made. *Ex. Ivory* (*adj.*) chessmen.

ivy (*y*-vi) *n.* The evergreen climbing plant often seen clinging to walls and old trees.

J

jack *n.* A tool for lifting heavy things, especially the wheel of a car off the ground.

jacket *n.* A short coat.

jade *n.* A hard, usually green, stone, used in jewellery and sometimes carved into figures.

jaded (*jay*-ded) *adj.* Worn out and weary. *Ex.* After a busy week we were feeling and looking rather *jaded.*

jagged (*jag*-ed) *adj.* Having a rough, uneven edge, like broken glass.

jaguar (*jag*-ew-ar) *n.* A fierce South American animal of the cat family, similar to the leopard but larger.

jail (jayl) *n. See* gaol.

jangle *n.* A mixture of sounds which is unpleasant to the ear, such as a badly rung peal of bells.

jaunt (jawnt) *n.* A short pleasure-trip.

jaw *n.* One of the two bones in the mouth in which the teeth are set.

jazz *n.* The dance-music developed by the American Negro, in which playing after the beat (syncopation) and improvising are the main features.

jealous (*jel*-us) *adj.* Being suspicious and resentfully envious, because someone has something you would like to have. *Ex.* She is *jealous* of her much prettier sister, and she shows her *jealousy* (*n.*).

jeans (jeenz) *n.* Strong close-fitting trousers made of denim.

jeer *v.* To laugh or scoff at unkindly.

jelly *n.* A sort of jam made of fruit juice boiled with sugar and then strained. *Ex. Bramble jelly. Table-jelly* is a stiff glassy-looking coloured mixture of fruit juice and gelatine.

jellyfish *n.* A small, umbrella-shaped sea-creature with a *jelly*-like body; some of them can give a painful sting.

jeopardy (*jep*-ard-i) *n.* Danger. *Ex.* He couldn't swim, so when he fell in the river his life was in *jeopardy*.

jerk 1. *n.* A sudden sharp movement. 2. *v.* To make such a movement. *Ex.* She *jerked* the skipping-rope out of my hand and ran off with it.

jersey *n.* A knitted jumper.

jest *n.* A joke. To say something in *jest* is to say it as a joke. Kings used to employ professional *jesters* (*n.*), who were given much freedom to *jest*, even about their masters.

jet *n.* (a) A hard shiny black stone used in jewellery etc. (b) A spout of liquid, gas or flame from a small opening. *Ex.* The fountain throws *jets* of water into the air.

jet-propelled *adj.* (Of aircraft) Moved forward by backward *jets* of hot gasses.

jetty *n.* A short pier.

jewel (*joo*-el) A precious stone, such as a diamond; an ornament containing precious stones. A *jeweller* (*n.*) is one who sells *jewels* or *jewellery* (*n.*).

jig *n.* A quick, lively dance or tune.

jockey *n.* The rider of a racehorse.

jog *v.* To run at a slow steady pace or *jog-trot*.

joint 1. *n.* (a) The place where two bones of the body meet. *Ex.* The *hip joint*. (b) The point at which any two parts or objects are joined together. *Ex.* Hose-pipes sometimes leak at the *joints*. (c) A piece of meat cut for roasting. *Ex.* A *joint* of beef. 2. *adj.*

Shared by two or more people etc. *Ex.* By their *joint* efforts they managed to pull him out of the river.

joist *n.* One of the beams on which a floor or ceiling is laid.

jolly *adj.* Merry, cheerful.

jolt (johlt) 1. *n.* A sudden jerk or bump. 2. *v.* To move in jerks or shakily. *Ex.* The bus *jolted* over the rough road.

jot *v.* To make a note of. *Ex.* I have *jotted* down the times of the return trains. Not a *jot* means not a bit.

journal (*jur*-nal) *n.* A magazine or diary. Newspapers were once called *journals*, and so one whose work is writing for newspapers and magazines is called a *journalist* (*n.*), and his work is *journalism* (*n.*).

journey (*jur*-ni) *n.* A trip from one place to another.

joy *n.* A feeling of great happiness. *Ex.* News that their son's baby was born brought great *joy* to its grandparents; it was *joyous* (*adj.*) news and made them feel *joyful* (*adj.*).

jubilant (*joo*-bi-lant) *adj.* Rejoicing, delighted. *Ex.* We were *jubilant* when our team won the cup.

jubilee (*joo*-bil-ee) *n.* A time for rejoicing; a special anniversary. *Ex.* A 25th anniversary is a silver *jubilee*, and a 50th a golden *jubilee*.

judge 1. *n.* An official appointed to hear cases in lawcourts and give decisions (*judgements*; *n.*) on them; someone asked to choose the winner in competitions etc. 2. *v.* To form an opinion on a particular thing and state what is good or bad about it. *Ex.* An artist is coming to *judge* the paintings and award prizes.

judicious (joo-*dish*-us) *adj.* Wise; able to form sensible judgements about things.

judo (*joo*-do) *n.* A sport based on a Japanese method of self-defence, using no weapons.

juggernaut (*jug*-er-nawt) *n.* A nickname for a giant-sized lorry.

juggle *v.* To toss several balls, plates etc. into the air, catch them, and toss them up again, keeping them all in motion all the time.

juice (joos) *n.* The liquid part of a fruit or vegetable. *Ex.* Most children like orange *juice* and *juicy* (*adj.*) apples.

jumble *n.* An untidy mixture of things. A *jumble sale* is a sale at which all sorts of things are sold, usually for charity.

jumbo *adj.* Very large. *Ex.* A *jumbo jet* is an airliner which takes a great many passengers. (*Jumbo* was the name of a famous zoo elephant.)

junction (*jungk*-sh'n)   *n.* The place where two or more things meet, such as roads or railway-lines.

jungle (*jung*-g'l)   *n.* Very thick, high forest of the kind common in tropical countries.

junior (*joon*-i-or)   *adj.* Younger; lower in rank.

junk   *n.* (a) A Chinese sailing-boat. (b) Odds and ends of rubbish.

junket   *n.* The thick curd of milk, sweetened and served as a pudding.

jurisdiction (joor-is-*dik*-sh'n)   *n.* Authority, especially of the law; the area in which it can be enforced.   *Ex.* My boss said 'Once you leave the office, you are outside my *jurisdiction*'.

jury (*joor*-i)   *n.* (a) A group of local citizens chosen at random to hear the evidence in certain cases in a lawcourt and give their verdict. (b) A similar group asked to judge competitions etc.

just   1. *adj.* Fair; honest; right and reasonable.   *Ex.* Our school rules are *just* and fair to us all. 2. *adv.* Exactly; barely.   *Ex.* We were late and *just* had time to buy our tickets.

justice (*jus*-tis)   *n.* Fairness; just treatment.   *Ex.* A court of law has to see that everyone gets *justice*.

justify (*jus*-ti-fy)   *v.* (a) To prove to be right and *just*.   *Ex.* The police were *justified* in arresting him, since he was found to have stolen goods on him. (b) To give a good excuse for doing something.   *Ex.* He *justified* his actions by saying that he had had to fight to defend himself.

jut   *v.* To stick out.   *Ex.* Land's End *juts* out from the coast of Cornwall.

juvenile (*joo*-ven-yl)   *adj.* Young; suitable for the young.   *Ex.* A *juvenile* court.

K

kangaroo (kan-gar-*oo*)   *n.* A large Australian animal with long hind legs, with which it makes long leaps. The female has a pouch in which she carries her young.

kapok (*kay*-pok)   *n.* A vegetable fibre used to stuff soft toys, pillows etc.

kayak (*ky*-ak)   *n.* A light, covered, one-man canoe.

keel   *n.* The lowest part of a ship, stretching the whole length and supporting the whole structure.

keen *adj.* Sharp, eager and interested; enthusiastic. *Ex.* On a cold day the wind is often *keen*. Birds have *keen* eyesight. Clare is *keen* on netball.

kennel *n.* A small house for a dog outdoors.

kerb (kurb) *n.* A stone edging to a pavement.

kernel (*kurn*-el) *n.* The inside part of a nut or fruit-stone etc.

khaki (*kah*-ki) 1. *n.* The yellowish-brown cloth used in making some uniforms. 2. *adj.* Of this colour.

kid *n.* A young goat.

kidnap *v.* To seize and carry away a person, usually to hold him to ransom.

kidney (*kid*-ni) *n.* One of the two glands in the body that extract liquid waste from the bloodstream.

kiln *n.* A closed oven or furnace, used to dry and bake bricks, pottery etc.

kilt *n.* A pleated skirt, usually of tartan cloth, worn by some Scotsmen.

kin *n.* People belonging to the same family; relations.

kindergarten (*kin*-der-gar-ten) *n.* A school for very young children.

kindle (*kin*-d'l) *v.* To set fire to. *Ex.* To light a camp fire, we begin by *kindling* the sticks.

kink *n.* A slight twist in a rope etc.

kiosk (*ki*-osk) *n.* (a) A covered stall or stand for selling papers, sweets etc. (b) A public telephone-box.

kipper *n.* A herring that has been dried and smoked.

kit *n.* The luggage and equipment of travellers, soldiers etc.

knack (nak) *n.* A way of being able to do a thing easily and well. *Ex.* To shake down the mercury in a thermometer you need not strength but the *knack*.

knead (need) *v.* To squeeze and press together, as in handling dough in bread-making.

knee (nee) *n.* The joint between the upper and lower leg. To *kneel* (*v.*) is to rest on one's knees.

knick-knack (*nik*-nak) *n.* A small ornament of little value except to the owner.

knight (nyt) *n.* A title given to a man by the monarch which makes him Sir instead of Mr. This honour is called a *knighthood* (*n.*).

knit (nit) *v.* To make a material by inter-looping wool or other yarn with *knitting needles* or on a *knitting-machine*.

knob (nob) *n.* The rounded handle used to open a door or a drawer etc.; a small hard lump of something, such as a *knob* of butter.

knock (nok) *v.* To strike or rap, as on a door. Sometimes a metal *knocker* is fixed on a house door for this purpose.

knot (not) *n.* (a) The twisting together of the ends of a rope, string etc., passing them through each other's loops and then drawing them tight together. *Ex.* There are different *knots* for special purposes, such as those used by sailors or scouts. (b) The seaman's unit of speed; one nautical mile per hour. (c) The base of a branch buried in a tree's later growth. When the tree is cut for timber, the *knot* may drop out and form a *knot-hole*.

knotty (*not*-i) *adj.* (Of a problem) Hard to solve.

knowledge (*nol*-ij) *n.* Knowing; what is known. *Ex.* His *knowledge* of French is good.

knuckle (*nuk*'l) *n.* A joint in the finger, especially the joint at the base of it.

L

label *n.* A small card or piece of paper fastened to something, to say what it contains (as on a bottle) or where it is to go (as on parcels or luggage).

laboratory (lab-*o*-ra-tor-i) *n.* A room fitted up with what is needed for scientific experiments.

labour 1. *n.* Work. 2. *v.* To work hard. A *labourer* (*n.*) is one who does heavy work, such as farming. A *laborious* (lab-*awr*-i-us; *adj.*) task is one that takes much hard work.

lace *n.* (a) Material made of an openwork pattern of threads, worked with a needle or by twisting threads round a pattern of pins (bobbin lace). (b) A cord threaded through eyelets to draw something together. *Ex.* A *shoe-lace*.

lack *n.* Want or need; shortage. *Ex.* There is no *lack* of food. This book is not a perfect copy—it *lacks* (*v.*) one page.

lacquer (*lak*-er) *n.* A hard glossy varnish used to decorate. *Hair-lacquer* is a spray to keep the hair set.

ladder *n.* Two long wooden or metal upright pieces joined by steps or bars (rungs) across them, for climbing.

laden *adj.* Carrying a load, usually heavy or bulky. *Ex.* The climbers were *laden* with equipment.

ladle *n.* A large deep spoon with a long handle, used to serve soup etc.

lady *n.* (a) A woman of good class or manners or education. (b) The title of the wife of a baronet or knight, and of certain peeresses. (c) A polite word for a woman.

ladybird *n.* A small, round, brightly coloured beetle, usually red and spotted, which feeds on greenfly.

lag *v.* (a) To linger or fall behind. (b) To cover a boiler or pipes with material to keep in the heat or to prevent freezing up.

lagoon (lag-*oon*) *n.* A shallow lake of salt water nearly or completely cut off from the sea by a strip of land, for instance by a sandbank or coral reef.

lair *n.* The home or bed of a wild animal, such as a lion.

lame *adj.* Unable to walk properly, usually owing to a leg injury etc.

lament (la-*ment*) *v.* To grieve about or show grief for. A *lament* (*n.*) is a mournful expression of sorrow in verse or music.

land 1. *n.* (a) The part of the earth not covered by sea. (b) A country, such as England, Sweden etc. 2. *v.* To come or bring into or on to land, from sea or air. *Ex.* Fishermen *land* their herring-catches here. We *landed* safely at the airport.

landing *n.* (a) The coming into or on to land. (b) The area at the top of a flight of stairs.

landlord *n.* A man who lets a house, lodgings or land to a tenant, or who keeps an inn. A *landlady* is a woman landlord, especially one who lets rooms to lodgers.

landmark *n.* Something noticeable and easily seen, such as a church tower, which can act as a guide to sailors or to travellers on land.

landscape (*lan*-skayp) *n.* A view of the countryside.

language (*lang*-gwij) *n.* The form of speech used by a particular group of people. *Ex.* The French *language*, Welsh *language* etc.

lantern *n.* A lamp enclosed in a case with transparent sides, suitable for carrying about.

lap 1. *n.* (a) The front part of the body from waist to knees, when one is sitting down, where a child or animal may be nursed. (b) One circuit (journey round) of a race-track. 2. *v.* To lick up with the tongue as an animal does when it drinks.

lapel (la-*pel*) *n.* The folded-back part of a jacket etc. at its neckline, above any fastening.

lapse *n.* (a) A slipping away. *Ex.* The *lapse* of time. (b) A small mistake. *Ex.* She had a *lapse* of memory and forgot the date of the concert.

larceny (*lar*-sen-i) *n.* The legal word for theft.

larch *n.* A cone-bearing tree which loses its needle-like leaves in winter.

lard *n.* Fat from the pig, melted down and used in cooking.

larder *n.* The storeroom in a house where food is kept.

lark *n.* A small ground-nesting bird of the fields which sings sweetly as it soars up into the sky.

larva (*lar*-va) *n.* An insect grub before it turns into its adult form. A caterpillar is the *larva* of a butterfly or moth.

laser (*lay*-zer) *n.* A specially intense beam of light which can be used for various purposes in medicine, in industry etc.

lash 1. *n.* (a) A whip or a stroke of a whip. (b) An eyelash. 2. *v.* To tie together with rope or cord. *Ex.* Robinson Crusoe *lashed* logs together to make a raft.

lasso (las-*oo*) *n.* A rope with a noose at one end, used by cowboys to catch cattle.

last 1. *adj.* After all the others. 2. *v.* To continue or hold out. *Ex.* We hope our stock of wood will *last* through the winter.

latch 1. *n.* A door or gate fastening consisting of a bar which drops into a catch or holder. 2. *v.* To use a latch to close a door.

late *adj.* (a) After the usual or expected time. *Ex.* The train was ten minutes *late*. (b) Recently dead. The *late* Mr Brown means the Mr Brown who recently died.

lath (lahth) *n.* A thin strip of wood used in plastering walls and in carpentry.

lathe (laydh) *n.* A machine with a revolving (turning) cutter, used to shape metal or wood.

lather (*lah*-dher) *n.* Froth made by rubbing soap in water.

latitude (*lat*-i-tewd) *n.* (a) The distance between a place and the Equator measured in degrees. Lines of *latitude* are imaginary lines round the globe north and south of the Equator, from which this distance can be worked out. *Ex.* London's *latitude* is about 51 degrees North. (b) Freedom of choice allowed. *Ex.* They were given great *latitude* in the choice of the sports or games they could play.

latter *adj.* The second of two things mentioned. *Ex.* He likes both apples and pears, but prefers the *latter* (pears). *Latterly* (*adv.*) means just recently, or nowadays.

laugh (lahf) *v.* To make the sounds (a *laugh*; *laughter*; *n.*) and wear the expression (smiling etc.) with which we show amusement, pleasure or scorn.

launch (lawnch) *v.* (a) To move a boat, especially one newly built, into the water. (b) To send up a space rocket etc. (c) To start something new. *Ex.* He *launched* a scheme for a lottery in aid of charity.

laundry (*lawn*-dri) *n.* A place where clothes etc. are washed.

lava (*lah*-va) *n.* The melted rock which flows from a volcano.

lavatory (*lav*-a-tor-i) *n.* A room with a water-closet (WC); a toilet.

lavender (*lav*-en-der) *n.* A sweet-smelling mauve-flowered garden plant, from which the scent (*lavender-water*) is made.

lavish (*lav*-ish) *adj.* Abundant or too abundant. *Ex.* A *lavish* spread of rich food was provided.

law *n.* The rules of a country or community which must be obeyed by all, for the good of all. *Lawful* (*adj.*) means according to the *law*; the opposite is *unlawful*. *Lawless* (*adj.*) people behave with no regard for the law.

lawn *n.* A level area of trimmed grass, a familiar feature in gardens.

lawyer (*law*-yer) *n.* A person trained in law who advises others about legal matters; a solicitor or barrister.

lax *adj.* So easy-going as to be careless. *Ex.* They had been *lax* in checking that the car was in good working order.

lay *v.* (a) To put down or place, as one *lays* a book or a cloth on a table. (b) To bring forth eggs, as birds do.

layer *n.* One thickness of anything. *Ex.* Put a *layer* of straw on top of each *layer* of apples in the box.

layette (lay-*yet*) *n.* A set of clothes, bedclothes and toilet articles for a new-born baby.

layman *n.* Anyone who is not a clergyman, or who is not an expert, especially in medicine or the law.

lazy *adj.* Not inclined to work or to be active.

leaflet *n.* A small printed sheet of paper. *Ex.* Here is a *leaflet* advertising the Town Hall concert.

league (leeg) *n.* (a) A group of people, cities etc. who agree to act together for a particular purpose. (b) An association of sports clubs who agree to play each other according to certain rules. *Ex.* The *Football League.*

leak 1. *n.* A hold or crack which lets liquid or gas run out. 2. *v.* To pass through or allow out in this way. *Ex.* This kettle has a *leak* (*n.*), and the water has all *leaked* out.

lean 1. *v.* To rest against, often in a sloping position; to bend over. *Ex.* Do not *lean* on the glass of the display case, as it might break. We *leant* over the wall to watch the trains. To have a *leaning* (*n.*) towards something is to have a liking for it. 2. *adj.* Not fat; thin. *Ex.* A piece of *lean* beef. A *lean* man.

leap *v.* To jump. *Ex.* He *leapt* (lept) over the fence. He made a *leap* (*n.*) into the air.

learn (lurn) *v.* To get knowledge or skill in a thing by study, experience or practice. *Ex.* Babies *learn* to speak by imitating and practising. *Learned* (*ler*-ned; *adj.*) means having *learnt* a great deal.

lease (lees) 1. *n.* A legal agreement about the rent to be paid by a tenant to a landlord. 2. *v.* To let (grant) a property on *lease*; to occupy a property on *lease*.

leash (leesh) *n.* The strap or chain by which one holds a dog. *Ex.* Dogs must be kept on a *leash* in this park. (Also called a *lead*.)

least (leest) *n.* The smallest in size, quantity, importance etc. *Ex.* We gave out some toffees; David had the most, Alan had less than he did, but John had the *least* of all.

leather (*ledh*-er) *n.* The skin of an animal, treated in a tannery so that it can be made into articles to use.

leave 1. *n.* Permission. *Ex.* Soldiers are on *leave* when they have permission to be absent from duty. 2. *v.* To go away from; to allow to remain. *Ex.* We are *leaving* the country to go abroad. When we sell our house, we are *leaving* the carpets and curtains.

lecture (*lek*-cher) *n.* A talk on a particular subject to an audience or class. *Ex.* He *lectured* (*v.*) on poetry. To *lecture* someone can mean to reprove him.

ledge (lej) *n.* A narrow shelf, such as a *window-ledge*.

ledger (*lej*-er) *n.* A large book in which money received and spent by a firm is recorded; an account book.

left 1. *v.* The past tense of to *leave*. 2. *adj.* Connected with the side of the body on which the heart is; the opposite of the right side. *Ex.* Turn *left* (*adv.*) at the Town Hall and then take the second turning on the *left* (*n.*).

legacy (*leg*-a-si) *n.* A gift to a person named in a will, to be handed over only after the death of the giver.

legal (*lee*-gal) *adj.* To do with the law; allowed by law, lawful.

Ex. It is not *legal* to ride a bicycle at night without a light; that is *illegal.*

legend (*lej*-end) *n.* A very old story about something, which may or may not be true. *Ex.* There is a *legend* that tells of a secret passage from the palace to the sea-shore.

legible (*lej*-i-b'l) *adj.* Easily read, as good handwriting is.

legislate (*lej*-is-layt) *v.* To make laws.

legitimate (lej-*it*-im-at) *adj.* Lawful; reasonable. *Ex.* He had a *legitimate* reason for being in the building, for he was working late.

leisure (*lezh*-er) *n.* Time free from work. *Ex.* She likes to knit in her *leisure* (*adj.*) hours. *Leisurely* (*adv.* and *adj.*) means without hurrying.

lemon (*lem*-on) *n.* An acid-tasting juicy fruit with a thick pale-yellow skin, useful for flavouring and making drinks.

lend *v.* To let a person have something for a time, after which he must return it. *Ex.* She *lent* me her umbrella.

length *n.* The distance that something measures from end to end. *Ex.* This stick is just one metre in *length.* To *lengthen* (*v.*) is to make longer. *At length* means at last, or for some time. *Ex.* He reached the top *at length*, after a long climb. It was hard to explain and he described it *at length.*

lenient (*lee*-ni-ent) *adj.* Mild, tolerant, not severe. *Ex.* The judge was too *lenient* with them.

lens (lenz) *n.* A piece of transparent material, usually glass, curved so as to bend light-rays, and used in cameras etc. The *lens* in our eyes, behind the pupil which lets in the light, enables us to focus a picture of what is before us.

Lent *n.* The 40 days before Easter Sunday, once a time of fasting.

leopard (*lep*-ard) *n.* A large wild animal, rather like a tiger but having spots instead of stripes.

less *adj.* Not so much. *Ex.* We had *less* rain than usual this year.

-less is a syllable sometimes added at the end of a noun and meaning 'without'. *Ex. Endless* (*adj.*) means without end or lasting a long time. *Noiseless* means without noise, quiet.

let *v.* (a) To allow. My mother won't *let* me go out in the boat until I can swim. (b) To allow someone to have the use of in return for payment of rent; to lease.

lethal (*lee*-thal) *adj.* Deadly. A *lethal* gas is a poisonous gas.

lettuce (*let*-is) *n.* A garden plant whose leaves are used in salads.

level 1. *n.* (a) A flat surface. (b) A height or position, especially in relation to others. *Ex.* The *level* of the lake is higher this year because of the heavy rains. 2. *adj.* Flat, having an even surface.

lever (*lee*-ver) *n.* A bar used to force up a weight. The bar moves on a point along it (the fulcrum), and when one end is pushed down, the other end with the weight on it rises.

liable (*ly*-a-b'l) *adj.* (a) Legally responsible. *Ex.* He was held *liable* for the damage he did. (b) Risking having to pay a penalty. *Ex.* Trespassers are *liable* to prosecution. (c) Likely to. *Ex.* She is *liable* to speak without thinking.

libel (*ly*-b'l) *n.* Something written about a person which is damaging to his character; an untrue and hurtful remark.

liberal (*lib*-er-al) *adj.* Generous, giving freely. *Ex.* There was a *liberal* supply of food at the party.

liberate (*lib*-er-ayt) *v.* To set free. *Ex.* He broke down the door and *liberated* the prisoners.

liberty (*lib*-er-ti) *n.* Freedom. To be *at liberty* to do something is to be free to do it.

library (*ly*-bra-ri) *n.* A collection of books; the room or building in which they are kept. A *librarian* (ly-*brair*-i-an) has the care of a library.

licence (*ly*-sens) *n.* Permission, usually granted after payment of a fee, to keep a dog, drive a car, run a television set etc. To *license* (*v.*) is to give such permission.

lichen (*ly*-ken) *n.* A kind of fungus plant, often grey or yellow, which grows over tree trunks and rocks.

lie *v.* (a) To say something which one knows is not true. To do this is to tell a *lie* (*n.*) and be a *liar* (*n.*). (b) To rest stretched out flat. *Ex.* I *lie* on a bed to sleep; last night I *lay* on it; I have always *lain* on it. (c) To be in a particular place. *Ex.* The village *lies* in a hollow.

lieu (lew) *n.* As a substitute for. *Ex.* He said he would take chocolates in *lieu* of money.

lieutenant (lef-*ten*-ant) *n.* A junior officer in the Army or Navy.

lifebuoy (*lyf*-boy) *n.* A belt made of cork or inflatable rubber which can support a body in water.

lift 1. *v.* To raise. 2. *n.* A sort of cage used in large buildings to carry people up and down from one floor to another.

ligament (*lig*-a-ment) *n.* A band of tough fibres in the body which links one bone to another.

light (lyt) 1. *n.* That which makes things visible, whether natural light from the sun, or artificial. 2. *v.* (a) To give light to; to make or become light. (b) To catch fire; to set fire to. *Ex.* We *lit* the sticks and the fire was soon *alight.* 3. *adj.* (a) Having plenty of light. (b) Having little weight; the opposite of heavy.

lighter (*lyt*-er) *n.* (a) A barge which carries goods from cargo-boat to shore. (b) A small container of fuel with a flint device which produces a flame to light cigarettes etc.

lighthouse (*lyt*-hows) *n.* A strong tower, either tall or in a high place, with a bright lantern on top to guide ships or warn them of danger-points off the coasts.

lightning (*lyt*-ning) *n.* The flash of electricity seen in thunderstorms.

lightship (*lyt*-ship) *n.* A ship carrying a powerful light, anchored in a place dangerous to shipping as a warning to other vessels.

likely *adj.* Probable; such as one would expect. *Ex.* The weather forecast says it is *likely* to be fine tomorrow.

likeness *n.* Something that is the same in appearance as something else. *Ex.* This painting is a good *likeness* of my father as he looked in old age.

lilac (*ly*-lak) *n.* A tree which in spring bears purple, mauve or white flowers with a delicate smell. *Lilac-coloured* means pale mauve.

limb (lim) *n.* An arm, leg or wing; one of the main branches of a tree.

lime *n.* (a) A tree with heart-shaped leaves and sweet-smelling yellow blossom. (b) The fruit of a tree, like a small and more acid lemon, whose juice is used to make a refreshing drink. (c) A white substance made by heating limestone.

limestone *n.* A kind of rock, used to make lime, cement and building stone.

limit (*lim*-it) 1. *n.* The boundary or farthest point. *Ex.* A fence marks the *limits* of the football ground. 2. *v.* To keep boundaries; to restrict. *Ex.* Each club was *limited* to two tickets for the match. A *limited* (*adj.*) space is one rather small for what is needed.

limp 1. *adj.* Not stiff or firm. To feel *limp* is to have no energy. 2. *v.* To walk as if lame.

limpet *n.* A small sea-creature with a cone-shaped shell, which clings very tightly to rocks.

linen (*lin*-en) *n.* Cloth made from flax.

linger (*ling*-ger) *v.* To delay or go very slowly. *Ex.* He was late, so did not *linger* on his way to school.

lingerie (*lan*-zher-i) *n.* Women's underwear.

linguist (*ling*-gwist) *n.* One who is quick to learn foreign languages.

lining *n.* The material placed on the inside of something, such as a box or garment.

link 1. *n.* (a) One of the rings of a chain. (b) Anything connected. *Ex.* The detectives think there is a *link* between the burglaries, as they are so similar. 2. *v.* To connect. *Ex.* The island is *linked* to the mainland by a bridge.

linoleum (lin-*oh*-li-um) *n.* A shiny covering for floors that is easily washed.

lint *n.* A soft kind of linen used to dress wounds.

lion *n.* A large fierce animal of the cat family, with thick hair on head and neck, and a loud roar. It is found mainly in Africa. The female is called a *lioness* (*ly*-on-es; *n.*).

liqueur (lik-*yoor*) *n.* A strong alcoholic after-dinner drink, strongly flavoured and sweetened.

liquid (*lik*-wid) *adj.* In the state between solid and gas, like water or oil; capable of flowing. A *liquid* sound is clear and musical. *Ex.* Water is a *liquid* (*n.*).

liquor (*lik*-or) *n.* Alcoholic drink; a liquid.

listen (*lis*-en) *v.* To hear with attention; to pay attention to. *Ex.* He *listened* to my advice and did as I suggested. Hearers of radio broadcasts are called *listeners* (*n.*).

listless *adj.* With no energy.

literary (*lit*-er-ar-i) *adj.* To do with literature. *Ex.* He followed a *literary* career, writing plays and poetry.

literature (*lit*-er-a-cher) *n.* (a) The art of good writing in prose or poetry. (b) Anything printed. *Ex.* There is a lot of *literature* published about the subject of pollution.

litre (*lee*-ter) *n.* A metric measure of capacity, equal to 1.76 pints.

litter *n.* (a) Straw or hay used as bedding for animals. (b) The family of puppies, pigs etc. born at one time. (c) Untidy bits of paper or other rubbish left lying about in streets and other public places.

liver (*liv*-er) *n.* A large and important organ of the digestive system; animal liver used as food.

live (lyv) *adj.* Living, not dead. To be *lively* (*adj.*) is to be active, gay and bright. The animals on a farm are called *livestock* (*n.*).

lizard (*liz*-ard) *n.* Small reptile with four short legs and a long tail.

load (lohd) 1. *n.* What is carried, especially something heavy or bulky. *Ex.* A *load* of hay. 2. *v.* To put a load on something.

loaf (lohf) 1. *n.* A piece of bread in the shape in which it was baked. 2. *v.* To spend time idly.

loan (lohn) *n.* The act of lending, or the thing lent. *Ex.* He asked for the *loan* of a book; the book, when he got it, was a *loan*, or *on loan*.

loath (lohth) *adj.* Unwilling. (Also spelt *loth*.)

loathe (lohdh) *v.* To hate, to feel disgust at. *Ex.* She *loathes* spiders; she thinks them *loathsome* (*adj.*).

lobby 1. *n.* An entrance hall, or the passage into which the front door opens. 2. *v.* To try to get someone, such as a Member of Parliament, interested in a cause or scheme.

lobster *n.* A large, long-tailed shellfish with two enormous claws like pincers. It is blue-black when alive, but bright red when boiled for eating.

local (*loh*-kal) *adj.* Connected with or belonging to some particular place. The *local* newspaper is one published in the *locality* (*n.*), that is, the town or district where you live.

location (loh-*kay*-sh'n) *n.* A geographical place. *Ex.* The *location* of the school is on the edge of the village; that is where it is *located* (*v.*).

loch *n.* The Scottish word for 'lake'. *Ex. Loch Lomond.*

lock 1. *n.* (a) A metal device fitted to a door etc. to keep it fastened until opened with a key. (b) A tuft of hair. 2. *v.* To fasten with a lock.

locket *n.* A small decorative metal case which may contain a photograph etc. and is worn round the neck on a chain.

locust (*loh*-kust) *n.* A member of the grasshopper family which sometimes migrates in huge swarms and can strip a whole area of all plant life.

lodge *v.* To live in a place for a time. A *lodger* (*n.*) is one who rents rooms in someone else's house, and has *lodgings* (*n.*) there.

loft *n.* A room or space right under the roof of a building; an attic, often used for storing things.

log *n.* (a) A large piece of wood such as is burnt in an open fireplace. (b) The daily record of a ship's voyage.

logic (*loj*-ik) *n.* The art of reasoning.

loiter *v.* To move in a lingering way; to dawdle.

loll *v.* To sit or lounge in a lazy attitude.

lonely *adj*. Alone and feeling sad about it. *Ex*. She is *lonely* now that her husband has died.

longing (*long*-ing) *n*. A great wish for. *Ex*. It was so hot in the classroom that everyone was *longing* (*v*.) to get out into the fresh air.

longitude (*lon*-ji-tewd) *n*. The distance of a place east or west of Greenwich (London), expressed in degrees. New York is about 74 degrees West.

loom *n*. A machine for weaving cloth.

loop *n*. The doubling over itself of a piece of string etc.; forming a bend or space inside. *Ex*. Every stitch in knitting is a kind of *loop*.

loose (loos) *adj*. Not tight; not fastened. *Ex*. You must sew on that *loose* button or you will lose it. To *loosen* (*v*.) is to make less tight.

loot *v*. To plunder or steal things during or after a catastrophe such as an earthquake or hurricane. Soldiers used to carry off their enemies' belongings as *loot* (*n*.) after a battle.

lop *v*. To cut off the branches and twigs of a tree.

lopsided *adj*. Having one side lower or smaller than the other, so that the thing is unevenly balanced.

lotion (*loh*-sh'n) *n*. A liquid which is used as a medicine or cosmetic.

lottery *n*. A way of raising money by selling numbered tickets, a few of which will be picked by chance and win their holders prizes.

lounge (lownj) 1. *n*. A room in a public place such as a hotel or liner, where one can relax in comfort; the sitting-room of a private house. 2. *v*. To sit back lolling.

lout *n*. A rough clumsy person with bad manners.

lovable (*luv*-a-b'l) *adj*. Good-natured and charming; deserving of love.

love 1. *n*. Strong, warm affection. 2. *v*. To be fond of. *Ex*. He does *love* his food.

lovely *adj*. Very beautiful, very attractive.

lower (*loh*-er) 1. *adj*. Further down; below the others. *Ex*. There is snow on the mountains, except on the *lower* slopes. 2. *v*. To let down; to make lower. *Ex*. The sailors *lowered* the cargo into the ship's hold.

lowly (*loh*-li) *adj*. Humble and simple, not grand.

loyal (*loi*-al)   *adj*. Faithful and true, worthy of being trusted. The opposite of *disloyal*.

lozenge (*loz*-enj)   *n*. Medicine in the form of a sweet which is meant to be sucked slowly. *Lozenge-shaped* is diamond-shaped (like the diamond on a playing card).

lubricate (*loo*-brik-ayt)   *v*. To make smooth and slippery with oil, as by oiling a lawn-mower.

lucid (*loo*-sid)   *adj*. Clear and easy to understand.

luck   *n*. Chance; something that happens by chance. You can have good *luck* (in which case you are *lucky*; *adj*.) or bad *luck* (and be *unlucky*).   *Ex*. It was only by *luck* that I found buttons to match the ones I had lost.

luggage (*lug*-ij)   *n*. The suitcases and other baggage in which one packs clothes etc. when travelling.

lukewarm (*look*-wawrm)   *adj*. Tepid, only slightly warm.

lull   *n*. A pause or interval.   *Ex*. There was a *lull* in the thunderstorm.

lullaby (*lul*-a-by)   *n*. A song to send a baby to sleep.

luminous (*loo*-min-us)   *adj*. Giving light; shining in the dark, as some clock-faces do.

lunacy (*loon*-a-si)   *n*. Madness. A *lunatic* (*n*.) is one who is mad.

lunch   *n*. The meal eaten in the middle of the day, sometimes called dinner. It is the short word for *luncheon*.

lung (lung)   *n*. One of the two organs of the body into and out of which we and other animals breathe air.

lurch (lerch)   *v*. To move unsteadily so as almost to fall, as one may on a ship's deck in rough weather. To leave someone in the *lurch* (*n*.) is to leave him without the help he expects from you.

lurid (*loor*-id)   *adj*. Glaringly bright; gaudily coloured; sensational.

lurk (lerk)   *v*. To lie hidden in wait.

luscious (*lush*-us)   *adj*. Delicious to eat; delightful; over-rich.

lustre (*lus*-ter)   *n*. A gleam on the surface of something; a glossy look.

luxury (*luk*-sher-i)   *n*. Great comfort, surrounded by rich and choice things; something which one would like to have but is expensive.   *Ex*. He lived a *luxurious* (luk-*shoor*-i-us; *adj*.) life in a *luxuriously* (*adv*.) furnished house.

lyric (*li*-rik)   1. *adj*. (Of poetry) Expressing the intense personal feelings of the poet. 2. *n*. (a) A lyric poem. (b) The words of a popular song.

M

macaroni (ma-ka-*roh*-ni) *n.* A food made of flour and water, shaped into thin tubes and cooked with savoury sauces.

macaroon (ma-ka-*roon*) *n.* A sweet biscuit made from ground almonds, egg-white etc. on a rice-paper base.

mace *n.* (a) An ornamental metal staff of office. (b) A spice made from the covering of the nutmeg kernel.

machine (ma-*sheen*) *n.* A device which uses power to do work, make things move etc., such as a *sewing-machine, machine-gun* etc. The moving parts of a machine are called *machinery*.

mackerel (*mak*-er-el) *n.* A beautifully marked eatable sea-fish living in large shoals.

mackintosh (*mak*-in-tosh) *n.* An overcoat made of a material which keeps out rain.

magazine (mag-a-*zeen*) *n.* (a) A storeroom for gunpowder or arms. (b) A periodical, a paper that comes out at a fixed time, usually weekly or monthly, containing articles, stories etc.

maggot *n.* The small grub or worm which will turn into a bluebottle or similar insect.

magic (*maj*-ik) *n.* (a) The ancient practice of trying or pretending to influence events or people by mysterious means, medicines, charms, words etc. or by such acts as sticking pins into the wax image of an enemy; witchcraft, sorcery. (b) The powers possessed by good or bad fairies in fairy-tales. (c) Conjuring tricks. *Magic* is practised by *magicians* (ma-*jish*-anz; *n.*), using *magic* (*adj.*) tricks.

magistrate (*maj*-is-trayt) *n.* A person appointed to act as a judge in a local lawcourt that deals with the less important offences.

magnanimous (mag-*nan*-i-mus) *adj.* Generous and forgiving.

magnet (*mag*-net) *n.* A piece of iron which has the power of drawing other pieces of metal towards it. This is done by *magnetism* (*n.*) and the iron is said to be *magnetic* (mag-*net*-ik; *adj.*).

magneto (mag-*nee*-to) *n.* A small device for making the electricity used to explode the petrol vapour in a car engine etc.

magnificent (mag-*nif*-i-sent) *adj.* Very splendid and grand. *Ex.* The Queen's coronation was a ceremony of great *magnificence* (*n.*).

magnify (*mag*-ni-fy) *v.* To make something seem larger, as a microscope will do to things that are very small.

magnitude (*mag*-ni-tewd) *n.* Size, largeness. *Ex.* The stars look small to us but are really of enormous *magnitude.*

magpie (*mag*-py) *n.* A black-and-white bird of the crow family, with a long tail and chattering call.

mahogany (ma-*hog*-an-i) *n.* A hard wood of reddish-brown colour much used for furniture.

maiden (*may*-den) *n.* An unmarried girl. A woman's *maiden name* is the surname she had before marriage. A *maid* (*n.*) is a female servant.

mail *n.* (a) Armour made of steel rings or plates, such as soldiers wore in olden times. (b) The letters and parcels sent by post.

maim (maym) *v.* To injure and cripple. *Ex.* He was *maimed* for life by a fall from a ladder.

main *adj.* Principal or chief. *Ex. Main* roads link cities and big towns.

mainland *n.* A country or continent, not including the islands off its shores.

mainstay *n.* Chief support to someone or something needing help. (Named after the rope which supports a ship's *mainmast.*)

maintain (men-*tayn*) *v.* (a) To support or keep something going. *Ex.* You can *maintain* a family, or a car. (b) To insist that something is true. *Ex.* He *maintained* that he had never been in the building, but the evidence was against him.

maize (mayz) *n.* Indian corn, a tall-growing cereal with large cobs of yellow grains, used as food for humans and animals.

majesty (*ma*-jest-i) *n.* (a) Dignity and grandeur. To have this is to be *majestic* (*adj.*). (b) The title used when speaking to or of a king or queen. *Ex.* Her *Majesty* the Queen.

major (*may*-jor) 1. *adj.* Greater or more important; chief, principal. *Ex.* '*Major* road ahead'. 2. *n.* An army officer next in rank above a captain.

majority (ma-*jo*-ri-ti) *n.* (a) The greater number or part of. *Ex.* The *majority* of the audience enjoyed the play; some didn't. (b) The full legal age (18 in Britain), at which, in the eyes of the law, a person becomes able to manage his own affairs.

malice (*mal*-is) *n.* Spite; the wish to do harm to someone.

malignant (ma-*lig*-nant) *adj.* Full of hatred; wanting to do harm; malicious.

mallet (*mal*-et) *n.* A wooden hammer. *Ex.* Croquet is played on a lawn with long-handled *mallets* used to drive balls through hoops.

malt (mawlt) *n.* Barley which has been prepared for brewing beer.

maltreat (mal-*treet*) *v.* To treat cruelly or roughly.

mammal (*mam*-al) *n.* An animal that suckles its young.

manage (*man*-ij) *v.* (a) To look after or control. *Ex.* The sailor *managed* the boat skilfully in the rough sea. (b) To be able to do something or to find a way of doing it. *Ex.* The wounded soldier *managed* to get back to camp. One who *manages* a shop, business etc. is a *manager* (*n.*) and the shop etc. is under his *management* (*n.*).

mane *n.* The long hair on the neck of a horse, lion etc.

manfully *adv.* Bravely and with determination.

manger (*mayn*-jer) *n.* The box or trough from which horses or cattle feed in a stable or cowshed.

mania (*may*-ni-a) *n.* (a) Madness. A *maniac* (*n.*) is a mad person. (b) Too much enthusiasm for something. *Ex.* She has a *mania* for jig-saws.

manicure (*man*-i-kewr) *n.* The care of hands and finger-nails. *Manicurists* (*n.*) are people who *manicure* (*v.*) hands as a profession.

manipulate (man-*ip*-ew-layt) *v.* To handle skilfully. *Ex.* The puppet-master *manipulated* his puppets very cleverly.

mankind *n.* All the people in the world.

manly *adj.* Like a man; having the good qualities of a man.

manner *n.* A way of behaving or doing anything. *Ex.* She has a pleasant, friendly *manner*. Courteous people are those who have good *manners*. She uses her free time in a sensible *manner*.

mannerism (*man*-er-izm) *n.* A trick of behaviour which has become a habit. Impersonators and mimics carefully observe the *mannerisms* of the people they imitate.

manoeuvre (man-*oo*-ver) *v.* To move in a clever way. *Ex.* Before the battle, our army *manoeuvred* to get on to hilly ground above the enemy. This was a skilful *manoeuvre* (*n.*).

mansion (*man*-sh'n) *n.* A large house.

mantelpiece *n.* The shelf above a fireplace.

manual (*man*-ew-al) 1. *n.* A book of instructions. *Ex.* New cars are supplied with *manuals* telling owners how to take care of them. 2. *adj.* Done by hand. *Ex.* Machines have replaced much *manual* labour.

manufacture (man-ew-*fak*-cher) *v.* To make goods in large quantities by machinery or by teams of manual workers. *Ex.* Britain *manufactures* cars. The owner of a factory is a *manufacturer* (*n.*).

manure (man-*ewr*) *n.* Anything dug into the ground to make it more fertile, especially animal dung.

manuscript (*man*-ew-skript) *n.* A book or paper written by hand and not printed.

maple (*may*-p'l) *n.* A tree common in North America, providing a fine wood for furniture and, in the case of the *sugar maple*, a syrup from the sap.

mar *v.* To spoil. *Ex.* Sports Day was *marred* by heavy showers.

marble *n.* A very hard and beautiful stone which can be polished and used for sculpture and in building. *Marbles* are small balls of stone or glass, used to play the game of *marbles*.

march 1. *v.* To walk as soldiers do, with regular steps. 2. *n.* A piece of music written to suit marching.

mare (mair) *n.* A female horse.

margarine (mar-jer-*een*) *n.* A substitute for butter made from various oils and fats.

margin (*mar*-jin) *n.* (a) The edge. *Ex.* The *margins* of a page are the blank spaces at each side of the print. (b) An extra allowance of time, space etc. to cover emergencies. *Marginal* (*adj.*) means on the borderline or on the edge.

marigold (*ma* ri-gohld) *n.* A common garden plant with bright orange-yellow flowers.

marine (ma-*reen*) 1. *adj.* Living in or connected with the sea. *Ex.* The whale is a *marine* mammal. 2. *n.* A soldier who serves in the navy.

mariner (*ma*-rin-er) *n.* A sailor.

marionette (ma-ri-on-*et*) *n.* A puppet made to move and dance by strings attached to it.

maritime (*ma*-rit-ym) *adj.* Connected with or bordering on the sea. *Ex.* Britain is a *maritime* nation. Sea holly is a *maritime* flower.

market *n.* A public place where goods are shown for sale.

marmalade (*mar*-ma-layd) *n.* A jam made from oranges or other citrus fruit.

maroon (ma-*roon*) 1. *adj.* A dark-red colour. 2. *v.* To put a person ashore on a desert island and leave him there as a punishment for mutiny etc.

marquee (mar-*kee*) *n.* A very large tent, especially one put up for a village fête etc.

marriage (*ma*-rij) *n.* The ceremony or religious service which makes a man and woman husband and wife; the relationship between husband and wife. They *marry* (*v.*) each other.

marrow (*ma*-ro) *n.* (a) A kind of fatty jelly found in the hollow part of bones, which manufactures blood-cells. (b) A large, long vegetable growing on the ground, green, white or striped, and soft and juicy when cooked.

marsh *n.* Very wet low-lying ground.

marsupial (mar-*soo*-pi-al) *n.* An animal whose young spends its early life in a pouch in the mother's body. Kangaroos and all other native Australian mammals belong to the *marsupial* (*adj.*) class.

martial (*mar*-shal) *adj.* Warlike. *Ex.* Regimental marches are *martial* tunes.

martin *n.* A bird of the swallow family, with a much shorter tail than the swallow and all-white underparts.

martyr (*mar*-ter) *n.* One who suffers hardships and even death because of his beliefs.

marvel (*mar*-vel) 1. *n.* Something wonderful or amazing. *Ex.* The shipwrecked sailor had a *marvellous* (*adj.*) escape from death. 2. *v.* To wonder or be astonished. *Ex.* We *marvelled* at his escape.

marzipan (mar-zi-*pan*) *n.* A paste for decorating cakes, or eating as a sweet, made of ground almonds, sugar and egg-white.

mascot *n.* Something which is supposed to bring luck to the person who wears or carries it.

masculine (*mas*-kew-lin) *adj.* Of the male sex; manly.

mash *v.* To beat down into a soft mass, as one *mashes* potatoes.

mask *n.* A covering which hides the face, used for various purposes such as at a masquerade for fun, at a hospital to prevent the spread of germs, or by a criminal to hide his identity.

mason (*may*-s'n) *n.* One who works with stone. Stonework is *masonry* (*n.*).

masquerade (mas-ker-*ayd*) 1. *n.* A party at which guests wear masks or other disguises. 2. *v.* To disguise oneself or pretend to be what one is not. *Ex.* The thieves *masqueraded* as guests at the hotel.

mass *n.* (a) A celebration of the Last Supper, especially in the

Roman Catholic Church. (b) A large amount or quantity. *Ex.* Great *masses* of snow still lay along the roadsides.

massacre (*mas*-a-ker) 1. *n.* The murder of a large number of people. 2. *v.* To murder in this way.

massage (*mas*-ahzh) 1. *n.* Rubbing and manipulating parts of the body to relieve pain or stiffness in the joints or muscles. 2. *v.* To apply *massage.* This is the work of a male *masseur* (mas-*er*) or female *masseuse* (mas-*erz*), or may be done by a physiotherapist.

massive (*mas*-iv) *adj.* Large and heavy; bulky. *Ex.* The doctor gave him a *massive* dose of pain-killer.

mast *n.* The tall pole on a ship or boat, which supports the sails.

master 1. *n.* (a) One who has control or authority over others. *Ex.* The *master* (captain) of a merchant ship. (b) One who is excellent at his art or craft. *Ex.* The painter Rembrandt was a *master* of his art. 2. *v.* To learn thoroughly how to do something extremely well. *Ex.* He has had a good piano teacher and now plays the piano in a *masterly* (*adj.*) way. A *masterpiece* (*n.*) is an excellent piece of work done by someone who is a *master* of his art.

masticate (*mas*-ti-kayt) *v.* To chew food.

match 1. *n.* (a) A small piece of wood tipped with a substance which lights when rubbed on a prepared surface. (b) A game between two sides, such as a *football match.* 2. *v.* To be the equal of someone or something. *Ex. Matching* (*adj.*) suitcases are of the same colour and design. *Matchless* (*adj.*) means perfect, without equal.

mate *n.* (a) The male or female of a pair in the animal world. (b) A fellow-worker or assistant. *Ex.* A plumber's *mate.* (c) The second in command (under the master) in a merchant ship.

material (ma-*teer*-i-al) *n.* (a) The stuff, especially a fabric, of which a thing is made. *Ex.* This *dress material* is washable. (b) Whatever is used or needed for a particular purpose. *Ex.* Drawing *materials*, photographic *materials.*

maternal (ma-*turn*-al) *adj.* Motherly; like a mother.

mathematics (math-e-*mat*-iks) *n.* The science that deals with numbers and space. Arithmetic is a branch of *mathematics.* A *mathematician* (math-e-mat-*ish*'n; *n.*) is a person skilled in things *mathematical* (*adj.*).

matinee (*mat*-in-ay) *n.* The afternoon performance at a theatre or cinema.

matrimony (*mat*-ri-mun-i) *n.* Marriage. *Ex.* Two people who are married are said to be joined together in *matrimony*.

matron (*may*-tron) *n.* (a) A married woman. (b) The head nurse in a hospital. (c) The woman who looks after domestic matters and the children's health at a boarding-school.

matted (*mat*-id) *adj.* Tangled, as hair may become if left unbrushed.

matter 1. *n.* (a) What things are made of. *Ex.* Everything is made of some kind of *matter*. (b) The subject being considered. *Ex.* We will talk about this *matter* later. 2. *v.* To be important. *Ex.* That doesn't *matter*, it's not worth bothering about.

mattress (*mat*-res) *n.* The soft part of a bed on which the sleeper lies.

mature (ma-*tewr*) *adj.* Ripe or fully grown. *Ex.* The pears have *matured* (*v.*) in the sun and are now ready to pick. They have come to *maturity* (*n.*).

maul (mawl) *v.* To attack savagely and injure. *Ex.* The tiger sprang on him and *mauled* him badly.

mauve (mohv) *adj.* Of a light purple colour.

maximum (*maks*-i-mum) *n.* The greatest number or amount. *Ex.* The *maximum* number of people this hall will seat is five hundred.

maybe (*may*-bee) *adj.* Perhaps.

mayonnaise (may-on-*ayz*) *n.* A thick creamy sauce made of egg-yolks, oil and vinegar, served with salads etc.

mayor (mair) *n.* The chief official of a city or borough corporation.

maze (mayz) *n.* A confusing arrangement of paths and turnings, from which it is difficult to find one's way out, designed as a puzzle in parks etc.

meadow (*med*-oh) *n.* A field of grass, usually grown to make into hay.

meagre (*mee*-ger) *adj.* Scarce; poor. *Ex.* The garret was *meagrely* (*adv.*) furnished, with nothing but a bed and chair.

meal *n.* (a) The food eaten at a certain time, such as breakfast or dinner. (b) Grain crushed into a rough powder. *Oatmeal* makes the best porridge.

mean 1. *adj.* (a) Poor, shabby. *Ex.* It was a *mean* street of poor and badly-kept houses. (b) The opposite of generous; stingy; malicious and cowardly. 2. *v.* To intend; to express. *Ex.* He *means* to be a doctor when he grows up. This book gives the *meanings* (*n.*) of words (the ideas that they express).

meander (me-*an*-der)　*v.* To take a winding course, as do some rivers.

means　*n.* (a) Income; the money one has to live on. (b) The method or way in which a thing is done.

meantime　*n.* The time when something else is happening.　*Ex.* I was buying the tickets, and in the *meantime* they were putting the luggage in the guard's van.

meanwhile　*adv.* While something else is happening; in the meantime.

measles (*meez*-l'z)　*n.* An infectious disease which causes a red rash on the skin, and occurs chiefly among children.

measure (*mezh*-er)　1. *v.* (a) To be of a certain size.　*Ex.* This carpet *measures* 4 metres each way. (b) To find out the size, amount or weight of a thing.　*Ex.* He *measured* the room before ordering the carpet; he took its *measurements* (*n.*). 2. A container that holds an exact amount; a tape or rod that *measures* an exact length.　*Ex.* A litre *measure*, a *tape measure*.

mechanic (me-*kan*-ik)　*n.* A person skilled in making, using or repairing machinery. A *mechanical* (*adj.*) toy is one worked by clockwork etc.

medal (*med*'l)　*n.* A piece of metal (bronze, silver or gold etc.), usually coin-shaped, and given as a reward for bravery or war service, as a prize, or in memory of some important event.

meddle (*med*'l)　*v.* To interfere.　*Ex.* It is wise not to *meddle* in other people's affairs.

media (*mee*-di-a)　*n.* The means by which news or other information is published, such as newspapers, television, radio etc.

medical (*med*-i-kal)　*adj.* Having to do with medicine and the treatment of illness.　*Ex.* He is having *medical* treatment.

medicine (*med*-sin)　*n.* (a) The art of curing the sick. (b) The substance a doctor prescribes to make a patient better.

mediocre (mee-di-*oh*-ker)　*adj.* Of moderate (not very good) quality.

meditate (*med*-it-ayt)　*v.* To think deeply, in an atmosphere of quiet. People of many religious beliefs practise *meditation* (*n.*).

medium (*mee*-di-um)　1. *adj.* Of middle quality, size etc.　*Ex.* She is of *medium* height, not tall or short. 2. *n.* The person or means through which something is done. *See also* media.

medley (*med*-li)　*n.* A mixture.　*Ex.* The band played a *medley* of old dance tunes.

meek *adj.* Humble, gentle.

megaphone (*meg*-a-fohn) *n.* A trumpet-shaped instrument for shouting through in order to make one's voice louder and heard at greater distance.

melancholy (*mel*-an-kol-i) *adj.* Sad and gloomy.

mellow (*mel*-o) *adj.* Ripe; soft and pleasant to taste or hear; having a nature softened by age and experience. *Ex.* Soft, ripe pears are *mellow*. She used to be too strict but has *mellowed* (*v.*) with age.

melodrama (*mel*-o-drah-ma) *n.* A sensational play with violent incidents and much sentimentality.

melody (*mel*-o-di) *n.* A tune. *Melodious* (*adj.*) means tuneful or making a sweet sound.

melon (*mel*-on) *n.* A large hard-skinned fruit which grows on the ground and has a pleasant flavour, though it consists mainly of water.

melt *v.* To make or become liquid. *Ex.* She *melted* the butter and sugar in a pan over a low flame. The snow *melted* when the sun came out.

member (*mem*-ber) *n.* One of a company, society or club. *Ex.* Our club has many *members*; it has a large *membership* (*n.*). A *Member* of Parliament is an elected representative in the House of Commons.

memento (me-*men*-toh) *n.* A souvenir.

memoir (*mem*-wahr) *n.* A biography; an account of events remembered by the writer.

memorable (*mem*-or-ra-b'l) *adj.* Worth remembering; not likely to be forgotten.

memorandum (mem-or-*ran*-dum) *n.* A note written to help one remember something; a brief account of a discussion etc. Often shortened to 'memo'.

memorial (mem-*awr*-ri-al) *n.* Something to remind us of a great person or event. *Ex.* The Monument in London is a *memorial* of the Great Fire of London in 1666.

memorize (*mem*-or-ryz) *v.* To learn by heart, as actors learn their lines in a play.

memory (*mem*-or-ri) *n.* (a) The part of the mind which remembers events of the past and stores, ready to be recalled, things that the mind has received in the way of experience, learning etc. *Ex.* My mother has a good *memory* for faces. (b) That which is remembered. *Ex.* We have happy *memories* of our holiday.

menace (*men*-is) *n.* A threat; a threatening danger. *Ex.* A man-eating tiger *menaced* (*v.*) a large district in India for a whole year.

mend *v.* To restore something to its original good condition; to repair.

mental *adj.* Connected with the mind. *Ex. Mental* arithmetic is worked out *mentally* (*adv.*) without anything being written down. One's *mentality* (men-*tal*-i-ti; *n.*) is the sort of mind one has.

mention (*men*-sh'n) *v.* To refer to or speak about. *Ex.* Don't *mention* this letter to anyone.

menu (*men*-yoo) *v.* A card or list stating the different foods which will be served at a meal.

mercenary (*mer*-sen-a-ri) *adj.* Working only for money; greedy for money. *Mercenaries* (*n.*) are hired soldiers who fight in foreign armies.

merchandise (*mer*-chan-dys) *n.* Goods that are bought and sold.

merchant (*mer*-chant) *n.* One who buys and sells goods, especially if trading with foreign countries. The *Merchant Navy* consists of shipping engaged in trade.

mercury (*mer*-kyU-ri) *n.* A heavy, silvery, poisonous metallic liquid, used in thermometers etc.; quicksilver.

mercy (*mer*-si) *n.* Pity for and forgiveness towards, shown by kindness. *Ex.* The prisoner begged his captors for *mercy.* One who shows *mercy* is *merciful* (*adj.*); one who does not is *merciless.*

mere (meer) *adj.* Nothing more than. *Ex.* It was *mere* chance that I met her. We *merely* (*adv.*) waved to each other, as we were too busy to stop.

merge (merj) *v.* To join into one. *Ex* The two rivers *merge* at this point.

meringue (me-*rang*) *n.* A light cake made of sugar and egg-white.

merit (*me*-rit) 1. *n.* (a) A good or praiseworthy quality; worth. *Ex.* He is a man of *merit.* (b) What one deserves. *Ex.* He should be judged according to his *merits* (deserts). *Meritorious* (*adj.*) conduct is conduct worthy of praise. 2. *v.* To deserve, to earn. *Ex.* His conduct *merits* severe condemnation.

mermaid (*mer*-mayd) *n.* An imaginary woman living in the sea, with the tail of a fish instead of legs.

merry *adj.* Gay and cheerful.

mesh (mesh) *n.* One of the open spaces in network. To become *enmeshed* is to be entangled in a net.

mesmerize (*mez*-mer-yz) *v. See* hypnotize.

mess *n.* (a) A state of untidiness and dirt; confusion. (b) A group of officers or men of the armed services who eat together; the place where they eat.

message (*mes*-ij) *n.* Information sent from one person to another. The person who carries the *message* is the *messenger* (*n.*).

metal (*met*-al) *n.* One of the elements of the earth. *Metals* are usually shiny, can be joined with another metal, and shaped into various objects. *Ex.* Iron, copper and gold are *metals*, or *metallic* (*adj.*) substances.

metaphor (*met*-a-for) *n.* A figure of speech in which something is described in words belonging to something else. *Ex.* When the politician spoke of 'moving into troubled waters', he meant 'expecting difficulties in the future'.

meteor (*mee*-ti-or) *n.* A mass of rock or metal from outer space, which gives off light as it enters the earth's atmosphere, and is often called a shooting star. A *meteor* does not reach the earth; a *meteorite* (*mee*-ti-or-yt; *n.*) does.

meteorology (mee-ti-or-*rol*-o-ji) *n.* The study of the state of the atmosphere, especially so that the weather can be forecast, by *meteorologists* (*n.*).

meter (*mee*-ter) *n.* An instrument which measures the amount of something used, such as gas or electricity.

method (*meth*-od) *n.* The way of doing something. *Ex.* There are many *methods* of cooking eggs. A *methodical* (meth-*od*-ik-al; *adj.*) person is one who does things in an orderly way.

metre (*mee*-ter) *n.* (a) The rhythm in poetry, which depends on the stress (emphasis) on the syllables. (b) A unit of length, about 39.37 inches.

metropolis (me-*trop*-o-lis) *n.* The chief city of a country. *Ex.* Paris is the French *metropolis*.

mettle (*met*'l) *n.* Character, spirit, courage. *Ex.* A man of *mettle*. To be on one's *mettle* means to be ready to do one's best. *Ex.* The football team will be on its *mettle* on Friday.

microbe (*my*-krohb) *n.* A tiny (microscopic) form of life, especially one that causes disease.

microphone (*my*-kro-fohn) *n.* The device into which a broad-caster etc. speaks and which converts the sounds into electrical pulses that are then passed on by radio.

microscope (*my*-kro-skohp) *n.* A magnifying instrument which makes it possible to see objects or details which cannot be seen by the naked eye.

mid- is a prefix meaning in the middle of. *Ex. Midday, midnight, midsummer, midway, midstream.*

middle *n.* The point half-way between the two ends of anything; the centre. *Ex.* There are three rocks in the *middle* of the stream, and I jumped on to the *middle* (*adj.*) one.

midge *n.* A tiny gnat-like insect, often found near water; some kinds sting.

midget (*mi*-jet) 1. *n.* A very small person. 2. *adj.* Very small. *Ex. Midget* submarines.

midwife *n.* A nurse who helps a mother at the birth of her baby.

might (myt) *n.* Power, strength. *Mighty* (*adj.*) means having great power or strength.

migrate (my-*grayt*) *v.* To leave a country and go to live in another. *Ex.* Swallows *migrate* from Africa to England every summer.

mild (myld) *adj.* Gentle in nature; gently and pleasantly affecting one's senses. *Ex.* The weather is *mild* enough to sit out of doors.

mile *n.* A measure of distance, about 1.6 kilometres. *Mileage* (*n.*) means the total number of miles. A *milestone* (*n.*) is a roadside stone showing the number of miles from that spot to near-by towns.

militant (*mil*-i-tant) *adj.* Aggressive; active in fighting for a cause.

military (*mil*-i-ta-ri) *adj.* Connected with soldiers, armies and warfare. *Ex.* A *military* hospital; *military* music.

mill *n.* A building in which certain kinds of work are done, such as grinding corn into flour, making cotton into cloth etc. A *miller* is a man who owns or manages a *flour-mill*.

million (*mil*-yon) *n.* A thousand thousands (1,000,000). A *million-aire* (*n.*) is one who owns a million pounds or more.

mime (mym) *v.* To express something by gesture and expression of the face only, without uttering words, especially as entertainment. *Mime* (*n.*) is used in ballet to show the characters' feelings and to help tell the story.

mince (mins) *v.* To chop into very small pieces.

mincemeat (*mins*-meet) *n.* A sweet mixture of chopped fruit, nuts etc., eaten in pies at Christmas.

mind 1. *n.* The part of ourselves by which we feel conscious, think, learn, feel and remember. To make up one's *mind* is to decide about something. 2. *v.* To pay attention to; to take care of. *Ex.* She is going to *mind* the baby while her mother is out. *Mindful* (*adj.*) means thoughtful, not forgetting.

mine *n.* (a) A place from which minerals are dug, often from deep below the earth's surface. A worker in a mine is called a *miner*. (b) A kind of bomb.

mineral (*min*-er-al) *n.* A substance found in or on the earth which is neither animal nor vegetable; anything dug from a mine, such as coal, iron, salt, gold etc.

mingle (*ming*-g'l) *v.* To mix. *Ex.* The thief escaped by *mingling* with the crowd.

miniature (*min*-ya-cher) 1. *adj.* Very small. 2. *n.* A very small painted portrait.

minimum (*min*-i-mum) *n.* The very smallest amount or size. *Ex.* The *minimum* club subscription is £1, but you may pay more if you wish. To *minimize* (*v.*) something is to treat it as lightly as possible. *Ex.* They were warned not to *minimize* the risk of fire.

minister (*min*-is-ter) 1. *n.* (a) The politician in charge of a government department. (b) A clergyman, usually of a Noncon-formist Church. 2. *v.* To serve or give help to. *Ex.* Doctors and nurses *minister* to the sick.

ministry (*min*-is-tri) *n.* (a) The work of a minister of a church. (b) A government department; the Cabinet. *Ex.* The *Ministry of Defence.*

mink *n.* An animal of northern forests, living near water, and related to the weasel. It is also bred on mink farms for its valuable fur.

minnow (*min*-oh) *n.* A small freshwater fish, often used as bait.

minor (*my*-nor) 1. *adj.* Small; not serious or important. *Ex.* He had only *minor* injuries. 2. *n.* A person not yet adult.

minority (myn-*or*-i-ti) *n.* The smaller number in a divided group. *Ex.* Most people agreed with him, but a *minority* disagreed.

mint 1. *n.* (a) A sweet-smelling herb used in cooking. (b) A government factory where coins are made. 2. *v.* To make coins.

minus (*my*-nus) *n.* A Latin word meaning less, used in arithmetic. *Ex.* Five *minus* three leaves two.

minute (my-*newt*) *adj.* Very small. *Ex.* There are *minute* living creatures in river water, which can be seen only under a microscope.

minute (*min*-it) *n.* (a) A sixtieth part of an hour. (b) *Minutes* (*pl.*) are the official record of what took place at a meeting.

miracle (*mi*-ra-k'l) *n.* A happening that does not obey the laws of nature; something very extraordinary or marvellous. *Ex.* We escaped by a *miracle*; it was a *miraculous* (mi-*rak*-ew-lus; *adj.*) escape.

mirror (*mi*-ror) *n.* A glass that reflects. *Ex.* If you look in a *mirror* you see your reflection.

mirth (murth) *n.* Fun and laughter.

mis- is a prefix which, placed before a verb, means badly or wrongly. *Ex.* To *mispronounce* is to pronounce wrongly. Similar words are: *misapply, miscount, misguide, misinform, misjudge, misplace, misread, mis-spell, mis-state, misunderstand, misuse.* When placed before a noun it means bad or wrong. *Ex.* A *misadventure* is an unlucky accident. Similar words are: *misconduct, misdeed, misrule.*

miscellaneous (mis-el-*ayn*-i-us) *adj.* Mixed, of different kinds. *Ex.* Her handbag was crammed with *miscellaneous* objects.

mischief (*mis*-chif) *n.* Harm, damage; fun of a kind that does no harm. *Mischievous* (*mis*-che-vus; *adj.*) means (a) doing harm; (b) full of fun, impish.

miser (*my*-zer) *n.* One who hoards money; an exceptionally stingy person.

miserable (*miz*-er-a-b'l) *adj.* Unhappy, wretched. *Misery* (*n.*) is unhappiness, the state of being miserable.

misfit *n.* That does not fit properly; used, for example, of clothes or of a person who does not fit into his job. *Ex.* He is a *misfit* in this office.

misfortune (mis-*fawr*-ch'n) *n.* A disaster; bad luck.

misgiving *n.* A fear of what may happen; suspicion; anxiety. *Ex.* I hope I've passed the exam, but I have *misgivings* about it

mishap (*mis*-hap) *n.* A small accident, such as knocking something over.

mislay (mis-*lay*) *v.* To put something in the wrong place and then be unable to find it.

mislead (mis-*leed*) *v.* To deceive, either on purpose or by mistake. *Ex.* She was *misled* into thinking it was too late.

missile (*mis*-yl) *n.* Something, usually a weapon, thrown or otherwise sent into the air; for instance, a spear thrown by hand, or a bomb launched by rocket.

mission (*mish*-'n) *v.* (a) A group of people sent abroad for a particular purpose. *Ex.* A scientific *mission* was sent to the Falkland Islands. (b) The purpose for which they are sent. (c) A group of missionaries; their headquarters.

missionary (*mish*-on-a-ri) *n.* A person sent on a mission, usually abroad, to spread religion.

mist *n.* A cloud of very fine drops of moisture in the air, making it difficult to see clearly. *Ex.* It is often *misty* (*adj.*) on the hills but quite clear lower down.

mistake (mis-*tayk*) 1. *n.* Something done wrongly or wrongly understood. 2. *v.* To make an error; to understand wrongly; to take one thing for another. *Ex.* It is easy to *mistake* a rook for a crow, they are so alike. One can be *mistaken* (*adj.*) about them.

mistletoe (*mi*-s'l-toh) *n.* A plant with poisonous white berries, which gets its nourishment from the tree it grows on, and is used as a Christmas decoration.

mix *v.* To put two or more things together so that they are spread about among each other to form a *mixture* (*n.*). One can make a *mixture* by stirring flour and sugar together, for example. *Mixed* (*adj.*) means consisting of different things; confused. *Ex.* I have *mixed* feelings about that.

moan (mohn) *n.* A low, sad cry, as from one in pain. *Ex.* The injured boy gave no answer, but went on *moaning* (*v.*).

moat (moht) *n.* A deep ditch filled with water as a defence round a castle. The castle could then be reached only if a hinged bridge (a drawbridge) was lowered.

mob *n.* A crowd, especially a disorderly one.

mobilize (*moh*-bil-yz) *v.* To make ready to move, especially the armed services when war is threatened.

mock 1. *v.* To make fun of and jeer at. 2. *adj.* Imitation, not real. *Ex.* Fencing is a *mock* duel.

mode (mohd) *n.* A way of doing something; a fashion. *Ex.* Living in a caravan is a *mode* of life that makes no appeal to me.

model (*mod'*l) 1. *n.* (a) A small but exact copy of something larger. *Ex.* He collects *model* railway engines. (b) One who poses for an artist, or to display clothes in a shop etc. 2. *v.* (a) To make into a shape. *Ex.* He *modelled* a duck in clay. (b) To wear a garment to show to customers. 3. *adj.* Good enough to be copied or imitated. *Ex.* This is a *model* sports centre, the best of its kind.

moderate (*mod*-er-at) *adj.* Reasonable, not excessive; of medium size; not very good. *Ex.* There was a *moderate* breeze, so they quite enjoyed their sail.

modern (*mod*-ern) *adj.* In or of recent times; not old-fashioned, in the style of today. To *modernize* (*v.*) something is to bring it up to date.

modest (*mod*-est) *adj.* Not conceited; not drawing attention to oneself. *Ex.* He showed great *modesty* (*n.*) when talking of his war service.

modify (*mod*-i-fy) *v.* To alter partly but not completely. *Ex.* He *modified* his design for a new aircraft, as he realized that it would cost too much.

moist *adj.* Damp. *Ex.* Postage stamps must be *moistened* (*v.*) before they will stick. The sun is drying up the puddles, but there is still *moisture* (*n.*) on the roofs.

mole *n.* (a) A small brown spot on the face or body. (b) A small black velvety-coated animal which burrows into holes.

molest (moh-*lest*) *v.* To pester and annoy; to interfere with aggressively. *Ex.* When they visited the market-place they were *molested* by beggars.

mollify (*mol*-i-fy) *v.* To calm, soothe or satisfy. *Ex.* The angry man was *mollified* when the boys apologized.

molten (*mohl*-ten) *adj.* Melted.

momentary (*moh*-men-ta-ri) *adj.* Lasting only for a moment. *Ex.* She felt only *momentary* pain when given an injection.

monarch (*mon*-ark) *n.* A king, queen or emperor. A *monarchy* (*n.*) is a country ruled by a *monarch*.

monastery (*mon*-as-ter-i) *n.* The building monks live in; a community of monks.

mongrel (*mung*-grel) *adj.* Of unknown mixed breed; not pure-bred. *Ex.* A dog bred from an Airedale and a wolfhound would be a *mongrel* (*n.*).

monitor (*mon*-i-tor) 1. *n.* A pupil at school who is made responsible for something. *Ex.* A *flower monitor*. 2. *v.* To check broadcasts for information or quality.

monk (mungk) *n.* A man who lives in a monastery according to a religious rule. He owns and earns nothing, does not marry, and spends his time in prayer and good works.

monkey (*mung*-ki) *v.* A long-tailed furry animal which can stand on its hind legs and use its forelegs much as we use our hands and arms.

monogram (*mon*-o-gram) *n.* Letters, especially a person's initials, interwoven into one design.

monopolize (mon-*op*-o-lyz) *v.* To take over entirely for oneself. *Ex.* He *monopolized* the lecturer's attention so that no one else could ask questions.

monotonous (mon-*ot*-on-us) *adj.* Dull; having no change or variety. *Ex.* He found his stay in hospital *monotonous*; every day seemed the same.

monsoon (mon-*soon*) *n.* A season in southern Asia when strong winds blow steadily in one direction for several months; the heavy rains brought by the south-west *monsoon*.

monster (*mon*-ster) 1. *n.* (a) A large imaginary creature, often made up of features from different animals. Myths and fairy-tales are full of monsters, such as the Giant that Jack killed. (b) A cruel, wicked person. *Ex.* Only a *monster* could have behaved with such cruelty. 2. *adj.* Huge.

monstrous (*mon*-strus) *adj.* (a) Having the qualities of a *monster*; horrible. (b) Huge.

monument (*mon*-ew-ment) *n.* A pillar, statue or other object, usually of stone, set up in memory of a person or event. *Ex.* The Cenotaph in London is a *monument* to honour the dead of the two World Wars.

mood *n.* A state of mind. You can be in a happy *mood*, a sad *mood* or a bad *mood*. To be *moody* (*adj.*) is to be inclined to have bad *moods*.

moon *n.* The planet (earth's satellite) which travels round the earth once every month. It reflects the light of the sun, which is what we call *moonlight* (*n.*).

moor 1. *n.* A high-lying region of uncultivated land growing little but heather and bracken. 2. *v.* To fasten a boat by rope or cable to a *mooring* (*n.*) ashore, or to a buoy afloat.

mope (mohp) *v.* To be sad and dull, usually because of loneliness. *Ex.* Our budgerigar is *moping* and listless since his mate died.

moral (*mo*-ral) 1. *n.* Kind of right behaviour pointed out by a story, as in Aesop's *Fables*. 2. *adj.* Of good and right behaviour; the opposite of *immoral* (*adj.*). *Immoral* means bad or wicked; *amoral* (*ay*-mo-ral; *adj.*) means with no sense of right and wrong at all. *Morals* (*pl.*) are the accepted standards of right and wrong; or a person's behaviour as judged by those standards. *Ex.* His *morals* are far from perfect.

morale (mo-*rahl*) *n.* The state of courage, discipline and confidence possessed, especially by soldiers and others in wartime. *Ex.* After their defeat, the army's *morale* was low.

morbid *adj.* Liking the gruesome and unwholesome; diseased in mind or body.

moreover (maw-*roh*-ver) *adv.* Also, besides. *Ex.* She is tall and fair and, *moreover*, beautiful.

Morse *n.* A code of dots and dashes standing for letters of the alphabet, used in sending messages by telegraph, radio, flashing lights etc.

morsel *n.* A small piece, usually of food.

mortal (*mawr*-t'l) 1. *adj.* Certain to die, as all living creatures are, one day; fatal. 2. *n.* A human being.

mortar (*mawr*-tar) *n.* A cement used to join bricks or stones in building.

mortgage (*mawr*-gij) *n.* The legal agreement between a house-owner and a lender of money (a building society, for example) by which many people buy their houses.

mosaic (moh-*zay*-ik) *n.* A kind of decoration for pavements etc., using small pieces of coloured stone, glass etc. to make a pattern or picture.

mosquito (mos-*kee*-to) *n.* A flying insect larger than a gnat, with an irritating bite which may cause disease, especially malaria.

moss *n.* A small green plant that grows in damp places, sometimes on trees, stones and walls.

moth *n.* An insect very like a butterfly, but seen mostly at night.

motion (*moh*-sh'n) *n.* Movement. *Ex.* The ship's rolling *motion* made some passengers sea-sick. *Motionless* (*adj.*) means making no movement.

motive (*moh*-tiv) *n.* Reason or purpose. *Ex.* We don't know his *motive* for selling his bicycle.

motor (*moh*-tor) *n.* An engine which supplies power for movement. It may be driven by petrol, electricity etc. A *motor-car* (more often called a car) is driven by petrol.

motorway *n.* A road especially built for fast traffic; it can be crossed only by bridge or tunnel.

mottled (*mo*-t'ld) *adj.* With coloured patches over the suface. *Ex.* His face was *mottled* with freckles. Some deer and other creatures have *mottled* skins.

motto (*mot*-oh) *n.* A short sentence which states a well-known truth or a rule of conduct, rather as a proverb does. *Ex.* 'Least said, soonest mended'. You may find a *motto* on a school badge or a coat of arms.

mould (mohld) 1. *n.* (a) A greenish fungus that appears on things left in a damp place; they are then said to be *mouldy* (*adj.*). (b) A shape into which a jelly etc. may be poured, the jelly setting into the shape of the mould. 2. *v.* To form into a shape.

moult (mohlt) *v.* (Of a bird) To shed old feathers before getting new ones; to shed hair, as a cat or dog may do.

mound (mownd) *n.* A heap of earth, stones, sand etc.

mount (mownt) 1. *n.* A mountain or high hill. 2. *v.* (a) To climb up on, as on to a platform or a horse. To get off a horse is to *dismount* (*v.*). (b) To put something on a background in order to display it; for example, a photograph on cardboard, a jewel on gold.

mountain (*mown*-ten) *n.* A large mass of high land, much bigger than a hill. *Ex* Switzerland is a *mountainous* (*adj.*) country. A *mountaineer* (*n.*) is a *mountain-climber*.

mourn (mawrn) *v.* To grieve or feel great sorrow, especially for someone's death. To be *mournful* (*adj.*) is to be sad.

mouse (mows) *n.* A small furry gnawing animal which lives in the fields or is a pest in houses.

moustache (mus-*tahsh*) *n.* The hair growing on a man's upper lip.

move (moov) 1. *v.* (a) To go, carry or take from one place to another. (b) To affect one's feelings. *Ex.* He was *moved* to tears by their kindness to him in his distress. 2. *n.* The act of *moving*. *Ex.* A group stood round the chess-board, watching the final *moves*. *Movable* (*adj.*) means able to be moved.

mow (moh) *v.* To cut down, as grass is cut for hay, or a lawn is cut by a *lawn-mower* (*n.*).

mucus (*mew*-kus) *n.* The slimy substance which covers, lubricates and protects the inner linings of various parts of the body, such as the nose and throat.

mud *n.* Wet earth. *Ex.* A football ground gets *muddy* (*adj.*) in wet weather.

muddle *n.* Untidiness or confusion. To be in a *muddle* is to have things lying about, all mixed up. To feel *muddled* (*adj.*) about something is to feel puzzled and confused.

muffin (*muf*-in) *n.* A thick, flat, bread-like cake, served toasted and buttered.

muffle (*mu*-f'l) *v.* (a) To wrap up in order to keep warm. *Ex.* He *muffled* himself in rugs to keep out the cold. A *muffler* (*n.*) is a warm scarf. (b) To wrap round in order to deaden sound. *Ex.* The church bells were *muffled* to make them sound less loudly.

multiply (*mul*-ti-ply) *v.* (a) To increase in number. *Ex.* Insects *multiply* quickly in hot weather. (b) To increase numbers in arithmetic by *multiplication* (*n.*).

multitude (*mul*-ti-tewd) *n.* A great number, a crowd.

mumble (*mum*-b'l) *v.* To speak indistinctly. *Ex.* I didn't hear what you said; you were *mumbling* so.

mummy (*mum*-i) *n.* A dead body preserved from decay by embalming; they have been found in Ancient Egyptian tombs.

munch *v.* To chew noisily.

municipal (mew-*nis*-i-p'l) *adj.* Connected with a town council or similar body.

munitions (mew-*nish*'nz) *n.* Weapons and equipment for waging war, such as guns or ammunition.

murder (*mur*-der) *v.* To kill a person deliberately, other than in warfare.

murky (*mur*-ki) *adj.* Dark and gloomy.

murmur (*mur*-mer) *v.* To speak in a low voice. *Ex.* The invalid's low *murmur* (*n.*) could only just be heard.

muscle (*mu*-s'l) *n.* One of the bundles of fibres in the body which make movement possible, by stretching or contracting. A very strong person is said to be *muscular* (*mus*-kew-lar; *adj.*).

museum (mew-*zee*-um) *n.* A building in which are displayed objects of interest connected with the past, natural history, art, science etc.

mushroom (*mush*-room) *n.* An edible umbrella-shaped fungus, which grows wild or may be cultivated.

music (*mew* zik) *n.* The art of combining sounds for voice or instrument in a way that will affect the listener by its beauty, emotional power etc. A person skilled and gifted in music is a *musician* (mew-*zish*-'n; *n.*).

mussel (*mus*'l) *n.* A small shellfish of salt and fresh water. The *sea-mussel*'s body is enclosed between two dark-blue shells, and is edible.

mustard (*mus*-tard) *n.* A yellow hot tasting powder, made from the seed of the *mustard plant*, and served as flavouring with beef etc.

muster *v.* To collect together, especially a group of people for inspection or roll-call.

musty *adj.* Stale and spoiled by damp; not fresh. *Ex.* The old house smelled *musty* after being shut up for so long.

mute (mewt) *adj.* Silent; dumb.

mutilate (*mew*-til-ayt) *v.* To injure seriously; to remove an essential part of. *Ex.* Two of the soldiers were badly *mutilated*, one having lost both legs and the other an arm.

mutiny (*mew*-tin-i) *n.* A refusal to obey orders, especially by members of a ship's crew or of the armed forces. One who *mutinies* (*v.*) is called a *mutineer* (*n.*).

mutter (*mut*-er) *v.* To speak in a low voice, hardly opening the mouth, and often in a complaining way.

mutton (*mut*-on) *n.* The flesh of the sheep used as food.

mutual (*mew*-tew-al) *adj.* Concerning something which two people both do, feel etc. towards each other. *Ex.* By *mutual* consent they agreed to share the prize-money.

muzzle (*muz*-'l) 1. *n.* (a) The part of an animal's head, including the nose and head, which sticks forward. (b) A sort of cage of straps and wire put over an animal's mouth to prevent it biting or eating. 2. *v.* To put a *muzzle* on an animal.

myriad (*mi*-ri-ad) *n.* Too large a number to be counted, as the grains of sand on a beach.

mystery (*mis*-ter-i) *n.* Something strange that cannot be understood or explained. *Ex. Mystery* (*adj.*) stories are exciting to read.

mystify (*mis*-ti-fy) *v.* To puzzle or confuse. *Ex.* The conjurer *mystified* the children, who could not see how the birds got into his hat.

myth (mith) *n.* (a) A story from the distant past in which men tried to explain natural happenings or an event in their lives. (b) An imaginary person, thing or event. *Mythology* (*n.*) is the study of myths.

N

nag 1. *n.* A small riding-horse; a poor-looking horse. 2. *v.* To be always finding fault.

naïve (nah-*eev*) *adj.* Innocently simple in outlook; without experience of the world; too ready to believe all one hears, and therefore likely to be deceived by rogues.

naked (*nay*-kid) *adj.* Having no clothes or covering on.

nape (nayp) *n.* The back of the neck.

napkin *n.* (a) A square cloth for wiping the fingers and lips at table. (b) A square of absorbent cloth folded to make panties for a baby. Often called a *nappy*.

narcissus (nar-*sis*-us) *n.* The scientific name of a large group of flowers, including the daffodils.

narcotic (nar-*kot*-ik) *n.* A drug that causes sleep, used in medicine.

narrate (na-*rayt*) *v.* To tell or give an account of. One who tells a story is a *narrator* (*n.*), and his story is a *narrative* (*na*-ra-tiv; *n.*).

nasal (*nay*-zal) *adj.* Connected with the nose.

nasty (*nah*-sti) *adj.* Not pleasant; the opposite of nice.

nation (*nay*-sh'n) *n.* The inhabitants of one country under one government.

national (*nash*-on-al) *adj.* Belonging to the whole nation. To belong to the British *nation* is to be of British *nationality* (*n.*). To *nationalize* (*v.*) an industry etc. is to take it out of private hands and put it under the ownership of the *nation*.

native (*nay*-tiv) 1. *n.* A person born in a particular place. *Ex.* He is a *native* of Birmingham. 2. *adj.* Belonging to the place where one was born. *Ex.* France is his *native* country and French his *native* language.

natural (*nach*-ral) *adj.* According to nature. *Ex.* It is *natural* for a dog to bark and a cat to mew. Her hair is *naturally* (*adv.*) curly; it has always been that way.

nature (*nay*-cher) *n.* (a) The world of things not made by man; animals, birds, plants, the sea, clouds etc. (b) A person's character or disposition. *Ex.* He was born with a kind, friendly *nature*.

naughty (*naw*-ti) *adj.* (Of children) Badly behaved, disobedient.

nautical (*naw*-ti-kal) *adj.* Connected with ships and travel by sea.

naval (*nay*-val) *adj.* Connected with the *navy*.

nave *n.* The main central part of a church where the congregation sits, from the west door up to the choir.

navel (*nay*-vel) *n.* The small hollow in the middle of the abdomen.

navigate (*nav*-i-gayt) *v.* To direct the course (way to go) of a ship or aeroplane, by charts, instruments, observations etc. This work is done by the *navigator* (*n.*). A *navigable* (*adj.*) river is one that can be used by shipping.

navvy (*na*-vi) *n.* A labourer who does the digging in making roads, railways etc.

navy (*nay*-vi) *n.* A country's ships of war and their crews. *Navy-blue* is the dark blue of *naval* uniforms.

neat *adj.* Tidy, carefully arranged; simply made. *Ex.* You can have a *neat* dress, or write *neatly* (*adv.*). The *neatness* (*n.*) of writing makes it easier to read.

necessary (*nes*-es-a-ri) *adj.* That which cannot be done without. *Ex.* Food and drink are *necessary* for life.

necessity (nes-*es*-i-ti) *n.* A thing that is a necessary; need.

nectar (*nek*-tar) *n.* The sweet substance which bees collect from flowers to make honey.

needless (*need*-les) *adj.* Unnecessary. *Ex.* My mother's worries about our safety were *needless*, for we are all good swimmers.

negative (*neg*-a-tiv) *n.* (a) A word or reply denying or forbidding. The word 'no' is a *negative*. *Ex.* When asked if he had seen an elephant he replied in the *negative*, meaning that he hadn't seen one. (b) A camera film showing a *negative* image, from which positive prints are taken.

neglect (neg-*lekt*) *v.* To pay no attention to; to treat without care or affection. *Ex.* He *neglected* his hamster, and it nearly died of *neglect* (*n.*).

negligent (*neg*-li-jent) *adj.* Neglectful; inclined to neglect. *Ex.* He is *negligent* in his duties as club secretary, and some letters never get answered.

negotiate (neg-*oh*-shi-ayt) *v.* To arrange something or try to come to an agreement by discussion. *Ex.* When the war was over a peace treaty was *negotiated*.

negro (*nee*-groh) *n.* A member of the black-skinned races of Africa, or of African origin; a black.

neigh (nay) *n.* The cry made by a horse.

neighbour (*nay*-bor) *n.* One who lives next door, or very near by.

neighbourhood (*nay*-bor-hUd) *n.* The district near a certain place. *Ex.* People usually use the schools, shops, doctor etc. in their own *neighbourhood*.

neither (*ny*-dher) *adj., pron.* and *conj.* Not either.

nephew (*nev*-ew) *n.* The son of a person's brother or sister.

nerve (nurv) *n.* One of the fibres which carry messages between the brain and other parts of the body. A *nervous* (*adj.*) person is one easily upset or frightened.

nest *n.* The home built by birds etc. in which to rear their young. A *nestling* (*nes*-ling; *n.*) is a very young bird not yet able to fly.

nestle (*nes*'l) *v.* To lie close and cosy, as a bird does in its nest or a baby in its mother's arms.

net *n.* Cord, thread etc. knotted to form equal-sized spaces linked together. *Ex.* A fishing *net*, tennis *net*, *hairnet*, wire *netting*.

nettle *n.* A weed with fine leaf-hairs which sting. When a person is irritated he can be said to be *nettled* (*v.*).

neurotic (newr-*ot*-ik) *adj.* Continually nervous; giving way to unnecessary worry, anxiety, suspicion etc.

neuter (*new*-ter) *adj.* Neither masculine nor feminine.

neutral (*new*-tral) *adj.* Not taking either side in a dispute, especially in a war. *Ex.* Switzerland was *neutral* throughout both World Wars.

nevertheless (nev-er-dhe-*les*) *adv.* In spite of that; all the same. *Ex.* We didn't enjoy the play, but we stayed till the end, *nevertheless*.

news *n.* Information about recent events. *Newspapers* are papers containing *news*, published daily or weekly and sold by *newsagents* (*n.*).

newt *n.* A small amphibian (able to live in and out of water) with a tail, and looking rather like a lizard.

nibble *v.* To take very small bites at.

niche (nich) *n.* A space hollowed out in a wall where a statue or ornament may be placed; a suitable position in life for a person, animal etc.

nickel (*nik*-'l) *n.* A silvery-white metal.

nickname *n.* An extra name which people may be called by, sometimes in friendly fun, sometimes in mockery. *Ex.* People with red hair may be *nicknamed* (*v.*) 'Carrots', 'Coppernob' or 'Ginger'.

nicotine (*nik* o-teen) *n.* A poisonous substance found in tobacco leaves.

niece (nees) *n.* The daughter of a person's brother or sister.

niggardly (*nig*-ard-li) *adj.* Not generous; mean.

nightingale (*nyt*-ing-gayl) *n.* A small brown bird, a summer visitor to Britain, with a beautiful song heard at night and also by day.

nightmare (*nyt*-mair) *n.* A frightening dream.

nil *n.* Nothing.

nimble *adj.* Able to move quickly and easily.

nitrogen (*nyt*-ro-jen) *n.* A gas which makes up about three-quarters of the air around us.

noble (*noh*-b'l) 1. *n.* A person (*nobleman* or *noblewoman*) with an inherited title, such as an earl or a duchess. They form the *nobility* (*n.*) of a country. 2. *adj.* (a) Belonging to the *nobility*. (b) Having or showing fine character or high ideals. *Ex.* He bore his misfortunes *nobly* (*adv.*), without complaint or resentment, showing great *nobility* (*n.*) of character.

nocturnal (nok-*tur*-nal) *adj.* Happening at night; active at night, as some creatures are, such as owls or bats.

nod *v.* To move the head quickly downward, in greeting, as a command or to mean 'yes'. *Ex.* He *nodded* his agreement; his reply was a *nod* (*n.*).

nominate (*nom*-in-ayt) *v.* To name for a particular post or job; to put someone up as a candidate. *Ex.* I was *nominated* for a seat on the committee; I don't know who made the *nomination* (*n.*).

nondescript (*non*-des-kript) *adj.* Having no distinguishing or striking feature or character. *Ex.* He was a *nondescript* individual, wearing *nondescript* clothes.

nonsense (*non*-sens) *n.* Words or ideas that make no sense and are absurd.

nook (nUk) *n.* A quiet and secluded corner.

noon *n.* Twelve o'clock in the middle of the day, when the sun reaches its highest point in the sky.

noose (noos) *n.* A loop of rope whose knot can be tightened when there is a pull on it, used in capturing cattle etc.

normal *adj.* Ordinary, usual. *Ex.* The *normal* time to start morning school is nine o'clock.

north *n.* The direction to a person's left if he is facing the rising sun. A *northerly* (*adj.*) wind comes from the north.

nostalgia (nos-*tal*-ji-a) *n.* A longing for past times; homesickness.

nostril (*nos*-tril) *n.* One of the openings in the nose.

notable (*noht*-a-b'l) *adj.* Important or remarkable.

notch *v.* To make a V-shaped cut in something, especially for a record, as Robinson Crusoe did to record the number of days he spent on his desert island.

note 1. *n.* (a) A short record of some fact to help remember it. (b) A short informal letter. (c) A *bank-note*. (d) A particular musical sound; its written sign. 2. *v.* (a) To make a *note* of. (b) To pay attention to.

noted *adj.* Famous, well known.

noteworthy *adj.* Worthy of being known and remembered.

notice (*noh*-tis) 1. *n.* A printed or written message placed where it will be easily seen. *Ex.* The *notice* in the gardens said 'No dogs allowed'. 2. *v.* To see and pay attention to. *Ex.* I *noticed* that she wasn't keen on the idea; her lack of enthusiasm was very *noticeable* (*adj.*).

notify (*noh*-ti-fy) *v.* To inform someone about something. *Ex.* Everyone was *notified* of the doctor's surgery hours.

notion (*noh*-shon) *n.* Idea or understanding of. *Ex.* She will never manage to cook the dinner; she has no *notion* of how to start.

notorious (noh-*tawr*-i-us) *adj.* Famous for bad qualities. *Ex.* Dick Turpin was a *notorious* highwayman.

nougat (*noo*-gah) *n.* A kind of white toffee made of sugar, almonds, honey and egg-white.

nought (nawt) *n.* Nothing; the figure '0'.

noun (nown) *n.* A word used to name a thing, person or place.

nourish (*nu*-rish) *v.* To feed with food good for the body's needs. This is *nourishment* (*n.*).

novel (*nov*-el) 1. *adj.* New or unusual. *Ex.* A trip in an aeroplane at the airshow was a *novel* way of celebrating his birthday; it was a *novelty* (*n.*). 2. *n.* A story long enough to fill a whole book. One who writes *novels* is a *novelist* (*n.*).

novice (*nov*-is) *n.* A beginner in anything; a monk or nun on probation.

nowadays *adv.* At the present time.

nozzle (*no*-z'l) *n.* The opening at the end of a pipe or tube to let the water etc. through.

nuclear (*new*-kli-ar) *adj.* To do with atomic energy; to do with the *nucleus* of something.

nucleus (*new*-kli-us) *n.* The central part of an atom, cell etc.

nude (newd) *adj.* Without clothing, naked.

nudge *v.* To push someone lightly with the elbow to draw his attention.

nugget (*nug*-et) *n.* A rough lump of gold as it is found when in the ground.

nuisance (*new*-sans) *n.* Something which is troublesome or annoying. *Ex.* What a *nuisance*! The milkman has left us no milk.

numb (num) *adj.* Having no feeling, usually because of cold. *Ex.* Our fingers were *numb* after snowballing.

numeral (*new*-mer-ral) *n.* A sign standing for a number, as the numeral '2' stands for 'two'.

numerous (*new*-mer-rus) *adj.* Many.

nun *n.* A woman who gives up her life to religion, following the rule of a religious order, as a monk does. *Nuns* live in convents or *nunneries* (*n.*).

nurse *v.* To take care of a sick person, or look after a baby in place of its mother. A person trained in this kind of work is a *nurse* (*n.*).

nursery *n.* (a) The room in a house where babies and young children are cared for and brought up. A *nursery school* is a school for the very young. (b) A place where young plants and seeds are grown ready for sale or for planting in the garden.

nutmeg (*nut*-meg) *n.* A seed from a tropical plant, ground and used as spice.

nutritious (new-*trish*-us) *adj.* Full of nourishment.

nylon (*ny*-lon) *n.* A synthetic (man-made) thread of great strength, used for many purposes, including making stockings or tights.

O

oak *n.* A large tree which lives to a great age and provides strong, hard wood. Its fruit are acorns.

oar (awr) *n.* A long pole with one end broad and flat, used for rowing small boats.

oasis (oh-*ay*-sis) *n.* A place in the desert where there are trees and water.

oat *n.* A cereal plant which provides valuable food for humans and animals. Porridge is made from *oats* or *oatmeal* (*n.*).

oath (ohth) *n.* A solemn promise. A witness in a lawcourt takes an *oath* to speak the truth, as if before God.

obey (oh-*bay*) *v.* To do as one is told. One is then *obedient* (*adj.*); the opposite is *disobedient*.

obituary (o-*bit*-ew-a-ri) *n.* Notice of death. *Obituary* (*adj.*) notices appear in newspapers.

object (*ob*-jekt) *n.* (a) A thing. (b) A purpose. *Ex.* What was her *object* when she said that?

object (ob-*jekt*) *v.* To say one disapproves or disagrees. *Ex.* Some people *object* to smoking and think it an *objectionable* (*adj.*) habit.

objective (ob-*jek*-tive) *n.* An aim in view. *Ex.* His *objective* is a career in engineering.

oblige (ob-*lyj*) *v.* (a) To force or compel. *Ex.* She was *obliged* to go to bed as she had a temperature. (b) To do something to please, as a favour. *Ex.* The salesgirl was very *obliging* (*adj.*) and helped us find what we wanted.

oblique (ob-*leek*) *adj.* Slanting.

obliterate (ob-*lit*-er-ayt) *v.* To blot out completely. *Ex.* The writing was *obliterated* by paint spilt on the page.

oblivious (ob-*liv*-i-us) *adj.* Not noticing at all. *Ex.* He was so interested in his book that he was *oblivious* to the fact that everyone else had gone.

oblong (*ob*-long) *adj.* Having a shape with four sides, rather like a square but longer than it is broad. *Ex.* Books and house-doors are *oblong.*

obscure (ob-*skewr*) 1. *v.* To make dark or dim. Ex. A fog came down and *obscured* everything. 2. *adj.* Not well known; not easy to understand. *Ex.* The meaning of this poem is *obscure.*

observatory (ob-*zur*-va-tor-i) *n.* A building which contains telescopes etc. for *observing* the stars.

observe (ob-*zurv*) *n.* (a) To notice or pay attention to; to obey or keep to. *Ex.* We must *observe* the rule of the road. An *observant* (*adj.*) person is one who is good at noticing things. (b) To make a remark. *Ex.* He *observed* that it was cold out.

obsolete (*ob*-so-leet) *adj.* Out of date, no longer used. *Ex.* Muskets and swords are *obsolete* weapons.

obstacle (*ob*-sta-k'l) *n.* Something which hinders or gets in the way. There may be *obstacles* to the flow of traffic (fallen trees etc.), or *obstacles* specially placed on a track for an *obstacle-race.*

obstinate (*ob*-stin-at) *adj.* Wanting one's own way and refusing to give way; stubborn. *Ex.* He *obstinately* (*adv.*) refused to say 'thank you for the party'; he showed great *obstinacy* (*n.*).

obstruct (ob-*strukt*) *v.* To get in the way or hinder; to block up with obstacles; to make difficult to get by. *Ex.* A fall of rock *obstructed* the road; this *obstruction* (*n.*) had to be moved before we could get by.

obtain (ob-*tayn*) *v.* To get. Things which you can *obtain* are *obtainable* (*adj.*).

obtuse (ob-*tews*) *adj.* (a) Stupid, dull in mind. *Ex.* He seemed very *obtuse* and couldn't see what I meant. (b) In geometry an *obtuse* angle is one greater than 90° but less than 180°.

obvious (*ob*-vi-us) *adj.* Easily seen or understood. *Ex.* It's *obvious* you don't want to go.

occasion (ok-*ay*-zh'n) *n.* (a) An opportunity. *Ex.* I thought it a suitable *occasion* to ask for more pocket-money. (b) A special event. *Ex.* Her wedding is a great *occasion* in any girl's life. (c) A reason or cause. *Ex.* We're early, so there's no *occasion* to hurry.

occasional (ok-*ay*-zhon-al) *adj.* Happening sometimes, but not regularly or often. *Ex.* There were *occasional* showers but it was mostly sunny.

occupation (ok-ew-*pay*-sh'n) *n.* Business, profession, employment; what one is doing.

occupy (*ok*-ew-py) *v.* (a) To live in or take possession of. *Ex.* This house has been *occupied* by Mr Brown for years; he is the *occupier* (*n.*) or *occupant* (*n.*). (b) To be busy with. *Ex.* We have been *occupied* with our homework all evening.

occur (ok-*ur*) *v.* (a) To happen. *Ex.* The factory fire was a terrifying *occurrence* (*n.*). (b) To come into one's mind. *Ex.* It has just *occurred* to me that we've missed the last train.

ocean (*oh*-sh'n) *n.* A huge area of sea. The five great *oceans* occupy three-quarters of the earth's surface.

octave (*ok*-tiv) *n.* (In music) The interval between one note and the note eight full tones above or below it; as from C to C, or doh to doh.

octopus (*ok*-to-pus) *n.* A sea creature having eight long arms with suckers on them, which surround its mouth.

oculist (*ok*-ew-list) *n.* A doctor who treats defects and diseases of the eye.

odd *adj.* (a) (Of a number in arithmetic) With a remainder left over when divided by 2. *Ex.* 3, 5, 7 are *odd* numbers. (b) An extra, or just one of a pair. *Ex.* An *odd* shoe is one without the other of the pair. (c) Strange, unusual. *Ex.* The clowns were *oddly* (*adv.*) dressed.

ode (ohd) *n.* A lyric poem addressed to someone or something. *Ex.* Keats's 'Ode to a Nightingale'.

odious (*oh*-di-us) *adj.* Hateful.

offend (of-*end*) *v.* (a) To hurt someone's feelings. *Ex.* He was *offended* because I wouldn't lend him my camera; he took *offence* (*n.*).

offensive (of-*en*-siv) 1. *adj.* Unpleasant, disgusting (often used to describe a smell). 2. *n.* An attack. *Ex.* The general massed all his troops for a final *offensive* against the city. An *offensive* (*adj.*) weapon is one that can be used to attack.

off-hand (of-*hand*) 1. *adj.* Careless, thoughtless, casual, curt. *Ex.* He was very *off-hand* when asked about his plans. 2. *adv.* Without preparation or thinking about beforehand. *Ex.* I must look it up; I can't tell you *off-hand*.

office (*of*-is) *n.* A room or building where business is done.

officer (*of*-is-er)   *n.* A person who holds a position of authority, especially in the armed services.

official (of-*ish*'l)   *n.* A person who holds a position of authority, especially in government employment. A *post-office* or *railway official* has *official* (*adj.*) duties.

officious (of-*ish*-us)   *adj.* Interfering; giving unwanted advice; bossy.

offspring   *n.* Children, or the young of animals.

ogre (*oh*-ger)   *n.* A man-eating giant of fairy tales.

oilskin   *n.* Waterproof clothing worn by sailors etc.

ointment (*oint*-ment)   *n.* An oily paste or cream used on the skin, as medicine or cosmetic.

olive (*ol*-iv)   *n.* A small long-lived tree of Mediterranean countries whose black fruit is edible and rich in oil, and whose green unripe fruit is pickled. *Olive* colour is yellowy-green.

omelette (*om*-let)   *n.* A dish, either sweet or savoury, made of eggs lightly beaten and fried.

omen (*oh*-men)   *n.* A sign or warning of something that is going to happen, either pleasant or unpleasant.   *Ex.* A red sky in the evening is often an *omen* of good weather.

ominous (*om*-in-us)   *adj.* Threatening or warning that something unpleasant will happen.   *Ex.* There were *ominous* black clouds threatening a storm.

omit (oh-*mit*)   *v.* To leave out; to fail to do.   *Ex.* I *omitted* to lock the door when I came out.

omnibus (*om*-ni-bus)   *n.* The full name for the large passenger vehicle usually called a *bus*. An *omnibus* (*adj.*) volume contains several books bound together.

onion (*un*-yon)   *n.* The strong-flavoured bulb of a plant which, sometimes with the leaves, is cooked as a vegetable or eaten raw in salads.

onslaught (*on*-slawt)   *n.* An attack.

ooze   *v.* To trickle or leak out slowly.

opal (*oh*-pal)   *n.* A gemstone with changing colours, ranging from milky-white to pink and greenish-blue.

opera (*op*-er-a)   *n.* A play set to music and performed with an orchestra, all or some of the words being sung instead of spoken.

operate (*op*-er-ayt)   *v.* (a) To put into action, or be in charge of.   *Ex.* They saw a man *operating* a television camera. (b) (Of a surgeon) To use instruments on a patient's body to cut out diseased parts, repair injury etc. by a surgical *operation* (*n.*).

opinion (o-*pin*-yon) *n.* A judgement or belief about a person or thing. *Ex.* What, in your *opinion*, should we do about it?

opponent (op-*oh*-nent) *n.* (a) Someone who is against one in a fight or game. (b) Someone who is against an idea or plan. *Ex.* We must try to persuade our *opponents* to stop *opposing* (*v.*) our scheme; but the *opposition* (*n.*) is strong.

opportunity (op-or-*tew*-ni-ti) *n.* A chance or a suitable time for doing something. *Ex.* Fine weather gave farmers a good *opportunity* to harvest the wheat.

opposite (*op*-o-zit) 1. *adj.* (a) On the other side. *Ex.* The house *opposite* yours is the house facing it. (b) Quite different, opposed to. *Ex.* He is in favour, but I take the *opposite* view. 2. *n.* The contrary. *Ex.* Sweet is the *opposite* of sour; north is the *opposite* of south.

oppress (o-*pres*) *v.* To treat cruelly; to bear heavily on, as a tyrant on his people.

optical (*op*-tik-al) *adj.* Connected with the sight of the eye. *Ex.* Telescopes are *optical* instruments. Spectacles are made by *opticians* (op-*tish*-anz; *n.*).

optimist (*op*-tim-ist) *n.* One who looks on the bright side of things and is ever hopeful. He shows *optimism* (*n.*).

option (*op*-sh'n) *n.* Choice. *Ex.* The competition winners had the *option* of taking as their prize either the car or its value in money.

oral (*awr*-al) *adj.* Spoken, not written. *Ex.* The *oral* exam tested our ability to carry on a conversation in French.

orange (*o*-ranj) 1. *n.* A reddish-yellow, sweet, juicy fruit with a thick skin, grown in warm climates. 2. *adj.* Of the colour of an *orange.*

orator (*o*-ra-tor) *n.* One who speaks well in public. *Oratory* (*n.*) is the art of doing this.

oratorio (o-ra-*tawr*-i-o) *n.* A musical composition, usually telling a Bible story, in which solo singers, a chorus and an orchestra all take part.

orbit (*awr*-bit) *n.* A curving track such as is made by the moon or an artificial satellite round the earth.

orchard (*awr*-cherd) *n.* A piece of land where fruit-trees are grown, especially apples, pears, plums or cherries.

orchestra (*awr*-kes-tra) *n.* A group of musicians who play together any of the string, woodwind, brass or percussion instruments used in *orchestral* (or-*kes*-tral; *adj.*) music.

ordain (awr-*dayn*) *v.* To make a man a priest of the Christian Church in a special religious ceremony.

ordeal (awr-*deel*) *n.* A severe testing; something endured. *Ex.* The kidnapped journalist survived his *ordeal* very well.

order (*awr*-der) 1. *n.* (a) The position of one thing or happening in relation to others. *Ex.* Words in this book are in alphabetical *order*. (b) Tidiness. The opposite is *disorder*. (c) A state of efficiency or control. *Ex.* The car is in excellent *order*. (d) An instruction or command. 2. *v.* (a) To give an order or command. (b) To instruct someone to supply goods.

ordinary (*awr*-din-a-ri) *adj.* Usual, not special, common. *Ex.* This is only *ordinary* china, for everyday use.

ore (awr) *n.* Metal in the state in which it is found in the ground.

organ (*awr*-gan) *n.* (a) A part of the body which has some special purpose, such as the eye or heart. (b) A large keyboard wind instrument with pipes that sound when air is forced into them.

organic (awr-*gan*-ik) *adj.* Relating to the *organs* of the body; having the characteristics of living things.

organism (*awr*-gan-izm) *n.* A living plant, animal or other creature.

organize (*awr*-gan-yz) *v.* To arrange business or work so that it can be done properly; to arrange with the co-operation of others. An *organization* (*n.*) is anything *organized*, or a group of people working together for some purpose. *Ex.* The *United Nations Organization*.

origin (*o*-ri-jin) *n.* The beginning of something. *Ex.* Jealousy over a girl was the *origin* of their quarrel; that is how it *originated* (*v.*).

original (o-*rij*-in-al) *adj.* (a) First. *Ex.* The *original* inhabitants of North America were Indians. (b) New; made, said or done for the first time; not copied from anything else. *Ex.* The building which won the prize was the most *original*, with many new features; the architect had shown great *originality* (*n.*).

ornament (*awr*-na-ment) 1. *n.* Something liked for its pleasing appearance and not because it is useful. 2. *v.* To make more attractive by adding decoration. *Ex.* The bridesmaids' caps were *ornamented* with pearls.

ornate (awr-*nayt*) *adj.* With much elaborate decoration.

orphan (*awr*-fan) *n.* A child whose parents are both dead.

orthodox (*awr*-tho-doks) *adj.* According to the official or accepted way.

ostentation (os-ten-*tay*-sh'n) *n.* The showing off of wealth and splendour etc. to get attention.

ostrich (*os*-trich) *n.* The largest of birds, found in Africa. It has long legs and neck, does not fly, but can run fast.

otter (*ot*-er) *n.* An aquatic fish-eating animal; it has webbed feet, sleek fur and is a splendid swimmer.

ought (awt) *v. Ought* followed by a verb expresses (a) duty. *Ex.* You *ought* to go and see her. (b) Probability. *Ex.* We *ought* to win on Saturday. (c) Desirability. *Ex.* You *ought* to have been there; you would have enjoyed it.

oust (owst) *v.* To turn someone out of the place he occupies. *Ex.* A baby cuckoo is strong enough to *oust* all the other young birds from the nest.

outcry *n.* A loud or general expression of disapproval or protest.

outfit *n.* The necessary clothes or equipment for some purpose. People often buy new *outfits* (clothes) for a holiday or wedding. An *outfitter* (*n.*) sells men's clothes.

outlaw *n.* A person outside the law's protection because of his wrong-doing; a bandit.

outlook *n.* What one sees on looking out or looking forward; a view from a window, for example, or the weather prospects.

outnumber *v.* To be more in number than. *Ex.* Sparrows *outnumber* all the other birds in our garden.

outrage (*owt*-rayj) *n.* A violent, horrifying act; a feeling of great anger and resentment. *Ex.* The killing of hostages is an *outrage*; it is *outrageous* (*adj.*).

outskirts (*owt*-skurts) *n.* The borders or edge of a city or other place.

outspoken *adj.* Spoken, or speaking, frankly and freely, perhaps without regard for the feelings of others. *Ex.* He was not very tactful, and his *outspoken* comments offended some.

oval (*oh*-val) *adj.* Having the shape of an egg or an ellipse.

oven (*uv*-en) *n.* The space in a cooker or stove where food is baked and roasted.

overall 1. *n.* A dress or suit (*overalls*) worn on top of other clothes to keep them clean. 2. *adj.* (a) (Of a measurement) From end to end. *Ex.* It measures 2 metres *overall*. (b) Sometimes used to mean complete, total, inclusive etc.

overbearing *adj.* Domineering, bullying.

overcast 1. *adj.* With a cloudy sky. 2. *v.* To stitch over the top of two edges of material, usually to prevent fraying.

overcome 1. *v.* To defeat or conquer. 2. *adj.* Feeling beaten or exhausted. *Ex.* She felt quite *overcome* by the heat, and nearly fainted.

overhaul (oh-ver-*hawl*) *v.* To examine in order to remove faults. *Ex.* That bicycle needs a complete *overhaul* (*n.*).

oversight *n.* A failure to see or think of something. *Ex.* Owing to an *oversight*, she wasn't invited to the party.

overtake *v.* To catch up with and pass. *Ex.* We soon *overtook* the walkers on our bicycles.

overthrow *v.* To defeat or overcome.

overture (*oh*-ver-tewr) *n.* A piece of music played at an opera before the curtain rises, or as a concert piece elsewhere.

overwhelm (oh-ver-*welm*) *v.* To cover completely, crush, over-power. A village may be *overwhelmed* by floods, or an army by a stronger force. We may be *overwhelmed* by powerful emotions.

owe (oh) *v.* To be under an obligation to pay or give back. *Ex.* I *owe* you 30p for the stamps you bought me. We *owe* them our gratitude for saving our lives. *Owing to* means because of, on account of. *Ex. Owing to* her cold she had to stay at home.

owl *n.* A bird of prey which hunts mainly at night. It has large eyes in a flat face, and hoots or screeches.

ox *n.* A kind of bull. In some countries *oxen* are used to pull carts or ploughs.

oxygen (*oks*-i-jen) *n.* A gas which makes up a fifth of the air and nine-tenths of water, and is essential to life.

oyster (*oi*-ster) *n.* A shellfish. One kind is fattened for food, and another produces pearls and mother-of-pearl.

P

pace (pays) *n.* (a) The speed at which one moves. (b) One step in walking. *Ex.* He *paced* (*v.*) up and down the room, which was only four *paces* long.

pacify (*pas*-i-fy) *v.* To calm down someone who is angry or excited. *Ex.* She *pacified* the baby with some orange juice. A *pacifist* (*n.*) is someone who refuses to fight in any circumstances.

pack 1. *n.* (a) A bundle of things wrapped up together for carrying. *Ex.* A *packhorse* (*n.*) is a horse used to carry goods. (b) A group of certain people, animals or things. We speak of a *pack* of hounds, wolves, thieves, playing-cards, Cub Scouts and so on. 2. *v.* To put things into a container for storing or travelling. *Ex.* He *packed* a suitcase for the weekend. A *package* (*n.*) or *packet* is a small parcel.

paddle (*pa*-d'l) *v.* (a) To walk barefoot in water. (b) To propel (move) a canoe with a short oar (*paddle*; *n.*), which may have a blade at either end.

paddock *n.* A small field where horses may be kept.

padlock *n.* A removable *lock* with a chain or metal hoop for a fastening.

pagan (*pay*-gan) *n.* A heathen.

page *n.* (a) One side of a sheet of paper or of a leaf of a book. (b) A serving-boy.

pageant (*paj*-ant) *n.* An entertainment, usually formed into a procession, in which historical scenes are shown in period costume.

pain *n.* A feeling in body or mind which causes suffering. To be *painstaking* (*adj.*) is to take trouble and care in doing something.

paint (paynt) 1. *n.* A coloured liquid substance for spreading on a surface. 2. *v.* To put paint on. A *painting* (*n.*) is a *painted* (*adj.*) picture.

palace (*pal*-is) *n.* A large and splendid house lived in by a king, bishop etc. A house as grand as a *palace* is said to be *palatial* (pal-*ay*-shal; *adj.*).

palate (*pal*-at) *n.* The roof of the mouth. *Palatable* (*adj.*) food means food that tastes nice.

pale *adj.* Without much colour.

palette (*pal*-et) *n.* A small board with a thumb-hole in it, which a painter holds when mixing colours on it.

pallid (*pa*-lid) *adj.* Pale. The state of being *pallid* is *pallor* (*n.*).

palm (pahm) *n.* (a) A tall tree with all its foliage at the top, which grows in warm climates. The date and coconut come from *palm trees*. (b) The soft inner surface of the hand.

palmistry (*pahm*-is-tri) *n.* Fortune-telling from the lines on the *palm* of the hand.

pamper *v.* To over-indulge or spoil someone, to give him everything he wants.

pamphlet (*pam*-flet) *n.* A small unbound booklet, usually one dealing with a political problem of the day.

pandemonium (pan-di-*moh*-ni-um) *n.* Great noise, confusion and excitement.

pane   *n.* A sheet of window-glass.

pang   *n.* A short sharp pain; a feeling of sorrow.   *Ex.* She felt a *pang* at parting with her dog for the holidays.

panic (*pan*-ik)   *n.* Great terror and alarm among people or animals, making them do things without thought or care in a *panic* (*adj.*) rush.

panorama (pan-or-*ah*-ma)   *n.* A wide view of sea or land.

pant   *v.* To breathe in quick gasps.   *Ex.* They ran up the hill and arrived *panting* at the top.

pantomime (*pan*-to-mym)   *n.* A light-hearted Christmas entertainment based on some well-known fairy-tale.

paper   *n.* The material made in thin sheets from rags, wood pulp etc., used for wrapping, writing on etc.

parable (*pa*-ra-b'l)   *n.* A story with a moral, used in religious education. The New Testament story of the Good Samaritan is a *parable*.

parachute (*pa*-ra-shoot)   *n.* A large umbrella-shaped stretch of nylon attached to a person by ropes, by which he can float down safely to earth from an aeroplane; also sometimes used to drop goods. One trained to use a *parachute* is a *parachutist* (*n.*). *Paratroops* (*n.*) are soldiers trained to land by *parachute*.

parade (pa-*rayd*)   *n.* A gathering of troops, usually for an inspection, on a *parade-ground* (*n.*); a display, often in the form of a procession.

paradise (*pa*-ra-dys)   *n.* The Garden of Eden; Heaven; a perfect place.

paraffin (*pu*-ra-fin)   *n.* A kind of oil used in lamps and stoves.

paragraph (*pa*-ra-grahf)   *n.* A section of a letter or other writing, dealing with one subject only. It is usual to start the first sentence of a new *paragraph* a little way in from the margin.

parallel (*pa*-ra-lel)   *adj.* Continuing along, always the same distance apart, as do railway lines.

paralysis (pa-*ral*-i-sis)   *n.* The loss of feeling and movement on one side or in one limb of the body, due to a stroke or other cause.

parapet (*pa*-ra-pet)   *n.* A low wall built for safety purposes on a bridge, balcony or roof.

paraphrase (*pa*-ra-frayz)   *n.* To put into other words but keep the meaning the same.

parasite (*pa*-ra-syt)   *n.* A living thing which gets nourishment from another living thing, and may be completely dependent on it.   *Ex.* Mistletoe is a *parasite* of trees, and fleas of animals.

parcel (*par*-sel) *n.* Goods wrapped up in paper to form a package for sending by post etc.

parched (parcht) *adj.* Very dry or thirsty. *Ex.* During the drought the garden was *parched* by the hot sun. He was *parched* with thirst.

parchment (*parch*-ment) *n.* A material formerly used to write on, made from animal skins.

pardon 1. *v.* To forgive. 2. *n.* The act of forgiving.

pare (pair) *v.* To trim by cutting the edges; to remove the skin of fruit or vegetables with a knife.

parish (*pa*-rish) *n.* A district with its own church and priest.

parliament (*parl*-i-ment) *n.* In Britain, a law-making council consisting of the monarch, the House of Lords and the House of Commons. There are similar councils in other countries.

parody (*pa*-ro-di) *n.* Something written in imitation of another work, in a lighthearted way or to ridicule it.

parole (pa-*rohl*) *n.* The word of honour of a prisoner that he will not try to escape.

parrot (*pa*-rot) *n.* A tropical bird of beautiful colouring, with a hooked beak. Some *parrots* can imitate the human voice.

parsley (*pars*-li) *n.* A bright green crinkly-leaved plant used to flavour and decorate food.

parsnip (*pars*-nip) *n.* A yellowish-white, carrot-shaped vegetable with a sweetish taste.

parson (*par*-son) *n.* A clergyman, the parish priest. His house is sometimes called the *parsonage* (*n.*).

partial (*par*-shal) *adj.* (a) Forming only a *part*. *Ex.* There was a *partial* thaw, so it was not safe to go on the ice. (b) Biased, favouring one side more than the other. *Ex.* A judge should always be *impartial* (not *partial*). (c) Having a fondness for. *Ex.* She is *partial* to cheese-cake.

participate (par-*tis*-i-payt) *v.* To take part in. *Ex.* Those *participating* in the play must come to all rehearsals.

particle (*part*-i-k'l) *n.* A very small piece, such as a *particle* of dust.

particular (par-*tik*-ew-lar) *adj.* (a) Special. *Ex.* One *particular* dog at the show seemed certain to win first prize. (b) Careful, very attentive. *Ex.* We have become very *particular* about locking up since our house was burgled.

partition (par-*tish*'n) *n.* A division or separation; a wall which divides a room into two.

partner (*part*-ner) *n.* Someone who shares work or other activity.

You can have a *dance partner*, a *business partner*, a *partner* in marriage etc.

partridge (*part*-rij) *n.* A plump brown game-bird.

party (*par*-ti) *n.* A number of people who have the same interest in something. *Ex.* A *party* of tourists; a political *party.* (b) A gathering of guests for entertainment.

pass 1. *n.* (a) A narrow gap through mountainous country. (b) A ticket allowing someone to enter a building etc.; a free ticket. 2. *v.* (a) To move on, go by. *Ex.* 'Pass right down the bus'. The train *passes* our station without stopping. (b) To hand over. *Ex.* If you want more tea, *pass* me your cup. (c) To get through, as a student in an exam, or a Bill in Parliament.

passable (*pahs*-a-b'l) *adj.* (a) Possible to *pass* through, as a road may be once more, after being blocked by snow. (b) Fair; not very good, not very bad. *Ex.* She speaks German only *passably* (*adv.*) well.

passage (*pas*-ij) *n.* (a) The act of *passing*; *passing* from one place to another. (b) A journey by sea. (c) A narrow corridor from which rooms lead off. (d) A portion of a book or speech. *Ex.* He quoted a *passage* from the Bible.

passenger (*pas*-en-jer) *n.* One who travels in a vehicle which someone else is driving.

passion (*pash*-on) *n.* Strong feeling of rage or love.

passive (*pas*-iv) *adj.* Doing nothing oneself but having something done to one. *Ex.* Everyone was cheering and slapping him on the back, but he remained *passive* in his chair.

passport (*pahs* pawrt) *n.* A government document essential for anyone wishing to travel in foreign countries.

password (*pahs*-wurd) *n.* A *word* or phrase which one used to have to say to a sentry in order to be allowed to *pass* into a military camp or guarded building.

pasteurize (*pahs*-ter-yz) *v.* To prevent milk from developing disease germs, by using a method of heating invented by Louis *Pasteur.*

pastime (*pahs*-tym) *n.* A game or amusement which *passes* the *time.*

pastry (*pays*-tri) *n.* A mixture of flour, fat and water baked in the oven.

pasture (*pahs*-cher) *n.* Grass fields where cattle can graze (feed). Also called *pasturage.*

patch 1. *n.* A piece of material sewn on to a garment etc. to mend a hole. 2. *v.* To mend in this way. *Patchwork* (*n.*) is fabric made up of *patches* of different materials.

pâté (*pat*-ay) *n.* A rich *paste* of finely minced meat or fish, usually containing liver.

paternal (pat-*urn*-al) *adj.* Fatherly, or to do with a father. *Ex.* Your *paternal* grandfather is your father's father. He patted the child on the head in a *paternal* way.

pathetic (path-*et*-ik) *adj.* Causing pity or sympathy. *Ex.* The half-drowned kitten was a *pathetic* sight.

pathos (*pay*-thos) *n.* Something that makes one feel pity.

patience (*pay*-shens) *n.* The ability to endure suffering without complaint, or to wait quietly for something. *Patient* (*adj.*) means having this quality. A *patient* (*n.*) is someone under the care of a doctor.

patriot (*pay*-tri-ot) *n.* One who loves his country and will do all he can to defend it. He is *patriotic* (pat-ri-*ot*-ik; *adj.*) and shows *patriotism* (*n.*).

patrol (pat-*rohl*) 1. *v.* To go round on guard or on a beat, as soldiers, police and watchmen do. 2. *n.* A group on *patrol duty*; a Scout group.

patron (*pay*-tron) *n.* One who helps and encourages another in some kind of work, often artistic. In Britain, the Arts Council is a *patron* to many small theatres. Regular customers of a shop are said to be its *patrons* and to *patronize* (*pat*-ron-yz; *v.*) it; but to be *patronising* (*adj.*) means to help someone in a superior, condescending way.

pattern (*pat*-ern) *n.* (a) Something used as a guide or model to be copied. *Ex.* The life of St Francis of Assisi is a *pattern* for Christians. I have a *pattern* to cut round, so I can make all these dolls' dresses alike. (b) The design or markings on material, carpets etc. *Ex.* Towels can be bought in plain colours or with *patterns* on them. (c) A small piece of cloth used as a sample.

pause (pawz) *v.* To stop doing for a short time; to make a *pause* (*n.*).

pavilion (pav-*il*-yon) *n.* A small building, especially at a cricket-ground, where players may change their clothes and store equipment; a very large tent.

pawn 1. *n.* In chess, one of the pieces of the smallest value. 2. *v.* To deposit something of value with a *pawnbroker* (*n.*) in return for a loan.

payment *n.* The act of *paying* (handing over money); the amount *paid* (*v.*).

peace (pees) *n.* Quiet, calm, freedom from war.

peach (peech) *n.* A soft-skinned fruit of a pinkish-yellow colour ripening to red, with sweet juicy flesh round a stone.

peacock *n.* A large bird. The male has beautifully coloured feathers, especially in its tail, which it can spread out like a fan. The female is called a *peahen.*

peak *n.* (a) The highest point of a mountain. (b) The front part of a cap that shades the eyes.

peal 1. *n.* The set of bells in a church tower; the sound they make when rung together. 2. *v.* To make this sound.

pear (pair) *n.* A tree-fruit about the size of an apple but oval; it is soft inside, with a sweet, delicate flavour.

pearl (purl) *n.* A small, round, shiny white precious stone found in the shells of oysters etc.

peat *n.* A kind of turf dug from bogs, which can be dried and burned like coal.

pebble *n.* A small stone worn smooth and round by water or ice. Some beaches are *pebbly* (*adj.*).

peculiar (pi-*kew*-li-ar) *adj.* (a) Strange, unusual. *Ex.* The plant had a *peculiar* smell. (b) Special to one person, place etc. *Ex.* This flower is *peculiar* to chalk downland.

pedal (*ped*-al) *n.* A lever pressed by the foot, either to work a machine (sewing-machine, bicycle etc.) or to make some part of a musical instrument work (organ, piano).

peddle (*ped*'l) *v.* To sell from door to door. One who does this is a *pedlar* (*n.*).

pedestrian (ped-*es*-tri-an) *n.* One who walks. *Ex. Pedestrian* (*adj.*) crossings are for *pedestrians* to use when crossing busy streets.

pedigree (*ped*-i-gree) *n.* A list of ancestors. A pure-bred dog has a *pedigree* to prove that its ancestors were of the same breed.

peel 1. *n.* The skin of a fruit or vegetable. 2. *v.* To remove this skin.

peep *v.* To look quickly, slyly or through a narrow opening. You can *peep* through your fingers or *peep* into a baby's room to check that he is asleep.

peer. 1. *n.* A person with a title and also with a right to sit in the House of Lords. 2. *v.* To look closely.

peevish *adj.* Cross, irritable.

pellet (*pel*-et) *n.* A little ball. You can make a *pellet* of paper or bread. The small lead shot used for shooting game-birds are called *pellets*.

penalty (*pen*-al-ti) *n.* A punishment, especially a fine; a disadvantage a player is put under for breaking a rule in a game.

pendulum (*pend*-ew-lum) *n.* A bar with a weight at the end that hangs down and swings to and fro, especially one which regulates a clock.

penetrate (*pen*-i-trayt) *v.* To pierce or push into. *Ex.* When he hammered in the nail it *penetrated* a water-pipe. *Penetrating (adj.)* voices can be heard through and above other sounds.

penguin (*pen*-gwin) *n.* A sea-bird found near the South Pole, which can walk upright but not fly, and uses its flipper-like wings to swim under water.

penicillin (pen-i-*sil*-in) *n.* A germ-killing drug which is made from a kind of fungus.

peninsula (pen-*in*-sew-la) *n.* A piece of land pointing out into the sea and almost surrounded by it. Italy is a *peninsula*.

penitent (*pen*-i-tent) *adj.* Sorry for something one has done or failed to do.

pennant (*pen*-ant) *n.* A long, usually pointed flag, often used for signalling.

pension (*pen*-sh'n) *n.* A regular payment, made by a government or former employer, to someone who is no longer working because of age, disablement etc.

pepper *n.* A plant from whose berries a hot spice is obtained, used to season foods.

perambulator (per-*ram*-bew-layt-or) *n.* A small carriage in which babies are pushed along by hand, often called a *pram*.

perceive (per-*seev*) *v.* To see or understand; to become aware of. *Ex.* It was easy to *perceive* that they were enjoying themselves, by the sound of their laughter. A thing that can be *perceived* is *perceptible (adj.)*.

perch (purch) 1. *n.* A small edible freshwater fish. (b) A bar or branch of a tree on which a bird rests. 2. *v.* To rest as on a *perch*.

perennial (pe-*ren*-i-al) *adj.* Lasting for several years, or for ever. Flowers which come up every year, such as primroses and daisies, are called *perennials (n.)*.

perfect (*pur*-fekt) *adj.* Complete; without a fault. *Ex.* It was a *perfect* day for the sports, not too hot or too cold.

perforate (*pur*-for-rayt)   *v.* To make holes in.   *Ex.* A sheet of postage stamps can be separated at the *perforations* (*n.*).

perform (per-*form*)   *v.* To do, carry out, act.   *Ex.* The soldiers *performed* their duties. Actors *perform* plays; surgeons *perform* operations. A *performance* (*n.*), such as a play, is something which is *performed*.

perfume (*pur*-fewm)   *n.* A sweet smell; a sweet-smelling liquid; scent.

peril (*pe*-ril)   *n.* Danger. A *perilous* (*adj.*) journey is a dangerous one.

perimeter (per-*rim*-e-ter)   *n.* The distance round an area; its boundary.   *Ex.* The sports-ground has a fence round its *perimeter.*

period (*peer*-i-od)   *n.* A portion of time.   *Ex.* Holidays only last for a certain *period.* The Elizabethan *period.* A *periodical* (peer-i-*od*-ik-al; *n.*) is a magazine which appears at regular times.

periscope (*pe*-ris-kohp)   *n.* An instrument containing mirrors which enables you to see what is happening on the other side of a wall or a crowd of people etc. Submarines have large *periscopes* in order to see what is happening on the surface of the sea when the boat is submerged.

perish (*pe*-rish)   *v.* To die or be destroyed.   *Ex.* Many people *perished* in the floods. *Perishable* (*adj.*) means likely to decay or become rotten quickly.

perjury (*pur*-jer-i)   *n.* Swearing that something is true when you know it to be false.

permanent (*pur* man-ent)   *adj.* Lasting; remaining the same for a long time or for ever.

permit   1. (per-*mit*) *v.* To allow.   *Ex.* No one is *permitted* to go beyond this point; no one has *permission* (*n.*) to do so. 2. (*pur*-mit) *n.* Written permission to do a thing.   *Ex.* We were given *permits* to visit the airfield.

permutation (per-mew-*tay*-sh'n)   *n.* The change of order in which you can arrange a set of objects, either actually or in maths. Change-ringing on church bells makes many *permutations* on the order in which the bells are rung.

perpendicular (per-pen-*dik*-ew-lar)   *adj.* Exactly upright.

perpetrate (*pur*-pet-rayt)   *v.* To do some bad deed.

perpetual (per-*pet*-ew-al)   *adj.* Never ending; lasting for ever.   *Ex.* The sea, even when calm, is in *perpetual* motion.

perplexed (per-*plekst*)   *adj.* Confused, puzzled, in doubt.   *Ex.* At the crossroads we were *perplexed* about which road to take. To be *perplexed* is to be in *perplexity* (*n.*).

persecute (*pur*-se-kewt) *v.* To treat with continual cruelty, especially for religious or political reasons; to keep on annoying and harassing. *Ex.* The early Christians often suffered *persecution* (*n.*) for their beliefs.

persevere (per-se-*veer*) *v.* To keep on trying. *Ex.* She *persevered* with her piano exercises, although she found them difficult.

persist (per-*sist*) *v.* To go on doing, firmly or obstinately. *Ex.* He *persisted* in asking for more money; he was very *persistent* (*adj.*).

personality (per-son-*al*-i-ti) *n.* All the qualities which make up a person's characteristics.

perspective (per-*spek*-tiv) *n.* The artist's way of showing the objects he draws so that they will look to be in the same relation to each other as they are in reality. To see things in *perspective* is to see them in their real order of importance.

perspire (per-*spyr*) *v. See* sweat.

persuade (per-*swayd*) *v.* To urge and coax a person into doing a thing. *Ex.* We *persuaded* our mother to let us stay up, and she gave in to our *persuasion* (*n.*).

pert (purt) *adj.* Cheeky, rude.

pessimist (*pes*-i-mist) *n.* Someone who always looks on the dark side of things. The opposite of an optimist.

pest *n.* A person, animal or insect that causes trouble and destruction. Mice, greenfly, rabbits etc. may all be *pests*.

pester *v.* To trouble and annoy persistently. *Ex.* The gipsy *pestered* us to buy flowers we didn't want.

petal (*pet*-al) *n.* One of the coloured or white leaves which make up a flower.

petition (pe-*tish*'n) *n.* A request, usually a written one signed by many people. *Ex.* Parents signed a *petition* demanding a pedestrian crossing outside the school.

petrify (*pet*-ri-fy) *v.* (a) To turn into stone. Fossils are *petrified* (*adj.*) plants and animals. (b) To paralyse or stun with fright or astonishment.

petrol (*pet*-rel) *n.* The spirit fuel used in the engines of cars, aeroplanes etc.

petroleum (pet-*roh*-li-um) *n.* The oil in its crude form as found in the ground, from which *petrol*, paraffin etc. are made.

petticoat (*pet*-i-koht) *n.* An underskirt.

petty *adj.* Unimportant, small. *Ex.* It was only a *petty* mistake.

Petty cash is money to spend on small items. *Petty-minded* means spiteful or mean.

pew *n.* A fixed wooden bench with a back, used in churches.

pewter *n.* An alloy of tin and lead. In olden days tableware was sometimes made of *pewter.*

phantom (*fan*-tom) *n.* A ghost or other imaginary figure.

pharmacy (*far*-mas-i) *n.* A place where drugs and medicines are made up and sold.

pheasant (*fez*-ant) *n.* A game-bird about the size of a hen, with a long tail, the cock bird having beautiful colouring.

phenomenon (fen-*om*-en-on) *n.* (a) Anything that is perceived by the senses, a natural *phenomenon. Ex.* The *phenomenon* of the rainbow. (b) An event, person or thing that is extraordinary. *Ex.* Mozart had a *phenomenal (adj.)* gift for music.

philosopher (fil-*os*-o-fer) *n.* One who searches for life's meaning by finding out what really exists and what (and how) we can know about it. One who accepts life's trials with resignation is said to be *philosophical (adj.).*

phonetic (fo-*net*-ik) *adj.* (Of a word) Spelt exactly as it sounds. One way to spell 'cough' *phonetically (adv.)* would be 'kof'.

photograph (*foh*-to-grahf) *n.* A picture made by the action of light on a camera film specially prepared to receive it. Such pictures are *photographed (v.)* by *photographers* (fo-*tog*-raf-erz; *n.*), whose work is called *photography (n.).*

phrase (frayz) *n.* A group of a few words, usually without a verb, forming only part of a sentence. *Ex.* Like the fox in the fable.

physical (*fiz*-ik-al) *adj.* To do with matter and what is actually in nature, including our bodies, but not with our minds and spirits. *Physical* exercise is exercise of the body.

physician (fiz-*ish*'n) *n.* A doctor.

physique (fiz-*eek*) *n.* The build and development of the body. *Ex.* Boxers and ballet dancers both need a strong *physique.*

piano (pe-*an*-oh) *n.* A musical instrument in which the notes are produced by hammers striking on wires when the keyboard is played. One who plays the *piano* is a *pianist* (*pee*-an-ist; *n.*).

picket *n.* (a) A group of workers on strike who post themselves at the entrance of their workplace and try to persuade others not to go in; they *picket (v.)* their place of work. (b) A pointed stake that forms part of a *picket fence.*

pickle 1. *n.* The vinegar, brine or other liquid in which vegetables or other foods are preserved; food so preserved, added to dishes at table. 2. *v.* To preserve in this way.

picnic (*pik*-nik) *n.* An outing with a meal out of doors.

picturesque (pik-cher-*esk*) *adj.* Attractive enough to make a good *picture* (*n.*). *Ex.* The thatched cottages on the village green looked very *picturesque.*

pied *adj.* Of two different colours, usually black and white, as is the magpie.

pier (peer) *n.* (a) A platform built out into the sea so that ships can come alongside, or as a place of amusement and recreation. (b) A large pillar to support a bridge or arch.

pierce (peers) *v.* To make a hole in.

piety (*py*-et-i) *n.* Devotion to religion. One so devoted is said to be *pious* (*adj.*).

pigeon (*pij*-on) *n.* A swift-flying, plump bird with a small head; some are wild, some domesticated. A dove is a small *pigeon.*

pike *n.* (a) A large, fierce freshwater fish. (b) A long wooden pole with a metal spike, once used as a weapon.

pilfer *v.* To steal in small amounts.

pilgrim (*pil*-grim) *n.* One who travels to a holy place as a religious duty. Such a journey is called a *pilgrimage* (*n.*).

pillar *n.* An upright column acting as a support or ornament in a building.

pillion (*pil*-yon) *n.* A seat for a second person behind the driver of a motor-cycle or rider of a horse.

pillow (*pil*-oh) *n.* A soft cushion on which to rest the head in bed.

pilot (*py*-lot) *n.* (a) One who controls an aeroplane. (b) One who guides ships in and out of harbour.

pimple *n.* A small raised spot on the skin, often infected.

pinafore (*pin*-a-fawr) *n.* An apron (a word not much used now). A *pinafore dress* is a sleeveless dress worn over a blouse or jumper.

pincers (*pin*-serz) *n. pl.* A metal tool for gripping tightly, used, for example, to pull out nails.

pine 1. *n.* An evergreen tree which bears cones and has leaves like needles. 2. *v.* To grow thin and ill because of sorrow.

pineapple (*pyn*-ap'l) *n.* A large, sweet, juicy fruit grown in warm climates; it has a thick knobbly skin and a cluster of small leaves on top.

pink 1. *n.* A red, white or pink garden flower resembling a carnation, with a sweet, sharp scent. 2. *v.* To snip three-cornered pieces from the edge of material etc. 3. *adj.* A pale red.

pinnacle (*pin*-ak'l) *n.* (a) The pointed ornamental top of a roof turret etc. *Ex.* Some church towers have a *pinnacle* at each corner. (b) The highest point.

pint (pynt) *n.* A measure for liquids equal to 568 millilitres or an eighth of a gallon. Milk is usually sold in *pint* bottles.

pioneer (py-on-*eer*) *n.* The first to undertake some enterprise or discovery, or one who plays a leading part in the development of something. *Ex.* The Wright brothers were *pioneers* of flying.

pious (*py*-us) *adj. See* piety.

piston *n.* The cylinder or disc moving to and fro inside a tube, which provides the driving force in a steam or petrol engine, pumps etc.

pitch 1. *v.* (a) To fling or toss. *Ex.* Many things were saved from the burning building by being *pitched* out of the windows. (b) To fix and put up, especially a tent. 2. *n.* (a) The place on which a stall is pitched (*v.*) or a game played. (b) A thick black substance like tar, used in road-making etc. (c) The high or low quality of a sound.

pitcher *n.* A large jug, usually earthenware.

pitfall *n.* (a) A covered pit to trap animals. (b) An unseen danger.

pith *n.* The soft white core of a plant stem; the white skin between the rind (peel) and flesh of an orange etc.

pitiful *adj.* Calling for pity. *Ex.* The starving refugees made a *pitiful* sight.

pittance (*pit*-ans) *n.* A very small amount of money on which to live.

pity 1. *n.* A kindly feeling (compassion) for the sufferings or sorrow of others. 2. *v.* To feel *pity* or sympathy for others.

pivot (*piv*-ot) *n.* A short shaft or pin on which something turns. *Ex.* He *pivoted* (*v.*) on his heel and went away.

placard (*plak*-ard) *n.* A large card or board containing a notice. *Ex.* Newsagents display *placards* which give a news headline from a particular newspaper.

placate (plak-*ayt*) *v.* To calm by yielding. *Ex.* We *placated* the crying child by promising him an ice-cream.

placid (*plas*-id) *adj.* Calm, peaceful. *Ex.* She had a *placid* nature and rarely got cross or excited.

plague (playg) 1. *n.* An epidemic disease of which many people die. *Ex.* The *Great Plague* of London in 1665. 2. *v.* To annoy or disturb. *Ex.* We were *plagued* by wasps at the picnic.

plaice (plays) *n.* A flat fish used as food.

plaid (plad) *n.* A long piece of woollen cloth of tartan pattern, worn wrapped round the shoulder by Scottish Highlanders.

plain (playn) 1. *n.* An area of flat land. *Ex. Salisbury Plain.* 2. *adj.* (a) Clear and simple. *Ex.* The instructions were *plainly* (*adv.*) written in a way we could understand. (b) Without decoration or ornament. *Ex.* She was *plainly* (*adv.*) dressed in a long brown coat. The food was *plain* but well cooked. (c) (Of the face) Neither ugly nor pretty.

plait (plat) *n.* A twisting together of three or more strands or strips of wool, hair etc. To do this is to *plait* (*v.*).

plane *n.* (a) A flat surface. *Ex.* The tail-*plane* of an aircraft. (b) A tool or machine for smoothing surfaces. (c) A tall tree often grown in towns, with leaves shaped like the maple leaf. (d) A short form of the word *aeroplane.*

planet (*plan*-et) *n.* A heavenly body, such as the earth, which revolves round the sun or another star.

plank *n.* A long flat piece of wood, such as a floor-board.

plantation (plan-*tay*-sh'n) *n.* An area planted with tea, tobacco, or cotton plants etc.

plaster (*plahs*-ter) *n.* (a) A mixture of lime, sand and water spread on the inside walls and ceilings of houses; one of various mixtures of powder and water which set hard when dry. (b) A piece of material specially prepared for placing over a cut or wound, sometimes called *sticking-plaster.*

plastic (*plas*-tik) 1. *adj.* Capable of being pressed into a shape. 2. *n.* Any of a group of chemically made substances which can be moulded to any shape, and take the place of natural products (wood, silk etc.) in manufactured goods.

plateau (*plat*-oh) *n.* A flat stretch of land, rather high above sea-level.

platform *n.* A raised flooring in a hall etc. *Ex.* We board trains from the *platform* at a railway-station.

platinum (*plat*-in-um) *n.* A valuable silvery-white metal, used in jewellery and in industry.

plausible (*plawz*-i-b'l) *adj.* Seeming reasonable and likely, but not always to be believed. *Ex.* She always had a *plausible* excuse for being late.

playwright (*play*-ryt) *n.* A writer of plays.

plead (pleed) *v.* To ask earnestly. *Ex.* The hostage *pleaded* to be set free.

pleasant (*plez*-ant) *adj.* Pleasing, enjoyable.

pleasure (*plezh*-er) *n.* Enjoyment, happiness.

pledge *n.* A promise. *Ex.* To *pledge* (*v.*) one's word is to make a solemn promise.

plenty *n.* Enough or more than enough. *Ex.* We have *plenty* of apples and can easily spare you some. We have a *plentiful* (*adj.*) supply.

pliable (*ply*-a-b'l) *adj.* Easily bent.

pliers (*ply*-erz) *n. pl.* A metal tool for bending and cutting wire etc.

plight (plyt) *n.* A difficult or sad situation. *Ex.* The knight rescued the lady in the dungeon from her unhappy *plight*.

plod *v.* To keep steadily on doing something, especially walking. *Ex.* We *plodded* on, though the hill was steep and slippery.

plot 1. *n.* (a) A small piece of land. (b) The story of a play, book, film etc. (c) A secret plan, usually to harm someone. *Ex.* The *Gunpowder Plot* (1605) was a plan to blow up the Houses of Parliament. 2. *v.* To make such a secret plan.

plough (plow) 1. *n.* A farming implement for cutting furrows in the earth and turning it over, before sowing seed in it. 2. *v.* To use such an implement.

pluck 1. *n.* Courage, bravery. *Ex.* Everyone admired the boy's *pluck*; he was very *plucky* (*adj.*). 2. *v.* (a) To pull off, as the feathers of a chicken before cooking it. (b) To pick, as flowers from a garden.

plum *n.* A small, usually purplish, fruit with thin skin and soft flesh round a stone.

plumber (*plum*-er) *n.* A worker who fits and mends water-pipes, gas-pipes and taps. His work is *plumbing* (*v.*).

plume (ploom) *n.* A large feather or tuft of feathers, worn as a decoration. *Ex.* The *plume* on a knight's helmet. The feathers of a bird are called its *plumage* (*ploom* ij; *n.*).

plump *adj.* Rather fat, with a lot of flesh on.

plunder *v.* To take goods by force, especially in war. What is taken is called *plunder* (*n.*).

plunge (plunj) *v.* (a) To push quickly or violently into. *Ex.* He *plunged* the burning cloth into the water. (b) To dive into. *Ex.* She *plunged* into the river from the bank.

plural (*ploor*-al) *n.* and *adj.* More than one. The singular (just one) of the word 'child' is 'child'; the *plural* (more than one) is 'children'.

ply *n.* One of the threads of anything spun which are twisted together to make rope, knitting yarn etc. *Ex.* Three-*ply* wool. *Plywood* (*n.*) is thin layers of wood glued together to form one thickness.

pneumatic (new-*mat*-ik) *adj.* Working by compressed air (*pneumatic* drill), or containing air (*pneumatic* tyre).

pneumonia (new-*mohn*-i-a) *n.* Serious inflammation of the lungs.

poach (pohch) *v.* (a) To cook an egg without its shell in water. (b) To trespass on to someone else's land to steal his game.

poem (*poh*-em) *n.* A piece of writing, using rhythm, rhyme, word pictures or patterned lines, which expresses the thoughts and feelings of a *poet* (*n.*); a piece of *poetry* (*n.*).

point 1. *n.* (a) The sharp tip of something. *Ex.* A *pencil point.* (b) A dot; a particular place or time. *Ex.* A *decimal point.* At the *point* of death. (c) A unit in counting a score in a game. 2. *v.* To show, with the finger, where a thing is, or the way to a place.

poise (poiz) *n.* Confident bearing and behaviour.

poison (*poi*-z'n) 1. *n.* A substance which will kill or do serious harm if taken into the body. 2. *v.* To give someone such a *poisonous* (*adj.*) substance.

polar (*poh*-lar) *adj.* Near, or connected with, the North or South Pole.

police (pol-*ees*) *n.* The official guardians of law and order.

policy (*pol*-is-i) *n.* (a) A plan of action or behaviour, by which governments, organizations, individuals etc. operate. *Ex.* It is the *policy* of this shop to please its customers. (b) The written agreement (contract) between an insurance company and the person it is insuring.

polish (*pol*-ish) 1. *n.* A smooth shining surface, or a substance that produces it. *Ex.* The shine on this table is very good because we have used a special wax *polish.* 2. *v.* To make a surface shine.

polite (pol-*yt*) *adj.* Courteous, showing good manners; showing *politeness* (*n.*).

political (pol-*it*-i-k'l) *adj.* To do with the state and its government. *Ex.* Members of Parliament belong to *political* parties (groups of *politicians* (*n.*) who hold similar opinions about *politics* (*n.*) or the business of governing).

pollen (*pol*-en) *n.* The powdery substance (male cells) of a plant, which is carried by wind, bees etc. to female plants in order to fertilize them. This process is called *pollination* (*n.*).

pollute (pol-*oot*) *v.* To make impure. *Ex.* Factory waste and chemicals may *pollute* a river.

polo (*poh*-loh) *n.* A team game played on horse-back, in which *polo-sticks* are used to drive a ball through goal-posts. *Water-polo* is a team game in which swimmers try to propel a large ball into a goal.

pomp *n.* A show of grandeur, such as a coronation.

pompous *adj.* Full of self-importance. *Ex.* The inspector spoke in a *pompous* way, as if only he was of any importance.

poncho (*pon*-choh) *n.* A piece of blanket with a slit through which to put the head, worn as a cloak. It came originally from South America.

pond *n.* A large pool of water, smaller than a lake.

ponder *v.* To think about carefully; to weigh in the mind. *Ex.* He *pondered* over the matter before making a decision. A *ponderous* (*adj.*) volume is a very heavy one.

pontoon (pon-*toon*) *n.* A flat-bottomed boat. *Pontoons* are sometimes fastened together to make a bridge that soldiers can use to cross a river.

pony (*poh*-ni) *n.* A small horse.

pool *n.* A small quantity of water on the ground; a very small pond; a puddle.

poplar (*pop*-lar) *n.* A tall slender tree, of which there are several kinds, including the aspen.

poppy *n.* A bright red field flower with black centre and thin silky petals. *Garden poppies* come in many bright colours.

populace (*pop*-ew-lis) *n.* Ordinary people.

popular (*pop*-ew-lar) *adj.* (a) Liked by many people. *Ex.* A *popular* song. A *popular* person. *Pop* stars enjoy much *popularity* (*n.*). (b) To do with the mass of ordinary people. *Ex. Popular* concern.

population (pop-ew-*lay*-sh'n) *n.* The number of people living in a place. *Ex.* The *population* of Great Britain is about 55 million.

porcelain (*pawr*-sel-in) *n.* A fine china through which you can see light, used to make tableware, ornaments etc.

porch *n.* A covered archway over a doorway. Many houses have *porches* so that people waiting to be let in are protected from the weather.

pore (pawr) 1. *n.* A tiny opening in the skin of animals or in the surface of plants, through which fluids can pass. *Ex.* We sweat through our *pores*. 2. *v.* To read or study something closely. *Ex.* They spent all afternoon *poring* over some old maps.

pork *n.* The flesh of the pig when used as food.

porous (*pawr*-us) *adj.* Letting liquid soak through, as a sponge does.

porpoise (*pawr*-pus) *n.* A small sea-mammal with a blunt nose, belonging to the dolphin family.

port *n.* (a) A harbour; a town which has a harbour. (b) A sweet red Portuguese wine. (c) The left side of a ship, when looking forward.

portable (*pawrt*-a-b'l) *adj.* Easily carried from place to place.

portcullis (pawrt-*kul*-is) *n.* A heavy iron grating in a castle doorway, which can be lowered to keep out an enemy.

porter *n.* A person employed to carry luggage etc., or as doorkeeper of a building.

porthole *n.* An opening or window in a ship's side.

portion (*pawr*-sh'n) *n.* A part or share of something, sometimes referring to a helping of food.

portrait (*pawr*-trayt) *n.* A picture or photograph of a person, usually the face only.

position (poz-*ish*'n) *n.* (a) The place where something is. *Ex.* The house is in a good *position*, with fine views. (b) The way a person or thing is placed. *Ex.* He was sitting in a comfortable *position*. (c) A job. *Ex.* He has a very good *position* as manager of a bank.

positive (*poz*-i-tiv) *adj.* Certain, sure. *Ex.* The postman is *positive* that he saw our dog a long way from home.

possess (po-*zes*) *v.* To have as one's own. Things which belong to you are your *possessions* (*n.*).

post (pohst) 1. *n.* (a) A long piece of wood or metal fixed into the ground, such as a *lamp-post* or *goal-post*. (b) The carrying and delivering of letters and parcels, done by *postmen (n.)* employed by the *Post Office*. (c) A job or employment. 2. *v.* To send by *post*; to put a letter in a *post-box*. You pay *postage (n.)* by putting a *postage stamp* on the letter. If you wish to send money by *post* you can use a *postal (adj.)* order.

post- (pohst) is a prefix meaning 'after', 'behind' or 'later than'. *Ex. Postscript*; *post-war*.

posterity (pos-*te*-rit-i) *n.* The descendants (those who will be born after) of a person, or all the generations yet to be born.

postpone (pohst-*pohn*) *v.* To put off till another (later) time. *Ex.* The party had to be *postponed* till the following week.

postscript (*pohst*-skript) *n.* A few lines written at the end of a letter, after it has been signed.

posture (*pos*-cher) *n.* The way a person holds his body. *Ex.* A good sitting *posture* may help to prevent backache.

posy (*pohz*-i) *n.* A small bunch of attractively arranged flowers.

potato (po-*tay*-toh) *n.* A vegetable brought to Europe from South America; it is the swollen part of the plant's underground stem, and contains starch.

potent (*poh*-tent) *adj.* Powerful. *Ex.* He exercised a *potent* influence behind the scenes. *Impotent* (*im*-po-tent; *adj.*) means powerless.

potential (po-*tensh*'l) *adj.* Having future possibilities. *Ex.* Petroleum has been found there, a *potential* source of wealth for that country.

pot-hole *n.* (a) A hole in a road caused by bad weather or heavy traffic. (b) An underground passage or hole in limestone areas which can be reached by a hole in the surface. *Pot-holing* is exploring *pot-holes*.

pottery (*pot*-er-i) *n.* Dishes or ornaments etc. made of clay baked hard in an oven.

pouch (powch) *n.* A small bag, such as a *tobacco-pouch*. The pocket in front of a kangaroo's body in which the baby lives is called a *pouch*.

poultry (*pohl*-tri) *n.* Domesticated birds such as hens, ducks, and turkeys, kept to produce eggs or to be eaten.

pounce (powns) *v.* To jump on and seize. *Ex.* The cat leapt from the wall and *pounced* on a mouse.

pound (pownd) 1. *n.* (a) The unit of British money, equal to 100 pence. (b) A unit of weight equal to 16 ounces or 454 grams. 2. *v.* To crush with a beater into small pieces or powder, in cooking, making medicine etc.

pour (pawr) *v.* To come or send streaming out. Water can be *poured* from a jug or pour over a waterfall; or it can *pour* with rain.

pout (powt) *v.* To push the lips forward to show discontent.

poverty (*pov*-er-ti) *n.* The state of being very poor.

power (powr) *n.* The ability to do something or make other people do something; energy, strength. Governments, men's minds, machines, natural forces (like wind or waves), all have *power*.

One who has great *power* or strength is *powerful* (*adj.*). One who is weak is *powerless* (without power).

practicable (*prak*-tik-a-b'l) *adj.* Possible to do; sensible to do. *Ex.* It was not *practicable* to take a small boat out in such a rough sea.

practical (*prak*-ti-kal) *adj.* Referring to the doing of something. *Ex.* She has *practical* experience of gardening, besides having studied the subject at college. *Practical* people tackle jobs with efficiency and common sense.

practice (*prak*-tis) *n.* (a) Regular habit or way of doing something. *Ex.* It is his *practice* to walk two miles a day, whatever the weather. (b) Repeated exercise in order to learn a skill. *Ex.* You need more *practice* if you are to swim well. (c) The work a doctor or lawyer does; their patients or clients as a whole.

practise (*prak*-tis) *v.* To do a thing regularly and repeatedly, so as to be skilled and keep at one's best in it. *Ex.* Musicians must *practise* regularly.

praise (prayz) *v.* To tell someone how highly you think of him, or to speak well of him to others. *Ex.* The brave rescuers received a lot of *praise* (*n.*).

prank *n.* A mischievous trick or game; a practical joke.

prawn *n.* A small edible shellfish, like a shrimp but larger.

pray *v.* (a) To turn oneself towards God in thought and often in words. A *prayer* (*n.*) is words used in *praying*. (b) To ask earnestly.

pre- is a prefix meaning 'before'.

preach (preech) *v.* To give a sermon, as a *preacher* (*n.*) does in church.

precaution (pri-*kaw*-sh'n) *n.* An arrangement to prevent trouble or danger. *Ex.* The hole in the road was roped off as a *precaution* against accidents.

precede (pree-*seed*) *v.* To go before. *Ex.* The Queen *precedes* others wherever she goes; those with her give her *precedence* (*pres*-i-dens; *n.*). The dinner consisted of roast beef *preceded* by soup.

precious (*presh*-us) *adj.* Valuable; worth a great deal; much loved. *Ex.* Diamonds are *precious* stones; children are *precious* to their parents.

precipice (*pres*-ip-is) *n.* A steep cliff.

précis (*pray*-see) *n.* A shortened version of a piece of writing or a speech, giving the main points but leaving out the details; a summary.

precise (pri-*sys*) *adj.* Exact. *Ex.* The Greenwich time-signal gives the *precise* time.

precocious (pri-*koh*-shus) *adj.* Showing an advanced development of mind or body at an unusually early age. *Ex.* Mozart as a child had a *precocious* talent in music.

predecessor (*pree*-de-ses-or) *n.* One who held a position before the present holder. *Ex.* The *predecessor* of the present headmaster had been in the school for 20 years.

predicament (pri-*dik*-a-ment) *n.* Awkward situation. *Ex.* They were in a *predicament* when they found themselves locked in.

predict (pri-*dikt*) *v.* To tell beforehand what will happen. *Ex.* rain is *predicted* for tomorrow.

preen *v.* To smarten up the feathers with beak, as birds do.

prefabricate (pree-*fab*-rik-ayt) *v.* To make up a building etc. in sections so that it can be put together quickly on the site.

preface (*pref*-is) *n.* A short introduction at the beginning of a book, explaining what it is about etc.

prefect (*pree*-fekt) *n.* An older pupil appointed to help with the responsibilities of running a school.

prefer (pri-*fur*) *v.* To like one thing better than another. *Ex.* He *prefers* soccer to rugger; he has a *preference* (*n.*) for it.

prefix (*pree*-fiks) *n.* A syllable placed at the beginning of a word to change its meaning. *Ex. Dis*appear, *il*legal, *un*true.

pregnant (*preg*-nant) *adj.* (Of a mother-to-be) carrying in her body a child yet to be born.

prehistoric (pree-his-*to*-rik) *adj.* Belonging to the time before *history* began to be written.

prejudice (*prej*-ew-dis) *n.* The state of a mind already made up about something (usually against it). *Ex.* Racial *prejudice* is *prejudice* against people of other races just because of their race, not for anything known against them.

prematurely (*prem*-a-tewr-li) *adv.* Too early or too soon. *Ex.* His hair became *prematurely* grey when he was only 25.

premier (*prem*-i-er) 1. *adj.* The first or chief. 2. *n.* A Prime Minister.

première (*prem*-i-air) *n.* The first performance of a play etc.

premises (*prem*-is-es) *n. pl.* A legal word meaning land with its buildings.

premium (*pree*-mi-um) *n.* The sum of money to be paid to insure something; a prize.

prepare (pri-*pair*) *v.* (a) To make ready. *Ex.* She *prepared* the supper. (b) To get ready for, as one can *prepare* for an examination or journey. To be *prepared* to do something is to be ready to. *Ex.* I am *prepared* to forgive him if he will apologize.

preposition (prep-o-*zish*'n) *n.* (In grammar) A word which shows the relationship between a noun and another noun or pronoun. *Ex.* Toast *with* marmalade. *Round* the lighthouse. *Through* the door. (With, round and through are *prepositions*).

prescribe (pri-*skryb*) *v.* To order. Often used of the order a doctor writes (*prescription*; *n.*) for medicine or other treatment.

presence (*prez*-ens) *n.* Being present. *Ex.* The ballet was performed in the *presence* of the princess.

present (*prez*-ent) *adj.* (a) In the place concerned; at hand. The opposite of absent. (b) The time now. *Ex.* 'I am too busy at *present*, but I will see you later on.' *Presently* (*adv.*) means before long; a short time from now.

present (pri-*zent*) *v.* (a) To give, usually on a formal occasion. *Ex.* The mayor *presented* the prizes. A *present* (*prez*-ent; *n.*) is a gift. (b) To introduce, especially an entertainment to the public.

preserve (pri-*zerv*) *v.* To keep safe from harm; to guard against decay. *Ex.* The life-jacket *preserved* his life, for he could not swim. Being made into jams and jellies *preserves* fruit; jams are sometimes called *preserves* (*n.*).

preside (pri-*zyd*) *v.* To be in charge at a meeting.

president (*prez*-i-dent) *n.* The elected head of a republic, or of an organization such as a sports club.

press 1. *v.* (a) To squeeze. *Ex.* To *press* the juice from a lemon. (b) To make smooth with an iron; this is done by applying *pressure* (*n.*) and heat. 2. *n.* (a) A place where books are printed; the machine that prints them. (b) Newspapers and journalists are often called the *press*.

pressure cooker (*presh*-er *kUk*-er) *n.* An airtight cooking-pot which *cooks* very fast under *steam pressure.*

prestige (pres-*teezh*) *n.* A high position in people's opinion because of success, power or influence. *Ex.* The rank of admiral carries *prestige.*

presume (pri-*zewm*) *v.* (a) To take for granted; to suppose something without having proof. *Ex.* I *presume* you visited Westminster Abbey, as I know of your interest in cathedrals. (b)

To do something without having the right to. *Ex.* It was *presumptuous* (*adj.*) of him to send those people away, for I had invited them to come.

pretend (pri-*tend*) *v.* (a) To make-believe, either in play or to deceive. *Ex.* In this game we are *pretending* to be Cavaliers and Roundheads. The thief *pretended* to be a window-cleaner, but we discovered the *pretence* (*n.*) in time. (b) To make claim to a throne etc. *Pretentious* (*adj.*) means claiming importance or fine qualities which are usually not deserved.

pretext (*pree*-tekst) *n.* An untrue reason given to hide the real one. *Ex.* I wanted to overhear them, so I came back on the *pretext* of looking for my gloves.

prevail (pri-*vayl*) *v.* To gain a victory; to be general, or the chief feature. *Ex.* Bad weather *prevailed* throughout February. We *prevailed* on (persuaded) him to get his hair cut.

prevent (pri-*vent*) *v.* To stop something happening or being done. *Ex.* This high fencing *prevents* balls going into other gardens.

previous (*pree*-vi-us) *adj.* Earlier; former. *Ex.* They remembered where the church was from a *previous* visit. We now live in London, but *previously* (*adv.*) we lived in Dorset.

prey (pray) *n.* A creature which is hunted and killed by another. *Ex.* An eagle is a bird of *prey*, killing for its food. Zebras are often the *prey* of lions and leopards.

price *n.* The money for which something is bought or sold; whatever is asked for in exchange for something. *Priceless* (*adj.*) means so valuable that no one can name a *price* for it.

pride (pryd) *n.* Having too high an opinion of oneself; feeling pleased with something one has done, or things that one can take credit for. *Ex.* He is a *proud* (*adj.*) man (full of *pride*), and thinks other people beneath him. We felt *proud* of (or full of *pride* for) our son when he won a medal.

priest (preest) *n.* A person appointed to perform religious acts (rites) and act as a go-between between a believer and a god; a clergyman.

prig *n.* A self-satisfied person who always behaves correctly.

prim *adj.* With very precise, formal manners; not acting in a natural, relaxed way.

primary (*prym*-a-ri) *adj.* First in order or in importance. *Ex.* A *primary* school is the first school to be attended. The *primary* reason for our not coming to the meeting is that we can't get a baby-sitter.

prime (prym) 1. *adj.* First in importance; of the best quality. *Ex.* The *Prime* Minister; a piece of *prime* beef. 2. *n.* The time at which a person or thing is at the best. *Ex.* In his *prime*, he was a great athlete.

primitive (*prim*-it-iv) *adj.* (a) To do with the earliest form of life on earth. (b) In the early stages of civilization. *Ex.* A *primitive* tribe. (c) Simple and crude, often because of being made long ago. *Ex. Primitive* pottery.

primrose (*prim*-rohz) *n.* A pale yellow Spring wildflower set in a rosette of leaves.

prince *n.* The son of a monarch; the ruler of a minor state. A *princess* is the daughter of a monarch or the wife of a *prince*.

principal (*prin*-sip-al) *adj.* Chief, most important. *Ex.* The *principal* building in our village is the church. The head of a college may be called the *principal* (*n.*).

principle (*prin*-si-p'l) *n.* (a) An implied rule. *Ex.* You should have obeyed the *principle* that one should ask permission first, before borrowing something. (b) Behaviour according to moral laws. *Ex.* He is a man of *principle* and will deal honestly with you.

print 1. *n.* (a) A picture or writing made by pressing an inked block on to paper. (b) Any mark made by pressure. *Ex.* A *finger-print*; a *footprint*. (c) A photograph made from a negative. 2. *v.* (a) To mark by pressing on something, used especially of *printed* (*adj.*) matter made by a *printing* (*adj.*) press. (b) To write in letters that are not joined together.

prism (*priz*'m) *n.* A specially-shaped glass object which can show light split into its separate (rainbow) colours.

prison (*priz*'n) *n.* A building to which those convicted of breaking the law, or awaiting trial, may be sent.

private (*pry*-vit) 1. *n.* A soldier of the lowest rank. 2. *adj.* Concerning oneself only. *Ex.* One's *private* life, *private* correspondence. (b) Confidential. *Ex.* The council held a *private* meeting, to which journalists were not admitted.

privilege (*priv*-il-ij) *n.* A special favour, advantage or right. *Ex.* We felt *privileged* when allowed to visit the castle's private apartments.

prize (pryz) *n.* An award or present for succeeding in something.

probable (*prob*-a-b'l) *adj.* Likely but not certain to happen. *Ex.* We shall *probably* (*adv.*) be in time; it is a *probability* (*n.*).

probation (proh-*bay*-sh'n) *n.* (a) A period of trial or testing. (b) A system under which a court allows an offender to live at home under the supervision of a *probation officer.*

problem (*prob*-lem) *n.* A question difficult to answer or make up one's mind about; a question for solving, such as a *maths problem.* *Ex.* It was a *problem* to find a way of feeding the refugees.

procedure (proh-*see*-jer) *n.* The way of doing something. *Ex.* The *procedure* for getting tickets is to apply for them by letter.

proceed (proh-*seed*) *v.* To move forward; to go on, continue. *Ex.* The concert *proceeded* after the interval.

process (*proh*-ses) *n.* A method of doing something. *Ex.* There is a *process* by which steel is made from iron.

procession (proh-*sesh*'n) *n.* A number of people proceeding together in an orderly way, as part of a ceremony, demonstration etc.

proclaim (proh-*klaym*) *v.* To announce officially. *Ex.* A public holiday was *proclaimed* for the Queen's Jubilee.

procure (proh-*kewr*) *v.* To get, obtain. *Ex.* It was difficult to *procure* lodgings in the crowded city.

prodigy (*prod*-ij-i) *n.* A wonder, especially a child of exceptional genius, such as Mozart.

produce (prod-*ews*) *v.* To make; to grow; to bring forth so that it can be seen. *Ex.* Our garden *produces* many vegetables. She *produced* cups and plates from the picnic basket. What a garden or farm *produces* is called its *produce* (*prod*-cws; *n.*).

profession (proh-*fesh*'n) *n.* An occupation requiring a high degree of learning and special training. *Ex.* He is a doctor by *profession.* A *professor* (*n.*) is a highly qualified teacher in a university.

proficient (proh-*fish*-ent) *adj.* Able to do something well.

profile (*proh*-fyl) *n.* The side view of a face.

profit (*prof*-it) 1. *n.* Something gained (usually money). *Ex.* I bought these flowers for 20p and sold them for 30p, making 10p *profit.* 2. *v.* To gain advantage; to receive a *profit.* *Ex.* She has *profited* from extra coaching in tennis. *Profitable* (*adj.*) means bringing in a good *profit.*

profound (proh-*fownd*) *adj.* Deep; deeply felt. *Ex.* His knowledge of maths is *profound.* His grief at her death was *profound.*

profuse (proh-*fews*) *adj.* Extremely plentiful; excessive.

programme (*proh*-gram)   *n.* A list of things to be done; a leaflet giving details of a play, concert etc.   *Ex.* TV *programmes* are printed in the newspapers.

progress (*proh*-gres)   1. *n.* A going forward; improvement.   *Ex.* We have made great *progress* in tidying up the garden. 2. *v.* (proh-*gres*) To go forward.

prohibit (proh-*hib*-it)   *v.* To forbid.

project   1. (*proj*-ekt)   *n.* (a) A planned course of action.   *Ex.* The council is working on a *project* to keep heavy lorries out of the city centre. (b) A piece of class-work in a school, done over several weeks on a particular subject. 2. (proh-*jekt*) *v.* To throw an image on to a background, as a film is *projected* on to a screen.

prolong (proh-*long*)   *v.* To lengthen.   *Ex.* We had to *prolong* our stay as we were snowed up.

promenade (prom-en-*ahd*)   *n.* A pedestrian way, usually by the sea, where people can enjoy a stroll.

prominent (*prom*-in-ent)   *adj.* Easily seen; jutting out; noticeable; distinguished.   *Ex.* The most *prominent* building in the High Street is the Town Hall. The mayor plays a *prominent* part in local affairs.

promise (*prom*-is)   *v.* To assure someone, or give him your word about something.   *Ex.* He *promised* to be home early, and he always keeps his *promises* (*n.*). *Promising* (*adj.*) means likely to do well or to improve.   *Ex.* The weather looks *promising*.

promote (prom-*oht*)   *v.* To raise to a higher rank or position.   *Ex.* An army corporal could get *promotion* (*n.*) to sergeant.

prompt   1. *adj.* Quick to act; done at once.   *Ex.* His *prompt* action in putting out the fire saved their lives. 2. *v.* To persuade to do something; to remind an actor of his words.   *Ex.* I don't know what *prompted* him to write such a letter.

prone (*prohn*)   *adj.* (*a*) Lying flat on one's face. (*b*) *Prone to* means inclined to, likely to.   *Ex.* He is *prone to* panic in emergencies.

prong   *n.* One of the sharp points of a fork or rake.

pronoun (*proh*-nown)   *n.* A word standing in place of a noun.   *Ex.* In 'Here is your cake, but don't eat it yet', *it* is the *pronoun* standing for the noun 'cake'.

pronounce (proh-*nowns*)   *v.* To utter the various sounds of speech. The way you *pronounce* words is your *pronunciation* (*n.*) of them.

proof   *n.* Something which shows the truth of a statement etc.   *Ex.* His footprints were *proof* that he had been there; they *proved* (*v.*) it.

prop 1. *n.* A stick or pole used to hold something up, as a *clothes-prop* does a clothes line. 2. *v.* To hold up, or act as a *prop.*

propaganda (prop-a-*gan*-da) *n.* Something written or spoken with the intention of making people believe what you want them to believe. It is used in wartime to mislead and dishearten the enemy.

propel (proh-*pel*) *v.* To make a thing move forward. *Ex.* This wheel-chair can be *propelled* by the person sitting in it.

propeller (proh-*pel*-er) *n.* A shaft with shaped blades, which turns in the water or air and drives a ship or aeroplane forward.

proper (*prop*-er) *adj.* Correct. *Ex.* Please hold your knife *properly* (*adv.*).

property (*prop*-er-ti) *n.* Something which a person owns. One who owns land or buildings is a *property-owner* and is the *proprietor* (*n.*) of them.

prophecy (*prof*-es-i) *n.* A statement of what will happen at some future time. *Ex.* In the Bible, the *prophet* (*n.*) Isaiah *prophesied* (*v.*) many things.

proportion (prop-*awr*-sh'n) *n.* (a) A fixed share. *Ex.* He gives a *proportion* of his earnings to charity. (b) Pleasing balance and harmony. *Ex.* Eighteenth-century town houses have pleasing *proportions.*

propose (prop-*ohz*) *v.* To suggest, offer, intend to; to offer marriage.

prose (prohz) *n.* Ordinary speech or writing, not poetry.

prosecute (*pros*-e-kewt) *v.* To take someone to law. *Ex.* She was *prosecuted* for neglecting her children.

prospect (*pros*-pekt) *n.* (a) A view. (b) What one expects, or seems likely, to happen. *Ex.* There was a red sky at sunset, so there is a *prospect* of fine weather tomorrow.

prosper (*pros*-per) *v.* To get on well and be successful. *Ex.* The new business is beginning to *prosper* and make money; the owner is getting quite *prosperous* (*adj.*) and may soon enjoy great *prosperity* (*n.*).

protect (proh-*tekt*) *v.* To guard or keep safe. *Ex.* Property is sometimes *protected* by guard-dogs. Umbrellas *protect* us from the rain.

protein (*proh*-teen) *n.* The body-building food needed by all living creatures, which forms part of all living cells.

protest (proh-*test*) *v.* To object or complain. *Ex.* He *protested* that his wages were too low; he made a *protest* (*proh*-test; *n.*) about it.

proud (prowd) *adj.* Full of pride.

prove (proov) *v.* To put to the *proof* (*n.*); to show that a thing is really so.

proverb (*prov*-urb) *n.* A well-known saying which states a simple truth, such as 'It's never too late to mend'.

provide (pro-*vyd*) *v.* To supply; to prepare for. *Ex.* Our hens *provide* us with eggs. We have *provided* ourselves with enough food (often called *provisions*; *n.*) for a three-day camping holiday. He *provided* for his old age by saving up; he made *provision* (*n.*) for it.

provoke (pro-*vohk*) *v.* To annoy, excite or make angry. *Ex.* They *provoked* the boys to attack by jeering at them; they gave *provocation* (*n.*).

prowl (prowl) *v.* To move about stealthily in search of prey, plunder etc.

prudent (*proo*-dent) *adj.* Cautious, wise. *Ex.* It was *imprudent* (not *prudent*) to climb the mountain without proper boots.

prune (proon) *n.* A dried plum.

pry *v.* To peer into or examine what is private.

psalm (sahm) *n.* A sacred song or hymn, especially one from the Old Testament Book of *Psalms*.

public (*pub*-lik) *adj.* Concerning everyone; not private. The *public* (*n.*) means all the people in a community.

publication (pub-lik-*ay*-sh'n) *n.* Any book, magazine etc. that is *published*; its production for sale.

publish (*pub*-lish) *v.* (a) To make known to the *public*. (b) To prepare books and other printed matter for sale.

pudding (*pUd*-ing) *n.* (a) A boiled, baked or steamed dish of pastry, suet or rice etc., often with stewed fruit or treacle etc., eaten as the last course of a meal. (b) Also used of a *steak-and-kidney pudding, Yorkshire pudding* etc.

puddle (*pud* 'l) *n.* A small pool of muddy water.

pulley (*pUl*-i) *n.* A wheel with a groove over which a rope runs so that a weight may be raised when the rope is *pulled*.

pulp (pulp) *n.* A soft moist mass of animal or vegetable matter. The inside of many fruits is *pulpy* (*adj.*).

pulpit (*pUl*-pit) *n.* A small high platform with a railing round it, from which the sermon is preached in church.

pulse (puls) *n.* The beating of the arteries, which can be felt at the wrist etc.; a throbbing or rhythmical beat.

pump (pump) *n.* A machine for lifting water to a higher level. *Ex.* Firemen use powerful *pumps* to direct water on to a fire.

punctual (*punk*-choo-al) *adj.* At the exact time; not late. *Ex.* The bus will leave *punctually* (*adv.*) at ten.

punctuation (punk-choo-*ay*-sh'n) *n.* The marking off of a sentence with commas, stops etc., to make it easier to follow the writer's meaning.

puncture (*punk*-cher) *v.* To pierce a small hole in something. *Ex.* Broken glass had made a *puncture* (*n.*) in the tyre.

punish (*pun*-ish) *v.* To make a person suffer in some way, for having done something wrong.

punt (punt) 1. *n.* A flat-bottomed boat with square ends, pushed in shallow waters by a pole. 2. *v.* To kick a football before it reaches the ground.

puny (*pew*-ni) *adj.* Small and weak.

pupil (*pew*-pil) *n.* (a) The round opening in the middle of the eye where light enters. (b) One who is being taught.

puppet (*pup*-et) *n.* A doll which is moved by strings, wires or hand, often used in toy theatres.

purchase (*pur*-chis) *v.* To buy. What one buys is a *purchase* (*n.*).

pure (pewr) *adj.* Clean, fresh, unspoiled; free from sin. *Ex. Pure* air; *pure-hearted. Impure* (not *pure*) water can be made pure by using a *purifier* (*n.*), which restores its *purity* (*n.*).

purple (*pur* p'l) *n.* A colour produced by mixing red and blue; a violet colour.

purpose (*pur*-pus) *n.* What is aimed at, the end wished for. *Ex.* The *purpose* of Columbus's voyage was to find a new way to India. To do a thing *on purpose* is to do it intentionally.

pursue (per-*sew*) *v.* To chase; to follow in order to catch. *Ex.* The police *pursued* the thieves, and others joined in the *pursuit* (*n.*).

putty (*put*-i) *n.* A paste of oil and whitening which is soft when put on but hardens later. It is used by glaziers to stick window-panes into their frames.

puzzle (*puz*'l) 1. *n.* Something which causes perplexity; a problem or toy which is meant to perplex for amusement, such as a *crossword* or *jig-saw puzzle.* 2. *v.* To make perplexed.

pyjamas (pa-*jah*-maz) *n.* A loose suit of jacket and trousers worn in bed.

pylon (*py*-lon)   *n.* A metal structure which supports electric power cables.

pyramid (*pi*-ram-id)   *n.* A shape on a square base with triangular sides meeting at a point.   *Ex.* The *Great Pyramid* of Egypt.

python (*py*-thon)   *n.* A large snake which coils round its victim and crushes it to death.

Q

quadruped (*kwod*-roo-ped)   *n.* A four-legged animal.

quaint (kwaynt)   *adj.* Odd and strange-looking but attractive; pleasantly old-fashioned.

quake (kwayk)   *v.* To shake, often with fear.

qualification (kwol-if-ik-*ay*-sh'n)   *n.* The proved ability which fits a person for a particular job. The winner of a round of a contest qualifies (*v.*) (becomes qualified) to go on to the next round.

quality (*kwol*-it-i)   *n.* The nature or character of a person or thing.   *Ex.* Clothes of good *quality* last longer.

qualm (kwahm)   *n.* An uneasy feeling, especially because of fear or doubt.

quantity (*kwon*-ti-ti)   *n.* The amount, bulk or number of a thing. *Ex.* If you don't want to get fat you should limit the *quantity* of sweets you eat.

quarantine (*kwo*-ran-teen)   *n.* Isolation to prevent the spread of an infection.

quarrel (*kwo*-rel)   *v.* To disagree angrily with someone.   *Ex.* They are always having *quarrels* (*n.*); they are *quarrelsome* (*adj.*).

quarry (*kwo*-ri)   *n.* (a) A surface pit from which building-stone or slate is dug. (b) A creature being hunted by animal or man.

quart (kwawrt)   *n.* A liquid measure equal to two pints or just over a litre.

quarter (*kwawrt*-er)   *n.* (a) A fourth part of anything. (b) A period of three months. (c) A district or direction.   *Ex.* We shall get no help from that *quarter*. (d) Mercy.

quaver (*kway*-ver)   1. *n.* A note of a certain length in music. 2. *v.* To tremble and shake, usually referring to the voice.   *Ex.* The old people sang with *quavering* voices.

queasy (*kwee*-zi)   *adj.* Inclined to feel sick.

queer (kweer) *adj.* Strange, odd.

quell (kwel) *v.* To put a stop to, to subdue. *Ex.* The rebellion was *quelled* by the army.

quench (kwench) *v.* To put out (a fire); to satisfy thirst.

query (*kweer*-i) *n.* A question.

quest (kwest) *n.* A search, especially an expedition to look for something.

question (*kwes*-chon) 1. *n.* The act of asking (for a reply); what is asked; the subject being discussed. *Ex.* The *question* is, what do we do next? 2. *v.* To ask; to express doubt. A *questionnaire* (kwest-yon-*air*) is a set of questions, usually printed, such as one used in a population census.

queue (kew) *n.* A number of people, vehicles etc. in line behind each other, awaiting their turn. To *queue* (*v.*) is to join a *queue*.

quicksand (*kwik*-sand) *n.* Soft wet sand into which a person would sink deep if he tried to walk on it.

quiet (*kwy*-et) *adj.* Without (or with little) noise or movement. *Ex.* We enjoyed the *quietness* (*n.*) of the countryside.

quill (kwil) *n.* A large stiff feather, the hollow stem of which was formerly used as a pen.

quilt (kwilt) 1. *n.* A bedcover made by stitching, in compartments, two pieces of cloth which enclose a layer of soft warm material. 2. *v.* To stitch something in this way.

quiver (*kwiv*-er) 1. *n.* A case to carry arrows. 2. *v.* To tremble, to quaver.

quota (*kwoh*-ta) *n.* A share to be given or received. *Ex.* Everyone had his *quota* of chores to do in camp.

quote (kwoht) *v.* To repeat something that has already been spoken or written. *Ex.* I can *quote* his exact words; I can give a *quotation* (*n.*) of them.

R

rabbi (*rab*-y) *n.* A Jewish priest or teacher of the law.

rabble (*rab*'l) *n.* A disorderly crowd of people.

rabies (*ray*-beez) *n.* A very dangerous virus disease, which can be caught by humans from infected animals.

race (rays) *n.* (a) A group of people who have many physical characteristics in common. *Ex.* The Jewish *race*. (b) A speed competition. Athletes, horses, boats etc. can all *race* (*v.*) to reach the winning-post first.

rack 1. *n.* A kind of shelf made of bars for holding tools, plates etc. 2. *v.* (a) To torture by stretching; to cause great pain. *Ex.* He is *racked* with rheumatism. (b) To stretch the mind to invent, or the memory to recall. *Ex.* I *racked* my brains to think of a way out of the difficulty.

racket *n.* (a) A banging, clattering noise. (b) An oval bat with tightly stretched crossed strings, used in tennis. (Also spelt *racquet*.)

radar (*ray*-dar) *n.* A form of radio equipment with a screen on which approaching aircraft, hazards to navigation etc. show up.

radiant (*ray*-di-ant) *adj.* Shining; beaming with happiness.

radiate (*ray*-di-ayt) *v.* To send out rays of light, heat etc. The sending out of such rays is called *radiation* (*n.*). A *radiator* (*n.*) spreads heat in a room; another type is used to cool car engines etc.

radio (*ray*-di-oh) *n.* A method of electrical communication without using wires; the apparatus used to receive such communication (a wireless-set, transistor etc.).

radioactivity (ray-di-oh-akt-*iv*-it-i) *n.* The continuous sending out of rays of energy, a feature of certain substances such as radium and uranium, and highly dangerous unless controlled.

radish (*rad*-ish) *n.* A small red root-vegetable with a white centre and a strong flavour.

radium (*ray*-di-um) *n.* A very rare metal which gives out energy rays which help to heal certain diseases.

radius (*ray*-di-us) *n.* A straight line drawn from the centre of a circle to its circumference; the length of such a line.

raffle (*raf*'l) *n.* A form of lottery used to sell things for charity; people buy numbered tickets, one of which is picked at random, and its holder wins the article *raffled* (*v.*).

raft (rahft) *n.* A number of logs etc. lashed together to form a floating platform.

rafter (*rahf*-ter) *n.* A sloping beam used to support a roof.

rage (rayj) *n.* Great anger. *Ex.* If you are in a *rage*, you *rage* (*v.*) about something and become *enraged* (*adj.*).

raid (rayd) *n.* A sudden attack.

rail (rayl) *n.* (a) A horizontal bar used as part of a fence; one of a pair of steel tracks for trains or trams. (b) Railway. *Ex*. Send it by *rail*.

rainbow (*rayn*-boh) *n*. An arch of coloured light, split into the seven colours of which light is made up, sometimes seen in the sky in sunshine after rain.

raise (rayz) *v*. (a) To lift up. (b) To rear animals or to get a crop to grow.

raisin (*rayz*-in) *n*. A dried grape, often put in cakes.

rake (rayk) 1. *n*. A garden tool with a long handle and sharp prongs, used to break up and smooth soil, gather leaves, weeds etc. 2. *v*. To pull together with (or as with) a *rake*.

rally 1. *v*. (a) To gather supporters, troops etc. round one in preparation for united action. *Ex*. The colonel *rallied* his scattered troops; they *rallied* round him. (b) To recover health or energy. 2. *n*. A mass meeting, as of Scouts, racing drivers etc.

ram 1. *n*. A male sheep. 2. *v*. To drive something in with heavy blows; to pack something into a container very tightly. *Ex*. Cotton waste had been *rammed* down the pipe and had blocked it. A *battering-ram* (*n*.) was formerly used to batter down castle walls.

ramble 1. *v*. (a) To stroll about for pleasure; to wander about. (b) To wander from the subject when talking. 2. *n*. A *rambling* (*adj*.) walk.

ramp *n*. A sloping path made where steps or stairs would not be suitable.

rampage (ram-*payj*) *v*. To behave in a violent, stormy way.

ranch (rahnch) *n*. A large livestock farm, especially in North America.

rancid (*ran*-sid) *adj*. (Of stale fat) Smelling or tasting unpleasant.

random (*ran*-dum) *adj*. Left to chance; without care, aim or thought. *Ex*. At bingo, the numbers called are chosen *at random* (*adv*.).

range (raynj) 1. *n*. (a) An enclosed fireplace with ovens etc. (b) A continuous line of mountains. (c) Unfenced grazing land (the cowboys' open *range*). (d) The farthest distance possible for something to reach. *Ex*. The *range* of this aeroplane is 3000 miles. (e) The full extent of anything within limits, for instance the *range* of a singing voice, or the daily *range* of temperature. 2. *v*. To roam about freely. *Ex*. The discussion *ranged* over many topics.

rank 1. *n*. (a) A row of things (such as taxis) or of people, especially soldiers. (b) A position or grade of importance in its relation to others, especially in the armed forces. *Ex.* An admiral *ranks* (*v.*) above a captain. 2. *adj.* Having a bad sour smell or taste.

ransack (*ran*-sak) *v.* To search very thoroughly, usually leaving mess and muddle behind.

ransom (*ran*-sum) *n.* The money paid to free a captive.

rapid *adj.* Quick; with great speed. *Rapids* (*n.*) are the part of a river where it descends steeply, often among rocks, and flows very *rapidly* (*adv.*).

rapture (*rap*-cher) *n.* Delight, tremendous joy.

rare (rair) *adj.* Unusual, or not numerous, and often therefore valuable.

rascal (*rah*-skal) *n.* A mischievous child; a rogue.

rash 1. *adj.* Hasty, acting without thinking. *Ex.* He was *rash* to rush off without checking that he had enough petrol. 2. *n.* Red spots on the skin, such as appear in measles.

raspberry (*rahz*-be-ri) *n.* A small red soft fruit growing on tall canes.

rat *n.* A long-tailed gnawing animal, similar to a mouse but much larger and more destructive.

rate *n.* (a) The relation between two amounts or values. *Ex.* Driving at the *rate* of 70 miles an hour. Wages at the *rate* of £3 an hour. The birth *rate*. (b) Class. *Ex.* A third-*rate* hotel. (c) Speed. *Ex.* He ran at a great (or slow) *rate*. (d) A local tax on property paid by householders etc.

ratio (*ray*-shi-oh) *n.* The proportion of one quantity to another. *Ex.* The grassed area of the playground is one-third of the whole playground, and so is in the *ratio* of 1 to 2.

ration (*rash*-on) *n.* A fixed allowance of food or other necessities. *Ex.* Water had to be *rationed* (*v.*) during the drought; the daily *ration* was small.

rational (*rash*-on-al) *adj.* Sensible.

rave *v.* To talk wildly, because of delirium, over-excitement etc.

raven (*ray*-ven) *n.* The largest of the crow family, an all-black bird with a hoarse croak, which feeds on meat.

ravenous (*rav*-en-us) *adj.* Extremely hungry.

raw *adj.* Uncooked; rough; in its natural state, as material may be before manufacture.

ray *n.* A line or beam of light or other energy.

rayon (*ray*-on) *n.* A man-made material similar to silk, used to make clothes, curtains etc. One kind is called viscose.

raze (rayz) *v.* To destroy completely, usually referring to buildings. *Ex.* The victors *razed* the city's walls to the ground.

razor (*ray*-zor) *n.* A sharp tool used to remove hair from face and body.

re- is a prefix meaning *back* or *again*. *Ex. Re*call, to call back; *re*count, to count again; *re*fresh, to make fresh again.

reach (reech) *v.* (a) To stretch out the hand to get. *Ex.* Can you *reach* that shelf and get me that book? (b) To arrive at. *Ex.* We *reached* London at five. (c) To extend to. *Ex.* Our line of pennies *reached* from the school gate to the main door. To be within *reach* (*n.*) means able to be *reached*.

react (re-*akt*) *v.* To do or say something in response to something. *Ex.* The children *reacted* with joy to the suggestion of a boat-trip. A *reaction* (re-*ak*-sh′n; *n.*) may be an action which goes the opposite way to something. *Ex.* After overdoing things he suffered a *reaction*, and had no energy at all.

ready (*red*-i) *adj.* Prepared, willing. *Ex.* Dinner is *ready* (prepared) and we are *ready* (willing) to help lay the table.

real (*ree*-al) *adj.* Actually existing, not imagined; not artificial; genuine. *Ex. Real* silk; *real* affection. Guy Fawkes *really* (*adv.*) lived.

reality (ree-*al*-i-ti) *n.* What is *real* or *really* so. *Ex.* He looks French but in *reality* he's Welsh.

realize (*ree*-al-yz) *v.* To understand clearly; to become fact. *Ex.* I didn't *realize* you two had met before. His hopes and ambitions were *realized*.

realm (relm) *n.* A kingdom.

reap (reep) *v.* To cut corn etc. at harvest time.

rear (reer) 1. *n.* The back part of a thing. 2. *v.* (a) To grow or nourish or bring up. *Ex.* You can *rear* puppies or a family of children. (b) To get up on the hind legs, as a horse can.

reason (*ree*-zon) *n.* (a) The power of drawing conclusions from what one knows. (b) The cause or explanation. *Ex.* We tried to find the *reason* for the noise. (c) Common sense, sensible behaviour, moderation. *Ex.* He wouldn't listen to *reason*. I'm sure you will behave *reasonably* (*adv.*). The price was *reasonable* (not excessive).

rebel (re-*bel*) *v.* To go against the rules and orders of those in authority. *Rebels* (*reb*-elz; *n.*) sometimes *rebel* against unjust laws; if organized they may take part in a *rebellion* (*n.*).

rebuke (ri-*bewk*) *n.* To reprove or scold. *Ex.* They were *rebuked* for being late.

recall (ri-*kawl*) v. (a) To call back. *Ex.* The teacher *recalled* the boy as he was leaving the room. (b) To call back to memory, to remember.

recede (ri-*seed*) *v.* To move back farther off. *Ex.* When the tide is going out, the sea *recedes*.

receipt (ri-*seet*) *n.* (a) The act of receiving. *Ex.* On *receipt* of his letter she telephoned him. (b) A written statement that money has been received. *Ex.* I paid my subscription and got a *receipt*.

receive (ri-*seev*) *v.* To get or be given. *Ex.* You can *receive* an invitation, a present or punishment etc.

recent (*ree*-sent) *adj.* Having happened only a short time ago. *Ex.* He is nearly better now, after his *recent* illness.

reception (ri-*sep*-sh'n) *n.* (a) The act of *receiving*. *Ex.* Our aunt gave us a warm *reception*. (b) A large, formal party at which many guests are *received* by the hosts.

recipe (*res*-i-pi) *n.* The rules for preparing a particular food or drink. Cookery books contain *recipes* giving the ingredients, quantities, method and time of cooking etc.

recital (ri-*syt*-al) *n.* A musical performance, often by a soloist. *Ex.* A piano *recital*.

recite (re-*syt*) *v.* To say aloud from memory. What one *recites* is called a *recitation* (res-i-*tay*-sh'n; *n.*).

reckless (*rek*-les) *adj.* Without care; thinking nothing of the danger or the consequence of what one does, as a *reckless* driver might.

reckon (*rek*-on) *v.* To count up; to suppose.

recline (ri-*klyn*) *v.* To lie back, as on a chair or sofa.

recognize (*rek*-og-nyz) *v.* To know again. *Ex.* I *recognized* him at once, by his long black coat. The *recognition* (*n.*) was mutual.

recoil (ri-*koil*) *v.* To draw back quickly, often in horror. *Ex.* She *recoiled* when she saw the snake. One can *recoil* at the idea of doing something horrible.

recollect (rek-o-*lekt*) *v.* To remember. *Ex.* She *recollected* where she had left her camera; she had a clear *recollection* (*n.*) of having put it on a rock.

recommend (rek-o-*mend*) *v.* To praise or speak favourably of, to others. *Ex.* Can you *recommend* a good book for me to read?

recompense (*rek*-om-pens) *v.* To pay back, reward or compensate. *Ex.* We *recompensed* the boys for their hard work by giving them a meal.

reconcile (*rek*-on-syl) *v.* To restore friendship after a quarrel. *Ex.* The two girls are now *reconciled* and greater friends than ever. To become *reconciled* to something disagreeable is to come to accept it or be resigned to it.

record 1. (ri-*kawrd*) *v.* (a) To set down in writing. (b) To transfer sound to a gramophone disc (*record*; *rek*-awrd; *n.*) or tape. 2. (*rek*-awrd) *adj.* The best so far. *Ex.* A *record* attendance at the cricket match. A *record* high jump, which breaks the *record* (*n.*).

recover (ri-*kuv*-er) *v.* (a) To get back what was lost. *Ex.* He soon *recovered* his temper and was his sunny self again. (b) To get better after an illness etc. *Ex.* She made a good *recovery* (*n.*) after her accident.

re-cover (ree-*kuv*-er) *v.* To put a new *cover* on, as on a cushion.

recreation (rek-ri-*aysh*'n) *n.* Pleasant occupation; relaxation and enjoyment from leisure activities, sport etc.

recruit (ri-*kroot*) 1. *n.* Someone who has just joined one of the armed services. 2. *v.* To get people to join one of the armed services.

rectangle (*rek*-tang-g'l) *n.* A four-sided figure or shape in which all four angles are right angles, such as a square or oblong.

rector (*rek*-tor) *n.* A vicar.

recuperate (ri-*kew*-per-ayt) *v.* To get back health after illness.

recur (ri-*kur*) *v.* To happen more than once. *Ex.* One type of malaria can *recur* throughout a person's life, once he has had it.

reduce (ri-*dews*) *v.* (a) To make less. *Ex.* To *reduce* one's weight. A *reduction* (*n.*) in price. (b) To alter shape, form etc. *Ex.* To *reduce* to powder. (c) To bring to some particular state. *Ex.* She was *reduced* to tears.

redundant (ri-*dun*-dant) *adj.* Superfluous. *Ex.* Workers may be made *redundant* when there is no longer enough work for them.

reef *n.* A line of rocks at or near the sea's surface, which can be a danger to shipping.

reek *v.* To smell strongly and unpleasantly; to give off fumes.

reel 1. *n.* (a) A small cylinder round which thread, film etc. is wound. *Ex.* A *cotton-reel.* (b) A lively Scottish or Irish dance. 2. *v.* To sway and stagger about as if dizzy.

refer (ri-*fur*) *v.* (a) To turn to for information; to direct someone to where he can get information. *Ex.* Nobody knew the answer, so he had to *refer* to a *reference* (*adj.*) book in the *reference* library to get the information he needed. (b) *Refer to* means to mention; to concern or apply to. *Ex.* He *referred to* his wartime experiences; he made several *references* (*n.*) to them. These regulations *refer to* motor-cyclists only.

referee (ref-er-*ee*) *n.* Someone who is *referred* to for his opinion or decision. In football and boxing the umpire is called a *referee*.

refine (ri-*fyn*) *v.* To make finer or purer. *Ex.* Petrol is petroleum (crude oil) *refined* in a *refinery* (*n.*).

reflect (ri-*flekt*) *v.* (a) To throw back light, heat or sound from a surface. *Ex.* When I look in a mirror I see my *reflection* (*n.*). (b) To think over. *Ex.* My grandmother often *reflects* on her past life, and sometimes chuckles at her *reflections* (*n.*).

reform (ri-*fawrm*) *v.* To make or become better. People who try to alter things for the better are called *reformers* (*n.*).

refrain (ri-*frayn*) 1. *n.* A chorus; the tune or words repeated at the end of each verse of a song or poem. 2. *v.* To stop oneself from doing something. *Ex.* The public is asked to *refrain* from walking on the grass.

refresh (ri-*fresh*) *v.* To make someone feel freshened and restored in strength. Food and drink are often called *refreshments* (*n.*).

refrigerator (ri-*frij*-er-ay-tor) *n.* A container for food kept at a low temperature, so that it is preserved longer. (Usually shortened to *fridge.*)

refuge (*ref*-ewj) *n.* A place of shelter or safety. One who takes *refuge* in another country from his own is a *refugee* (ref-ew-*jee*; *n.*).

refund (ree-*fund*) *v.* To pay back money. *Ex.* When rain prevented the match, ticket-holders had their money *refunded.*

refuse (ri-*fewz*) *v.* To say 'no' to what has been asked. *Ex.* He *refused* to come back with us, and his *refusal* (*n.*) offended us.

refuse (*ref*-ews) *n.* Rubbish, waste material.

regain (ree-*gayn*) *v.* To get back.

regal (*ree*-gal) *adj.* Like or connected with a monarch.

regard (ri-*gard*) 1. *n.* Respect; kindly feeling. '(Kind) *regards*', often written in letters, means 'friendly feelings'. *Ex.* He sent his *regards* to you. 2. *v.* To consider; to look upon as. *Ex.* I *regard* her as my best friend.

regiment (*rej*-i-ment) *n.* A group of soldiers commanded by a colonel.

region (*ree*-jon) *n.* (a) A large area of land or sea which is distinguished in some way from neighbouring areas. *Ex.* The Arctic *regions.* (b) A district. *Ex.* The Midland *region.*

register (*rej*-is-ter)   *n.* A list of persons kept for record purposes. *Ex.* A school attendance *register*; a hotel *register* which lists guests' names etc.

regret (ri-*gret*)   *n.* A sorrowful wish that a thing had been different. You can *regret* (*v.*) having left your umbrella at home, or *regret* (more deeply) someone's death.

regular (*reg*-ew-lar)   *adj.* (a) According to rule. (b) Not changing. *Ex.* His pulse beats *regularly* (*adv.*). (c) Happening at fixed times. *Ex.* There is a *regular* train service to Birmingham.

regulate (*reg*-ew-layt)   *v.* To make *regular* or keep in good order. Clocks need to be *regulated* to keep them accurate.

regulation (reg-ew-*lay*-sh'n)   *n.* A rule for controlling an organization or the running of something. *Ex.* The railway *regulations* say that every passenger must have a ticket.

rehearse (ri-*hurs*)   *v.* To practise something, usually for a public performance. These practices are called *rehearsals* (*n.*).

reign (rayn)   *v.* To rule as monarch. *Ex.* Queen Victoria's *reign* (*n.*) lasted 63 years.

rein (rayn)   *n.* One of the straps used to guide a horse.

reindeer (*rayn*-deer)   *n.* A hardy Arctic deer with large antlers; some are domesticated, some wild.

reinforce (ree-in-*fors*)   *v.* To strengthen by adding something. *Ex.* Concrete can be *reinforced* by putting steel bars in it.

reject (ri-*jekt*)   *v.* To throw out or refuse to have. *Ex.* She *rejected* his offer of marriage.

rejoice (ri-*jois*)   *v.* To feel joy and gladness. *Ex.* Everyone *rejoiced* when the trapped miners were rescued.

relapse (ri-*laps*)   *v.* To slip back into illness, or a life of crime. *Ex.* He seemed to be making a good recovery, but then had a *relapse* (*n.*).

relate (ri-*layt*)   *v.* (a) To tell a story. (b) To have some connection with or reference to.

relation (ri-*lay*-sh'n)   *n.* (a) A connection. *Ex.* Your story bears no *relation* to the truth. (b) Someone connected with the family by birth or marriage, such as a cousin, mother-in-law etc. Also called a *relative* (*rel*-a-tiv; *n.*).

relax (ri-*laks*)   *v.* To loosen; to take things easily. *Ex.* You can *relax* your grip on a rope, or *relax* body and mind on holiday.

relay 1. (*ree*-lay) *n.* A fresh supply of horses etc. to replace tired ones. A *relay-race* is run by *relays* of runners, each running over only part of the course. 2. (ree-*lay*) *v.* To pass on. *Ex.* He *relayed* the information that the dustmen were going on strike again.

release (ri-*lees*) *v.* To set free. *Ex.* They petitioned for the *release* (*n.*) of the prisoner.

relegate (*rel*-i-gayt) *v.* To remove to a lower place. *Ex.* A football team may be *relegated* to a lower division.

relent (ri-*lent*) *v.* To change one's mind and be less severe. *Ex.* At first the farmer would not let us camp on his land, but later he *relented*.

relief (ri-*leef*) *n.* A freeing from suffering, anxiety etc. *Ex.* It was a *relief* to learn that he was better. The dentist *relieved* (*v.*) my toothache.

religion (ri-*lij*-on) *n.* (a) A belief in an unseen higher power which governs the universe and our lives. Christianity, Buddhism, Islam etc. are great *religions*. (b) The rituals, moral behaviour etc. associated with a *religion* and observed by *religious* (*adj.*) people.

relish (*rel*-ish) *v.* To enjoy, especially food.

reluctant (ri-*luk*-tant) *adj.* Unwilling. *Ex.* She showed great *reluctance* (*n.*) to go to bed.

rely (ri-*ly*) *v.* To count on, depend on. *Ex.* We can *rely* on him to play well in goal; he is a *reliable* (ri-*ly*-a-b'l; *adj.*) goalie.

remain (ri-*mayn*) *v.* To stay or continue. *Ex.* The weather *remains* cold. What *remains* over is called the *remainder* (*n.*) or the *remains*.

remark (ri-*mark*) *v.* To say something about what one has noticed. *Ex.* The postman *remarked* on our lovely roses; we appreciated his *remarks* (*n.*).

remedy (*rem*-ed-i) *n.* A cure.

remember (ri-*mem*-ber) *v.* To keep in mind; not to forget.

remind (ri-*mynd*) *v.* To make a person remember something. *Ex. Remind* me to buy bread; without a *reminder* (*n.*) I'm sure to forget.

remittance (ri-*mit*-ans) *n.* Money sent. *Ex.* Enclose a stamped addressed envelope with your *remittance*.

remnant (*rem*-nant) *n.* Something left over. *Ex.* The *remnants* of a defeated army. The *remnants* at the ends of rolls of materials, which drapers sell cheap.

remorse (ri-*mawrs*) *n.* Bitter regret for wrongs done.

remote (ri-*moht*) *adj.* Far away, in a lonely position. *Ex.* He lives in a *remote* part of the Scottish Highlands.

remove (ri-*moov*) *v.* To take or move away. *Ex.* We used to live in London, but have *removed* to Manchester. Reference books must not be *removed* from the library.

rendezvous (*ron*-day-voo) *n.* A meeting-place agreed upon; an arranged meeting.

renew (ri-*new*) *v.* (a) To restore. *Ex.* He came back from holiday with *renewed* strength. (b) To replace with something new. *Ex.* It's time we *renewed* this worn carpet. (c) To begin again. *Ex.* He *renewed* his complaints. (d) To repeat or prolong. *Ex.* I *renewed* my subscription.

rent *n.* (a) Regular payment for the use of something, such as a flat or TV set. (b) A tear.

repair (ri-*pair*) *v.* To mend.

repeal (ri-*peel*) *v.* To cancel and abolish. Sometimes Parliament *repeals* laws that it once made.

repeat (ri-*peet*) *v.* To say again. *Repeatedly* (ri-*peet*-ed-li; *adv.*) means often. *Ex.* They *repeatedly* warned us of the danger.

repel (ri-*pel*) *v.* To push or drive back. *Ex.* The army *repelled* the invaders, who had to retreat to their ships.

repent (ri-*pent*) *v.* To be sorry for what one has done or failed to do. *Ex.* He showed such *repentance* (*n.*) for the trouble he had caused that they forgave him.

repetition (rep-et-*ish*'n) *n.* A repeating.

replace (ri-*plays*) *v.* (a) To put back. *Ex.* If you don't want the book, please *replace* it on the shelf. (b) To get something to take the *place* of. *Ex.* If you break this cup I shall have to *replace* it.

report (ri-*pawrt*) 1. *v.* To describe, or make known information on a subject. One makes a *report* (*n.*) on it. *Reporters* (*n.*) *report* news to their papers; people who wish to complain about a thing often *report* it to those who can do something about it. School *reports* (*n.*) *report* to parents on the work and behaviour of their children. 2. *n.* A loud bang.

repose (ri-*pohz*) *v.* To rest. *Ex.* You can enjoy a time of *repose* (*n.*) after work, or *repose* on a bed when tired.

represent (rep-ri-*zent*) *v.* (a) To stand for. *Ex.* In this book *dh* *represents* the sound of *th* in *there*. (b) To act as an agent or spokesman. *Ex.* An ambassador acts as his county's chief *representative* (*n.*) abroad. (c) To give a likeness of. *Ex.* This painting *represents* Rembrandt as a young man.

repress (ri-*pres*) *v.* (a) To put down by force. *Ex.* The army *repressed* the rebellion. (b) To hold back. *Ex.* She *repressed* her tears.

reprieve (ri-*preev*) *v.* To cancel a punishment or delay it for a while.

reprisal (ri-*pryz*-al) *n.* An act of revenge.

reproach (ri-*prohch*) *v.* To express disappointment and disapproval. *Ex.* She *reproached* him for neglecting his mother.

reproduce (ree-prod-*ews*) *v.* (a) To copy. *Ex.* Photography can be used to make copies (*reproductions*; *n.*) of paintings etc. (b) To have young. *Ex.* Mice *reproduce* very frequently, producing several families a year.

reprove (ri-*proov*) *v.* To blame, scold or rebuke.

reptile (*rep*-tyl) *n.* A class of cold-blooded animals with scaly skins, which crawl without legs (snakes) or on very short legs (crocodiles, lizards etc.).

republic (ri-*pub*-lik) *n.* A country whose head of state is not a monarch but an elected president. France and the United States of America are *republics*.

repulsive (ri-*puls*-iv) *adj.* Making one turn away in disgust, often because of an ugly appearance.

reputation (rep-ew-*tay*-sh'n) *n.* The character a person is believed to have. *Ex.* I haven't met him, but I know he has the *reputation* of being kind.

request (ri-*kwest*) *v.* To ask for; to make a *request* (*n.*).

require (ri-*kwyr*) *v.* To demand something of a person; to need. *Ex.* The law *requires* you to pass a test before you can get a driving licence. This bicycle *requires* an overhaul.

rescue (*res*-kew) *v.* To save from danger or harm.

research (ri-*surch*) *n.* Investigation, especially the serious study of a subject with a view to making new discoveries.

resemble (re-*zem*-b'l) *v.* To look like. *Ex.* The twins *resemble* each other very much; the *resemblance* (*n.*) is very great.

resent (ri-*zent*) *v.* To feel indignation or bitterness about; to take offence. *Ex.* The workers *resented* having to work late, and showed their *resentment* (*n.*).

reserved (ri-*zurvd*) *adj.* (a) Not saying all one thinks or feels. (b) Put aside or kept back for a special purpose. *Ex. Reserved* seats in the front row were kept for us.

reservoir (*rez*-er-vwar) *n.* A large artificial lake which provides the water-supply for a district.

residue (*rez*-i-dew) *n.* What is left, the remainder. *Ex.* There is a *residue* of coffee-grounds in the pot.

resign (ri-*zyn*) *v.* To give up one's position or work. *Ex.* He has *resigned* as headmaster because of ill-health; his *resignation* (rez-ig-*nay*-sh′n; *n.*) has just been announced.

resigned (ri-*zynd*) *adj.* Accepting some situation, news etc. without complaining, because nothing can be done to alter things. *Ex.* He is *resigned* to having to give up games until his ankle is better.

resist (ri-*zist*) *v.* To oppose or be against, sometimes using force. *Ex.* I *resisted* the temptation to eat too many sweets when I was training. The prisoner *resisted* arrest, but the police overcame his *resistance* (*n.*).

resolution (rez-o-*loo*-sh′n) *n.* (a) Determination. *Ex.* He tackled the job with *resolution.* (b) A firm intention. *Ex.* Some people make New Year *resolutions* to alter their behaviour for the better.

resolve (ri-*zolv*) *v.* To determine, to decide. *Ex.* He *resolved* to save money to buy a guitar.

resort (ri-*zawrt*) *n.* A place people go to for holidays. *Ex.* A seaside *resort.*

resourceful (ri-*sawrs*-fUl) *adj.* Clever at thinking of ways to overcome difficulties.

respect (ri-*spekt*) *v.* To look up to. *Ex.* He had great *respect* (*n.*) for his uncle, who had given him much sound advice. The opposite of *respect* is *disrespect* (*n.*).

respectable (ri *spek* ta-b'l) *adj.* Decent; accepted by people as being of good social standard. *Ex.* Do try and make yourself *respectable*—you look positively disreputable!

respiration (res-pi-*ray*-sh′n) *n.* Breathing.

respond (ri-*spond*) *v.* To answer; to give a *response* (*n.*).

responsible (ri-*spon*-si-b'l) *adj.* Answerable for the occurrence, success or failure of something; trustworthy and reliable. *Ex.* He was held *responsible* for their bad behaviour. She is a *responsible* person, and will see that everything is left in good order.

restaurant (*rest*-er-ron(g)) *n.* A place in which meals are provided for customers who pay for them.

restless *adj.* Uneasy, never still. *Ex.* The children became *restless* on the long train journey.

restore (ri-*stawr*) *v.* To give back; to make look like new again.

Ex. The lost child was *restored* to his parents. The new owner *restored* the old house to its original splendour.

restrain (ri-*strayn*) *v.* To hold back; to repress. *Ex.* The dog had to be *restrained* from chasing the rabbits. She was so upset that she had difficulty in *restraining* her tears.

restrict (ri-*strikt*) *v.* To limit. This playground is *restricted* to use by children under twelve only.

result (ri-*zult*) *n.* The consequence or end. *Ex.* The *result* of the match was a draw. She got up late, and that *resulted* (*v.*) in her missing the bus.

resume (ri-*zewm*) *v.* To begin again. *Ex.* At the Test Match, play was *resumed* after the tea interval.

resurrect (rez-er-*rekt*) *v.* To bring to life again. *Ex.* The *Resurrection* (*n.*) of Jesus Christ is celebrated at Easter.

retail (ree-*tayl*) *v.* To sell goods in small quantities, usually in shops. *Ex.* Shopkeepers buy goods wholesale (in bulk) and *retail* them to their customers; they sell them *retail* (*ree*-tayl; *adv.*).

retain (ri-*tayn*) *v.* To keep. *Ex.* The doorman tore our tickets in half and told us to *retain* one half.

retaliate (ri-*tal*-i-ayt) *v.* To hit back in revenge.

retard (ri-*tard*) *v.* To slow up. *Ex.* A slow puncture *retarded* his progress, and he was late arriving.

retinue (*ret*-in-ew) *n.* Attendants and followers who accompany a monarch etc. on state occasions.

retire (ri-*tyr*) *v.* To go back, to withdraw; to withdraw to a private place; to give up one's occupation on reaching the age of *retirement* (*n.*); to go to bed.

retort (ri-*tawrt*) 1. *n.* A quick, often sharp, reply which turns the argument against the person spoken to. 2. *v.* To make such a reply.

retreat (ri-*treet*) *v.* To go back, to retire, as when an army gives up its position on the battlefield.

retrieve (ri-*treev*) *v.* To save after apparent loss. *Ex.* They managed to *retrieve* some of the furniture from the fire. A *retriever* (*n.*) is a dog trained to fetch birds, rabbits etc. that have been shot.

reveal (ri-*veel*) *v.* To disclose or make known. *Ex.* The searchlight *revealed* the boys crouching on a cliff-ledge.

revel (*rev*-el) *v.* To have a good time, with merrymaking etc.; to enjoy oneself. *Ex.* The boys *revelled* in the snow.

revenge (ri-*venj*)   *v.* To do injury in return to someone who has injured you. If you do this you take your *revenge* (*n.*).

revenue (*rev*-en-ew)   *n.* Income from owning property or other sources of wealth, especially the income a government gets from taxing people, goods etc.

revere (ri-*veer*)   *v.* To respect and honour.   *Ex.* Solemn occasions such as coronations are observed in a *reverent* (*adj.*) manner. 'The *Reverend*' (*adj.*) is used instead of 'Mr' in addressing an envelope to a clergyman. People, places and things are held in *reverence* (*n.*) by those who look on them as sacred or worthy of high respect.   *Ex.* Christians feel *reverence* for the Bible.

reverse (ri-*vers*)   1. *n.* (a) The opposite.   *Ex.* We expected the evening to be boring, but the *reverse* was the case. (b) A misfortune or a defeat in battle. 2. *v.* To change something the other way round.   *Ex.* He *reversed* the car and turned back.

review (ri-*vew*)   1. *v.* To look over again carefully. A formal *review* (*n.*) or inspection of troops etc. is held on various state occasions. 2. *n.* A critic's published or broadcast opinion of a book, play etc.

revise (ri-*vys*)   *v.* To read over so that one can correct; to study again, as one revises what one has learnt before an exam.

revive (ri-*vyv*)   *v.* To come or bring back to life and strength.   *Ex.* The drooping plant soon *revived* when watered.

revolt (ri-*vohlt*)   *v.* To rebel. A *revolt* (*n.*) is a rebellion. *Revolting* (*adj.*) means disgusting.

revolution (rev-ol-*ew*-sh'n)   *n.* (a) A great change, affecting the lives of many people.   *Ex.* The *Industrial Revolution*. (b) The violent overthrow of a government, or an attempt at it.   *Ex.* The *French Revolution* of 1789. (c). *See* revolve.

revolve (ri-*volv*)   *v.* To turn or move round a centre or axis, as a wheel turns.   *Ex.* A car engine makes so many *revolutions* (*n.*) per minute.

revolver (ri-*vol*-ver)   *n.* A kind of pistol which can fire several shots, from a revolving cylinder, without having to be reloaded.

reward (ri-*wawrd*)   *n.* Something given in return for some service etc. You can be *rewarded* (*v.*) for returning lost property, or for helping the police to arrest a criminal.

rheumatism (*roo*-ma-tizm)   *n.* A disease that causes inflammation and swelling of the joints or muscles of the body, giving the sufferer *rheumatic* (roo-*mat*-ik; *adj.*) pains.

rhinoceros (ry-*nos*-er-os)   *n.* A large thick-skinned animal with horns growing from its nose, found in Africa and Asia.

rhododendron (roh-do-*den*-dron) *n.* An evergreen shrub with big flowers, pink, red, purple or white.

rhubarb (*roo*-barb) *n.* A plant whose juicy pinkish-green stalks are stewed and eaten as a sweet-course.

rhyme (rym) *n.* (a) The relationship between words whose endings sound similar. *Ex.* 'Boat' and 'goat', 'sleep' and 'weep' *rhyme* (*v.*) with each other. (b) A poem or piece of verse.

rhythm (*ridh*'m) *n.* Regular beat in music or verse.

rib *n.* One of the curved bones reaching from the backbone to the upper part of the front of the body, making a kind of cage to enclose the heart and lungs.

rice (rys) *n.* A cereal crop of warm countries, whose small white seeds may be ground into flour or cooked and eaten whole.

rid *v.* To make a person or place free from. You can get *rid* (*adj.*) of a cold, or *rid* the roses of greenfly.

riddle *n.* (a) A puzzling question with a pun or other trick in it. *Ex.* What is black and white and read all over? A newspaper. (b) Something puzzling or mysterious.

ridge *n.* (a) A long narrow line of hills. (b) A raised edge, such as the *ridge* along a roof-top, or a raised line on a surface.

ridicule (*rid*-i-kewl) *v.* To make fun of, to mock. *Ex.* People once *ridiculed* the idea that the earth revolved round the sun; they said it was a *ridiculous* (*adj.*) idea.

rifle (*ry*-f'l) *n.* A gun with a long barrel which has grooves inside to make the bullets rotate and keep steady in flight.

rigging *n.* The ropes and wires used to support the masts and spars of a sailing ship, and to raise (hoist) the sails.

right (ryt) 1. *adj.* (a) Morally correct, being true and just, not wicked. *Ex.* The *right* thing to do. (b) Logically correct. *Ex.* The *right* answer to a sum. (c) On the opposite side of the body to the heart. 2. *adv.* Towards the *right*. *Ex.* Turn *right* at the T-junction. 3. *v.* To put to *rights* (*n.*) or in the proper position. *Ex.* When they had shifted the cargo the ship *righted* herself again.

rigid (*rij*-id) *adj.* Stiff, firm, not easily bent or moved.

rim *n.* The edge, for instance a cup's *rim*, from which one drinks.

rind (rynd) *n.* The outer covering of a fruit such as an orange or a lemon.

rinse (rins) *v.* To wash out in water. You can *rinse* out an empty milk bottle, or *rinse* detergent out of washed clothes.

riot (*ry*-ot) *n.* A noisy quarrel or disturbance caused by a number of people.

ripe (ryp) *adj.* Fully grown and developed. *Ex.* Fruit is not ready to eat until it is *ripe*, or has *ripened* (*v.*).

ripple *v.* To flow in little waves. *Ex.* A stone dropped in a pond causes *ripples*.

risk 1. *n.* Danger; chance of loss. *Ex.* A *risk* of getting hurt; a *risk* of losing one's money. 2. *v.* To take a chance of endangering oneself or losing something. *Ex.* The firemen *risked* their lives by going into the burning building.

ritual (*rit*-ew-al) *n.* An ordered ceremony, especially formal acts of worship or *rites* (*n.*).

rival (*ry*-val) *n.* One who competes against another for a prize or other distinction they both want. *Ex.* There is friendly *rivalry* (*n.*) between the two.

rivet (*riv*-et) *n.* A bolt which is hammered flat at the ends, used to fasten metal plates etc. together.

roast (rohst) *v.* To cook (especially a joint) in a very hot oven.

robot (*roh*-bot) *n.* A mechanical man.

robust (roh-*bust*) *adj.* Healthy and vigorous.

rocket *n.* (a) A large jet-powered launcher for a spacecraft. (b) A firework that shoots into the air by *rocket-propulsion*, used for distress signals at sea or in firework displays.

rodent (*roh*-dent) *n.* An animal with chisel-like teeth used for gnawing. Rats and beavers are *rodents*.

roe (roh) *n.* (a) The eggs of certain kinds of fish. (b) A kind of small deer.

rogue (rohg) *n.* A dishonest person. But *roguish* (*roh*-gish; *adj.*) means full of mischievous fun.

role (rohl) *n.* The part an actor plays; the part anyone plays on a particular occasion. *Ex.* The *role* of a peacemaker in a quarrel between others.

romance (roh-*mans*) *n.* (a) A story of adventure and love, often with a happy ending and set in surroundings remote from everyday life. *Ex. Romeo and Juliet* is a *romantic* (*adj.*) story with a tragic ending. (b) A tender love affair.

romp *v.* To play vigorously, running, tumbling about etc.

rook (rUk) *n.* A large black bird of the crow family, which nests in large groups in a *rookery* (*n.*).

roost *v.* To rest or sleep as birds do, on a perch. Cocks are sometimes called *roosters* (*n.*).

root *n.* The parts of a plant which reach down into the soil to absorb water and nourishment, and to hold the plant in place.

rotate (roh-*tayt*) *v.* To turn round or revolve on an axis, as the earth does once every 24 hours. To do a thing in *rotation* (*n.*) is to do it in turn. *Ex.* There is no permanent club secretary, so we all do the work in *rotation*.

rotten *adj.* Decayed and going bad, as fallen fruit may be.

rough (ruf) *adj.* With an uneven and rugged surface; not smooth. The ground or the sea can be *rough*. *Rough* notes are hastily written without much care.

rouse (rowz) *v.* To wake from sleep; to excite. *Ex.* We crept in quietly, so as not to *rouse* the sleepers. We gave the conquering hero a *rousing* (*adj.*) welcome.

route (root) *n.* The way to somewhere. *Ex.* What is the shortest *route* home from here?

routine (roo-*teen*) *n.* A set way of doing a thing, often repeated and sometimes boring. *Ex.* Sister made a *routine* (*adj.*) round of the ward.

row (row) *n.* A noisy quarrel.

row (roh) 1. *n.* A line of things. *Ex.* The front *row* at the theatre. 2. *v.* To move a boat with oars.

rowdy (*row*-di) *adj.* Noisy and disorderly.

royal (*roi*-al) *adj.* Connected with a monarch. Any member of a *royal* family can be called *royalty* (*n.*).

rubbish (*rub*-ish) *n.* Anything that is of no use or value; refuse; nonsense.

ruby (*roo*-bi) *n.* A deep-red precious stone.

rucksack (*ruk*-sak) *n.* A back-pack for walkers and climbers.

rudder *n.* The flat piece of wood or metal, like a fin, at the stern (back) of a ship or aircraft, by which they can be steered.

ruffian (*ruf*-i-an) *n.* A rough, violent man, who might commit any crime.

ruffle 1. *v.* To disturb, as the wind does hair. 2. *n.* A frill at wrist or neck.

rugby (*rug*-bi) *n.* A kind of football, using an oval ball which may be handled during play. Usually called *rugger*.

rugged (*rug*-ed) *adj.* Rough, uneven. Hills and coastlines can be described as *rugged*; also a person's features.

ruin (*roo*-in) 1. *v.* To spoil or destroy. *Ex.* The film was *ruined* because light had got into the camera. 2. *n.* (a) A state of decay. (b) The remains of a building etc. that has been damaged or partly destroyed, by war, fire or the passage of time. (c) Disaster, usually financial.

rummage (*rum*-ij) *v.* To search in a rather wild way, turning things upside down.

rumour (*roo*-mer) *n.* A piece of news or gossip, which may or may not be true.

rung *n.* A step of a ladder.

runway *n.* The straight, smooth track made for aircraft to take off from and land on.

rural (*roor*-al) *adj.* Concerning the countryside. *Ex.* Farming is a *rural* occupation.

rust *n.* The reddish-brown coating which forms on iron and steel when long exposed to moisture and air.

rustic (*rus*-tik) *adj.* Having to do with the countryside. *Ex.* Town-dwellers sometimes dream of retiring to a *rustic* cottage with a thatched roof and roses round the door.

rustle (*rus*'l) *v.* To make a soft noise as of leaves in the wind, or tissue paper being crumpled.

ruthless (*rooth*-les) *adj.* Without pity, cruel.

rye *n.* A cereal crop used for fodder, and for making a dark-coloured bread.

S

sabotage (*sab*-o-tahzh) *n.* Deliberate damage to machinery, railways or other property, done by guerrillas, resistance fighters or political agitators.

saccharin (*sak*-ar-in) *n.* A white substance used as a substitute for sugar. *Saccharine* (sak-ar-*een*; *adj.*) means sugary, over-sweet or sickly.

sacrament (*sak*-ra-ment) *n.* A Christian rite. Holy Communion and baptism are *sacraments*.

sacred (*say*-krid) *adj.* Holy, connected with the worship of a god.

sacrifice (*sak*-ri-fys) *v.* To give up, especially to a god. People may *sacrifice* their lives for others, or make smaller *sacrifices* in their everyday lives. *Ex.* She *sacrificed* her holiday to look after us when we were ill.

saddle 1. *n.* A seat on a horse's back, or on a cycle etc. 2. *v.* To put a saddle on a horse.

safari (saf-*ahr*-i) *n.* A hunting expedition in Africa. *Safari parks* are large parks where wild animals may be watched from the safety of cars.

safe (sayf) 1. *adj.* Free from danger. 2. *n.* A fire-proof and burglar-proof container where money and valuables can be kept in *safety* (*n.*).

sage (sayj) 1. *adj.* Wise in judgement. 2. *n.* A herb with fragrant leaves, used to flavour savoury dishes.

sail 1. *n.* A piece of canvas, nylon etc. fixed to supports, which catches the wind and drives a boat along. 2. *v.* (a) To travel by boat; to manage a *sailing-boat.* (b) To glide through the air.

saint (saynt) *n.* A person whom the Christian Church has named as most holy.

sake (sayk) *n. For the sake of* means in the interest of, on behalf of. *Ex.* He hurried home *for the sake of* his tired children.

salad (*sal*-ad) *n.* A cold dish of, usually, raw vegetables, served with a dressing (sauce). A *fruit salad* is a *salad* of different fruits, fresh or tinned.

salary (*sal*-a-ri) *n.* Money paid, usually monthly, to an employee whose work is not manual work.

saline (*say*-lyn) *adj.* Containing salt, as does sea-water.

salmon (*sam*-on) *n.* A large edible game-fish with pink flesh, which from the sea comes up the same river to breed at intervals of a year or more.

saloon (sa-*loon*) *n.* (a) The first-class lounge in a liner. (b) A public room used for a particular purpose, such as a *billiard saloon.* A *saloon bar* is the first-class bar in a public house. A *saloon car* is an ordinary family motor-car.

salute (sa-*loot*) *v.* To greet, sometimes formally. A man may *salute* a woman by raising his hat, a soldier give an officer a military *salute* (*n.*), or a gun fire blank rounds as a form of *salute.* Saying 'good morning' is one form of *salutation* (*n.*).

salvage (*sal*-vij) *n.* What has been saved or *salvaged* (*v.*) from destruction by fire, shipwreck etc.

salvation (sal-*vay*-sh′n) *n.* Being saved from destruction; the saving of a soul from sin.

sample (*sahm*-pl) 1. *n.* A small part of something which shows what the whole is like. *Ex.* She sent for *samples* of curtain-material, to see what there was to choose from. 2. *v.* To see what the quality of something is; to test a part of. *Ex.* A food inspector may *sample* the food provided by a restaurant.

sanction (*sangk*-sh′n) *n.* (a) Permission. *Ex.* We have to get the council's official *sanction* before we can build a garage. (b) (Usually plural) Measures, such as cutting off supplies, taken by one country against another to force it to stop doing something regarded as wrong.

sanctuary (*sangk*-tew-a-ri) *n.* (a) A holy place, especially where the altar is in a church. (b) A place of refuge. (c) An area where animals and birds can breed in safety.

sandal (*san*-dal) *n.* A light shoe with no upper part, being only a sole fastened to the foot by straps.

sandwich (*san*-wij) *n.* Two slices of bread with a filling between them of egg or meat etc. To be *sandwiched* (*v.*) between two things is to be squeezed between them.

sane *adj.* Healthy in mind, sensible. The opposite is *insane.*

sanitary (*san*-it-ar-i) *adj.* To do with health and providing hygienic conditions, especially drainage, refuse disposal and pure water.

sapphire (*saf*-yr) *n.* A deep-blue precious stone.

sarcasm (*sar*-kazm) *n.* Making hurtful and scornful remarks, sometimes meaning the opposite of what is actually said. *Ex.* 'I didn't know you owned the place' is a *sarcastic* (sar-*kas*-tik; *adj.*) remark.

sardine (sar-*deen*) *n.* A very small sea-fish, usually tinned in oil.

sash *n.* (a) A window-frame that can be slid up and down. (b) A broad band of ribbon or silk, worn round the waist as part of a dress, or over the shoulder as a badge of honour.

satchel (*sach*-el) *n.* A bag, usually hung from the shoulder, such as school children sometimes use to carry books.

satellite (*sat*-el-yt) *n.* A natural or man-made body rotating in orbit round a planet.

satin (*sat*-in) *n.* Silk cloth glossy on one side.

satisfy (*sat*-is-fy) *v.* To make pleased or contented. When you have what you want or enough of something, you are *satisfied* (*adj.*); that gives you *satisfaction* (*n.*). *Ex.* We have had a *satisfactory* (*adj.*) football season, only losing three matches.

saturate (*sat*-ewr-ayt) *v.* To soak thoroughly. *Ex.* Anything left soaking in water becomes *saturated* with it.

sauce (saws) *n.* A specially prepared liquid served with meat, puddings etc. to add flavour.

saunter (*sawn*-ter) *v.* To walk slowly for pleasure. *Ex.* They *sauntered* along the seaside promenade.

sausage (*sos*-ij) *n.* A mixture of chopped and seasoned meat put into a thin tube-like skin.

savage (*sav*-ij) 1. *adj.* Wild, fierce, untamed. 2. *n.* A human who lives in a wild state; a fierce, cruel person.

saviour (*sayv*-yer) *n.* Someone who *saves* another from death or harm. *Ex.* He was regarded as the *saviour* of his country.

savoury (*sayv*-or-i) *adj.* With an appetizing taste or smell. A *savoury* (*n.*) is a light snack, often salty, sometimes eaten as the final course of a meal.

saxophone (*saks*-o-fohn) *n.* A brass wind instrument with one reed, played in all kinds of bands.

scaffolding (*skaf*-ohld-ing) *n.* The structure of poles and planks which workmen stand on when building or repairing buildings. A *scaffold* (*n.*) is also a raised platform where people are executed.

scald (skawld) *v.* To burn the body with hot liquid or steam.

scale (skayl) 1. *n.* (a) A machine for weighing things. (b) One of the small thin plates which form the skin of a fish or reptile. (c) A number of musical sounds, arranged in order of highness of tone. (d) The markings on a map or drawing to say how distance and size are shown. 2. *v.* To climb up something steep.

scallop (*skol*-op) 1. *n.* A shellfish which lives enclosed between two ridged, fan-shaped shells with wavy edges. 2. *v.* To trim material with a *scallop*-shaped edging.

scalp (skalp) *n.* The hairy skin of the head.

scamper *v.* To run about as children do, or animals which have been disturbed.

scandal (*skan*-dal) *n.* Unkind gossip; something that makes people indignant. *Ex.* It was *scandalous* (*adj.*) to go away and leave the dog to starve.

scanty (*skan*-ti) *adj.* Hardly enough.

scar *n.* A mark left on the skin by a healed cut or burn.

scarce (skairs) *adj.* Not many; rare. *Ex.* Strawberries are *scarce* this year; there is a *scarcity* (*skair*-sit-i; *n.*) of them.

scarcely (*skairs*-li) *adv.* With difficulty; only just. *Ex.* She could *scarcely* reach the letter-box and had to stand on tip-toe.

scare (skair) *v.* To frighten. A *scarecrow* (*n.*) is an arrangement of old clothes on a pole to look like a man, put in fields to *scare* birds off crops.

scarlet (*skar*-let) *adj.* Bright red.

scatter *v.* (a) To throw about. *Ex.* We *scattered* crumbs in the yard for the birds. (b) To move apart. *Ex.* The crowd *scattered* when the bull got into the market-place.

scene (seen) *n.* (a) A place where something happens, either in reality or on the stage. *Ex.* When I arrived on the *scene* the cows had already wandered into the garden. (b) A part of a play where something happens at a particular place and time. *Ex.* Act I, *Scene* 2: A Woodcutter's Cottage, in the evening. (c) A view. (d) An emotional outburst which makes others feel uncomfortable. *Ex.* When he found that he had tickets for the wrong day, he made a *scene* at the box-office.

scenery (*seen*-er-ri) *n.* (a) Views of beautiful landscapes or seascapes. (b) The painted boards, curtains etc. on a stage, meant to represent the place where the scene is set.

scent (sent) *n.* (a) A smell, especially a sweet one; perfume. (b) The sense of smell.

schedule (*shed*-ewl) 1. *n.* A list. *Ex.* A *schedule* of duties for the day. 2. *v.* To arrange the time of a coming event. *Ex.* A dance display is *scheduled* for Friday.

scheme (skeem) 1. *n.* A plan or plot. *Ex.* There is a *scheme* to build a motorway near here. 2. *v.* To plot.

scholar (*skol*-ar) *n.* (a) A pupil. (b) A learned person. (c) The holder of a *scholarship* (*n.*).

scholarship (*skol*-ar-ship) *n.* (a) The learning of a *scholarly* (*adj.*) person. (b) A grant of money won by examination, which helps a student to pay for his education.

science (*sy*-ens) *n.* The knowledge of things that exist in nature, whether the stars, insects, the human body, electricity etc., which man gets by observation, study and experiment. Such knowledge is *scientific* (sy-en-*tif*-ik; *adj.*), and one learned in *science* is a *scientist* (*n.*).

scissors (*siz*-orz) *n.* A cutting tool with two sharp blades, often used for cutting paper, nails, hair etc.

scoff (skof) *v.* To jeer.

scold (skohld) *v.* To rebuke angrily.

scone (skon) *n.* A plain flat cake made with little fat, best eaten freshly baked and buttered.

scoop (skoop) 1. *n.* A concave holder of any size, from the one on a giant digger to a serving *scoop* for ice-cream. 2. *v.* To gather up into a *scoop* or to hollow out with one. *Ex.* We used our hands to *scoop* out a hole in the sand and bury the rubbish.

scope (skohp) *n.* Range, extent; opportunity. *Ex.* The job was varied and he had *scope* for using all his skills.

scorch (skawrch) *v.* To burn slightly on the surface, as you can a garment with an iron that is too hot.

score (skawr) *n.* (a) A record of the number of runs, points or goals *scored* (*v.*) in a game. *Ex.* The *score* was 5–1. (b) Twenty.

scorn (skawrn) *n.* Contempt, disdain. To be *scornful* is to look on. *Ex.* He *scorned* (*v.*) the paddling-pool now he could swim.

scoundrel (*skown*-drel) *n.* A mean and contemptible person capable of wicked behaviour.

scout (skowt) *n.* (a) A soldier or other person sent out to bring back information. (b) A member of the *Scouts* Association.

scowl (skowl) *v.* To frown in a threatening or discontented way. *Ex.* They said nothing, but had threatening *scowls* (*n.*) on their faces.

scramble (*skram*-b'l) *v.* (a) To hurry along, sometimes climbing and crawling on hands and feet. (b) To put together in a jumbled (*scrambling*) way. *Ex.* You can *scramble* eggs by stirring them together with milk and butter.

scrap *n.* A small piece. *Ex.* We saved all our *scraps* of material to make a patchwork quilt.

scrape *v.* (a) To clean a surface with a knife or other sharp tool, so as to leave it smooth. *Ex.* He *scraped* the mud off his shoes. (b) To scratch along the surface of something. *Ex.* The car *scraped* the wall.

scratch *v.* To mark the surface of something with a sharp point or one's nails.

scrawl *v.* To write badly and untidily.

scream *v.* To utter a sharp cry, usually from fright or pain. Such a cry is a *scream* (*n.*).

screech *n.* A harsh, shrill, sharp cry.

screw (skroo) *n.* A kind of nail which, because it has spiral grooves, cannot be pulled out except by a turning tool called a *screwdriver* (*n.*).

scribble *v.* To write or draw hastily and untidily.

scrub *v.* To clean by rubbing hard with a *scrubbing* brush etc.

scruff *n.* The back of the neck.

scuba (*skew*-ba) *n.* An aqualung.

scullery (*skul*-er-i) *n.* A small room near a kitchen, where there is a sink for washing up.

sculptor (*skulp*-tor) *n.* An artist who carves in stone, wood etc.; his work is called *sculpture* (*skulp*-cher; *n.*).

scum *n.* A sort of froth which rises to the surface of boiled liquids etc. *Ex.* When making jam, you take off the *scum* before putting the jam into jars.

scurry (*sku*-ri) *v.* To move in a hurry, in a flustered way. *Ex.* The mouse *scurried* into its hole.

scuttle (*skut'*l) 1. *n.* A small fireside bin for coal. 2. *v.* To make holes in a ship in order to sink her. (b) To scurry.

scythe (sydh) *n.* A tool with a long curved blade, for cutting grass etc.

seal 1. *n.* An animal with smooth fur, and flippers instead of legs, which lives mainly in the sea. 2. *v.* To close up firmly and completely. You can *seal* a letter with *sealing-wax* (*n.*).

seam (seem) *n.* (a) The line of sewing etc. which marks where two pieces of material have been joined together. (b) A layer of coal, ore etc. in rock.

search (surch) *v.* To look for something with thoroughness. To do this is to make a *search* (*n.*) for it. A *searchlight* (*n.*) is a moveable lamp which sends out a powerful beam for a very long distance.

season (*see*-zon) 1. *n.* One of the four parts into which the year is divided: Spring, Summer, Autumn, Winter. The *football season* or the *holiday season* etc. is the part of the year suitable for such things. *Seasonable* (*adj.*) means natural to, or suitable for, a season. *Ex. Seasonable* weather is the kind natural to that *season.* You are not dressed *seasonably* if you wear a cotton frock in winter. 2. *v.* To add salt, pepper etc. to food to bring out its flavour.

seaworthy (*see*-wur-dhi) *adj.* (Of a boat) Fit to put to sea in any weather.

secluded (si-*klood*-id) *adj.* Shut off from sight, remote; withdrawn from the world, solitary. *Ex.* He lives a *secluded* life in a *secluded* spot in the country; he lives in *seclusion* (*n.*).

second (*sek*-ond) 1. *n.* A division of time; there are 60 seconds in a minute. 2. *adj.* Next after the first. A *second-hand* (*adj.*) book is one that belonged to someone else before you bought it. 3. *v.* To support, or agree formally with, a suggestion at a meeting. *Seconds* (*n.*) attend and support boxers or duellers.

secret (*seek*-rit) *adj.* Kept hidden or private; known only to few.

Ex. The pirates had a *secret* hiding-place which they kept a *secret* (*n.*).

secretary (*sek*-re-ta-ri) *n.* Someone who attends to the personal concerns of an employer, dealing with letter-writing, making appointments, keeping records etc.

section (*sek*-sh'n) *n.* One of the parts into which a whole thing can be divided. *Ex.* The bookcase was made in *sections* and can easily be put together.

secure (si-*kewr*) *adj.* Safe; firmly fixed. *Ex.* The baby was *securely* (*adv.*) fastened into her pram. To know that you are safe gives you a feeling of *security* (*n.*).

sediment (*sed*-i-ment) *n.* Any solids that drop to the bottom of a liquid; dregs.

seedling *n.* A very young plant.

seek *v.* To look for, as one looks for the one who is hiding in *hide-and-seek.*

segregate (*seg*-re-gayt) *v.* To keep apart. *Ex.* The children who had measles were *segregated* from the rest, to stop the disease spreading.

seize (seez) *v.* To take possession of; to snatch. *Ex.* The thieves *seized* the jewellery and ran off with it.

seldom (*sel*-dom) *adv.* Not often. *Ex.* It *seldom* rains in the desert.

select (si-*lekt*) *v.* To choose. *Ex.* From the many books (a large *selection*; *n.*) we could *select* only one each.

selfish *adj.* Only concerned with one's own needs and wishes, and not thinking of others.

semi- is a prefix meaning half. A *semicircle* is half a circle. A *semi-detached* house is detached on one side only, its other side being joined to another house.

senile (*see*-nyl) *adj.* Old and failing in mind and body.

senior (*see*-ni-or) *adj.* Older, or higher in rank. *Ex.* She is my *senior* by two years.

sensation (sen-*say*-sh'n) *n.* (a) A feeling which comes through one of the five *senses*; a feeling of the mind. *Ex.* A pleasant *sensation* of warmth, or of happiness. (b) Excited interest. *Ex.* The news of the murder caused a *sensation* in the village; it was a *sensational* (*adj.*) case.

sense *n.* (a) The power of feeling *sensations*. The five *senses* are: sight, hearing, taste, touch and smell. (b) An emotional feeling. *Ex.* A *sense* of dread. (c) Good judgement. *Ex.* They had the *sense* to slow down at the blind corner.

sensible (*sen*-si-b'l) *adj.* Having good sense. *Ex.* She is a *sensible* girl and not likely to do anything foolish.

sensitive (*sen*-sit-iv) *adj.* Having strong and easily roused feelings; too easily affected or hurt. *Ex.* Being a *sensitive* man, he was upset by the disaster.

sentence (*sen*-tens) *n.* (a) A group of words which makes complete sense by itself. *Ex.* 'John walked home from school' is a *sentence*, but 'when John was walking home' is not. *Sentences* begin with a capital letter and end with a full stop. (b) The punishment which a court orders for a person found guilty of crime.

sentiment (*sen*-ti-ment) *n.* (a) A view or opinion. *Ex.* I agree with you, those are my *sentiments* too. (b) Feeling. *Ex.* The music expressed *sentiments* of gaiety and joy. *Sentimental* (*adj.*) means showing too much feeling in a sloppy sort of way.

sentry (*sen*-tri) *n.* A soldier etc. stationed on guard.

separate (*sep*-a-rayt) 1. *adj.* Divided, not joined together. *Ex.* The teams had *separate* changing-rooms. 2. *v.* To divide, to make *separate*. *Ex.* He *separated* the fighting dogs.

sequel (*see*-kwel) *n.* (a) Anything that follows (especially as a result). *Ex.* I lost my purse, and the *sequel* was that I had to walk all the way home. (b) A continuation of a story, especially a second novel which deals with the further adventures of characters from the first novel.

serenade (se-ren-*ayd*) *n.* Music played or sung as a form of courtship, beneath a girl's window, in the evening.

serene (se-*reen*) *adj.* Calm and peaceful. *Ex.* A *serene* September; a *serene* temperament.

sergeant (*sar*-jent) *n.* A non-commissioned officer, next in rank above a corporal; a police officer next in rank below inspector.

serial (*seer*-i-al) *adj.* Published or broadcast in instalments, as are many television or magazine stories.

series (*seer*-eez) *n.* A number of similar or related things which follow each other in order. *Ex.* The vines grow up the hill on a *series* of terraces.

serious (*seer*-i-us) *adj.* (a) Grave, not light-hearted; worthy of earnest thought and attention. (b) Important, and likely to be dangerous. *Ex.* The increase in crime is a *serious* matter. A *serious* illness is one that is bad enough to be dangerous.

sermon (*sur*-mon) *n.* An address (speech) given by a clergyman as part of a church service.

serrated (se-*rayt*-id)   *adj.* With notches cut in the edge like the side of a saw.

service (*sur*-vis)   *n.* (a) The act of working for or helping another. (b) Public work, especially by a government department; the department etc. which carries out such work.   *Ex.* The *Civil Service*; the *armed services*. (c) The organized supply of a public need.   *Ex.* A *bus service*; a *telephone service*. (d) Public worship. *Ex. Morning service*; a *thanksgiving service*. (e) Waiting at table. *Ex.* The *service* at this restaurant is quick and efficient. (f) A set of plates, cups etc.   *Ex.* A *tea-service*.

serviceable (*sur*-vis-a-b'l)   *adj.* In working order.

session (*sesh*'n)   *n.* The period during which Parliament sits.

settlement (*se*-t'l-ment)   *n.* (a) A place where people have *settled* (*set* up their homes). (b) Something decided on, which ends a dispute etc.   *Ex.* After long discussion, a *settlement* was reached between the two sides.

several (*sev*-er-al)   *adj.* Some; more than two but not many.

severe (si-*veer*)   *adj.* (a) Hard to bear.   *Ex.* Bad burns cause *severe* pain. (b) Very strict.   *Ex.* He was *severe* but just in dealing with wrong-doers.

sew (soh)   *v.* To fasten together with needle and thread. This is called *sewing* (*n.*).

sewer (*sew*-er)   *n.* An underground tunnel that carries away waste material from drains, which is then dealt with in *sewage* (*sew*-ij; *n.*) *works*.

shabby (*shab*-i)   *adj.* Showing signs of wear, especially referring to clothes, furniture etc.

shack   *n.* A roughly put-up shed.

shade   *n.* (a) A kind of colour.   *Ex.* The poppy is a lovely *shade* of red. (b) A place on which the sun is not directly shining.   *Ex.* When it is very hot, *shady* (*adj.*) places are cooler; they are in the *shadows* (*n.*) made when something blocks the light and its image is cast on to something.

shaft   *n.* (a) A ray of light.   *Ex.* A *shaft* of sunlight lit up the picture. (b) The long straight handle of various tools, weapons etc. (c) A vertical passage, leading down to a mine etc.   *Ex.* A *lift shaft*. (d) One of the two bars of a cart, between which the horse is harnessed.

shaggy (*shag*-i)   *adj.* Having long, uneven, untidy hair, as have many dogs.

shallow (*shal*-oh)   *adj.* Not deep.

sham 1. *adj.* False; imitation. *Ex.* Fencing is *sham* fighting. 2. *v.* To pretend, as some animals *sham* being dead to escape their enemies.

shambles *n.* Utter disorder and confusion. *Ex.* The deck was a *shambles* after the battle.

shame *n.* The feeling of regret and humiliation, or of having disgraced oneself. *Shameful* (*adj.*) means causing *shame* or disgrace; disgraceful. *Ex.* It is a *shameful* thing to neglect a pet animal.

shampoo (sham-*poo*) *n.* A kind of soap for washing the hair. There are also *shampoos* for cleaning carpets.

shamrock *n.* A three-leaved plant like the clover, the national emblem of Ireland.

share *n.* A part of something allotted to anyone. *Ex.* Here is your *share* of the toffee; we will *share* (*v.*) it equally.

shark *n.* A flesh-eating fish, often large and dangerous.

sharp *adj.* (a) Having a fine point or cutting edge. *Ex.* A *sharp* pencil; a *sharp* knife. (b) Seeming pointed or cutting to our senses. *Ex.* Lemons have a *sharp* taste.

shatter *v.* To break in pieces *Ex.* The mirror fell to the floor and was *shattered.*

shave *v.* (a) To remove hair from the body, especially from the face, with a razor. (b) To just touch something in passing.

shawl *n.* A piece of material, often knitted, worn round the shoulders.

sheaf *n.* A bundle of things bound together, especially corn.

shear *v.* To cut off. *Ex.* Sheep are *sheared* every summer with *shears* (*n.*) which cut off their wool.

sheath (sheeth) *n.* A case into which a knife or sword is *sheathed* (sheedhd; *v.*) or put.

shed *n.* A small house or hut, usually of wood.

sheepish *adj.* Embarrassed at having done something silly.

sheer *adj.* (a) Steep, like a precipice. (b) Utter, complete. *Ex.* It was *sheer* joy to watch the dolphins.

sheet *n.* A thin flat broad piece of material (paper, steel, cloth etc.), or one of the *sheets* of cotton or linen used on a bed.

shelf *n.* A narrow piece of board fixed to a wall to hold books, dishes etc. Many cupboards contain *shelves*.

shell *n.* (a) The hard outer covering of various things such as eggs, nuts or shellfish. Creatures, such as snails, turtles and tortoises, have *shells* also. (b) A metal case in which explosives are placed, and which is then fired from a gun.

shelter 1. *n.* (a) Protection. *Ex.* Ships take *shelter* in harbour during storms. (b) A building designed to give protection from weather etc. 2. *v.* To protect from danger or weather.

shepherd (*shep*-erd) *n.* The man who looks after *sheep* on a farm.

sherry (*she*-ri) *n.* A strong Spanish wine, often drunk to arouse the appetite.

shield (sheeld) 1. *n.* A large piece of metal or other material, held in front or over the body to ward off weapons; any object placed so as to protect something from harm or damage. *Ex.* The *heat-shield* on a spacecraft. 2. *v.* To protect by *shielding*. *Ex.* Dark glasses *shield* the eyes from sun-glare.

shift 1. *v.* To change the position of, as one can *shift* a table to another part of the room. 2. *n.* A group of workers taking turns with other groups to do the same job. *Ex.* She is on *night-shift* at the hospital, and has to sleep during the day.

shin *n.* The front bone of the lower part of the leg.

shine *v.* To give out light, as the sun does. *Ex.* Her face *shone* (shon) with happiness.

shingle *n.* (a) Small round pebbles, often mixed with sand on the shore. (b) A roof tile, usually of wood.

ship *n.* A large sea-going boat. *Shipping* (*n.*) means *ships*, especially *ships* belonging to a particular company or nation.

shirk (shurk) *n.* To avoid doing something you do not want to do. *Ex.* The work was tiring, but none of them *shirked* it.

shiver (*shiv*-er) *v.* To shake or tremble, as when feeling cold or frightened.

shoal (shohl) *n.* (a) A part of the sea or a lake which is shallow because of sandbanks. (b) A great number of fish swimming together. *Ex.* A *shoal* of mackerel.

shock *n.* A sudden blow to the emotions (as, the *shock* of bad news); or to the nerves (as, an electric *shock*); the helpless state brought about by injury or distress of mind etc.

shoddy *adj.* Of poor quality, usually referring to cloth or other material.

shoot 1. *n.* A small piece of new growth on a plant. 2. *v.* To fire with a gun etc. *Ex.* He *shot* an arrow at the target.

shore (shawr) *n.* The land at the edge of the sea or a lake.

shoulder (*shohld*-er) *n.* The joint that connects the arm to the body.

shout (showt) *n.* A loud cry, a yell. *Ex.* They *shouted* (*v.*) with joy.

shove (shuv) *v.* To push, often roughly.

shovel (*shuv*'l) *n.* A large spade-like tool, used to lift earth, coal etc.

shower (showr) *n.* A fall of rain that is soon over. The word also means *shower-bath*, in which the water falls from above, like rain.

shred 1. *n.* A tiny torn-off bit of something. 2. *v.* To tear into *shreds*.

shrewd (shrood) *adj.* Sharp-witted; having sound judgement and common sense.

shriek (shreek) *n.* A sharp scream of pain, surprise, or even of laughter.

shrill *adj.* Making a loud high sound, as some people's laughter does.

shrimp *n.* A small, thin, edible shellfish with a long tail.

shrink *v.* (a) To become smaller or shrivelled up, as some fabrics do after washing. (b) To draw back in fear or shyness. *Ex.* She *shrank* back when the dog growled at her.

shrivel (*shriv*'l) *v.* To go into wrinkles, often through having dried up, as the skin of fruit may do.

shrub *n.* A bushy plant which has several branches growing from the root. A *shrubbery* (*n.*) is a part of a garden planted with many *shrubs*.

shrug *v.* To raise the shoulders in a movement meant to show that one doesn't know or doesn't really care.

shudder *v.* To tremble with fear or horror.

shuffle (*shuf*'l) *v.* (a) To drag the feet along the ground, without lifting them properly. (b) To alter the order in which things are placed, as when *shuffling* playing-cards.

shun *v.* To avoid.

shunt *v.* To move railway trucks and carriages from one line to another.

shutter *n.* (a) A cover for a window, usually of wood. (b) The cover behind a camera lens, which opens when taking a photograph.

shuttle *n.* The instrument carrying the thread which a weaver passes to and fro, to make the weft (crossways threads) when weaving cloth. A *shuttle-service* (*n.*) of transport travels to and fro in short trips like a weaver's *shuttle*.

shy 1. *adj.* Shrinking away from notice, especially the notice of strangers. 2. *v.* To move quickly to one side, as a frightened horse may do.

sickle *n.* A curved knife with a short handle, used to cut grass or tall weeds.

sideboard *n.* A piece of dining-room furniture, useful both as cupboard and side-table.

siege (seej) *n.* The surrounding and cutting off of a castle or town by attackers, in order to make it surrender.

siesta (see-*es*-ta) *n.* An afternoon sleep taken in countries where the hottest part of the day is the early afternoon.

sieve (siv) *n.* A container with fine wire or nylon network at the bottom, so that finer particles will fall through the holes and the larger ones remain on top. *Sieves* are used in kitchens to strain foods such as flour, and liquids such as vegetable soup.

sift *v.* (a) To separate the fine grains of anything from the coarser ones by passing them through a sieve. *Ex.* Sugar can be *sifted* on to a cake from a *sugar-sifter* (*n.*), which is a jar with holes in the top. (b) To examine the contents of anything very carefully. *Ex.* All the documents were *sifted* through, in the search for a will.

sigh (sy) *v.* To take a deep breath rather loudly, because of feeling sad, tired or relieved. *Ex.* He heaved a *sigh* (*n.*) of relief.

sight (syt) *n.* (a) The power of seeing, one of the five senses. (b) The thing that is seen. *Ex.* The rose garden was a beautiful *sight* in June.

sign (syn) *n.* (a) Something that conveys a meaning, such as a gesture. *Ex.* A nod of the head is a *sign* meaning 'yes'. (b) A written notice. *Ex.* A *traffic sign.* (c) A mark having meaning. *Ex.* A *plus sign* (+) in arithmetic. (d) A picture-board on an inn or shop giving its name or the name of the trade practised. 2. *v.* To write your name at the end of a letter etc. This is called your *signature* (*sig*-na-cher; *n.*).

signal (*sig*-nal) *n.* A sign made with lights, flags etc. which conveys a message, sometimes a warning, over a distance. *Ex.* 'Mayday' is the international radio distress *signal* for ships and aircraft. (b) A post of coloured lights used on railways to show train-drivers whether the line is clear. (c) A message sent, using a *signal* code such as the Morse code. 2. *v.* To send such a message.

significant (sig-*nif*-i-kant) *adj.* (a) Having definite and special meaning. *Ex.* A *significant* look from her mother meant 'Look after the guests'. (b) Important. *Ex.* His opinions have little *significance* (*n.*).

signify (*sig*-ni-fy) *v*. (a) To mean. *Ex*. A large 'L' on a car *signifies* that its driver is a learner. (b) To make known. *Ex*. We knew that her smile *signified* that she was pleased with us.

signpost (*syn*-pohst) *n*. A post at crossroads, having wooden arms painted with the names of places the roads lead to.

silage (*sy*-lij) *n*. Winter fodder, stored in a *silo* (*n*.) when still green, and left to ferment.

silence (*sy*-lens) *n*. Complete quiet.

silhouette (sil-oo-*et*) *n*. (a) A shadow-portrait of a person's profile, usually cut out from black paper and put on a white background. (b) The outline of a person or thing seen against the light.

silk *n*. A soft, glossy cloth made from threads produced by the caterpillar of the *silkworm moth*.

sill *n*. The bottom ledge of a window.

silver 1. *n*. A valuable white metal, used in making spoons, forks, jewellery etc. 2. *adj*. Of the colour of silver.

similar (*sim*-il-ar) *adj*. Resembling; like each other.

simile (*sim*-il-i) *n*. A figure of speech in which a thing is likened to something else. *Ex*. 'The surface was as slippery as ice'.

simmer *v*. To boil gently.

simple *adj*. (a) Easy. (b) Plain. *Ex*. *Simple* food is ordinary food, not elaborately cooked. She dressed with *simplicity* (sim-*plis*-it-i; *n*.) in good plain clothes. To make a thing *simple* is to *simplify* (*v*.) it.

simultaneous (sim-ul-*tayn*-i-us) *adj*. Happening at the same time. *Ex*. Pianists use both hands *simultaneously* (*adv*.) on the keyboard.

since 1. *conj*. (a) Seeing that, because. *Ex*. *Since* I'm not busy I have time to help you. (b) Between a certain time and now. *Ex*. I have not seen him *since* I was in London. 2. *prep*. *Ex*. *Since* Easter. 3. *adv*. We visited him last summer and have gone once a week ever *since*.

sincere (sin-*seer*) *adj*. True in speech or feeling; free from any pretence.

sinew (*sin*-ew) *n*. The fibre-like tissue which joins muscles to bones.

singe (sinj) *v*. To burn on the surface; to scorch.

single *adj*. One; for one only. *Ex*. We didn't see a *single* car on the road. A *single* bed. An unmarried woman is said to be *single*.

singular (*sing*-gew-lar) *adj*. (a) (Grammar) Applying to one only; the opposite of plural. *Ex*. 'Child' is the *singular* (*n*.) of 'children'.

(b) Strange, remarkable. *Ex.* The sunset was *singularly* (*adv.*) beautiful.

sinister (*sin*-is-ter) *adj.* Threatening evil; evil-looking.

sink 1. *n.* A fixed basin in a kitchen where dishes are washed. 2. *v.* (a) To go down in water, as a stone does; to become submerged. (b) To drop or push down into anything. One can *sink* into a chair, *sink* a well, see the sun *sink* below the horizon, or have one's heart *sink* if one feels discouraged.

sip *v.* To drink in very small mouthfuls.

sir *n.* A form of polite address to a man, used when speaking to him, or in a formal letter to a stranger. (b) The title used before the Christian name of a knight or baronet. *Ex. Sir* Winston Churchill.

siren (*syr*-en) *n.* A horn or loud whistle, which sounds by the escape of steam or air, and can be heard a long distance away.

site (syt) *n.* The position or ground where a building stands or is to stand.

situated (*sit*-ew-ay-ted) *adj.* Placed.

situation (sit-ew-*ay*-sh'n) (a) Position. *Ex.* The cottage is in a beautiful *situation.* (b) Employment.

size (syz) *n.* The dimension or bigness of anything.

skate 1. *n.* A steel edge fitted underneath boots for moving quickly and easily over ice. (b) A large flat fish. 2. *v.* To move on *skates.*

skein (skayn) *n.* A coil of yarn or thread.

skeleton (*skel*-e-ton) *n.* The bones of a human being or animal which support or protect the other parts.

sketch. 1. *n.* A drawing which is not yet a completed picture. 2. *v.* To draw the first outlines of a plan or picture.

skewer (*skew*-er) *n.* A thick pin to hold a piece of meat together while being cooked.

ski (skee) *n.* A long flat runner of wood or metal, fastened under the boot to enable a *skier* (*n.*) to slide over snow.

skid *v.* To slip sideways on a slippery road, as a car will do if the wheels cannot grip the ground.

skill *n.* Ability to do something well, usually after study and practice. *Ex.* The *skilful* (*adj.*) doctor performed a successful operation, for he was very *skilled* (*adj.*) in his profession.

skim *v.* (a) To take off the surface layer of a liquid, as cream is *skimmed* off milk. (b) To glide lightly over, as a swallow *skims* over water, or a reader *skims* a book by skipping through it.

skip 1. *v.* (a) To hop along on first one foot and then the other. (b)

To jump over and over a *skipping* (*adj.*) rope which is turned over the *skipper's* (*n.*) head. (c) To omit something or doing something, such as *skipping* attendance at a meeting, or *skipping* (not reading) a few pages of a book. 2. *n.* A large container which builders use for rubble etc.

skirmish (*skur*-mish) *n.* A short fight between two groups of soldiers.

skulk *v.* To wander about furtively, hoping not to be seen.

skull *n.* The bony covering of the head.

skylight *n.* A window in a house roof.

skyscraper *n.* A very tall building of many storeys.

slab *n.* A flat piece of stone; a thick slice (of cake etc.).

slack *adj.* (a) Loose. *Ex.* This belt is too *slack*. To *slacken* (*v.*) is to make a thing slack. (b) Lazy, careless.

slam *v.* To shut (a door or gate etc.) noisily.

slander (*slahn*-der) *n.* An untrue, spiteful statement meant to harm a person. *Ex.* She *slandered* (*v.*) him and damaged his reputation.

slang. *n.* Words and phrases commonly used in informal everyday speech and writing but not accepted as correct usage of the language. *Ex.* 'Fuzz' is a *slang* (*adj.*) name for the police.

slant *v.* To have one end lower than the other; to slope. *Ex.* Some roofs are flat but most are *slanting*, or on a *slant* (*n.*).

slap *n.* A blow with the open hand. To give such a blow is to *slap* (*v.*).

slash *v.* To cut roughly with a knife. *Ex.* The seats of the railway-carriage had been *slashed*.

slate *n.* A smooth, usually greyish blue rock which splits easily into thin flat pieces, used for roofing.

slaughter (*slaw*-ter) *n.* Killing in large numbers. *Ex.* There was great *slaughter* in the battle. Animals are *slaughtered* (*v.*) for food in *slaughter-houses* (*n.*).

slave (slayv) *n.* Someone owned by someone else and made to work for him. This condition is called *slavery* (*n.*).

slay *v.* An old word meaning to kill. *Ex.* In the fairy-tale Jack *slew* the Giant; the Giant was *slain* by Jack.

sledge *n.* A vehicle consisting of planks of wood laid across runners (instead of wheels), which can be dragged or ridden over snow and ice.

sleek *adj.* Having a smooth and glossy surface, as an animal's coat after grooming.

sleeper *n.* (a) One who sleeps. (b) One of the wooden beams joining two lines of railway track. (c) A railway *sleeping-car*.

sleet *n.* A mixture of snow and rain falling at the same time.

sleigh (slay) *n.* A light sledge used in winter sports. *Ex. A bobsleigh.*

slender *adj.* Thin, narrow, slim.

sleuth (slooth) *n.* A detective.

slice (slys) *n.* A thin but wide piece of something that has been cut off, such as a *slice* of cake. To *slice* (*v.*) something is to cut off such a piece.

slide *v.* To move smoothly; to glide, especially over ice.

slight (slyt) 1. *adj.* (a) Slender. (b) Little, not important, not much, trifling. *Ex.* There is not the *slightest* danger. 2. *v.* To ignore or snub rudely, and thus make someone feel slighted.

slim 1. *adj.* Slender, very thin. (b) Slight. *Ex.* There was only a *slim* chance of success. 2. *v.* To diet and exercise in order to become *slim*.

slime *n.* A slippery sort of mud etc.

sling *n.* (a) A band passed round something in order to lift it. *Ex.* Heavy loads are lifted on to ships by *slings*. A *sling* can be hung round the neck to support an injured arm. (b) A simple weapon used in the past to hurl a stone with force, such as was used by David to kill Goliath; a catapult.

slink *v.* To move about in a sneaking way. *Slinky* (*adj.*) means weaving about in a supple way, like a snake.

slip 1. *n.* (a) A petticoat. (b) A narrow piece of paper etc. (c) A small error. 2. *v.* (a) To move something quickly and easily. *Ex.* To *slip* on a coat. (b) To slide on losing one's balance. *Slippery* (*adj.*) means having a surface one is likely to *slip* on.

slipper *n.* A light shoe for wear indoors.

slipshod *adj.* Careless, untidy.

slit 1. *n.* A narrow cut or opening. *Ex.* The boys watched the match through a *slit* in the fence. 2. *v.* To make a narrow cut, to split open. *Ex.* To *slit* open an envelope.

slither (*slidh*-er) *v.* To slide on a slippery surface.

sloe (sloh) *n.* The black fruit of the blackthorn.

slogan (*sloh*-gan) *n.* A motto or phrase used in advertising, political campaigns etc. *Ex.* 'Post early for Christmas'.

slope *v.* To slant. There was a *slope* (*n.*) down to the beach instead of steps.

slot *n.* A cut made in something into which something else can be fitted. *Ex.* Coins can be put in the *slots* of public telephones.

slouch (slowch) *v.* To stand or walk carelessly, with head and shoulders bent.

slovenly (*sluv*-en-li) *adj.* Untidy and careless about dress and appearance.

slug *n.* A snail-like creature which has no shell.

sluice (sloos) *n.* A kind of door placed across a river etc. to control the flow of water.

slum *n.* An overcrowded, badly kept housing area.

slumber *v.* To sleep.

slush *n.* Melting snow; very soft mud.

sly *adj.* Secretive, crafty; meaning something not openly expressed. *Ex.* She gave me a *sly* look.

smack *n.* (a) A slap. (b) A small fishing-boat.

smart 1. *adj.* (a) Well-dressed. *Ex.* A *smart* business-suit. (b) Quick, business-like, efficient. *Ex.* A *smart* salute. 2. *v.* To cause or feel a stinging pain. *Ex.* A nettle-sting *smarts*.

smash 1. *n.* The act of striking something with force and breaking it to pieces, as in a car-*smash*. 2. *v.* To break into pieces, to shatter.

smattering *n.* A very little knowledge of a subject. *Ex.* I have only a *smattering* of French.

smear *v.* To spread something dirty, greasy or sticky over.

smirk (smurk) *v.* To smile foolishly.

smith *n.* A worker in metals, such as a *blacksmith* or *silversmith*.

smock 1. *n.* A loose shirt-like garment, such as an artist wears to protect his clothes. 2. *v.* To decorate cloth with stitching which gathers up the fullness.

smoke 1. *n.* The gases, dust etc. that rise from a burning fire. 2. *v.* To give out *smoke*; to draw *tobacco-smoke* from a cigarette etc. and then breathe it out.

smooth (smoodh) *adj.* Having a flat, even surface without roughness. *Ex.* Silk has a *smooth* surface. The sea may be *smooth* when there is no wind. An iron will *smooth* out creases in clothes.

smother (*smudh*-er) *v.* To suffocate.

smoulder (*smohl*-der) *v.* To burn slowly without flame.

smudge *v.* To make a dirty mark on something, as with ink or paint on paper.

smug *adj.* Feeling very pleased with oneself and showing it in an irritating manner.

smuggle *v.* To bring into the country, or take out of it, things which the government has banned (such as drugs or animals), or taxed goods without paying tax on them.

smut   *n.* A spot of dirt which a burning fire sometimes throws off in the smoke.

snack   *n.* A light meal.

snag   *n.* An unexpected difficulty.   *Ex.* The *snag* about the picnic was the wasps.

snail (snayl)   *n.* A small creature which creeps slowly along the ground, and has a shell on its back into which it can withdraw.

snake   *n.* A scaly, flesh-eating reptile with a long legless body. Many have poisonous fangs.

snare (snair)   *n.* A kind of trap set to catch animals, such as rabbits.

snarl   *v.* To growl and show the teeth as a dog may do; to show anger by the savage way one speaks.

snatch   *v.* To seize quickly, usually without the owner's permission.

sneak (sneek)   *v.* To creep stealthily.

sneer   *v.* To make scornful remarks about someone; to jeer, and show by an unpleasant expression on the face that one despises someone.

sneeze   *v.* To make a sudden kind of cough through the nostrils, because something irritates the lining of the nose.

sniff   *v.* To draw in the breath through the nose, as one does in smelling a flower; to draw up the moisture in the nostrils as one may when one has a cold or is crying.

snip   *v.* To cut as with scissors. A *snippet* (*n.*) is a small piece *snipped* off.

snipe (snyp)   1. *n.* A marsh bird with a very long beak. 2. *v.* To shoot from a concealed place. One who does this is a *sniper* (*n.*).

snivel (*sniv*'l)   *v.* To cry in a sniffing, whining way, often to get attention.

snob   *n.* A person who values people for their high position in society, likes to be thought one of them, and alters his behaviour according to the kind of people he is with.   His behaviour is *snobbish* (*adj.*).

snore   *v.* To breathe noisily with open mouth when asleep.

snorkel   *n.* (a) The tubes on a submarine which can let in fresh air and let out impure gases when the submarine is submerged. (b) A swimmer's air-tube for underwater swimming.

snort   *v.* To make an angry noise through the nostrils, a noise similar to that made by a horse.

snout *n.* The long nose of an animal such as a pig.

snow (snoh) *n.* Moisture in the atmosphere that has frozen, and falls to earth as small white flakes.

snowdrop *n.* A small white flower, grown from a bulb, which appears very early in the year.

snub *v.* To treat someone in an unfriendly and humiliating way. *Ex.* We asked them to tea, but they *snubbed* our offer.

snug *adj.* Warm, comfortable. *Ex.* It was *snug* by the fire.

soak *v.* To wet thoroughly. *Ex.* Clothes may be *soaked* in water to get stains out.

soap *v.* A substance made of fats etc. and used with water to wash hands, clothes etc.

soar (sawr) *v.* To rise high, as a bird may *soar* on an upward current of air.

sob 1. *v.* To catch the breath sharply when crying. 2. *n.* The sound made when doing this.

sober (*soh*-ber) *adj.* Calm and serious; not drunk.

sociable (*soh*-shi-a-b'l) *adj.* Friendly and fond of being with friends and acquaintances.

socialism (*soh*-shi-al-izm) *n.* A system of managing the wealth of a country in which the government owns all the main industries, services, banks etc., and runs them for the good of everybody, instead of letting them be privately owned for private profit (which would then be capitalism).

society (so-*sy*-e-ti) *n.* (a) The whole of the people of a country etc. (b) Companionship. *Ex.* He enjoyed the *society* of his fellow workers. (c) Fashionable people. (d) An organization to which people belong. *Ex.* A *debating society*.

socket *n.* A hollow construction made to take something fitted into it, such as an electrical *socket* for a plug.

sod *n.* A piece of grass with its roots and earth; turf.

soda *n.* A chemical used in the manufacture of glass, soap etc. *Baking soda* is bicarbonate of *soda*. *Soda-water* is water made fizzy by putting in carbon dioxide under pressure.

sofa (*soh*-fa) *n.* A long, upholstered seat with back and arms.

soft *adj.* With a surface which is easily pressed down; smooth to the touch; quiet in tone; the opposite of hard. To *soften* (*v.*) is to make *soft*.

soil 1. *n.* The earth in which plants grow. 2. *v.* To make dirty.

solar (*soh*-lar) *adj.* To do with the sun.

sole 1. *n.* (a) A flat fish which is almost circular, and very good to eat. (b) The under-part of the foot, on which we walk. 2. *adj.* Only. *Ex.* He was the *sole* survivor of the wreck.

solemn (*sol*-em) *adj.* Very serious, grave and dignified. *Ex.* The funeral was a *solemn* occasion.

solicitor (sol-*is*-it-or) *n.* A person trained to advise on matters of law.

solid (*sol*-id) *adj.* Firm all the way through; not hollow or liquid.

soliloquy (sol-*il*-o-kwi) *n.* A speech made by a character in a play, as if he were thinking aloud.

solitary (*sol*-it-a-ri) *adj.* Alone or lonely. *Ex.* He led a *solitary* life after his wife died.

solitude (*sol*-it-ewd) *n.* Loneliness; being alone, seclusion.

solo (*soh*-lo) *n.* A piece of music for one player or singer, sometimes with an accompaniment; a performance or activity by one person only. *Ex.* A *dance solo*. A *solo* flight in an aeroplane.

soluble (*sol*-ew-b'l) *adj.* Capable of being dissolved, as sugar is in hot water. (b) Capable of being solved, as a crossword is.

solution (sol-*ew*-sh'n) *n.* Any solid or gas turned into liquid form, such as salt dissolved in water. *See also* solve.

solve (solv) *v.* To explain or find the answer, which is called the *solution* (*n.*). Mysteries or puzzles may have *solutions*; they may be *solved*.

sombre (*som*-ber) *adj.* Gloomy, dark, sad.

somersault (*som*-er-sawlt) *n.* A turning head-over-heels.

somewhat *adv.* Slightly, rather. *Ex.* Although it was August, it was *somewhat* cold.

sonata (son-*ah*-ta) A piece of music for one or two instruments, divided into three or four parts (movements).

sonic (*son*-ik) *adj.* Referring to sound-waves. *See also* supersonic.

sonnet *n.* A poem of 14 lines.

soot (sUt) *n.* A fine black dust formed by burning coal or other fuels.

soothe (soodh) *v.* To calm or quieten; to make pain easier to bear.

soprano (sop-*rahn*-oh) *n.* The highest singing voice of a woman.

sorcerer (*sor*-ser-er) *n.* A magician.

sordid *adj.* Mean, poor, dirty.

sore *adj.* Painful.

sorrow (*so*-roh) *n.* Grief, sadness. To be *sorry* (*adj.*) is to feel regret, grief or pity.

soul (sohl) *n.* The part of a person which some believe lives on after death; the spirit.

sound (sownd) 1. *n.* Noise; what is heard by our ears. 2. *adj.* In good condition. *Ex.* He was *sound* in mind and body.

soup (soop) *n.* A liquid food made by stewing meat, vegetables or fish with water etc.

sour (sowr) *adj.* Tasting sharp or bitter; not sweet. *Ex.* He has a *sour* temper.

source (sawrs) *n.* (a) The point at which a river begins. *Ex.* The *source* of the Thames is a spring in the Cotswold Hills. (b) The beginning or cause of something. *Ex.* His long illness was the *source* of his financial troubles.

south (sowth) *n.* The direction faced when the setting sun is on one's right. A *southerly* (*sudh*-er-li; *adj.*) wind comes from the *south*. *Southern* (*sudh*-ern; *adj.*) means on the *south*.

souvenir (*soo*-ven-eer) *n.* A thing kept as a remembrance. People bring back *souvenirs* from holiday.

sovereign (*sov*-rin) 1. *n.* (a) The ruler of a state, especially a monarch. (b) A gold coin worth £1. 2. *adj.* Free to act independently. *Ex.* A *sovereign* state.

sow (sow) *n.* A female pig.

sow (soh) *v.* To plant seeds.

soya (*soi*-a) *n.* A bean grown in Asia and elsewhere which is a valuable source of protein. It provides flour, oil, fodder and fertilizer.

spa (spah) *n.* A resort where there is a spring of mineral water supposed to be good for the health.

space *n.* (a) Room for something. *Ex.* There isn't enough *space* for a tennis court in our garden. *Spacious* (*adj.*) means having plenty of room. (b) The area outside the Earth's atmosphere. A *spaceship* or *spacecraft* is a rocket-launched vehicle which travels to the moon or the planets; a *spaceship* is a manned *spacecraft*, but a *spacecraft* may have no crew.

spade *n.* A long-handled tool with a wide flat blade, for digging.

spaghetti (spa-*get*-i) *n.* A thin kind of macaroni.

span *n.* Extent; the distance between the two ends of anything. *Ex.* The bridge which *spans* (*v.*) this river has a *span* of half a kilometre.

spaniel (*span*-yel) *n.* A dog kept by sportsmen or as a pet, which has drooping ears and a silky coat.

spank *v.* To slap a person's bottom.

spar *n.* A pole on a ship which supports a sail.

spare 1. *adj.* Extra, not needed at the time. *Ex.* A *spare* bedroom is one not used until a guest comes to stay. 2. *v.* (a) To be able to give up or do without. *Ex.* I can *spare* you a pound of sugar, as I have plenty. (b) To refrain from harming, or from taking someone's life. *Ex.* He *spared* his prisoners' lives.

spark *n.* A particle of light and heat thrown off from a burning fire; or by two hard substances struck together (as in a cigarette-lighter); or by electricity.

sparkle *v.* To shine or glitter, like a diamond or a star.

sparrow *n.* A small brown bird of the finch family, very common in gardens and in towns.

sparse *adj.* Thinly scattered over an area; not growing thickly.

spate *n.* A sudden flood, especially of a river after heavy rain.

spatter *v.* To splash about, in small drops.

spawn *n.* The tiny eggs of fish, frogs etc., collected in a jelly-like mass.

spear *n.* A long pole with a sharp iron point, used as a weapon.

special (*spesh*-al) *adj.* Of a different or particular kind, or intended for a particular purpose, *Ex.* A *special* bus was provided for the school outing. A *specialist* (*n.*) is one who has made a *special* study of one branch of knowledge. *Ex.* An *ear specialist* is a doctor who is an expert on diseases of the ear. An engineer may *specialize* (*v.*) in aero-engines.

speciality (spesh-i-*al*-it-i) *n.* The feature which is special. *Ex.* The *speciality* of that school is its musical activities. This restaurant's *speciality* is shellfish.

species (*spee*-sheez) *n.* (a) A group of creatures or plants with similar characteristics, which do not usually breed with other species. (b) A kind or sort.

specify (*spes*-i-fy) *v.* To state definitely and most clearly. *Ex.* The customer *specified* the exact kind of notebook he wanted. A *specification* (*n.*) is a list which a builder or engineer etc. makes to show the materials, measurements and processes used to do a particular job.

specimen (*spes*-i-men) *n.* One of its kind taken as a sample. *Ex.* There were *specimens* of all the new cars at the motor show.

speck *n.* A small spot; a tiny bit of something. *Ex.* A *speck* of dust.

speckled *adj.* Marked with specks or dots. *Ex.* A *speckled* hen.

spectacle (*spek*-tak'l) *n.* A large public display, such as a circus or a Red Arrows aerial display; a sight.

spectacles (*spek*-tak'lz) *n.* Glasses (a pair of lenses in a frame with bars which rest on the ears), designed to correct what is wrong with a person's eyesight, or to protect his eyes from sun-glare.

spectator (spek-*tay*-tor)   *n.* One who looks on, especially at a game or performance of some kind.

spectre (*spek*-ter)   *n.* A ghost.

speech   *n.* (a) The power of being able to talk. (b) A talk given by one person on a definite subject to an audience. To be *speechless* (*adj.*) means that your feelings are so strong that you can't for the moment say anything.

speed   *n.* Quickness of movement. A *speedometer* (speed-*om*-e-ter; *n.*) is an instrument which measures the speed of a vehicle and shows it on a dial.

spell   1. *v.* To write or name correctly the letters which make up a word. 2. *n.* (a) The words of a magic charm. (b) A short period of time or turn at work.   *Ex.* A *spell* in hospital. We each took a *spell* at baling out the water from the boat.

spellbound   *adj.* Bound as by a spell, and so, fascinated, intensely interested.   *Ex.* The children were *spellbound* by the magic show.

spend   *v.* (a) To use money for buying things, etc. (b) To use time for some purpose.   *Ex.* I *spent* an hour picking mushrooms. A *spendthrift* (*n.*) is an extravagant person.

sphere (sfeer)   *n.* A completely round object like a ball.

spice (spys)   *n.* Strongly flavoured seeds, roots etc. of certain plants, used to season and flavour food.

spider (*spy*-der)   *n.* A small animal with eight legs, which spins webs in which it traps flies for its food.

spike   *n.* A sharp point, such as one sees on top of railings.

spill   *v.* To allow liquid to overflow or splash down.

spin   *v.* (a) To make thread by drawing out and twisting strands of cotton, wool etc., either by hand or machine.   *Ex.* Webs are *spun* by spiders. (b) To turn round, or cause to turn round. You yourself can *spin* round, or you can make a top *spin*.

spinach (*spin*-ij)   *n.* A green leaf-vegetable.

spine (spyn)   *n.* The backbone of the body; a thorn, the long points on a hedgehog, porcupine etc.

spinster   *n.* A woman who is not married.

spiral (*spyr*-al)   *adj.* Winding like the thread of a screw. A *spiral* staircase in a tower goes up *spirally* (*adv.*).

spire (spyr)   *n.* A tall tapering structure, often on a church tower.

spirit (*spi*-rit)   *n.* (a) A ghost. (b) The soul. (c) A mood.   *Ex.* You may do a thing in a kindly *spirit*, or be in high *spirits* (very cheerful). (d) Certain alcoholic drinks (whisky etc.) and other distilled liquids are called *spirits*.

spiritual (*spi*-rit-ew-al) *adj.* Connected with the soul or *spirit*.

spite (spyt) *n.* Ill-will or unkindness towards someone. A *spiteful* (*adj.*) person wants to hurt someone. *In spite of* means not taking any notice of. *Ex.* She went out *in spite of* the heavy rain.

splash 1. *v.* To move water etc. about, often with hands or feet, making the drops fly about. *Ex.* Babies like to *splash* their bathwater about. 2. *n.* The act of *splashing*.

splendid *adj.* Magnificent, very fine. *Ex.* The gala-night at the opera was a scene of great *splendour* (*n.*).

splinter *n.* A small sharp piece of wood, glass etc. which has been broken off something.

split *v.* To divide into parts. *Ex.* One can *split* logs for the fire, or *split* a class into two.

spoil 1. *n.* Things stolen or captured in war. 2. *v.* To do harm to. *Ex.* Flowers may be *spoiled* by frost, or a child have his character *spoiled* by being over-indulged.

spoke (spohk) *n.* One of the bars or rods which join the centre of a wheel to the rim.

spokesman (*spohks*-man) *n.* One member of a group chosen to speak for the others, or to make public statements for them.

sponge (spunj) 1. *n.* (a) A soft skeleton of a certain sea-creature called a *sponge* (or some rubber or other substitute), which absorbs and holds water and is used in washing. (b) A soft cake of flour, beaten eggs and sugar. *Ex.* A *sponge cake*. 2. *v.* To wash with a *sponge*.

spontaneous (spon-*tay*-ni-us) *adj.* Done without planning or prompting. *Ex.* They cheered him *spontaneously* (*adv.*).

spool *n.* A reel on which thread etc. is wound.

spout (spowt) *n.* A pipe or tube from which liquid can pour. *Ex.* A *rainwater spout*; the *spout* of a kettle.

sprain *v.* To pull or tear the muscles and ligaments of a joint, especially the ankle or wrist.

sprat *n.* A sea-fish like a very small herring.

sprawl *v.* To spread out the limbs in an awkward and ungraceful position.

spray 1. *n.* (a) A quantity of liquid in tiny drops. *Ex.* Waves breaking on rocks send up showers of *spray*. (b) A small branch with flowers on it. 2. *v.* To scatter liquid as a *spray*, often from a special container.

spread (spred) *v.* (a) To open out. *Ex. Spread* the map out so that we can all read it. (b) To cover with a layer of something. *Ex.* To *spread* butter on bread.

sprightly (*spryt*-li) *adj.* Lively and active.

spring 1. *n.* (a) A stream of water which comes up out of the ground. (b) The season between Winter and Summer. 2. *v.* To leap or jump. *Ex.* The cat *sprang* on the mouse.

sprinkle (*spring*-k'l) *v.* To scatter in tiny drops or pieces. *Ex.* They *sprinkled* sugar on their cereal.

sprout (sprowt) 1. *v.* To begin to grow by putting forth shoots. 2. *n.* Sprout, or *Brussels sprout*, is an edible plant which bears buds like little cabbages.

spruce (sproos) 1. *n.* A kind of fir tree. 2. *adj.* Very tidy and neatly dressed.

spur *n.* A sharp metal instrument fastened on the heel of a rider's boot, which is pressed against the horse's side to make it move on.

squabble (*skwob*'l) *v.* To quarrel in a noisy, childish way.

squad (skwod) *n.* A small group of men organized to work together.

squadron (*skwod*-ron) *n.* A military unit, a number of cavalry, ships, tanks or aircraft under one command.

squalid (*skwol*-id) *adj.* Poor, dirty and uncared for.

squall (skwawl) *n.* (a) A sudden gust of wind. *Ex.* A *squall* hit the dinghy and overturned her. (b) A harsh scream.

squander (*skwon*-der) *v.* To spend too much, wastefully. Both time and money can be *squandered*.

square (skwair) *n.* (a) A shape which has four sides of the same length and all the corners right angles. (b) The roughly *square*-shaped space, with buildings all around, found in many cities. *Ex. Trafalgar Square.*

squash (skwosh) 1. *n.* (a) A drink made by squeezing the juice out of a fruit. (b) *Squash-rackets*, a game played by two with a soft ball hit by rackets against the walls of a four-sided court. 2. *v.* To crush or pack in tightly. *Ex.* He *squashed* all his clothes into one small case.

squeak *n.* A small cry on a high note. *Ex.* A mouse *squeaks*.

squeal *n.* A cry louder than a squeak, expressing either pain or joy. *Ex.* A pig *squeals*.

squeamish (*skweem*-ish) *adj.* Easily inclined to feel sick; easily put off by a feeling of disgust.

squeeze *v.* To press or crush. *Ex.* We *squeezed* lemons to make lemonade.

squint (skwint) *v.* To be cross-eyed; to be unable to focus both eyes on a thing at the same time. To *squint* is to have a *squint* (*n.*).

squire (skwyr) *n.* A name sometimes given to the chief landowner in a parish.

squirm (skwurm) *v.* To wriggle and twist as though uncomfortable.

squirrel (*skwi*-rel) *n.* A bushy-tailed rodent which lives in trees.

squirt (skwurt) *v.* To eject a liquid in a thin stream, as a water-pistol does.

stab *v.* To pierce with something sharp such as a dagger.

stable 1. *n.* A building where horses are kept. 2. *adj.* Steady and not about to change. *Ex.* A *stable* working-top is one that does not wobble.

stack 1. *n.* (a) A group of chimneys, or a steamship's funnel. (b) A large, orderly pile of something, such as books, hay etc. 2. *v.* To make into a pile or heap.

stadium (*stay*-di-um) *n.* A sports ground with tiers of seats for spectators.

staff (stahf) *n.* (a) A stick carried in the hand, either to help the walker or to show authority. *Ex.* A mayor's mace is a *staff* of office. (b) A pole (*flagstaff*) to which a flag can be fastened. (c) The group of people employed by one firm, school, factory etc.

stag *n.* A male deer.

stage *n.* (a) The platform in a theatre etc. where the acting is done. (b) The theatrical profession. *Ex.* He wants to go on the *stage.* (c) A certain point reached in a process or journey. *Ex.* He is in the early *stages* of learning the piano.

stagger *v.* To walk unsteadily, as if about to fall.

stagnant (*stag*-nant) *adj.* Not flowing along, but still, dirty and smelly, as a pond may be.

stain 1. *n.* A mark, usually a dirty mark. 2. *v.* To make such a mark. *Ex.* If you pick blackberries you are bound to get your hands *stained.*

stake *n.* A sharp-pointed stick driven into the ground, to support something or to mark a boundary etc.

stale *adj.* No longer fresh.

stalk (stawk) 1. *n.* The stem of a leaf or flower. 2. *v.* (a) To creep quietly up to an animal you are hunting, so that it does not hear you. (b) To walk away haughtily, showing anger.

stall (stawl) 1. *n*. (a) A compartment in a stable or shed for one animal. (b) A table or bench from which things are sold at a market or fair. (c) A seat with arms, either in a church choir, or in a theatre near the stage. 2. *v*. To cause an engine to stop by accident, or an aeroplane to lose the speed necessary to keep it up.

stalwart (*stawl*-wert) *adj*. Strong and sturdy.

stamen (*stay*-men) *n*. The male organ of a flower, which contains the pollen.

stammer *v*. To speak in a hesitating way, finding it hard to go on to the next syllable or word.

stamp (stamp) *v*. (a) To strike the ground heavily with the foot. (b) To show official approval by putting a mark on something. *Ex*. A bus pass can be *stamped*. A *postage stamp* on a letter shows that postage has been paid.

stampede (stam-*peed*) *n*. A sudden rush of a number of animals that have been frightened.

stanch (stahnch) *v*. To stop the flow of blood from a wound.

standard *n*. (a) The typical specimen or example in any group. *Ex*. The *standard* (*adj*.) way to begin a business letter is 'Dear Sir'. (b) A particular grade. *Ex*. His work is of a high *standard*. (c) A flag.

staple (*stay*-p'l) *n*. (a) A U-shaped metal loop with pointed ends. *Ex*. He fixed the electric flex to the wall with *staples*. (b) A wire clip to fasten papers together. (c) The main product or food of a country. *Ex*. The *staple* (*adj*.) diet in India is rice.

star *n*. A heavenly body which shines with its own light, such as we see in the sky after dark. *Star-shaped* (*adj*.) usually means having five points, like a *starfish*.

starboard *n*. The right side of a ship when looking forward.

starch *n*. A food stored in plants (cereals, potatoes etc.), which our bodies convert into sugar and energy. *Starch* can also be used as a stiffener when washing cotton, linen etc.

stare (stair) *v*. To gaze with a fixed look and wide-open eyes.

starling *n*. A smallish dark bird with iridescent feathers.

start *v*. (a) To begin. (b) To make a sudden movement from surprise or fear.

startle *v*. To surprise or frighten.

starve *v*. To be in great need of food; to die of hunger.

state 1. *n*. Condition. *Ex*. This carpet is in a bad *state*. (b) A country with its own government; a nation. (c) A partly independent member of a federation. *Ex.* The *state* of Maryland, U.S.A. 2. *v.* To express in speech or writing, often formally. *Ex.* The label *stated* that the contents were poisonous. A *statement* (*n.*) is what has been *stated*, often a public announcement. *Ex.* The Prime Minister made a *statement* on his return from the conference.

statesman *n.* One who has won a high reputation as a politician.

station *n.* (a) A *railway-station.* (b) A centre for a particular activity. *Ex.* A *police station*; a *broadcasting station*; a *filling station* (for petrol).

stationary (*stay*-shon-ar-ri) *adj.* Staying in one place; not moving.

stationery (*stay*-shon-er-ri) *n.* Writing materials, especially writing-paper and envelopes, sold by *stationers* (*n.*).

statistics (stat-*ist*-iks) *n.* Information collected in the form of figures rather than words.

statue (*stat*-ew) *n.* The figure of a person carved in stone or made in metal etc.

staunch (stawnch) *adj.* Loyal and faithful.

steady (*sted*-i) *adj.* Firm, not moving. *Ex.* This table is not *steady*; it wobbles.

steak (stayk) *n.* A thick slice of meat (especially beef) or fish.

steal (steel) *v.* (a) To take what belongs to someone else. (b) To move stealthily. *Ex.* He *stole* into the house one night.

stealthy (*stel*-thi) *adj.* Secret, furtive. *Ex.* We heard *stealthy* footsteps outside, and thought it was a burglar.

steel *n.* Iron that has been treated to make it specially hard and strong.

steep 1. *adj.* Rising sharply. *Ex.* These stairs are *steep.* 2. *v.* To soak.

stem *n.* A stalk.

stencil (*sten*-sil) *n.* A thin sheet of plastic etc. with cut-out letters or designs through which ink is transferred to paper etc.

stereophonic (ste-ri-o-*fon*-ik) *adj.* (Of sound) Appearing to come from more than one direction, as from a radio with two loudspeakers.

sterile (*ste*-ryl) *adj.* (a) Made antiseptic (free of germs). (b) Unable to produce young.

stern (sturn) 1. *n.* The back end of a ship. 2. *adj.* Having a severe expression, manner or outlook.

stew 1. *v.* To cook meat, vegetables or fruit slowly in water. 2. *n.* A dish of meat and vegetables so cooked.

steward (*stew*-ard) *n.* (a) The man who attends to the food and comfort of passengers in a ship or aircraft. A *stewardess* is a woman steward. (b) One who helps to organize a wedding, dance, sports-meeting etc.

stiff *adj.* Difficult to bend or move. *Ex.* You can have a *stiff* leg; or a *stiff* window which is hard to open. To *stiffen* (*v.*) is to make *stiff*.

stifle (*styf*'l) *v.* To deprive of fresh air.

stile (styl) *n.* Steps in a wall or fence to allow people, but not cattle etc., to get over.

still 1. *adj.* Quiet, peaceful, without movement. 2. *adv.* Even now. *Ex.* Do you *still* want to try?

stimulate (*stim*-ew-layt) *v.* To rouse. Your interest can be *stimulated* by a television programme, or your appetite by the smell of food.

sting 1. *n.* (a) The sharp organ containing poison or irritant which some insects (such as bees) and other creatures have. (b) A sudden sharp pain which feels like a sting. 2. *v.* To wound with a *sting*. Some plants, such as nettles, *sting* when touched.

stingy (*stin*-ji) *adj.* Mean over money matters.

stint 1. *v.* To be too sparing with something and not use enough. *Ex.* When making the trifle, don't *stint* the cream. 2. *n.* A period of work. *Ex.* We all had to do our *stint* of housework.

stir (stur) 1. *n.* Excitement; much activity. *Ex.* There is always a great *stir* in the town on market-day. 2. *v.* (a) To mix something, especially food, with a spoon etc. (b) To move. *Ex.* I haven't *stirred* from my chair all afternoon.

stirrup (*sti*-rup) *n.* A metal ring hung from the saddle of a horse, in which the rider puts his foot.

stitch *n.* (a) One loop made in sewing or knitting. To make these stitches is to *stitch* (*v.*). (b) A sudden sharp pain in the side, caused by violent exercise.

stoat (stoht) *n.* A small wild animal related to the weasel, which hunts rats, rabbits etc.

stock *n.* (a) A quantity or supply. Large *stocks* of goods, especially those for sale, are stored in *stockrooms* until needed. (b) The *livestock* (animals) of a farm. (c) A sweet-scented summer garden flower of various pale colours.

stodgy (*sto*-ji) *adj.* Heavy and dull. Uninteresting food can be called *stodgy*, and so can a dull person.

stoke *v.* To feed a furnace with fuel.

stole *n.* A strip of fur or other material, worn by women round the shoulders.

stolid (*stol*-id) *adj.* Dull, not easily excited.

stomach (*stum*-ak) *n.* The organ of the body in which food is digested; the belly.

stool *n.* A small seat with no back.

stoop *v.* (a) To bend one's body forwards. *Ex.* He had to *stoop* to get through the low doorway. (b) To lower oneself by behaviour. *Ex.* We did not think he would *stoop* to such meanness.

store 1. *n.* (a) A stock of things; supplies kept together. (b) A shop, especially a *department store*. 2. *v.* To keep supplies of something until needed. *Ex.* Our furniture is being *stored* until we get our new house.

storey *n.* One floor of a building. High-rise flats are in buildings of many *storeys*.

storm *n.* Bad weather such as high winds, heavy rain or snow, or thunder. A *stormy* (*adj.*) sea is one that has large waves. In deserts, wind can raise *sand-storms*.

stout 1. *adj.* Fat and bulky of figure; brave and undaunted. 2. *n.* A heavy dark beer.

stove (stohv) *n.* Apparatus for cooking or heating.

stow (stoh) *v.* To pack or put in a suitable place, especially cargo on board a ship.

stowaway (*stoh*-a-way) *n.* A person who hides in a ship or aircraft so as to travel without paying the fare.

straggle *v.* To lag behind a main group, as some cross-country runners, or tired soldiers on the march, may do.

straight (strayt) *adj.* Direct; not bent or curved. You might draw a *straight* line, or walk along a *straight* road. To come *straight* home means to come home in the most direct way, without dawdling. To *straighten* (*v.*) is to make *straight*. To be *straightforward* (*adj.*) is to be frank and honest; not complicated.

strain (strayn) 1. *n.* Injury, caused by too much effort, to body, mind or emotions. You can *strain* (*v.*) a muscle or your memory, or suffer *strain* of mind from worry. 2. *v.* (a) To stretch or make the greatest use of; to make a great effort. *Ex.* We *strained* our ears in the hope of hearing an answering call. (b) To put through a sieve.

strait *n.* A narrow piece of water joining two seas. *Ex.* The *Straits* of Gibraltar, between the Mediterranean and the Atlantic.

strange (straynj) *adj.* (a) Unusual; extraordinary. (b) Not seen before; unfamiliar. *Ex.* The handwriting was *strange* to me. A *stranger* (*n.*) is a person one does not know.

strangle (*strang*-g'l) *v.* To kill by gripping the throat tightly.

strap *n.* A narrow leather band, usually with a buckle for fastening.

stratagem (*strat*-a-jem) *n.* A carefully planned trick to gain something. *Ex.* The Greeks' *stratagem* of the Wooden Horse enabled them to capture Troy.

strategy (*strat*-e-ji) *n.* The art of planning and directing forces in war or in other activities where *strategic* (strat-*ee*-jik; *adj.*) moves have to be made (football, chess etc.).

straw *n.* The dried stalk of corn.

strawberry (*straw*-be-ri) *n.* A sweet, soft, red fruit with tiny yellow seeds, growing close to the ground.

stray 1. *v.* To wander. 2. *adj.* Having wandered off, as a *stray* animal may.

streak *n.* A line of different colour or kind from its background. *Ex.* The sunset sky was *streaked* (*v.*) with pink and mauve. A *streak* of lightning.

stream 1. *n.* A small river. 2. *v.* To flow or come out like a *stream*. *Ex.* After the show, people *streamed* out of the theatre.

streamer *n.* A long ribbon fixed at one end and allowed to *stream* out in the wind.

streamlined *adj.* Having a smooth outline with as little as possible sticking out to catch wind or water and lessen the speed (of a car, yacht, aeroplane, fish etc.).

strength *n.* The quality of being *strong* (*adj.*). To *strengthen* is to make stronger.

stretch *v.* (a) To make longer or wider by pulling out. *Ex. Stretch* (*adj.*) fabric is specially made to *stretch* and make for a close fit. (b) To reach or hold out. *Ex.* They *stretched* out their hands for the sweets.

stretcher *n.* A cloth-covered frame to carry the sick or wounded.

strict *adj.* Exact, regular; enforcing the rules. *Ex.* The conductor was *strict* about the players being on time for rehearsals; he conducted the music in *strict* (regular) time.

stride (stryd) *n.* A long step in walking. To *stride* (*v.*) is to walk with long steps.

strife (stryf) *n.* Quarrelling and fighting.

strike (stryk) *v.* (a) To hit or knock against. *Ex.* He *struck* the ball hard. You *strike* a match on a matchbox. (b) To sound the hours. *Ex.* The clock *struck* ten. (c) To stop work until a dispute has been settled; this is called going on *strike* (*n.*). (d) To occur to the mind. *Ex.* It *strikes* me that I've heard that story before.

striking (*stryk*-ing) *adj.* Remarkable, very noticeable. *Ex.* There was a *stiking* resemblance between them.

string *n.* The thin cord used for tying etc.; the wire, nylon etc. used on *stringed* (*adj.*) musical instruments.

strip 1. *n.* A long narrow piece of anything. *Ex.* A *strip* of land; a *strip* of plaster for a cut finger. 2. *v.* To take or pull off. You can *strip* paper off a wall, or *strip* off your clothes for a swim.

stripe (stryp) *n.* A band or line of a different colour from the background. *Ex.* A blue and white *striped* (*adj.*) shirt.

stroke 1. *n.* (a) The act of *striking*; a hit. *Ex.* The batsman played some good *strokes*. (b) A mark made by pencil or pen. (c) An attack of a paralysing illness. 2. *v.* To rub the hand gently along, as one *strokes* a cat.

stroll (strohl) *v.* To walk slowly for pleasure; to take a *stroll* (*n.*).

structure (*struk*-cher) *n.* A building; anything constructed or put together.

struggle *v.* To make an energetic effort. *Ex.* He *struggled* to lift the heavy weight; it was a hard *struggle* (*n.*).

stubble *n.* The short stalks left in the ground after corn has been cut.

stubborn (*stub*-ern) *adj.* Determined not to give way; obstinate. *Ex.* My grandmother would be safer living with us, but she *stubbornly* (*adv.*) refuses.

student (*stew*-dent) *n.* One who studies, especially at college.

studio (*stew*-di-oh) *v.* The room where an artist or photographer works, or from which television and radio programmes are broadcast.

studious (*stew*-di-us) *adj.* Given to study and learning.

study (*stud*-i) 1. *v.* To give one's mind to learning, especially from books. 2. *n.* A room set apart for *study*.

stuff 1. *n.* (a) Cloth. (b) Rubbish. *Ex.* What's all this *stuff* in your wardrobe? 2. *v.* To fill a thing tightly with something, as in *stuffing* a cushion with feathers. The skins of birds can be *stuffed* so that they look much as they did when alive. *Stuffing* (*n.*) is the material used to *stuff* things with. *Ex.* The savoury *stuffing* of a roast turkey.

stuffy *adj.* Having no fresh air coming in.

stumble *v.* To trip and almost fall; to walk awkwardly.

stump 1. *n.* (a) (Cricket) One of the posts which form a wicket. (b) The part left when the rest has been cut or broken off. *Ex.* A *tree stump.* 2. *v.* To walk heavily and stiffly.

stun *v.* To make unconscious by a blow on the head, or make bewildered by noise, shock etc.

stunt 1. *n.* A daring trick or other sensational act done to attract attention. 2. *v.* To stop the growth of a thing. *Ex.* Lack of light and water *stunted* the plant's growth.

stupefy (*stew*-pi-fy) *v.* To make dull, sleepy or almost unconscious with drugs, alcohol etc.; to make *stupid* with shock.

stupendous (stew-pend-us) *adj.* Amazing, especially because of size. *Ex.* The Grand Canyon is a *stupendous* river gorge. The conquest of Everest was a *stupendous* feat.

stupid (*stew*-pid) *adj.* Not clever or intelligent; foolish. *Ex.* It is *stupid* not to use pedestrian crossings when they are provided.

sturdy *adj.* Strong and healthy.

stutter *v.* To stammer.

sty *n.* (a) An enclosed area for pigs. (b) A painful swelling on the eyelid (also spelt *stye*).

style *n.* (a) A way of doing something, often special to one person. *Ex.* A cricketer's batting *style*; a writer's *style*. (b) A fashion, or fashionable look. *Ex.* The *styles* this season are very full-skirted. She follows the fashions and is always *stylishly* (*adv.*) dressed.

sub- is a prefix usually meaning *under* or *below*. *Ex.* A *sub*marine is a warship which moves under the sea.

subdue (sub-*dew*) *v.* (a) To conquer, get the better of or tame. *Ex.* The rebels were soon *subdued* by the army. (b) To make softer or more gentle. *Ex. Subdued* (*adj.*) lighting is soft, not brilliant.

subject (*sub*-jekt) *n.* (a) One who is under the authority of another. *Ex.* The king's *subjects.* (b) The person or thing that is being written about, spoken of, dealt with, or represented in art. *Ex.* The *subject* for your next essay is Village Life. (c) The branch of learning being taught. *Ex.* Maths and geography are school *subjects.* (d) (Grammar) The *subject* of a sentence is the noun that governs the verb. *Ex.* In 'The cat lapped the milk', 'cat' is the *subject* and 'milk' the *object*.

submarine (sub-ma-*reen*) 1. *adj.* Under the sea. *Ex. Submarine* photography. 2. *n.* A warship that can stay under the sea for long periods.

submerge (sub-*merj*) *v.* To put or go completely under water. *Ex.* A submarine can *submerge*.

submit (sub-*mit*) *v.* (a) To give way or yield. (b) To offer something to someone, for his decision or acceptance. *Ex.* Competition entries must be *submitted* by April 1st.

subordinate (sub-*awr*-din-it) *adj.* Lower in rank or importance. *Ex.* In the army, a private is *subordinate* to a corporal.

subscribe (sub-*skryb*) *v.* To agree to something by signing one's name. You can *subscribe* to a society, promising to pay the *subscription* (*n.*) money and so become a member.

subside (sub-*syd*) *v.* To sink down. *Ex.* When the waters *subsided*, Noah's Ark came to rest on the land.

substance (*sub*-stans) *n.* The material or matter of which a thing is made. Rock, sugar, rubber, silver are all *substances*, with their own different qualities or characteristics. *Ex.* Sugar is a sweet *substance*.

substantial (sub-*stan*-shal) *adj.* (a) Strong, solid, well-constructed. *Ex.* The lighthouse is a *substantial* building. (b) Of real importance; a good amount. *Ex.* He made a *substantial* contribution to the debate.

substitute (*sub*-stit-ewt) *n.* A person or thing put or used in place of another. *Ex.* Margarine is a *substitute* for butter in cooking; you can *substitute* (*v.*) it for butter.

subterranean (sub-ter-*ray*-ni-an) *adj.* Underground. *Ex.* A secret *subterranean* passage led from the castle to the chapel.

subtle (*sut'l*) *adj.* Clever in a shrewd, ingenious or cunning way; not obvious. *Ex.* A *subtle* difference. A *subtle* chess-player.

subtract (sub-*trakt*) *v.* To take away a part from the rest. *Ex.* *Subtracting* 2 from 5 leaves 3.

suburb (*sub*-urb) *n.* An outlying part of a city. *Ex.* Hampstead is a London *suburb*; it is a *suburban* (*adj.*) district.

subway *n.* An underground passage for pedestrians, going under a road or railway.

succeed (suk-*seed*) *v.* (a) To follow after. *Ex.* King Edward VII *succeeded* Queen Victoria. (b) To get on well; to manage to do what one aimed to do. *Ex.* He *succeeded* in swimming 100 metres.

suck *n.* To draw into the mouth etc., as a baby does its milk. Vacuum cleaners remove dirt by *suction* (*n.*).

suckle *n.* To feed the newly-born with its mother's milk.

sudden *adj.* Quick; not expected. *Ex.* A *sudden* clap of thunder startled us.

suds (sudz) *n.* Soapy water.

sue (sew) *v.* (a) To take someone to law, to prosecute. (b) To plead or ask for. *Ex.* The defeated enemy *sued* for peace.

suede (swayd) *n.* Kid-skin used to make shoes, bags, gloves etc.

suet (*sew*-it) *n.* The hard fat found near an animal's kidneys, used in cooking.

suffer *v.* To feel pain; to be made to bear some kind of injury, misfortune etc. *Ex.* He *suffered* from toothache. The house *suffered* damage in the storm.

sufficient (su-*fish*-ent) *adj.* Enough. *Ex.* It is a large cake, *sufficient* for everybody.

suffix (*suf*-iks) *n.* A syllable added to the end of a word, which alters its meaning. *Ex.* The *suffix* 'er' added to 'fight' changes it to 'fighter', the one who does the fighting.

suffocate (*suf*-o-kayt) *v.* To kill by depriving of air. *Ex.* In a fire, people are sometimes *suffocated* by smoke.

suggest (su-*jest*) *v.* To offer an opinion, or make a person consider an idea. *Ex.* It was *suggested* that I learn riding, and I liked the *suggestion* (*n.*).

suicide (*soo*-i-syd) *n.* The act of killing oneself.

suit (soot) 1. *n.* (a) A set of clothes made to be worn together. *Ex.* A matching jacket and trousers (or skirt) is a *suit*. (b) Any of the four sets (spades, hearts, diamonds, clubs) that make up a pack of playing-cards. 2. *v.* To be convenient, to please, to satisfy. *Ex.* We decided to leave at ten, a time which *suited* us all; it was the most *suitable* (*adj.*) time.

suitcase (*soot*-kays) *n.* A case in which clothes are carried when travelling.

suite (sweet) *n.* (a) A set of furniture for one room. (b) A set of rooms, especially in a hotel.

sulky (*sul*-ki) *adj.* Silent and gloomy from bad temper.

sullen (*sul*-en) *adj.* Very sulky indeed.

sultana (sul-*tah*-na) *n.* A small seedless raisin.

sultry (*sul*-tri) *adj.* Very hot, with the air feeling damp and heavy, as before a thunderstorm.

summary (*sum*-a-ri) *n.* A short statement of facts without details.

summit (*sum*-it) *n.* The highest point, especially of a mountain.

summon (*sum*-on) *v.* To send for someone over whom one has authority. *Ex.* The general *summoned* his officers to his headquarters.

sumptuous (*sump*-tew-us) *adj.* Very rich and grand in style. *Ex.* The rich merchant gave a *sumptuous* feast for the princes.

sundae (*sun*-day) *n.* An ice-cream dish with fruit, nuts etc.

sundial (*sun*-dy-al) *n.* A dial marked with the hours, on which the sun casts a shadow which indicates the time.

sunstroke *n.* An illness caused by exposing oneself too long in hot sun.

superb (soo-*purb*) *adj.* Splendid, magnificent, excellent.

superfluous (soo-*per*-floo-us) *adj.* Not needed; more than enough. *Ex.* We gave away our *superfluous* rhubarb.

superintend (soo-per-in-*tend*) *v.* To be in charge of, or to direct, any kind of work. One who does this is a *superintendent* (*n.*).

superior (soo-*peer*-i-or) *adj.* Higher; better in quality.

supermarket *n.* A large self-service store that sells food and household goods.

supernatural (soo-per-*nach*-ral) *adj.* Not according to the laws of nature; that cannot be explained in any natural way. *Ex.* Ghosts are *supernatural* beings.

supersede (soo-per-*seed*) *v.* To replace, especially something out-of-date. *Ex.* This cooker *supersedes* last year's model.

supersonic (soo-per-*son*-ik) *adj.* Above the speed of sound.

superstition (soo-per-*stish*-on) *n.* Belief in the supernatural. *Ex. Superstitious* (*adj.*) people think it unlucky to walk under a ladder.

supervise (*soo*-per-vyz) *v.* To superintend. A *supervisor* (*n.*) is one who *supervises*.

supple (*sup*'l) *adj.* Able to bend easily. *Ex.* Leather has to be specially treated to make it *supple*.

supplement (*sup*-li-ment) 1. *n.* Something added. Some newspapers have separate *supplements*, printed in colour. 2. *v.* To add something. *Ex.* He *supplements* his pension by taking on odd jobs.

supply (su-*ply*) *v.* To give what is needed; to provide with. *Ex.* He *supplies* us with vegetables from his garden; we get our *supplies* (*n.*) from him.

support (su-*pawrt*) *v.* (a) To carry the weight of; to prevent from falling. A table is *supported* by legs. (b) To provide something, such as money to live on, or encouragement etc. *Ex.* The widow worked hard to *support* her children and her brother was a great *support* (*n.*) to her.

suppose (su-*pohz*) *v.* To believe to be true or probable. *Ex.* I don't *suppose* he will stay for long. *Supposing* can also mean 'if'. *Ex.* What will you do *supposing* you miss your train?

suppress (su-*pres*) *v.* (a) To put down and stop forcibly. *Ex.* The troops *suppressed* the rebellion. (b) To withhold. *Ex.* News of the king's escape was *suppressed.*

supreme (su-*preem*) *adj.* Highest, greatest. *Ex.* He was in *supreme* command of land, sea and air forces.

surcharge (*sur*-charj) *n.* An extra charge, such as one for an additional service, or for an unexpected expense.

surf *n.* Waves of the sea breaking in foam on the shore. To *surf* (*v.*) or *surf-ride* is to ride such waves balanced on a narrow *surfboard* (*n.*).

surface (*sur*-fis) *n.* The outside or top layer of anything. On the *surface* means not going beneath the top layer or skin.

surfeit (*sur*-fit) *n.* Too much, especially of eating and drinking.

surgeon (*sur*-jun) *n.* A doctor who relieves or cures illness not by giving medicines but by operating, using *surgical* (*adj.*) instruments.

surgery (*sur*-je-ri) *n.* (a) The work done by a *surgeon.* (b) The room where a doctor gives treatment or advice to his patients.

surly (*sur*-li) *adj.* Bad-tempered, rude, sullen.

surname (*sur*-naym) *n.* A person's last or family name. *Ex.* Beatrix Potter's *surname* is Potter.

surpass (sur-*pahs*) *v.* To be beyond or better than. *Ex.* The beauty of this countryside *surpasses* any I have seen.

surplus (*sur*-plus) *n.* What is left over and not needed. *Ex.* We sold our *surplus* (*adj.*) vegetables to the greengrocer.

surprise (sur-*pryz*) *n.* Something unusual or unexpected; the feeling caused by this. *Ex.* We were *surprised* (*v.*) to see snow on the hills.

surrender (su-*ren*-der) *v.* To give in after defeat; to give up possession of.

surround (sur-*rownd*) *v.* To be all around. *Ex.* Our house is *surrounded* by green fields.

survey 1. (ser-*vay*) *v.* To look at or look over. *Ex.* We *surveyed* the countryside from the hill-top. 2. (*sur*-vay) *n.* A detailed map or examination.

survive (ser-*vyv*) *v.* To live on after, as a person does who lives longer than another, or *survives* an accident. *Ex.* He was the sole *survivor* (*n.*) of the shipwreck.

suspect (su-*spekt*) *v.* To be inclined to believe something without having certain knowledge; especially to think someone may be guilty. *Ex.* The police *suspected* the children were guilty because their stories differed; they were *suspicious* (*adj.*) of them.

suspend (su-*spend*) *v.* (a) To hang from above. *Ex.* Strings of onions were *suspended* from the kitchen ceiling. (b) To stop something for a time. *Ex.* The air-service was *suspended* because of fog.

suspense (su-*spens*) *n.* Anxious uncertainty while waiting for news. *Ex.* Waiting for the exam results kept us in *suspense*.

sustain (su-*stayn*) *v.* To support, to keep going; to provide with nourishment. *Ex.* The men were *sustained* by their emergency rations; their courage was *sustained* by their cheerful leader. *Sustenance* (*n.*) is food which *sustains*.

swagger *v.* To walk along in a conceited, 'showing off' way.

swallow 1. *n.* A small bird with long wings and forked tail, which migrates south for the winter. 2. *v.* To allow food or drink to pass down the throat into the stomach.

swamp (swomp) 1. *n.* Marsh. 2. *v.* To flood over.

swan (swon) *n.* A large white water-bird with a long gracefully curving neck.

swarm (swawrm) 1. *n.* A great number of insects etc., such as bees, ants or locusts. 2. *v.* To come together in great numbers.

sway 1. *n.* Rule, government. 2. *v.* To move this way and that, as tree branches in wind.

swear (swair) *v.* (a) To promise solemnly; to take an oath, as in a lawcourt. *Ex.* The witness *swore* that he was telling the truth. (b) To use bad language.

sweat (swet) *n.* A natural moisture which comes out through the pores of the skin, especially after hard bodily work, or in hot weather. This is also called *perspiration* (pur-spi-*ray*-sh'n), and to *sweat* (*v.*) is to *perspire*.

sweater (*swet*-er) *n.* A thick jersey.

swede (sweed) *n.* A large turnip, sweetish in taste.

sweep 1. *n.* A man who cleans chimneys. 2. *v.* To gather up dust etc. with a broom or brush.

swell 1. *v.* To grow greater in size, loudness etc. *Ex.* A balloon *swells* as it is blown up. A *swollen* (*swoh*-len; *adj.*) part of the body is called a *swelling* (*n.*). 2. *n.* Long, unbroken sea-waves.

swelter *v.* To be or feel very hot indeed.

swerve (swurv) *v.* To turn aside suddenly. *Ex.* The horse *swerved* off the path, frightened.

swift 1. *n.* A migrant bird, rather like a swallow, with very long wings, living much of its life in the air. 2. *adj.* Quick.

swindle *v.* To cheat someone, usually out of his money. A *swindle* (*n.*) is such cheating.

switch *n.* A small knob, button, handle etc. to turn electricity on or off.

sword (*sawrd*) *n.* A weapon like a very long knife, once used in war but now only in a ceremonial way or, specially blunted, in the sport of fencing.

syllable (*sil*-a-b'l) *n.* A part of a word that can be pronounced separately. *Ex.* Sep-a-rate-ly has four *syllables*.

symbol (*sim*-bol) *n.* Something which stands for or represents something else. *Ex.* The *symbol* for 'is equal to' (=).

sympathetic (sim-pa-*thet*-ik) *adj.* Sharing the feelings of someone, especially someone in trouble or sorrow. To have this feeling is to *sympathize* (*v.*) or to show *sympathy* (*sim*-path-i; *n.*).

symphony (*sim*-fon-i) *n.* A musical composition, usually in three or four movements, written for an orchestra.

symptom (*simp*-tom) *n.* A sign or change in the body, showing that there is some illness or something wrong; an outward sign. *Ex.* Toothache could be a *symptom* of tooth decay.

synagogue (*sin*-a-gog) *n.* (a) A meeting of Jews for worship and teaching. (b) The building where such meetings take place.

synthetic (sin-*thet*-ik) *adj.* Man-made, in imitation of the natural. *Ex.* Nylon is a *synthetic* fabric.

syringe (*si*-rinj) 1. *n.* A tube with a piston, into which liquid is drawn up and then squirted out. Gardeners and nurses both use *syringes*. 2. *v.* To use a *syringe*.

syrup (*si*-rup) *n.* A thick sweet liquid consisting wholly or partly of dissolved sugar.

system (*sis*-tem) *n.* A connected set of parts which work together for one purpose. *Ex.* The digestive *system*; a railway *system*.

T

tabby *n.* A cat with dark wavy stripes on brown or grey fur.

tablet (*tab*-let) *n.* A slab of wood, metal or stone with an inscription on it, often fixed to a wall. (b) A small flat slab of soap, chocolate etc. (c) Medicine compressed into flat round shapes for ease of swallowing.

tack 1. *n.* (a) A short nail with a flat head, such as is used to nail down carpets. (b) A long loose holding-stitch put in temporarily when dressmaking. 2. *v.* (Of sailing vessels) To change course across the wind.

tackle 1. *n.* Tools or whatever is needed for some special purpose. *Ex.* Fishing *tackle* consists of rods, reels, lines etc. 2. *v.* (a) To try hard to accomplish a thing. You can *tackle* a difficult job, or *tackle* a player in soccer to get the ball from him.

tact *n.* The art of knowing the most fitting thing to say or do. *Ex.* She was too *tactful* (*adj.*) to tell them they had come on the wrong day!

tactics (*tak*-tiks) *n. pl.* The art of arranging a plan of battle; ways of defeating opposition or tackling a tricky problem.

tadpole *n.* A frog, toad etc. just hatched from the egg, and living entirely in water like a fish.

tailor *n.* One who makes suits, usually for men.

talent (*tal*-ent) *n.* A special ability in some particular field. *Ex.* Some people have a *talent* for drawing.

talkative (*tawk*-a-tiv) *adj.* Inclined to talk a great deal.

talon (*tal*-on) *n.* The sharp claw of a bird of prey. *Ex.* An eagle can carry off a lamb in its *talons*.

tambourine (tam-bor-*een*) *n.* A thin drum made of parchment set into the top of a wooden hoop, with jingles on the rim; it can be beaten or shaken.

tame *adj.* (Of wild creatures) Used to man and not frightened by him. Domesticated animals and pets were once wild species, but are now *tame*.

tamper *v.* To meddle or interfere with something. *Ex.* The mower won't work, someone must have *tampered* with it.

tan 1. *n.* The brown colour one's skin gets from being in the sun; sunburn. 2. *v.* To make animal skin into leather; this is done in a tannery (*n.*).

tandem *adj.* (Of harnessed horses) One behind the other. A *tandem* bicycle is for two cyclists so arranged.

tangent (*tan*-jent) *n.* A line touching a surface but not crossing it. To go off at a *tangent* is to turn suddenly from a subject to something else.

tangerine (tan-jer-*een*) *n.* A small sweet kind of orange.

tangle (*tang*-g'l) *v.* To twist into an untidy muddle. *Ex.* Our kitten has been playing with a ball of wool, and it is now in a hopeless *tangle* (*n.*).

tank *n.* (a) A large container for holding water, oil or other liquid. A *tanker* (*n.*) is a ship or lorry which carries liquids in bulk. (b) An armoured car with a gun and tracked wheels, able to move over rough country.

tantalize (*tan*-tal-yz) *v.* To tease someone by offering something pleasant but preventing him from getting it.

tantrum *n.* A childish display of bad temper.

tap 1. *v.* To hit gently. You can *tap* someone on the shoulder to get his attention, or *tap* the keys of a typewriter, etc. 2. *n.* A short pipe by which water etc. can be run off as wanted.

tape *n.* (a) A long narrow strip of cotton cloth etc., used by dressmakers, or for tying things. (b) Magnetic metal *tape* on which music etc. can be recorded to be played back in a *tape-recorder*.

taper (*tay*-per) 1. *n.* A long thin candle; a long wick, covered with wax, used to light lamps etc. 2. *v.* To become thinner gradually towards the end, as does a church spire.

tapestry (*tap*-es-tri) *n.* A heavy cloth, usually of wool, with a pattern or picture woven into it, used in the past to cover the walls of a room. Nowadays, embroidered and machine-made material, in imitation of this, is called *tapestry* and used for curtains etc.

tar *n.* A thick, black, sticky liquid made from coal, wood etc., used in road-making and as a protective covering for wood.

target (*tar*-get) *n.* Anything that is aimed at, either in shooting or in work. *Ex.* When you play darts, the dart-board is your *target*.

tariff (*ta*-rif) *n.* A list of prices or charges for goods or services, such as hotels put out.

tarnish *v.* To become dull and badly coloured, as silver does when exposed for some time to the air.

tart 1. *n.* A flat pie with fruit etc. in it. 2. *adj.* Having a sharp taste, sharp tongued.

tartan (*tart*-an) *n.* A woollen cloth with a pattern of stripes of various colours crossing each other, used for kilts.

task (tahsk) *n.* A piece of work that has to be done.

tassel (*tas*'l) *n.* A gathered fringe hanging from a knot, used to decorate an end or edge.

taste (tayst) 1. *v.* To get the flavour of food by putting in the mouth. 2. *n.* The ability to find and enjoy beauty in the arts; having an understanding of what is fitting and most pleasing in dress, behaviour, furnishing etc. To have bad *taste* is to lack this understanding.

tatters *n. pl.* Torn, ragged clothing.

tattle *n.* Gossip, idle talk.

tattoo (ta-*too*) 1. *n.* (a) A rhythm beaten on a drum. (b) A show, with music etc., given by soldiers, at night out of doors. 2. *v.* To make a picture on a person's skin by pricking it with a needle and then rubbing colours into the outline.

taunt (tawnt) *v.* To mock or jeer.

taut (tawt) *adj.* Stretched tightly, as a wire or a muscle might be.

tawdry *adj.* Showy and gaudy, but worth very little.

taxi (*tak*-si) 1. *n.* A car whose driver can be hired to take passengers for (usually) short journeys. 2. *v.* (Of aircraft) To move across the ground before take-off or after landing.

team *n.* A group of people acting together in a game or at work.

tear (teer) *n.* One of the drops of water that appear in the eye when crying. To be *tearful* (*adj.*) is to be inclined to weep.

tear (tair) *v.* To pull apart or to pieces; to make a *tear* (*n.*) or slit in.

tease (teez) *v.* To annoy in a playful, sometimes irritating way.

technical (*tek*-ni-kal) *adj.* (a) Having to do with an art, craft or science, or the skill (*technique*) needed for it. (b) Having to do with the application of scientific and mechanical knowledge in industry. *Ex.* Engineering may be taught in a *technical* college.

technique (tek-*neek*) *n.* (a) A method used in the skilful performance of a particular activity. (b) The skill required for this. *Ex.* However musical you may be, you must first master the *technique* of playing an instrument.

tedious (*teed*-i-us) *adj.* Going on too long, boring, tiring. *Ex.* We had to listen to a *tedious* speech at the meeting.

teem *v.* (a) To be very numerous; to be full of. *Ex.* There were quantities of frog-spawn, so now the pond *teems* with tadpoles. (b) To pour with rain.

tele- (*tel*-i) is a prefix meaning far away, at a distance.

telegram (*tel*-i-gram) *n.* A message sent by telegraph.

telegraph (*tel*-i-grahf) *n.* An electrical instrument for sending messages instantly over long distances by wire.

telephone (*tel*-i-fohn) *n.* An electrical instrument which makes it possible for people to speak to each other across a great distance, by wire or by radio.

telescope (*tel*-i-skohp) *n.* An instrument which makes it possible to see things which are a long way off, by the use of lenses and mirrors, which make the thing seen look much bigger.

television (tel-i-*vizh*'n) *n.* An electrical invention which brings a picture of what a camera photographs on to a screen at any distance from it, using wireless waves.

temper *n.* A state of mind, which can be good or bad.

temperament (*tem*-per-a-ment) *n.* The tendency with which a person is born which makes him act in certain ways to whatever happens to him. He might have a calm *temperament* or a fiery one.

temperate (*tem*-per-it) *adj.* Moderate. *Ex.* Europe has a *temperate* climate compared with that of the Arctic or the tropics.

temperature (*tem*-pri-cher) *n.* The amount of heat or cold in the atmosphere, the human body or any other object. *Ex.* He has a *temperature* of 102°.

tempest (*tem*-pest) *n.* A severe storm, with high winds.

temple *n.* A building used for worship.

temporary (*tem*-por-ra-ri) *adj.* Lasting only for a time. *Ex.* We made a *temporary* hutch for our rabbit.

tempt (temt) *v.* To entice or encourage someone to do something, often something he should not do. *Ex.* The cakes looked so *tempting* that it was hard to pass them by.

tenant (*ten*-ant) *n.* A person who pays a rent for the use of a room, house or land.

tend *v.* (a) To look after or take care of. *Ex.* Nurses *tend* the sick. (b) To be inclined to. *Ex.* In autumn the weather *tends* to become colder; the weather has this *tendency* (*n.*).

tender *adj.* (a) Soft and easily injured; easily moved to pity and concern; gentle and affectionate. *Ex.* He looked after her *tenderly* (*adv.*). (b) Soft and easily chewed, as meat may be.

tennis *n.* A game for two or four, in which rackets are used to hit a ball over a net stretched across a court.

tenor (*ten*-or) *n.* A man's high singing voice.

tense (tens) 1. *adj.* Not relaxed; anxiously alert, strained. *Ex.* The crowd at the pit-head was *tense*, waiting for news of the trapped miners. 2. *n.* (Grammar) The form of a verb which shows whether the action took place in the past (I was), is taking place now (I am), or will take place in the future (I shall).

tent *n.* A shelter made of canvas, nylon etc. stretched over poles and fastened to the ground by guy-ropes.

tentacle (*ten*-tak'l)   *n.* A sensitive feeler in certain sea creatures etc., which it uses to grasp its prey or feel its way.   *Ex.* An octopus has eight *tentacles.*

tepid (*tep*-id)   *adj.* Slightly warm.

term (turm)   *n.* (a) A definite period of time, such as the *summer term* at school. (b) A word or words that have a particular meaning.   *Ex.* 'Polar regions' is a *term* applied to the area round either of the Poles. (c) *pl.* The conditions, often including price, which are required.   *Ex.* We asked him the *terms* on which he would rent us the cottage.

terminate (*tur*-min-ayt)   *v.* To come or bring to an end.   *Ex.* The party *terminated* with a firework display.

terminus (*tur*-min-us)   *n.* The end of a railway line, air route or bus route.

terrace (*te*-ris)   *n.* (a) A row of town houses joined together. (b) A raised lawn or paved path at the front or back of a building, which often looks on to a view.

terrible (*te*-ri-b'l)   *adj.* Dreadful; causing terror.

terrier (*te*-ri-er)   *n.* A small dog of a kind originally bred to dig out rats, rabbits etc.

terrific (te-*rif*-ik)   *adj.* Terrifying, dreadful; especially dreadfully big.   *Ex.* The waves were *terrific.*

terrify (*te*-ri-fy)   *v.* To fill with great fear.

territory (*te*-ri-tor-ri)   *n.* A large area of land; an area under the rule of one authority. Birds and animals may have *territories* which they claim as theirs to feed and breed in.

terror (*te*-ror)   *n.* Great fear.

test   *v.* To examine or make trial of the quality of a thing, or a person's knowledge etc.   *Ex.* Old cars have to pass a yearly *test* (*n.*) of their efficiency.

testify (*test*-i-fy)   *v.* To give evidence or to be evidence of.   *Ex.* Both witnesses *testified* that they had seen the accident.

testimonial (test-i-*mohn*-i-al)   *n.* A written statement about a person's character or ability.

tether (*tedh*-er)   *v.* To tie a grazing animal by a rope etc.

text   *n.* (a) The main part of a book (excluding preface, index etc.). (b) A verse or phrase from the Bible used as the theme of a sermon.

textile (*teks*-tyl)   *n.* Woven fabric. Weaving, tapestry and fabric printing are *textile* (*adj.*) crafts.

texture (*teks*-cher)   *n.* The quality and feel of something, especially of a fabric.   *Ex.* Silk has a soft, smooth *texture*.

thatched (thachd)   *adj.* Roofed with a careful arrangement of reeds or straw.

thaw (thaw)   1. *n.* The melting of snow and ice after the weather has got warmer. 2. *v.* To bring ice and snow to a melting state; to become warm enough to melt ice and snow.

theatre (*thee*-a-ter)   *n.* (a) A building where plays are performed. (b) An area where an activity takes place.   *Ex.* A *theatre* of war; an *operating theatre* in a hospital.

theft   *n.* Stealing.

theme (theem)   *n.* The subject or topic of a play, book or lecture etc.; a recurring melody.   *Ex.* The *theme* of his lecture was that crime does not pay.

theology (thee-*ol*-o-ji)   *n.* The study of religion.

therapy (*the*-ra-pi)   *n.* Healing; treatment in order to cure. Occupational *therapy* helps sick people get better by giving them craftwork to occupy their minds. *Physiotherapy* (*phiz*-i-o-*the*-ra-pi; *n.*) is treatment by exercise, massage, heat etc., especially of injured or defective limbs.

thermometer (ther-*mom*-e-ter)   *n.* An instrument for measuring temperature.

thicken (*thik*-en)   *v.* To make or become thicker. You can *thicken* soup by adding flour; a fog can *thicken*.

thicket (*thik*-et)   *n.* A place where trees and bushes grow very closely together.

thief (theef)   *n.* One who steals. To steal is to be guilty of *thieving* (*n.*) or *theft* (*n.*).

thigh (thy)   *n.* The thick part of the leg between the knee and the hip.

thimble (*thim*-b'l)   *n.* A small metal cap for the middle finger, used by people when sewing to help them push the needle through the cloth.

thirst (thurst)   *n.* The desire to drink. One who feels this need is *thirsty* (*adj.*).

thistle (*this*'l)   *n.* A wild plant with prickly leaves and purple flowers; the national emblem of Scotland.

thorn   *n.* A prickle or sharp point found on the stems of roses and other plants.

thorough (*thu*-ro)   *adj.* Complete; done with care and attention to detail. *Ex.* During the spring-cleaning, every room was *thoroughly* (*adj.*) cleaned.

thoroughfare (*thu*-ro-fair) *n.* A road open at both ends, which traffic can pass through. 'No *thoroughfare*' means that there is no way through for traffic.

thoughtful (*thawt*-fUl) *adj.* (a) Deep in thought; thinking carefully. (b) Showing consideration for others. *Ex.* It was *thoughtful* of you to realize that we would be without milk and to bring us some. The opposite of *thoughtful* is *thoughtless* (*adj.*).

thrash *v.* To beat with a stick or whip.

thread (thred) 1. *n.* (a) A fine line of cotton etc. which can be used to sew or weave with. (b) A ridge winding round and round upwards from the point of a screw. 2. *v.* To pass *thread* through something, such as the eye of a needle. *Threadbare* (*adj.*) describes the old and shabby look of cloth when the fluffy surface has worn off and the *threads* are left *bare*.

threat (thret) *n.* A promise of punishment or injury. To make a threat is to *threaten* (*v.*).

thresh (thresh) *v.* To beat the grain out of the ears of corn.

threshold (*thresh*-hohld) *n.* The piece of stone etc. lying at the doorway of a house, over which you step as you enter.

thrifty *adj.* Being careful with money and goods, and not wasting them; economical.

thrill *n.* A feeling of nervous excitement. *Ex.* Ski-jumping is a *thrilling* (*adj.*) sport. Exciting stories are called *thrillers* (*n.*).

thrive (thryv) *v.* To develop well and grow up strong; to prosper. *Ex.* All our chickens are *thriving*.

throat (throht) *v.* The front of the neck; the passage for breathing and swallowing which runs through the neck.

throb *v.* To beat strongly, as the heart does.

throne (throhn) *n.* A special decorative chair used by a monarch on certain state occasions.

throng *n.* A crowd of people. *Ex.* After the test match the streets outside the cricket-ground were *thronged* (*v.*) with people.

throttle 1. *n.* The part of an engine (a valve) which controls the amount of fuel used, so that speed can be increased or decreased. 2. *v.* To choke by squeezing the windpipe.

through (throo) *prep.* (a) From end to end. *Ex.* He slept soundly *through* the thunderstorm. (b) Because of. *Ex.* It was *through* the manager's kindness that we had free tickets.

thrush *n.* A brown garden song-bird with a speckled breast.

thrust *v.* To push or drive through or into, often with some force. *Ex.* They *thrust* their way through the crowd.

thud *n.* A dull sound as of a bump or fall. *Ex.* A mass of snow fell off the roof with a *thud*.

thumb (thum) *n.* The shortest and thickest finger.

thunder *n.* The loud noise which comes with lightning, but is heard after the flash is seen.

thwart (thwawrt) 1. *v.* To put difficulties in the way and stop something being done. *Ex.* He *thwarted* our plan to go on the lake by not letting us have the key to the boat-house. 2. *n.* A seat across a boat for a rower.

thyme (tym) *n.* A herb, growing wild or in the garden, with strongly scented leaves, used to season food.

tick *v.* (a) To make the small noise that a clock does. (b) To make a small mark against items when checking a list, or against a total or other answer if it is correct.

ticket *n.* (a) A label or card on something, giving information about price etc. (b) A slip of paper etc. giving the holder the right to make a railway journey, go to the theatre etc.

tickle *v.* To touch lightly with the fingers so as to excite the nerves under the skin, usually causing helpless laughter in the person tickled.

tide (tyd) *n.* The rise and fall of the sea, under the moon's influence; there are two high and two low *tides* each 24 hours.

tidy (ty-di) *adj.* Neat and in good order. *Ex.* He *tidied* (*v.*) up the room.

tie 1. *n.* A strip of material worn round the neck (a necktie), knotted or made into a bow. 2. *v.* (a) To secure, fasten or join together. You can *tie* a knot, or a boat to a jetty. (b) To equal someone in the number of votes, goals etc. obtained.

tier (teer) *n.* A row or layer, usually placed above another one. Theatre seats are arranged in *tiers*, each higher than the one in front.

tiger (*ty*-ger) *n.* A large wild animal of the cat family, with a striped body, found in Asia.

tight (tyt) *adj.* Fitting very closely. To make tighter is to *tighten* (*v.*). *Tights* (*n. pl.*) are a close-fitting garment, usually of nylon, which completely covers the body from waist to toe.

tile *n.* A flat piece of baked clay or similar material, used to cover roofs, floors, walls etc.

till 1. *n.* A drawer in which shopkeepers keep the money they take from customers. 2. *v.* To cultivate the land.

tiller *n.* The handle which moves a boat's rudder.

tilt *v.* To lean, to slope.

timber *n.* Wood used in building and construction.

timetable *n.* A list showing the times at which certain things happen or have to be done, for instance the times at which trains arrive and depart.

timid (*tim*-id) *adj.* Inclined to be afraid.

tinge (tinj) *n.* A trace or tiny amount of a colour, sound, emotion etc. *Ex.* His voice was *tinged* (*v.*) with sadness.

tingle 1. *n.* A slight prickling of the skin, from cold or a blow etc. 2. *v.* To thrill. *Ex.* They were *tingling* with excitement.

tinsel *n.* Tiny metallic shreds bound round a cord and used for Christmas decorations.

tint *n.* A variety or tinge of a particular colour. *Ex.* The paper was pale blue, *tinted* (*v.*) a darker blue at the edge.

tip 1. *n.* (a) The pointed end of a thing. *Ex.* The *tip* of the nose. (b) A small extra payment to a waiter, porter etc. who has done something for you. 2. *v.* (a) To give a *tip*. (b) To push lightly against and knock over, as one might *tip* over a glass of water. (c) To empty out by tilting. *Ex. Tip* the contents of the packet into the basin.

tiresome (*tyr*-sum) *adj.* Wearisome, irritating. *Ex.* She has a *tiresome* habit of forgetting her key.

tissue (*tis*-ew) *n.* (a) The substance of plant and animal bodies. (b) A paper handkerchief. *Tissue-paper* is very thin, soft paper, used to wrap gifts, pack clothes etc.

tithe (tydh) *n.* The tenth part of what a man produces from his land, formerly given to the parson or the parish.

title (*tyt'*l) *n.* (a) The name of a book, play, picture etc. (b) A name showing rank or social position, such as Admiral or Duke.

titter (*tit*-er) *v.* To giggle, usually quietly.

toad (tohd) *n.* A small amphibian rather like a frog (though it does not have to spend all its life by the water), which lives mainly on insects.

toadstool (*tohd*-stool) *n.* A fungus which looks very like a mushroom but is often poisonous.

toast (tohst) *n.* (a) Bread browned on both sides under a grill or in a *toaster* (*n.*). (b) A goodwill wish to someone or to some plan, offered as a drink is taken.

tobacco (to-*bak*-oh) *n.* The dried leaves of a plant, smoked in a pipe, cigarette etc. One who sells tobacco is a *tobacconist* (*n.*).

toboggan (to-*bog*-an) *n.* A small sledge for sliding downhill in snow.

toddle (*tod*'l) *v.* To walk with short uncertain steps, as a child (sometimes called a *toddler*; *n.*) when learning to walk.

toffee (*tof*-i) *n.* A sweet made by boiling sugar and butter.

toil *n.* Work which is long and hard. *Ex.* They *toiled* (*v.*) up the steep hill.

toilet *n.* (a) The actions of washing, dressing etc. (b) Another name for a lavatory.

tolerate (*tol*-er-ayt) *v.* To bear or put up with. *Ex.* I cannot *tolerate* his conceit.

toll (tohl) 1. *n.* A tax paid for the use of some bridges and roads. 2. *v.* To ring a bell slowly, as when a church bell is *tolled* for a funeral.

tomato (tom-*ah*-toh) *n.* A thin-skinned roundish red or yellow fruit, used in salads etc.

tomb (toom) *n.* A grave. A *tombstone* (*n.*) is a stone set up on a grave, with an inscription on it.

tone *n.* (a) The special quality of a sound; the sound that a particular note makes. *Ex.* The *tone* of her violin playing was sweet and sad. (b) A shade of colour. *Ex.* The sunset *tones* were pink and mauve.

tongs *n.* An instrument for picking up things which it is convenient not to have to handle. Lump sugar, cakes at a shop, and coal are all picked up by some kind of *tongs*.

tongue (tung) *n.* The organ in the mouth which we use in tasting food and in speaking. The *tongues* of some animals are used by us as food.

tonic (*ton*-ik) *n.* A medicine (or some other thing) which strengthens a person, when recovering from illness, for example.

tonsil *n.* One of the two glands at the back of the throat.

tool *n.* An implement, usually a hand implement, used to do a particular job. Hammers, spades, spanners are examples.

topic (*top*-ik) *n.* A subject being talked about etc. A *topical* (*adj.*) matter is an up-to-date matter.

topography (top-*og*-raf-i) *n.* Geographical description of a place, pointing out its various features, such as mountains, rivers etc.

topple *v.* To fall over. *Ex.* She put the last toy brick on clumsily, and the whole tower *toppled* over.

topsy-turvy *adj.* Turned upside down; disordered.

torch *n.* A small battery-operated electric lamp, to carry in the hand.

torment (*tawr*-ment) *n.* Extreme pain of body or mind. *Ex.* He was tormented (tawr-*ment*-ed; *v.*) by doubt.

tornado (tawr-*nay*-doh) *n.* (a) A violent, destructive whirlwind, occurring in central U.S.A. (b) A brief but violent storm in West Africa.

torpedo (tawr-*peed*-oh) *n.* A self-propelled underwater weapon with an explosive head which goes off when it hits a ship.

torrent (*to*-rent) *n.* A very fast-flowing stream. *Torrential* (*adj.*) rain is rain which pours down heavily.

tortoise (*tawr*-tus) *n.* A small reptile whose back is covered by a thick rounded shell, under which it can hide its head and legs.

torture (*tawr*-cher) 1. *n.* Very great physical or mental pain. 2. *v.* To inflict such pain for cruel reasons.

toss *v.* To throw, usually upwards. You can *toss* a ball into the air, a horse can *toss* its head, or you can *toss* a coin to decide something.

total *adj.* All, complete, whole. *Ex.* The *total* amount (or *total*; *n.*) collected was £53.

totter *v.* To walk unsteadily.

touch (tuch) 1. *n.* (a) The sense of feeling. (b) Contact between two things. (c) A slight amount. *Ex.* A *touch* of paint on the door. 2. *v.* (a) To come against gently. *Ex.* The two boats just *touched* each other, and no damage was done. (b) To affect the feelings, especially feelings of pity. *Ex.* Hers was a *touching* (*adj.*) story.

tough (tuf) *adj.* Hard, strong; difficult to break down or cut through etc. *Ex.* He is very *tough*, and so recovered quickly from his night on the mountain. *Tough* meat is difficult to cut and chew.

tour (toor) *n.* A journey, often on holiday, to several different places. One who *tours* (*v.*) is a *tourist* (*n.*).

tournament (*toor*-na-ment) *n.* A set of games or matches to decide which of the competitors are the champions or winners. *Ex.* A tennis *tournament*.

tow (toh) *v.* To pull along with a rope, as one boat or car may *tow* another.

towel (*tow*-el) *n.* A cloth on which to dry something after washing.

tower (*tow*-er) *n.* A tall building standing alone; a tall structure forming part of a building. A *tower* may be built for defence, as are those on a castle; or to hold bells, as does a *church tower*.

trace 1. *n.* A mark left by something. *Ex.* There were *traces* of fingerprints on the desk. 2. *v.* (a) To follow, by looking for marks, signs or information. *Ex.* The police are trying to *trace* the man last seen near the house. (b) To draw the outlines of something seen underneath clear (*tracing*; *adj.*) paper.

track 1. *n.* (a) A path or rough road. (b) Any mark or sign on the ground, such as tyre-marks, foot or hoof prints etc. (c) A railway line. 2. *v.* To follow the *tracks* of someone or something.

tractor *n.* A motor vehicle used, chiefly on farms, to pull ploughs and other farm implements or trailers.

trade *n.* (a) The business of buying and selling, whether retail, wholesale or export and import. A shopkeeper can be called a *tradesman* (*n.*). (b) The work a person does for his living, usually skilled work of a practical kind, such as carpentry, printing etc.

tradition (trad-*ish*-on) *n.* An experience, belief or story of the past, handed on from generation to generation. *Ex.* Fairy stories and playground games are *traditional* (*adj.*).

traffic *n.* The coming and going of people and goods in all sorts of transport.

tragedy (*traj*-ed-i) *n.* (a) A very sad event. (b) A play written with serious purpose and ending in sadness. Such events and plays are *tragic* (*tra*-jik; *adj.*).

trail 1. *v.* To drag behind; to follow as if dragged. A *trailer* (*n.*) is a vehicle towed by another. 2. *n.* (a) A track which can be followed. *Ex.* The 'hares' in the paperchase left a *trail* of paper for the 'hounds' to follow. (b) A track or pathway through rough countryside.

train 1. *n.* (a) A railway engine with its carriages or trucks. (b) The end of a robe which trails on the ground behind the wearer. 2. *v.* To get ready for something by coaching and practice; to control, teach or guide a person, animal or plant. You can *train* to be a dancer, *train* a horse to jump, or *train* a plant to grow along a wall.

traitor *n.* One who betrays his country.

tramp *n.* (a) A long walk, usually for pleasure. (b) A person who has no fixed home and wanders about, often begging.

trample *v.* To walk heavily over, often doing damage.

trance (trahns) *n.* An unconscious state, in which a person may seem to be asleep but can respond to voices, etc. *See* hypnotize.

tranquil (*trang*-kwil) *adj.* Calm and peaceful. A *tranquillizer* (*n.*) is a drug that calms the nerves.

trans- is a prefix meaning through, across or over.

transfer (*trans*-fur) *v.* To move or hand over from one place or person to another. *Ex.* We had to *transfer* from the train to a bus, and our luggage had to be *transferred* also.

transform (trans-*form*) *v.* To change completely. *Ex.* In 'Beauty and the Beast', the Beast is *transformed* into a handsome prince.

transistor (tran-*sis*-tor) *n.* (a) A device which controls the flow of electricity, a substitute for the bulkier valves of earlier days. (b) A portable radio set, containing *transistors*.

translate (trans-*layt*) *v.* To put into another language; to make a *translation* (*n.*).

transmit (trans-*mit*) *v.* To send or pass on. *Radio transmitters* (*n.*) send out radio-waves that can be picked up by radio receivers.

transparent (trans-*pair*-rent) *adj.* Able to be seen through, as glass is.

transplant (trans-*plahnt*) *v.* To take up and plant in another place. Organs of the body can be *transplanted* by surgeons, taking them from one body and placing them in another.

transport (trans-*pawrt*) *v.* To take something from one place to another, often on a vehicle. Cars, buses and lorries are examples of *road transport* (*trans*-port; *n.*).

trap *n.* A means of catching some creature. *Ex.* A *mousetrap*.

trapeze (trap-eez) *n.* A swinging bar on which gymnastics can be performed.

trapdoor *n.* A small door in a roof or floor, usually just big enough to get through.

trash *n.* Rubbish.

travel (*tra*-vel) *v.* To go on a journey; to move. *Ex.* That car was *travelling* too fast.

trawler *n.* A small steam or motor vessel which pulls (*trawls*; *v.*) a large fishing net behind it along the sea bottom.

tray *n.* A flat piece of metal, wood, plastic etc., with a low rim, used to carry dishes of food, china etc.

treacherous (*trech*-er-us) *adj.* False, deceitful, disloyal. A *treacherous* person is one who cannot be trusted, or a *traitor* (*n.*). *Treachery* (*n.*) is *treacherous* conduct.

treacle (*tree*-k'l) *n.* A sweet, thick, dark-coloured syrup.

tread (tred) 1. *n.* A way of walking. *Ex.* They heard the heavy tread of the returning guard. (b) Each step of a stair. 2. *v.* To set the foot down on something; to walk. *Ex.* Don't *tread* on this carpet with your muddy shoes.

treason *n.* The crime of a traitor.

treasure (*trezh*-er) *n.* A store of things of great value. Many adventure stories tell of hidden *treasure.*

treasurer (*trezh*-er-er) *n.* The officer of a club etc. in charge of money and accounts.

treat (treet) 1. *n.* A pleasure. 2. *v.* (a) To act towards, in a certain way. *Ex.* To *treat* a person or pet well; to *treat* something as a joke. *Treatment* (*n.*) is the way a person or thing is *treated.* (b) To deal with illness by giving medicines etc. as *treatment.* (c) To pay for something that gives pleasure to someone. *Ex.* Our uncle *treated* us to a speed-boat trip.

treaty (*tree*-ti) *n.* An agreement, usually between nations.

treble (*treb*'l) 1. *n.* (a) A boy's singing voice. (b) The top part in harmonized music. 2. *adj.* Three times as much, as many or as big.

trellis *n.* A light, flat screen of crossed strips of wood etc., against which plants can be trained.

tremble *v.* To shake with cold, fear or excitement.

tremendous (trem-*en*-dus) *adj.* Awe-inspiring because of great size, noise etc.

trench *n.* A long narrow cut in the ground, such as a gardener may dig for his plants.

trespass (*tres*-pas) *v.* To go on land where one has no right to be, and so become a *trespasser* (*n.*). In the Bible, the word means to sin.

trial (*try*-al) *n.* Putting someone or something to the test. Wrong-doers can be brought to *trial* by the courts, or a new aeroplane model can have *trial* (*adj.*) flights to test performance.

triangle (*try*-ang-g'l) *n.* A three-sided figure. *Triangular* (*adj.*); means having this shape.

tribe (tryb) *n.* A group of people of the same race, customs and beliefs and under one chief.

tributary (*trib*-ew-ta-ri) *n.* A stream that flows into a larger one.

trick 1. *n.* (a) Something done to deceive. (b) Some amusing and surprising thing done by a conjurer etc. 2. *v.* To deceive or cheat.

trickle *v.* To flow slowly in small drops.

trifle (*try*-f'l) *n.* (a) A matter of little importance. (b) A cold pudding made of custard, sponge-cake, fruit and cream.

trigger *n.* The steel lever on a gun which has to be pulled to fire it.

trinket *n.* A small and not very expensive ornament or piece of jewellery.

trip 1. *n.* A journey taken for pleasure. 2. *v.* To catch one's foot in something and fall or nearly fall.

tripe (tryp) *n.* The stomachs of cattle cooked for food.

triumph (*try*-umf) *n.* Victory, success; a feeling of joy at being successful.

trivial (*triv*-i-al) *adj.* Of little importance.

trolley (*trol*-i) *n.* A small container or table on wheels or castors, pushed by hand and used to move a number of things together, such as luggage or a meal.

trombone (trom-*bohn*) *n.* A brass musical instrument with a sliding tube which alters the notes.

troop *n.* A band of people, especially soldiers, or a group of Scout patrols. *Troops* means soldiers.

trophy (*troh*-fi) *n.* Something to show that one has won, usually in a sports competition. A silver cup is a common *trophy*.

tropics (*trop*-iks) *n.* The hot countries in the middle belt on either side of the Equator. *Tropical* (*adj.*) climates can be very hot.

trot *n.* A pace between running and walking; a horse's pace between a walk and a canter.

trouble (*trub'*l) 1. *n.* Something disturbing, annoying or worry-ing. *Ex.* She has *trouble* at home, for her sister is very ill. This is the second time he has been in *trouble* with the law. 2. *v.* To disturb, annoy or worry. *Ex.* I'm sorry to *trouble* you when you are so busy. To cause *trouble* is to be *troublesome* (*adj.*).

trough (trof) *n.* A large open vessel, often used to hold food or water for horses and cattle.

troupe (troop) *n.* A troop of actors, acrobats or dancers.

trout (trowt) *n.* An edible freshwater fish of the salmon family.

trowel (*trow*-el) *n.* A short-handled tool: like a small scoop for gardeners, and like a small, flat, pointed spade for plasterers.

truant (*troo*-ant) *n.* A child who stays away from school without permission.

truce (troos) *n.* An agreement to stop fighting for a time, usually with the hope of getting both sides to end the fighting altogether.

truck *n.* A railway goods wagon with an open top; a lorry; a kind of barrow.

trudge (truj) *v.* To walk in a heavy, tired way.

trumpet *n.* A brass wind instrument with a loud, ringing tone.

truncheon (*trun*-sh'n) *n.* A short heavy stick carried by police.

trundle *v.* To roll something along, usually something heavy which is awkward to move.

trunk *n.* (a) The main stem of a tree; the body of an animal, apart from head and limbs. (b) The long snout of an elephant. (c) In *trunk-road, trunk-line* and *trunk-call* (telephone) *trunk* means main.

trust *v.* To rely on. *Ex.* We can *trust* him to look after the house, as he is *trustworthy* (*adj.*). *Distrust* (*n.* and *v.*) is the opposite of *trust.*

tube (tewb) *n.* A hollow length of metal, rubber, glass etc. *Ex.* A *tube* of toothpaste.

tuber (*tew*-ber) *n.* The swollen underground stem of a plant. A potato is a *tuber.*

tuft *n.* A bunch of such things as hair or grass, growing closely together.

tug 1. *n.* A steamboat used to tow other boats or ships behind it, especially a large ship out of a harbour. 2. *v.* To pull hard.

tuition (tew-*ish*'n) *n.* Teaching, usually by a teacher instructing one pupil.

tulip (*tew*-lip) *n.* A spring bulb whose cup-like flowers come in many different colours.

tumble *v.* To fall over.

tumbler *n.* (a) A large drinking-glass. (b) An acrobat.

tune (tewn) *n.* Musical notes arranged in such a way that they make a complete pattern which can be remembered and repeated.

tunic (*tew*-nik) *n.* (a) A sleeveless frock-like garment worn by Ancient Greeks and Romans. (b) A soldier's or policeman's close-fitting jacket.

tunnel (*tun*-el) *n.* A passage cut underground, such as a *railway tunnel* running through a hill.

turban (*tur*-ban) *n.* A long strip of material wound round and round the head, worn by men in some Muslim (Mohammedan) countries, and by Sikhs.

turbine (*tur*-byn) *n.* A motor operated by water, steam or gas pressure, used to power ships, produce electricity etc.

turbot (*tur*-bot) *n.* A large flat sea-fish, much liked as food.

turf (turf) *n.* Earth covered with grass, especially a square of it cut out from the ground.

turkey (*tur*-ki) *n.* A large bird of the pheasant family, reared for food.

turmoil (*tur*-moil) *n.* Noise and confusion.

turnip (*tur*-nip) *n.* A vegetable for man and animals, consisting of a roundish root with a sweetish taste.

turnstile (*turn*-styl) *n.* A gate which allows only one person at a time to pass through.

turquoise (*tur*-kwoiz) *n.* (a) A bluish-green precious stone. (b) Its colour.

turret (*tu*-ret) *n.* (a) A small tower, often part of a castle, and containing a spiral staircase. (b) A movable housing for a gun, on tanks, warships and aircraft.

turtle (*tur*-t'l) *n.* A reptile, usually aquatic, with a soft body, like a large tortoise. The word usually means a *sea-turtle*, though there are freshwater kinds as well.

tusk *n.* A long tooth sticking out beyond the mouth, such as elephants and wild boars have.

tussle *v.* To wrestle and struggle, usually in fun.

tutor (*tew*-tor) *n.* Someone who teaches a pupil at his home.

twang *n.* (a) The ringing, vibrating sound a string of a musical instrument makes when plucked. (b) The nasal sound of some speaking voices.

tweed *n.* A strong, rough-surfaced woollen cloth from Scotland, used to make coats and suits.

tweezers (*twee*-zerz) *n.* Small tongs for gripping something very small. *Ex. Eyebrow tweezers.*

twilight (*twy*-lyt) *n.* The time when daylight is fading and darkness is coming on.

twin *n.* One of two children born of the same mother at the same time.

twine (twyn) 1. *n.* Strong thread or string. 2. *v.* To twist round, as ivy may *twine* round a tree.

twinge (twinj) *n.* A sudden short pain.

twinkle *v.* To shine with a sparkling light, as stars do.

twist *v.* (a) To turn or bend. *Ex.* I have *twisted* my ankle. (b) To *twist* together. *Ex.* Rope is made by *twisting* lengths of cord together.

twitter *v.* To make tiny chirping sounds, as birds do.

type 1. *n.* (a) A kind or sort. *Ex.* There are many *types* of footwear. (b) Letters made in metal to print from. *Ex.* Different kinds of *type* are used on this page. 2. *v.* To print with a typewriter.

typewriter *n.* A small machine with a keyboard, used for printing what would otherwise be written by hand. *Typists* (*n.*) use *typewriters*.

typhoon (ty-*foon*) *n.* A violent storm, especially in the China Sea.

typical (*tip*-i-kal) *adj.* Characteristic of someone or something. *Ex.* He is a brave man and that rescue was *typical* of him.

tyrant (*tyr*-ant) *n.* A ruler who has complete power and uses it cruelly to oppress. People suffer under his *tyranny* (*ti*-ran-i; *n.*).

tyre *n.* The rubber tube on the wheel of a vehicle.

U

udder *n.* The organ which holds the milk of such animals as cows.

ugly *adj.* Unpleasant or frightful to look at; the opposite of beautiful.

ulterior (ul-*teer*-i-or) *adj.* (Of motives) Not disclosed, kept secret. *Ex.* He said he was going to London on business, but we think he has an *ulterior* motive for going.

ultimate (*ult*-im-it) *adj.* The last, the farthest away. *Ex.* The *ultimate* goal of the space-probe is to reach Saturn, after passing by Jupiter.

ultimatum (ult-im *ay* tum) *n.* Final offer of conditions; often by one nation to another, which if refused would mean that negotiations had failed and war become a possibility.

umbrella (um-*brel*-a) *n.* A circular piece of silk, nylon etc. stretched over a light metal frame, held over the head as a protection from rain.

umpire (*um*-pyr) *n.* The person who enforces the rules of a game and decides any disputed points.

un- is a prefix meaning *not* when placed before adjectives or adverbs. *Ex. Unfair* means not fair. Placed before a verb it makes the meaning the opposite of what it was. *Ex.* To *undress*, to *unfasten*.

unanimous (ew-*nan*-i-mus) *adj.* All having the same opinion. *Ex.* We were *unanimous* in our opinion, not one of us disagreeing.

uncanny (un-*kan*-i) *adj.* Mysterious and perhaps rather frightening. *Ex.* The house was said to be haunted, and *uncanny* noises were heard at night.

uncle *n.* The brother of one's father or mother.

uncouth (un-*kooth*) *adj.* Awkward, ill-mannered and ungracious.

undergo *v.* To endure; to experience. *Ex.* He has to *undergo* an operation on his eyes.

understand *v.* To grasp with the mind; to have knowledge of or information about. You can *understand* the reason for an action, *understand* German, or have an *understanding* (*n.*) of physics.

understudy *n.* One who learns the part of an actor in a play, so that he can take over the part if the actor falls ill etc.

undertake *v.* To agree to do; to be responsible for. *Ex.* He has *undertaken* to weed the garden once a week.

undertaker *n.* Someone employed to manage funerals.

uneasy *adj.* Restless, troubled, anxious.

unfurl *v.* To open out a flag or umbrella etc.

ungainly (un-*gayn*-li) *adj.* Awkward.

unicorn (*ew*-ni-kawrn) *n.* An imaginary beast, like a horse with a single horn in the middle of its forehead.

uniform (*ew*-ni-fawrm) 1. *n.* Special dress worn by all the members of a group to show that they all belong; especially the *uniform* of the armed services and official organizations. *Ex.* Naval *uniform*; police *uniform*. 2. *adj.* Exactly the same, not varying. *Ex.* For the sake of fairness, all the equipment in sports competitions must be *uniform*.

unit (*ew*-nit) *n.* (a) A fixed amount by which to measure something. *Ex.* A volt is the *unit* of measurement for electric power. (b) A group of people, things etc., designed to work together as one.

unite (ew-*nyt*) *v.* To join two or more into one. *Ex.* The United States of America is a *union* (*n.*) of all the states under one government. People employed in the same trade can join a *trade union*.

universe (*ew*-ni-vurs) *n.* The whole of creation. *Universal* (*adj.*) means applying to everything, everywhere.

university (ew-ni-*vur*-si-ti) *n.* A number of colleges joined together for higher (advanced) education.

unwieldy (un-*weel*-di) *adj.* Difficult to handle or manage because of size, shape etc. *Ex.* The parcel was too *unwieldy* to send by post.

upholstery (up-*hohl*-ster-i) *n.* Curtains, carpets; the covers and padding of chairs, cushions etc.

upright *adj.* (a) Standing straight up. (b) Honourable, honest.

uproar *n.* Loud noise and disturbance.

upset (up-*set*) *v.* (a) To knock over. (b) To cause physical or mental distress. You can have an *upset* (*adj.*) stomach, or be *upset* by bad news.

upside-down *adj.* (a) Having the upper side below and the under side on top. (b) Untidy, in confusion. *Ex.* He ransacked his room for the missing book, and left it *upside-down.*

urban (*ur*-ban) *adj.* To do with a town or city. *Ex. Urban* populations live on the produce grown in rural areas.

urge (urj) *v.* To earnestly persuade or encourage someone. *Ex.* We *urged* him to see a doctor.

urgent (*ur*-jent) *adj.* Needing attention immediately. *Ex.* It is a matter of *urgency* (*n.*).

urn (urn) *n.* A large vessel for making tea or coffee in bulk; a large vase.

use (ewz) *v.* To work with, avail oneself of or employ; to make use (ews; *n.*) of. You *use* a knife to cut with, a pen to write with, or a dictionary to look up the meaning of a word. These are *useful* (*adj.*) things; but a blunt knife is *useless* (*adj.*).

usual (*ew*-zhoo-al) *adj.* According to custom or habit; normal. *Ex.* He came home at six, as *usual.*

utensil (ew-*ten*-sil) *n.* A dish, container, tool etc. used in the kitchen; any other useful piece of equipment.

utility (ew-*til*-i-ti) *n.* Usefulness.

utmost (*ut*-mohst) *adj.* The most that is possible. *Ex.* Emergencies have to be tackled with the *utmost* speed.

utter (*ut*-er) 1. *v.* To give voice to. *Ex.* He *uttered* a cry of pain. 2. *adj.* Complete, total. *Ex.* He talked *utter* nonsense.

V

vacant (*vay*-kant) *adj.* (a) Empty. (b) Foolish and meaningless. *Ex.* Her *vacant* stare showed that she had understood nothing. There is a *vacancy* (*n.*) in our office for a typist.

vacation (va-*kay*-sh'n) *n*. A holiday; the holiday period between university terms.

vaccination (vak-sin-*ay*-sh'n) *n*. Inoculation against smallpox etc.

vacuum (*vak*-ew-um) *n*. A space with no air in it.

vague (vayg) *adj*. Indistinct, not precise, not clearly understood. *Ex*. He had only a *vague* idea where he was.

vain *adj*. (a) Conceited, especially about one's appearance. (b) Useless, without success. *Ex*. He searched for his atlas *in vain* (*adv*.).

valiant (*val*-i-ant) *adj*. Brave, heroic.

valid (*val*-id) *adj*. Legally in order. *Ex*. Rail passengers must have *valid* tickets.

valley *n*. A piece of land between hills.

valour (*val*-or) *n*. Courage, heroism.

value (*val*-ew) *n*. Worth, importance; the price of a thing. *Ex*. The chief *value* of my bicycle is that it gets me to school quickly; I find it *valuable* (*adj*.) for other reasons, too. Its *value* in money is £40; that is what it is *valued* (*v*.) at.

van *n*. (a) The front, usually of an advancing army. (b) A road vehicle for carrying goods. *Ex*. A *delivery van*; a *removal van*. (c) A railway carriage for luggage.

vandal (*van*-dal) *n*. Someone who destroys things of value, through spite, envy or ignorance.

vanilla (van-*il*-a) *n*. A plant of the orchid family whose pods produce a sweet essence used to flavour ice-cream, custard etc.

vanish (*van*-ish) *v*. To disappear.

vanity (*van*-it-i) *n*. The state of being vain.

vanquish (*van*-kwish) *v*. To conquer.

vapour (*vay*-por) *n*. Steam, mist, cloud or fog; any heated liquid turning into a gas-like state in the air.

varnish *n*. A special coating, often used to protect wood, which gives a hard, shiny surface.

vary (*vair*-i) *v*. To become changed; to make or become different; to be of different kinds. *Ex*. The weather *varies* from day to day; it is *variable* (*adj*.). A *variety* (va-*ry*-e-ti; *n*.) of food to choose from.

vase (vahz) *n*. A tall vessel of silver, glass, pottery etc., used to hold flowers or as an ornament.

vast (vahst) *adj*. Very large, usually in area.

vault (vawlt) 1. *n*. An arched room, usually underground; the strongroom of a bank. 2. *v.* To leap over, with the help of hands or a pole.

veal *n.* The flesh of a calf when used as food.

veer *v.* To change direction, as the wind may do.

vegetable (*vej*-e-ta-b'l) *n.* A plant; any part of a plant which can be eaten, especially if it is not a fruit.

vegetarian (vej-e-*tair*-i-an) *n.* One who eats no meat.

vegetation (vej-e-*tay*-sh'n) *n.* Plant life.

vehicle (*vee*-ik'l) *n.* Any form of transport on wheels which can carry people or goods.

veil (vayl) 1. *n.* A transparent covering which goes over the head and hangs in front of the face, such as brides wear. 2. *v.* To cover with, or as if with, a veil.

vein (vayn) *n.* (a) One of the small tube-like vessels that carry blood back to the heart from all parts of the body. Leaves are also ribbed with *veins*, which carry vital nourishment. (b) A layer of mineral in a rock. *Ex.* A *vein* of gold.

velocity (ve-*los*-i-ti) *n.* Speed.

velvet (*vel*-vet) *n.* A soft woven material, often of silk, with closely cut threads standing up on one side of it to make it smooth to the touch.

veneer (ve-*neer*) *v.* To cover wood with a thin layer of another, usually finer, wood.

venerable (*ven*-er-a-b'l) *adj.* Worthy of respect (of being *venerated*; *v.*), especially on account of old age.

vengeance (*ven*-jans) *n.* Revenge.

venison (*ven*-zun) *n.* The flesh of the deer when used as food.

venom (*ven* om) *n.* Poison, which some *venomous* (*adj.*) snakes use to kill their prey. Some spiders and insects also secrete *venom*.

ventilate (*ven*-til-ayt) *v.* To let fresh air come in, as when opening the window of a stuffy room to improve the *ventilation* (*n.*).

ventriloquist (ven-*tril*-o-kwist) *n.* One who can speak without moving the lips and make people believe that the voice comes from a dummy or from another person.

venture (*ven*-cher) *v.* To risk or dare; to do something daring. *Ex.* I don't dare *venture* on such thin ice.

veranda (ve-*ran*-da) *n.* A roofed terrace attached to a house.

verb (vurb) *n.* A word which expresses action, either done by or done to someone or something. In 'She opened her presents', 'opened' is the *verb*.

verdict (*vur*-dikt) *n.* A judgement or decision, especially that of a jury as to whether a person is guilty or not.

verify (*ve*-ri-fy) *v.* To check or prove the correctness of. *Ex.* We had to *verify* the facts before we wrote our report.

vermin (*vur*-min) *n.* Destructive or harmful creatures (rats, lice etc.) which can damage crops or endanger health.

versatile (*vur*-sa-tyl) *adj.* Able to do a variety of things. *Ex.* He is *versatile*, being good both at languages and at games.

verse (vurs) *n.* Poetry; one of the groups of lines (stanzas) into which some poems are divided.

version (*vur*-shon) *n.* One of differing accounts of the same event. *Ex.* That's your story—but I have heard a different *version.*

versus (*vur*-sus) *prep.* Against. *Ex.* Oxford *versus* Cambridge in the Boat Race.

vertebrate (*vur*-ti-brayt) *n.* An animal which has a backbone.

vertical (*vur*-ti-kal) *adj.* Straight up and down, like a telegraph pole.

vessel (*ves*'l) *n.* (a) A boat or ship. (b) Anything that can hold liquid, such as a cup, bowl, jug or kettle. Our veins are called *blood-vessels.*

vestibule (*ves*-ti-bewl) *n.* The hall or lobby between the front door of a house and the inside.

vestige (*ves*-tij) *n.* A trace. *Ex.* An hour after the sun came out, not a *vestige* of snow remained.

vestry (*ves*-tri) *n.* A small room in a church for the use of clergy, choir and those dealing with parish business.

veteran (*vet*-er-ran) 1. *n.* One who has given many years of service, especially an old soldier. 2. *adj.* Having given long service, whether a person or an object. *Ex.* A *veteran* car is one made before 1918.

veterinary (*vet*'n-ri) *adj.* Concerned with the diseases of domestic animals. A *veterinary* surgeon (*vet*) is an animal-doctor.

veto (*vee*-toh) *v.* To use one's right to stop a law or decision from being put into practice; to forbid absolutely.

vex *v.* To annoy, to irritate. *Ex.* Mothers get *vexed* with their children if they behave badly.

viaduct (*vy*-a-dukt) *n.* A bridge carrying a road or railway over a valley.

vibrate (vy-*brayt*) *v.* To shake from side to side, to quiver, as do the strings of a musical instrument when touched.

vicar (*vik*-ar) *n*. A clergyman in charge of a parish.

vice (vys) *n*. (a) Wickedness; a depraved habit or practice. *Ex*. The *vice* of drug-taking. (b) A bench tool for gripping an object on which a carpenter, metal-worker etc. is working.

vice- is a prefix meaning *in place of*. *Ex*. A *vice-captain* takes over the team when the captain is absent.

vicinity (vi-*sin*-i-ti) *n*. The neighbourhood. *Ex*. There are beautiful country walks in the *vicinity* of this town.

vicious (*vish*-us) *adj*. Spiteful and cruel.

victim (*vik*-tim) *n*. Someone who has to suffer death, injury or ill-treatment. *Ex*. The *victims* of the crash were brothers.

victor (*vik*-tor) *n*. The conqueror in a battle or contest.

view (vew) 1. *n*. What is seen; scenery. 2. *v*. To look. *Ex*. Those who watch television are called *viewers* (*n*.).

vigour (*vig*-or) *n*. Physical energy and strength. *Ex*. He made a *vigorous* (*adj*.) effort to knock out his attacker.

vile (vyl) *adj*. Evil, horrible.

villain (*vil*-an) *n*. A wicked person, especially the bad man in a story or play whom the hero has to struggle against.

vindictive (vin-*dik*-tiv) *adj*. Full of spite and the desire for revenge.

vine (vyn) *n*. A plant that climbs and twines, especially the *vine* on which grapes grow. A *vineyard* (*vin*-yard; *n*.) is an area planted with *grape-vines*.

vinegar (*vin*-e-gar) *n*. An acid liquid made from beer or wine and used in pickling or seasoning.

viola *n*. (a) (vi-*oh*-la) A stringed orchestral instrument, a little larger than a violin. (b) (*vy*-o-la) The family which includes pansies and violets; a garden variety which may resemble either of these.

violence (*vy*-o-lens) *n*. Rough and cruel behaviour; the use of force to injure others. *Ex*. The men had a *violent* (*adj*.) quarrel, and both got hurt.

violet (*vy*-o-let) *n*. (a) A small purple spring wildflower with a sweet scent. (b) Its colour.

violin (vy-o-*lin*) *n*. A stringed instrument played with a bow.

viper (*vy*-per) *n*. An adder.

virtue (*vur*-tew) *n*. Goodness. To have this quality is to be *virtuous* (*adj*.).

virus (*vyr*-us) *n*. A microscopic creature which lives in human, animal and plant cells, and causes many serious diseases.

visible (*viz*-i-b'l) *adj*. Able to be seen. *Ex*. In fog, *visibility* (*n*.) is poor.

vision (*vizh*-on) *n*. (a) The power of seeing. (b) Something seen in the imagination or in a dream. *Ex*. He is a man of *vision*, who looks far ahead.

visit (*viz*-it) 1. *v*. To go to see someone or something. You can *visit* a friend, or the theatre. 2. *n*. A call on a person; a temporary stay at a place. *Ex*. He paid a *visit* to his old school. People who *visit* are *visitors* (*n*.).

vital (*vy*-tal) *adj*. Necessary for life, as are air and water; energetic and lively. A lively person has great *vitality* (*n*.).

vitamin (*vit*-a-min) *n*. One of several substances essential for health, all of them found in a normal diet.

vivid (*viv*-id) *adj*. Very clear and bright to the sight; lively and realistic to the imagination. *Ex*. Many parrots are *vividly* (*adv*.) coloured. She gave us a *vivid* description of her travels.

vocabulary (voh-*kab*-ew-la-ri) *n*. (a) All the words used or understood by a particular person. *Ex*. He has a very small *vocabulary*, but he is young yet. (b) A list of technical or difficult words used in a textbook, with their meanings, sometimes found at the end of the book.

vocal (*voh*-kal) *adj*. To do with the voice. *Ex*. The *vocal* cords.

vocation (voh-*kay*-sh'n) *n*. A feeling of being drawn towards a particular occupation, by preference, natural ability or temperament. *Ex*. She has a *vocation* for nursing.

volcano (vol-*kay*-noh) *n*. A mountain, formed by the lava that has poured out from a crack in the earth's surface, from which flames and more lava may pour from time to time.

volley (*vol*-i) *n*. (a) The firing of several rifles together. (b) (Tennis) The return of a ball before it bounces.

volume (*vol*-ewm) *n*. (a) A book. (b) An amount of anything or the space taken up by its bulk; the loudness of a sound. *Ex*. Turn down the *volume* of the radio, it's far too loud.

voluntary (*vol*-un-ta-ri) *adj*. Given of one's own free will; given willingly without thought of payment. *Ex*. *Voluntary* workers at hospitals give their services free; they are *volunteers* (*n*.).

vote *v*. To express one's wish by raising the hand, marking a paper etc.

vouch (vowch) *v*. To be a guarantee for. *Ex*. I can't *vouch* for the truth of what I was told.

voucher (*vow*-cher) *n*. A coupon with which one can get something cheap or free. *Ex.* A *luncheon voucher* can be offered in part payment for lunch.

vow *n.* A solemn promise. *Ex.* I *vow* (*v.*) I will never go there again!

vowel (*vow*-el) *n.* A sound which, unlike a consonant, can be drawled or drawn out. The main *vowels* in English are a,e,i,o,u.

voyage (*voi*-ij) *n.* A long journey, usually by sea.

vulgar (*vul*-gar) *adj.* Coarse, offensive, not polite.

vulnerable (*vul*-ner-ra-b'l) *adj.* Open to the danger of being attacked or hurt. *Ex.* She is very *vulnerable* to criticism, and easily hurt.

vulture (*vul*-cher) *n.* A large bird that lives mainly on carrion, which it finds by its exceptionally keen sense of smell and sight.

W

waddle *v.* To walk as a duck does, with short steps, moving the body from side to side.

wade (wayd) *v.* To walk through water.

wafer (*way*-fer) *n.* A very thin, light, crisp biscuit, such as is served with ice-cream.

waft (wahft) *v.* To move gently through the air, or on water, as a feather, perfume, a seed or a toy boat may be floated along.

wage (wayj) *v.* To carry on a war.

wages (*way* jez) *n. pl.* Money paid, usually weekly, for work done.

wagon (*wag*-on) *n.* A vehicle for carrying heavy loads; a railway truck.

wagtail *n.* A small, elegant, often black-and-white bird, which continually *wags* its long *tail* as it walks.

wail *v.* To show grief by crying loudly.

waist *n.* The narrowest part of the body, below the ribs.

wait *v.* (a) To stay in one place. (b) To watch for, to expect. *Ex.* She is *waiting* for the results of her exams. (c) To attend or serve someone at table, as a *waiter* or *waitress* (*n.*) does.

wake *v.* To come out of sleep; to rouse someone from sleep. To *waken* (*v.*) has the same meaning.

wall (wawl) *n.* Something built upwards of bricks, stone etc., to enclose, to act as a boundary or to divide off parts of a house etc.

wallet (*wol*-et) *n.* A pocket case, usually leather, to carry money and papers.

walnut (*wawl*-nut) *n.* A large tree which produces good timber and nuts (*walnuts*) that are good to eat.

walrus (*wawl*-rus) *n.* A large sea-animal with long tusks.

waltz (wawls) *n.* (a) A dance in triple time (three beats to a bar) for couples who themselves circle round while circling the dance-floor. (b) Music for a waltz.

wand (wond) *n.* A long thin stick, such as the one a fairy waves to make magic.

wander (*won*-der) *v.* To walk or roam about without plan; to move restlessly from place to place.

wane (wayn) *v.* To become smaller, less strong, less bright etc. *Ex.* After finding that digging was such hard work, her interest in gardening *waned*. The moon *wanes* as it appears to get smaller after full moon.

want (wont) 1. *n.* Need, poverty. 2. *v.* To wish for; to need. *Ex.* We all *want* the television on, but our father *wants* quiet, because he *wants* (needs) to study.

warble (*wawrb'*l) *v.* To sing quaveringly; to sing as a bird does. *Warblers* (*n.*) are small singing-birds of the thrush family.

ward (wawrd) *n.* A bedroom for patients in a hospital.

warden (*wawr*-den) *n.* An official with special duties who is responsible for seeing that rules are kept. *Ex. Game-warden, traffic-warden.*

warder (*wawr*-der) *n.* The guard in charge of prisoners in a prison.

wardrobe (*wawrd*-rohb) *n.* A large cupboard in which clothes are hung up.

ware (wair) *n.* Things for sale (used more often in the plural, *wares*). Depending on what they are made of, some things are called *silverware, earthenware, ironware,* etc. *Wares* are often stored in *warehouses* (*n.*).

warn (wawrn) *v.* (a) To draw someone's attention to what may happen as the result of an act, especially to *warn* of danger etc. (b) To tell someone something beforehand. *Ex.* There was a *warning* (*adj.*) notice on the beach about the dangers of bathing there. He *warned* them that he would not be coming next week.

warp (wawrp) 1. *v.* To cause wood to go out of shape, by damp, great heat etc.; to go out of shape in this way. A twisted and diseased mind is sometimes called *warped*. 2. *n*. The up-and-down threads on a loom.

warrior (*wo*-ri-er) *n*. A fighting man.

wart (wawrt) *n*. A small hard lump on the skin, harmless but unsightly.

wary (*wair*-i) *adj*. Careful and on the look out for danger.

wash (wosh) *v*. To clean oneself or anything with soap and water. *Washing* (*n*.) is clothes etc. to be *washed*.

wasp (wosp) *n*. An insect, striped black and yellow, which can give a painful sting.

waste (wayst) 1. *adj*. No longer of use and therefore thrown away. *Ex. Waste* paper. 2. *v*. To use needlessly and carelessly, which is to be *wasteful* (*adj*.).

watch (woch) 1. *n*. A small clock worn on the wrist or carried in the pocket. 2. *v*. To look at with attention, as one would a tennis-match. A *watchman* (*n*.) is a guard who takes care of a building when it is empty.

water-colour *n*. (a) Paint mixed with water instead of oil. (b) A picture painted with this.

waterfall *n*. A steep drop in a stream or river.

waterproof *adj*. Keeping water from getting in or through. A raincoat made of such material can be called a *waterproof* (*n*.).

watt (wot) *n*. The unit for measuring electrical power. *Ex.* A 100-*watt* light bulb.

wave 1. *n*. (a) A rising of the water into ridges, especially on the sea. (b) The invisible band in which light or sound travels. 2. *v*. To move to and fro in the air, as a flag *waves* in the wind, or as you *wave* your hand.

waver (*way*-ver) *v*. To hesitate, to be in doubt.

wax 1. *n*. A yellow substance made by bees and used to make the honeycomb in which they store honey; any of various similar substances. 2. *v*. To get larger, as the moon appears to do after it has become a crescent.

waylay *v*. To lie in wait for, in order to rob or kill, or merely to talk to.

weak *adj*. Feeble, with no strength.

wealth (welth) *n*. Riches, great possessions. Someone with *wealth* is *wealthy* (*adj*.).

weapon (*wep*-on) *n*. Anything which can be used to attack, or to defend oneself, with. Swords and spears are old-fashioned *weapons*; a nuclear bomb is a modern *weapon*.

wear (wair) 1. *v.* To have on the body as clothes. Old clothes become *worn* (*adj.*) because they have been *worn out*. 2. *n.* Deterioration through being used. *Ex.* This carpet already shows signs of *wear*.

weary *adj.* Tired.

weasel (*wee*-zel) *n.* A small fierce animal with a thin body, which preys on other animals.

weather (*wedh*-er) *n.* The condition of the atmosphere around us, which changes frequently. The *weather* may be cold, changeable, rainy, sunny etc.

weathercock (*wedh*-er-kok) *n.* A metal pointer, often in the shape of a cock, placed on top of a building; it turns in the wind, thus showing the direction it is blowing from.

weave (weev) *v.* To make cloth by means of threads passing over and under each other in a loom. Other material (such as straw) can be interlaced in this way to make *woven* (*adj.*) articles.

web *n.* (a) The trap spun by a spider to catch insects. (b) A kind of skin which stretches between the toes of water-birds, to help them swim.

wed *v.* To marry. The day on which a couple *weds* is called their *wedding-day* (*n.*).

wedge 1. *n.* A piece of something which is thick at one end and slopes down into a thin edge, used as a tool to widen cracks, jam things tightly etc. 2. *v.* To apply a *wedge* to something (to stop a window rattling, for example).

weed *n.* A wild plant which a gardener does not want in his garden; he *weeds* (*v.*) the garden to remove it.

week *n.* The period of seven days, especially from Sunday to Saturday. Something done each *week* is done *weekly* (*adj.*). Each day of the *week* except Sunday is a *weekday* (*n.*). The *week-end* is from Friday evening to Monday morning.

weep *v.* To cry and shed tears. *Ex.* She *wept* like a child when he'd gone.

weft *n.* The crossways threads woven into the warp (up-and-down ones) on a loom.

weigh (way) *v.* To measure how heavy a thing is on some kind of scales. The heaviness of a thing is its *weight* (wayt; *n.*). *Ex.* I *weighed* this parcel and its *weight* is two kilograms.

weir (weer) *n.* A dam across a river to keep the water back and control its flow.

weird (weerd) *adj.* Strange, uncanny.

welcome (*wel*-kum) *v.* To show pleasure when someone visits, and to receive him gladly. This is called giving him a *welcome* (*n.*).

weld *v.* To join metals by heating their ends so that they melt together.

welfare (*wel*-fair) *n.* Happiness, contentment; health and good living conditions, things which a '*Welfare State*' tries to provide for its citizens.

well 1. *n.* A deep hole dug in the ground, from which water can be drawn up. 2. *adj.* In good health. 3. *adv.* In a good, satisfactory, thorough or successful way. *Ex.* He draws *well*. We have heard from the hospital, and all is going *well*. He speaks Italian *well*. He has done *well*, and is now a doctor.

west *n.* The direction in which the sun sets.

whale *n.* The largest sea-animal, the blue *whale* being the largest animal in the world today.

wharf (wawrf) *n.* A part of a harbour, dock etc. where ships can moor alongside and load or unload their cargoes.

wheat (weet) *n.* A cereal from which bread is made.

wheel *n.* A round flat frame turning about a central pivot or axis. A car moves on *wheels*, is steered by a *wheel*, has *gear-wheels* and a *flywheel* as part of its machinery. The uses of the *wheel* are numberless.

wheeze *v.* To breathe noisily with a hissing sound, often because of a chest infection.

whether (*wedh*-er) *conj.* A word used when alternative possibilities are suggested, even if the second one is not actually mentioned. *Ex.* I wonder *whether* he'll come (or *whether* he won't). I doubt *whether* he will come (I don't think he will come).

whimper *v.* To cry in a whining, complaining way.

whine 1. *n.* The long drawn out wail of a dog when it's unhappy. 2. *v.* To make childish complaints in a fretful voice about small matters.

whirl (wurl) *v.* To swing or turn round quickly, as when a high wind sweeps dead leaves about.

whirlwind (*wurl*-wind) *n.* A great storm of wind made by a *whirling* column of air spiralling upwards. A *whirlpool* is water moving round and round a centre, owing to a meeting of currents etc.

whisk 1. *n.* A kitchen implement for beating eggs. 2. *v.* To beat with a *whisk* in order to make a frothy mixture. (b) To remove something with one quick movement. *Ex.* She *whisked* the cloth off the table.

whiskers *n.* The hairs which grow on either side of some animals' mouths; hair growing on a man's cheek.

whisky *n.* An alcoholic spirit distilled from grain (barley etc.).

whisper *v.* To speak so softly that the sound is made by the breath only and not the voice.

whistle (*wis'l*) 1. *n.* A sharp musical sound made by forcing the breath through one's lips when they are almost closed. 2. *v.* To make such a sound in this way, or with a small stopped intrument called a *whistle* (*n.*).

whiting (*wyt*-ing) *n.* A small edible sea-fish.

whole *adj.* All, the complete amount. *Ex.* The *whole* class, and not just some of them.

wholesale *adj. See* retail.

wholesome (*hohl*-sum) *adj.* Good for the body or mind because it is healthy. *Ex.* Brown bread and cheese is *wholesome* food.

whoop (hoop) 1. *n.* A shout of joy. 2. *v.* To give such a shout.

whooping-cough (*hoop*-ing-kof) *n.* An infectious disease of children, which makes them draw in the breath loudly when coughing.

wick *n.* Twisted threads of cotton, used in candles and oil-lamps, which burn when lit.

wicker *adj.* Made of twigs, as baskets are.

wicket *n.* (a) A small gate. (b) (Cricket) The three stumps with their bails on top; the pitch; the condition of the pitch.

widow (*wid*-oh) *n.* A woman whose husband has died. A man whose wife has died is a *widower* (*n.*).

width *n.* The distance between the sides of a thing. *Ex.* The *width* of the table is 1 metre; it is 1 metre *wide* (*adj.*).

wield (weeld) *v.* To use something with skill and control, as a fireman *wields* a hose, for example.

wig *n.* A false covering of hair for the head, made of real or artificial hair; it is worn because of baldness, or because of fashion, or as part of ceremonial dress (a judge's *wig*, for instance).

wilderness (*wil*-der-nes) *n.* A large tract of waste land; a desert.

wilful *adj.* Obstinate, determined to go one's own way.

will *n.* (a) The power of the mind by which one decides what one means to do; what one wants done. (b) A written document stating what a person wishes to have done with his property after his death.

willow *n.* A tree, usually growing near rivers, with graceful, bending branches and tear-shaped leaves.

wily (*wy*-li) *adj.* Cunning.

wind l. (wind) *n.* Air that is moving. 2. (wynd) *v.* (a) To roll up or make tight. *Ex.* To *wind* up a car window, or the spring of a clock. (b) To twist and turn, as a river *winds* in a turning course.

windpipe *n.* The passage at the back of the throat down which air travels to the lungs.

wing *n.* The organ of birds and insects with which they fly; something which looks or behaves like a *wing*. *Ex.* An aeroplane's *wing*.

wink *v.* To open and close one eye quickly.

wire *n.* Metal drawn out into long threads.

wireless 1. *n.* (a) A way of communicating by electromagnetic waves, without the use of wires. (b) A radio, a *wireless set.* 2. *adj.* Relating to radio, *wireless* telegraphy and telephony. *Ex.* A *wireless* S.O.S. was sent from the ship before she sank.

wisdom (*wiz*-dum) *n.* Knowledge and judgement.

wise *adj.* (a) Learned and knowing many things. *Ex.* A *wise* professor. (b) Sensible and able to judge the right thing to do. *Ex.* It was *wise* of you to put off the sports until a finer day.

witch *n.* A woman supposed to have magic powers, usually to do evil. She is supposed to practise *witchcraft* (*n.*).

withdraw *v.* To take away or draw away. *Ex.* He *withdrew* his offer of help when he found no one wanted him to join in. He *withdrew* to a quiet corner to open his presents.

wither (*widh*-er) *v.* To fade or shrivel.

withstand *v.* To stand up against. *Ex.* The sea wall was strengthened so that it could *withstand* the winter storms.

witness (*wit*-nes) *n.* A person who sees a thing happen. You can *witness* (*v.*) a signature (see it being signed), or *witness* a road accident.

witty *adj.* Amusing in a clever way.

wizard (*wiz*-erd) *n.* A man who is supposed to have magic powers. There are many *wizards* in fairy-tales.

wolf (wUlf) *n.* A fierce wild animal, like a large dog. *Wolves* hunt in packs.

woman (*wU*-man) *n.* A grown-up female human being.

womb (woom) *n.* The organ in a female mammal's body where the young child or animal grows until it is born.

wonder (*wun*-der) 1. *n.* A feeling of surprise, admiration and delight. Something causing this is said to be *wonderful* (*adj.*). 2. *v.* To feel *wonder*; to ask oneself questions; to be puzzled or curious. *Ex.* I *wonder* if I can save up enough money to buy it. She *wondered* how he could have got home so quickly.

woodpecker *n.* A colourful, woodland bird with a bill that can bore into tree-trunks to get out the insects with its long tongue.

wool (wUl) *n.* The special curled hair of an animal such as the sheep; the thread made from this. *Woollen* (*adj.*) things are those made of *wool*.

word (wurd) *n.* A sound or sounds made by the voice which have a special meaning, and can be written down by the use of letters, so that a reader can say them and recognize their meaning. Babies say *words* before they can read or write any.

work (wurk) *n.* An effort made by the mind or body to do something for a special purpose. People everywhere *work* (*v.*) to earn a living.

world (wurld) *n.* The earth on which we live; the people on it.

worm (wurm) *n.* The *earthworm*, or one of various other kinds of long-bodied crawling creatures; it has a segmented body and moves over the ground like a snake.

worry (*wu*-ri) *v.* To feel anxious and troubled. *Ex.* We were *worried* by my father's illness, and it was a *worry* (*n.*) to him not to be able to do his work.

worse (wurs) 1. *adj.* More bad. *Ex.* A *worse* winter than usual. 2. *adv.* More badly. Ex. It snowed *worse* than ever.

worship (*wur*-ship) *v.* To reverence and honour a god; to feel adoration for a person. A church service is public *worship* (*n.*).

worthless (*wurth*-les) *adj.* Of no value. *Ex.* 'Play-money' can't be used in shops, because it is *worthless* and has no value as real money.

worthy (*wur*-dhi) *adj.* Deserving. *Ex.* We gave money to the Mayor's Christmas fund, as it is a *worthy* cause.

wound (woond) *n.* Any outer damage to the body from cuts, bruises etc. *Ex.* Many people were *wounded* (*v.*) in the raid and some died from their *wounds*.

wrangle (*rang*-g'l) *v.* To quarrel or argue, but not very seriously.

wrap (rap) *v.* To put a cover round something. Parcels are usually *wrapped* in brown paper.

wrath (rawth) *n.* Great anger.

wreath (reeth) *n.* Flowers and leaves arranged in a circle. *Wreaths* are put on graves and war memorials; also on doors as a Christmas decoration.

wreck (rek)   *n.* Destruction, especially of a ship (*shipwreck*).

wren (ren)   *n.* A very small brown bird with a short tail and a surprisingly loud song for its size.

wrench (rench)   1. *v.* To pull with a twist, often using force.   *Ex.* A handle was *wrenched* off the door. A parting with a loved one can be a *wrench* (*n.*) also. 2. *n.* A tool for gripping and turning nuts etc., like a very strong spanner.

wrestle (*res'*l)   *v.* To fight with a person by gripping him round the body and trying to throw him to the ground.

wretched (*rech*-id)   *adj.* Unhappy, miserable.

wriggle (*rig'*l)   *v.* To move the body about, twisting and turning it.

wring (ring)   *v.* To squeeze by twisting, especially to squeeze out water.   *Ex.* When she had *wrung* the cloth dry, she hung it on the line.

wrinkle (*ring*-k'l)   *n.* A crease. Skin becomes *wrinkled* (*v.*) with age, and cloth is usually *wrinkled* after washing.

wrist (rist)   *n.* The joint between arm and hand.

write (ryt)   *v.* (a) To form letters or words with pen or pencil. (b) To compose.   *Ex.* She *wrote* a very good story. She has just *written* a letter to her mother.

writhe (rydh)   *v.* To roll around and double up the body, usually in pain.

X

X-rays   *n. pl.* Rays which can pass through thicknesses that light cannot penetrate. They are used to photograph broken bones and other things inside the body.

xylophone (*zy*-lo-fohn)   *n.* A musical instrument consisting of wooden bars laid out on a flat surface and tuned to a scale, played by being struck with wooden hammers.

Y

yacht (yot)   *n.* A boat, usually a sailing-boat, used for racing or for pleasure trips.

yard   *n.* (a) A length of 3 foot (91 centimetres). (b) An enclosed piece of ground, usually adjoining a building. (c) An enclosed *yard* for various purposes.   *Ex.* A *churchyard, graveyard, dockyard, farmyard* etc.

yarn   *n.* (a) Thread for weaving and knitting. (b) A story, especially one told by a traveller.

yawn   *n.* A deep breath taken through the wide-open mouth, usually due to sleepiness.

yearn (yurn)   *v.* To wish or long for something.

yeast (yeest)   *n.* A fungus which causes fermentation, and enables bread to rise, beer to be brewed etc.

yew   *n.* An evergreen tree with red berries, which lives to a great age.

yield (yeeld)   *v.* (a) To produce.   *Ex.* This field has *yielded* a good crop of wheat. (b) To give in or surrender, as a beaten army may do.

yodel (*yoh*-del)   *v.* To call or sing (as do Swiss mountaineers) in a voice which keeps changing from its usual pitch to the falsetto (high) range, and carries over distances.

yoga (*yoh*-ga)   *n.* A Hindu system in which exercises for the body and mind, combined with meditation, aim at increasing health and contentment.

yoghurt (*yog*-urt)   *n.* A food, resembling junket, made from fermented milk.

yoke (yohk)   *n.* (a) A wooden frame fitted across the necks of animals to join them together as they pull a load; a similar frame fitted across a person's shoulders, to help him balance two weights which he is carrying. (b) The top part of a fitted garment to which a lower part is sewn.

yolk (yohk)   *n.* The yellow part of an egg.

youth (yooth)   *n.* (a) Being young.   *Ex.* In his *youth* he was an athlete. (b) A young man.   *Ex.* A *youth* of about sixteen. (c) Young people.   *Ex.* The *youth* of today have many opportunities to travel.

yuletide (*yool*-tyd)   *n.* An old word for Christmas-time.

Z

zeal (zeel) *n.* Keenness or eagerness in doing some work or supporting some cause.

zebra (*zee*-bra) *n.* An African animal of the horse family, with black or brown stripes on a white or fawn body.

zenith (*zen*-ith) *n.* The part of the sky directly overhead; the highest point.

zero (*zeer*-oh) *n.* The figure nought (0), meaning 'nothing'; the point marked 0 on a thermometer.

zest *n.* Enjoyment and enthusiasm. *Ex.* He trained for the sports with *zest*.

zigzag *n.* A crooked line which turns alternately from side to side, making sharp corners.

zinc (zingk) *n.* A white metal rather like tin, which does not rust.

zither (*zidh*-er) *n.* A musical instrument whose metal strings, set into a frame, are plucked as it lies flat on a table.

zodiac (*zoh*-di-ak) *n.* An imaginary band in the sky which contains the path of the sun, moon and planets, divided into twelve equal parts, each named after a constellation.

zone (zohn) *n.* One of the five geographical bands into which the earth is divided by temperature; one is hot, two cold and two temperate; a region; a strip of land used for a particular purpose.

zoo *n.* A short name for *zoological gardens*, where collections of animals from all over the world are kept. *Zoology* (zoh-*ol*-o-ji; *n.*) is the study of animal life.